W9-AKZ-567

THE POLITICS
OF RIOT
COMMISSIONS,
1917–1970

FROM THE RESEARCH PROGRAM OF

The Center for the Study of Law and Society University of California, Berkeley

---

CONTRIBUTORS

Elliott Currie
Robert M. Fogelson
Norman D. Humphrey
Paul Jacobs
Andrew Kopkind
Alfred McClung Lee
Alain Locke
Anthony Platt
Elliott M. Rudwick
Arthur I. Waskow

THE POLITICS
OF RIOT
COMMISSIONS
1917-1970

A Collection of
Official Reports and
Critical Essays

EDITED AND INTRODUCED BY
Anthony Platt

COLLIER BOOKS, NEW YORK, NEW YORK

Copyright © 1971 by Anthony M. Platt

All rights reserved. No part of this book may be reproduced or transmitted
in any form or by any means, electronic or mechanical, including photocopy-
ing, recording or by any information storage and retrieval system, without
permission in writing from the Publisher.

The Macmillan Company
866 Third Avenue, New York, N.Y. 10022
Collier-Macmillan Canada Ltd., Toronto, Ontario

The Politics of Riot Commissions, 1917–1970 is also published in a hard-
cover edition by The Macmillan Company.

Library of Congress Catalog Card Number: 79–150069

First Collier Books Edition 1971

Printed in the United States of America

COLBY COLLEGE LIBRARY
Withdrawn

Contents

Preface

This is *not* another book about "riots." It is about *official* interpretations and investigations of "riots." The collection includes selections from the final reports of official riot commissions between 1917 and 1970, as well as critical essays written by persons unconnected with commissions.

The collection has three general purposes. First, it assembles a series of official documents of considerable historical and political importance. Some of these documents are not generally available, some are often difficult to find, and others are rarely presented in their original form. Secondly, the collection has an analytical purpose. It is designed to assess critically the political implications and internal dynamics of riot commissions, with a view to generalizing about their nature and impact. And finally, this collection has an important educational function—namely, to teach the "consumers" of official reports how to evaluate their assumptions, scientific validity, and competence.

The idea for this collection was suggested during my participation in the writing of *The Politics of Protest,* a task force report on group protest and violence prepared for the Violence Commission. The discovery of the suppressed report of the 1935 Harlem Commission also encouraged my interest in the politics of riot commissions.

I am grateful to a number of people for their help in determining the formulation and content of this collection: C. R. Carey, Michael Couzens, Elliott Currie, Renetia Martin, Sheldon Messinger, Alan Sutter, and Jerome Skolnick. My special thanks to Chuck Carey for his help with the original research, to Elliott Currie for his dependable and perceptive advice, and to Jerome Skolnick for introducing me to commissions and teaching me so much about critical analysis.

My thanks also to Gabriella Duncan and Sandra Dasmann for their efficient secretarial assistance and help with the tedious tasks involved in organizing a collection.

Finally, I would like to thank my colleagues at the Center for the Study of Law and Society—particularly its chairman Philip Selznick and vice-chairman Philippe Nonet—for their interest and spirit of cooperation as well as intellectual support. My thanks to the Center for funding the research for this collection, with the help of a grant from the Ford Foundation.

Anthony Platt

University of California
Berkeley
September 1970

I

Introduction

I.

ANTHONY PLATT

The Politics of Riot Commissions, 1917–1970: An Overview

Definitions

Collective violence by black Americans has always been a source of anxiety for whites and established authorities. It is neither a new phenomenon nor intrinsic to urban life. As Herbert Aptheker and others have noted, contemporary black protesters are the "inheritors and continuers of a great tradition of militancy,"[1] a tradition which encompasses numerous Southern slave insurrections, the abolitionist crusade, various nationalistic and Third World movements dating back to Martin Delaney and the American Colonization Society in the eighteenth century, the civil rights movement of the NAACP, SNCC, and CORE in the 1950s and early 1960s, and the recent black liberation movement which has brought attention to the more intractable sources of institutional racism.[2]

Black militancy cannot be explained in simple evolutionary or linear terms. "The history of black protest," suggests the Skolnick Report to the Violence Commission, "is the history of the temporary decline, fall, and resurgence of almost every conceivable means of achieving black well-being and dignity within the context of a generally hostile polity, and in the face of unremitting white violence, both official and private."[3] The black writer, Arna Bontemps, similarly observed in 1968, over thirty years after the publication of his novel about Gabriel's slave rebellion in Virginia, that self-assertion by black men is a persistent theme in American political history. "Time is not a river," he noted after the black riots of the 1960s. "Time is a pendulum."[4]

Although collective violence and self-defense by blacks is as old as slavery, the riot commission is a twentieth-century phenomenon which promises to become a traditional institution and routine feature of the governance of civil disorders. Riot commissions are authoritative tribunals, financed and/or supported by a governmental body, established temporarily to investigate and explain specific outbursts of illegal collective violence by private citizens, notably urban blacks.

Riot commissions are *authoritative* in the sense that they are created at the request of or with the approval of governmental representatives and are composed of professional experts, "leading citizens," and high-level members of political, economic, and religious interest groups. While riot commissions share many common features in terms of their organization, ideology, and findings, the sources of their authority and their composition are quite varied. Commissions may be sponsored by city government (for example, the 1935 Mayor's Commission on Conditions in Harlem and the 1968 Chicago Riot Study Committee), by state government (for example, the 1943 Governor's Committee to Investigate Riot Occurring in Detroit and the 1965 Governor's Commission on the Los Angeles Riots), by the federal government (for example, the 1917 Special Committee Authorized by Congress to Investigate the East St. Louis Riots), or by the President (for example, the 1969 National Commission on the Causes and Prevention of Violence). Although most riot commissions are financed by public funds, there is an important exception in the 1919 Chicago Commission on Race Relations, which was supported by private contributions despite the fact that the commission was appointed by the Governor and included an elected state official. Finally, the racial composition of riot commissions varies considerably, from the all-white 1943 Detroit Committee, the balanced composition of the 1919 Chicago Commission, to the predominantly black membership of the 1935 Harlem Commission.

Riot commissions are *temporary organizations* because they are part of the emergency apparatus of government, hastily assembled in times of public crisis and charged with completing their investigation within a short period of time. Aside from the fact that riot commissions are usually appointed under dramatic conditions during or soon after a civil disorder, commissioners do not derive either their income or their occupational identification from their association with a commission. Appointment to a commission brings prestige and publicity to its members but does not require long-term obligations and duties which might interfere with their routine work.

Riot commissions are primarily concerned with the *illegal, domestic, and collective violence of private citizens*. Riot commissions are not established to investigate "lawful" collective violence, such as an athletic event, the conduct of the military in foreign wars, or acts of illegal violence committed by individuals and small groups; nor do riot commissions investigate the collective violence of public officials, such as the police or national guard, except insofar as that violence is pertinent or incidental to the main focus of their inquiry. It is the job of riot commissions to study and explain episodes of collective behavior which public officials, primarily the police, have previously designated as "riots."

Finally, riot commissions are invariably synonomous with the study of *collective black violence*, even to the extent that "riots" and "ghettos" have become popularly and semantically associated. That riot commissions are primarily concerned with *black* civil disorders is self-evident from even a cursory glance of their reports. While it is true that official investigations of "rioting" have been expanded recently to include the disturbing collective behavior of youth (especially students) and even police,[5] it is also evident that, from the perspective of official authority, urban blacks continue to be the most problematic "rioters."[6] Moreover, authoritative studies of collective violence involving students and youth derive many of their ideological and theoretical assumptions from commissions investigating black violence.[7]

Although riots are a cause of general concern and alarm to the mass media and general public, the proliferation of riot commissions in recent years indicates that government officials are optimistic about the possibility of developing institutional structures to predict and control such outbursts. It is an irony of riot commissions that, while they may memorialize riots as a symptom of profound despair and alienation, they also testify to the capacity of the modern state to "rationalize" rebellions and to swiftly restore order and regularity to the political process. As Harold Cruse has perceptively commented:

The American propaganda apparatus has created the great social myth that the Negro protest movement is, in fact, the Black Revolution in progress. This is stretching the word revolution to include anything from 'pray ins' to the March on Washington. It is true, that, to many whites, the very fact that so many Negroes are protesting all at one time in so many different places, is unsettling enough to induce certain opinion-molders to believe their own alarmist propaganda. Ghetto uprisings like Harlem and Watts lend credence to the spectre of revolution even more. But as long as these uprisings are sporadic, the American capitalistic welfare state will absorb them and, more than that, pay for the damage in the same way the government pays for the destruction caused by hurricanes and floods. Uprisings are merely another form of extreme protest action soon to be included under the heading of Natural Calamities.[8]

The commission is becoming a permanent feature of the political response to riots (see Table 1). In 1968, for example, there were numerous local commissions in addition to the national Kerner Commission: Following the riots after the murder of Martin Luther King, Mayor Daley appointed a Riot Study Committee in Chicago and the Mayor of Pittsburgh appointed a Special (investigative) Task Force; several specialized commissions were also established to investigate the response of the judicial system to riots in Baltimore, Cincinnati, New York, and Washington, D.C.[9] The proliferation of riot commissions, and especially their repetitive quality prompted Kenneth Clark to observe in his testimony to the Kerner Commission that "it is a kind of Alice in Wonderland—with the same moving picture reshown over and over again, the same analysis, the same recommendations, and the same inaction."[10] After serving on the 1969 Violence Commission, United States District Judge A. Leon Higginbotham Jr. proposed "a national moratorium on any additional temporary study commissions to probe the causes of racism, or poverty, or crime, or the urban crisis. The rational response to the work of the great commissions of recent years is not the appointment of still more commissions to study the same problems—but rather the prompt implementation of their many valuable recommendations."[11]

Less than six months later, President Nixon appointed a nine-member national commission to investigate "campus unrest" and the deaths of six students at Kent State University and Jackson State College.

Studying Riot Commissions

The study and analysis of riot commissions has three general implications and justifications:

(1) As political and policy-making organizations, riot commissions deserve careful assessment as to their effectiveness and impact on the political process. How are they appointed? What is the source of their political authority and legitimacy? To what extent are they representative of various constituencies and interest groups? In what ways, if at all, do they innovate or modify public policies? Do riot commissions serve any symbolic purposes in the political process, such as testifying to the flexibility and persistence of orderly government or communicating the impression that grievances are being redressed? All these questions address the political character of riot commissions and direct our attention to a more comprehensive examination of the governance of riots.

(2) A study of riot commissions is inevitably a study also of the relationship between government and social scientists, for at least since the 1919 Chicago Commission on Race Relations, social-scientific theories of collective behavior have influenced the ideological and theoretical assumptions underlying official reports on civil disorders. In addition to the 1919 Chicago Commission, social scientists played a leading role in the 1935 Harlem Commission, the 1965 McCone Commission, the 1968 Kerner Commission, and, in 1969, they were finally appointed to the executive staff of the Violence Commission. An examination of riot commissions therefore, should involve a consideration of the differences and similarities between official and social-scientific theories of riots, as well as of the ethical and political obligations of social scientists involved in government-sponsored research.

(3) As Howard Zinn has pointed out, "there is an underside to every age about which history does not often speak, because history is written from records left by the privileged. We learn about politics from the political leaders, about economics from the entrepreneurs, about slavery from the plantation owners, about the thinking of an age from its intellectual elite."[12] Similarly, we learn about riots from riot commissions. Their descriptions of riots, their compilation of "relevant" facts, and their analysis of underlying social and economic

Table 1

SIGNIFICANT RIOT COMMISSIONS 1917–1970

Year	Place	Name	Appointed by	Chairman	Final Report
1917	East St. Louis	Special Committee Authorized by Congress	House of Representatives	Ben Johnson	*Report*
1919	Chicago	The Chicago Commission on Race Relations	Governor Frank Lowden	Edgar A. Bancroft	*The Negro in Chicago: A Study of Race Relations and a Race Riot*
1935	New York	The Mayor's Commission on Conditions in Harlem	Mayor Fiorello LaGuardia	Charles Roberts	*The Negro in Harlem: A Report on Social and Economic Conditions Responsible for the Outbreak of March 19, 1935*
1943	Detroit	Governor's Committee to Investigate Riot	Governor Harry Kelly	Herbert J. Rushton	*Final Report*

Year	Location	Commission	Appointed by	Chairman	Report
1965	Los Angeles	Governor's Commission on the Los Angeles Riots	Governor Edmund Brown	John A. McCone	*Violence in the City—An End or a Beginning?*
1968	Washington, D.C.	National Advisory Commission on Civil Disorders	President Lyndon B. Johnson	Otto Kerner	*The Kerner Report*
1968	New Jersey	Governor's Select Commission on Civil Disorders	Governor Richard J. Hughes	Robert D. Lilley	*Report for Action*
1968	Chicago	Chicago Riot Study Committee	Mayor Richard J. Daley	Richard B. Austin	*Final Report*
1969	Washington, D.C.	National Commission on the Causes and Prevention of Violence	President Lyndon B. Johnson	Milton S. Eisenhower	*To Establish Justice, To Insure Domestic Tranquility*
1970	Washington, D.C.	National Commission on Campus Unrest	President Richard M. Nixon	William W. Scranton	*The Scranton Report*

conditions, have become widely accepted as authoritative and objective historical documents. The reports of the 1917 Congressional Committee, the 1919 Chicago Commission and the 1968 Kerner Commission are used widely by scholars and students interested in American race relations, urban history and riots. Given this use and interpretation of riot commission reports by scholars and policymakers, it is especially important to assess the political and ideological dynamics of "official" history.[13] An understanding of riot commissions, therefore, should provide not only an appreciation of how the "official" history of black riots is written, but also suggest alternative interpretations and explanations of black history.

With these general implications in mind, the following analysis examines four critical areas in the politics of riot commissions: (1) the origins and mandates of commissions, (2) their internal organization and staff relationships, (3) their conceptions and theories of riots, and (4) the nature and effectiveness of their recommendations.

The data for this paper were collected in a number of ways. It is primarily a historical analysis, based on library research and documentary evidence. Analysis of the 1935 Harlem Commission, the 1969 Violence Commission and the 1970 Scranton Commission is for the most part based on first-hand research; analysis of other commissions relies extensively on secondary sources and critiques. The author's participation in a task force for the Violence Commission is another source of data. It should be noted, however, that the following analysis is *not* the result of personal observations or interviews. Like most historical research, it suffers from a lack of first-hand appreciation of informal processes.

ESTABLISHING COMMISSIONS

Profile of Commissioners

The appointment of riot commissions is invariably accompanied by a statement from a government official exhorting commissioners to approach their task "with an open mind"[14] or "to make publicly known the whole truth"[15] or "to make an objective and dispassionate study."[16] These instructions are designed to affirm the idea that riot commissions are *representative* and *impartial* tribunals, created in order to provide *authoritative* documentation of the causes of riots and to suggest policy recommendations for preventing their recurrence. The appointment of a commission is itself a symbolic dramatization of the realization that "riots" can not be managed or understood within the "normal channels" of the political process. Controversies about the political significance of riots, about the relationship between rioters and agencies of social control, and about the response of the wider community and mass media prompt government officials to establish special investigative commissions whose findings hopefully will be received as objective, authoritative, and uncontaminated by vested interests and partisan politics. Thus, President Johnson instructed the Kerner Commission:

> One thing should be absolutely clear: this matter is far, far too important for politics. It goes to the health and safety of all American citizens—Republicans and Democrats. It goes to the proper responsibilities of officials in both of our Parties. It goes to the heart of our society in a time of swift change and of great stress. I think the composition of this Commission is proof against any narrowness of partisanship. . . . We are looking to you, not to approve our own notions, but to guide us and to guide the country through a thicket of tension, conflicting evidence and extreme opinion. So . . . let your search be free. Let it be untrammeled by what has been called the "conventional wisdom." As best you can, find the truth, the whole truth, and express it in your report.[17]

The transformation of political rhetoric into policy and action is accomplished in the context of a pluralist model of government and power. Pluralism, as a political philosophy, suggests that government policy emerges as a result of bargaining and compromises between organized interest groups which are in turn responsive to and representative of various mass publics. Riot commissioners are therefore selected on the basis of their membership in a major interest group— industry, labor, Republicans, Democrats, etc.—and are thus to be regarded as "a microcosm of the interest groups and hereditary groups which, according to pluralism, constitute American society."[18] Presumably, commissions are expected to produce a report which is both politically representative and scientifically objective, a report based on adversary debates and negotiations between commissioners of diverse backgrounds and interests.

Pluralist imagery of a society regulated by countervailing checks and balances leads us to expect commissions composed of elite representatives from major blocs of cultural, economic, and political power, each bloc equally or proportionally represented, facing one another as ideological combatants until harmony is reached through compromise and mediation. The following analysis examines the extent to which riot commissions conform to a pluralist model and then raises some critical questions about the political limitations of such a model.

Analysis of the background and occupations of eighty-six persons who served on nine riot commissions between 1917 and 1970 (see Table 2) indicates that (1) commissioners are predominantly male (only five women), middle-class, and middle-aged (average age is 54.3 years), (2) sixty commissioners are white and twenty-six are black, (3) forty-nine (57%) were trained professionally as lawyers, and (4) almost two-thirds were political representatives or governmental employees either before or at the time of their appointment as commissioners.

In the selection of commissioners, it is evident that government officials regard some interest groups as more significant and established than others. Industry and business provided three times as many commissioners as organized labor; lawyers far outnumbered the combined total of all other professional representatives from religion, education and medicine; for every black commissioner there were at least three white commissioners; and only 6 percent of all commissioners were women. Even if we were to accept the pluralist assumption that only representatives of *established* and *powerful* interest groups merit appointment, it is clear that in the case of riot commissions this principle has operated selectively and conservatively to favor established groups with predominant economic and political power—politicians, lawyers, and businessmen. Nor does it appear that riot commissions are becoming more balanced and representative over time: the 1935 Harlem Commission had the highest percentage of black members; a woman was appointed to commissions in 1935, 1965, 1968, 1969, and 1970; the 1943 Detroit Commission had the highest percentage of members under fifty years of age; and lawyers have consistently dominated the professional composition of commissions since 1917 (See Table 3.)

Aside from the fact that some "established" groups are over-represented and others under-represented in the composition of commissions, the group to which commissioners are supposedly affiliated is often ambiguous. For example, a commissioner may be selected because he is distinguished and black, yet he may regard his racial

Table 2

PROFILE OF EIGHTY-SIX RIOT COMMISSIONERS, 1917–1970
(BY SEX, AGE, AND RACE)
N = 86

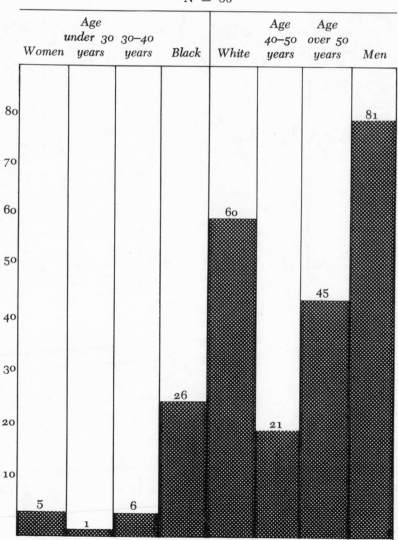

Table 3
Profile of Nine Riot Commissions, 1917–1970
(by race, sex, age and profession)

Commission	Number of Commissioners	Black	Female	Age under* 50 Years	Lawyers
East St. Louis 1917	4	0	0	0	3 (75%)
Chicago 1919	13	6 (46%)	0	2 (22%)	8 (62%)
New York 1935	13	7 (54%)	1	6 (55%)	6 (46%)
Detroit 1943	4	0	0	3 (75%)	3 (75%)
Los Angeles 1965	8	2 (25%)	1	2 (40%)	2 (25%)
Kerner 1968	11	2 (18%)	1	5 (45%)	7 (64%)
Chicago 1968	11	3 (27%)	0	1 (11%)	8 (73%)
Violence 1969	13	2 (15%)	1	4 (31%)	9 (69%)
Scranton 1970	9	4 (44%)	1	4 (57%)	3 (33%)
Totals	86 (100%)	26 (30%)	5 (6%)	27 (37%)	49 (57%)

* The percentages in this column are based on ages of 73 commissioners. Data are not available on ages of 13 commissioners.

identity as irrelevant or peripheral to his occupational identity. The appointment of Benjamin O. Davis to the Scranton Commission on Campus Unrest is a case in point. Davis recently retired from the Air Force a Lieutenant General—the highest ranking black officer—after nearly forty years of service. He was later appointed Public Safety Director in Cleveland, a position from which he quickly retired on the grounds that the city's black mayor, Carl Stokes, was providing "support and comfort" to "enemies of the police."[19] From what is known about Davis' career and public statements, it is more accurate to regard him as a "representative" of the military and law enforcement groups rather than as a spokesman for the "black community."

On the other hand, a black commissioner may regard himself as a representative of blacks, whereas he may be regarded by his constituency as an "Uncle Tom" or as an ineffective leader. Thus, two of the three black members of the 1968 Chicago Commission, George Leighton and Ralph Metcalfe, are "machine" Democrats who represent only a narrow segment of the black community in that city. Similarly, of seven blacks on the 1935 Harlem Commission, three were active in partisan politics at the time of their appointment.

Among twenty-six black commissioners who served on commissions between 1917 and 1970, only five were active in civil rights organizations (such as the NAACP and Urban League) preceding their appointment and thus representative of a broad cross section of the black community. Of the remainder, most were involved in law, business, and politics and, consequently, represented middle-class and professional interests. The possibility that black commissioners may be selected for their class and professional interests, as opposed or in addition to their racial identity, is confirmed by the fact that racial composition is not necessarily indicative of the scholarly or political quality of a commission's report. The Kerner Commission, with only two blacks and nine whites, produced one of the most liberal and scholarly reports. Whereas the McCone Commission on the Watts riots, with two blacks and six whites, produced one of the most conservative and superficial reports.

The question of representativeness does not apply to black members alone. Can it be said, for example, that Eric Hoffer (1969 Violence Commission) "represents" organized labor and the working classes because he happens to be, *inter alia*, a longshoreman? Does James Ahern (1970 Scranton Commission) "represent" professional law enforcement or the city of New Haven where he is Chief of Police? Was Julius Rosenwald asked to serve on the 1919 Chicago Commission because of his vast business interests or as a "representative" of en-lightened philanthropy? Whatever the answers to these questions, it is apparent that the determination of the group affiliation of commis-sioners is not always straightforward and self-evident but may be a matter of political interpretation. Government officials who appoint commissioners do not call attention to the problematic nature of group affiliation, for it is their hope that such appointments will convey the impression that commissions are unquestionably repre-sentative, impartial, and authoritative. In this respect, commissions are an example of what Murray Edelman has called symbolic politics: "The assumption by the mass public that what administrators do is ordained by a legislative and public 'will' sanctifies administrative actions and helps make them acceptable. . . . It is through speeches, gestures, and settings that evoke reassuring anticipations that men's political claims are limited and public order maintained."[20]

Competition and conflict are indispensable features of pluralist imagery. Groups with conflicting interests and competing constituen-cies—business and labor, law and medicine, liberals and conserva-tives, etc.—strive for power, mediate differences, negotiate and com-promise, thus achieving a situation of orderly accommodation and harmony. When applied to commission politics, then, we would ex-pect to find commissioners engaged in vigorous representation of their unique interests with the result that, as in an ideal criminal trial, they are able to reach a verdict which reflects not only the full participa-tion of all parties but also an accurate and honorable decision. The model for this perspective is the British Royal Commission:

> It represents a collective, balanced, not an individual or seg-mental, approach to social problems. It is based on the as-sumption that even the best-trained mind is auto-biographi-cally biased, that the individual group, no matter how large or dominant, is also situationally restricted in its view of reality. Its arrangement of members, of unquestioned integ-rity and competence, with least self-interest in the problem, yet bringing to its consideration the viewpoints of important interests; its mediating chairman; its impartial expert assist-ants; its evidence from every source of relevant information and bias; its due process and cross-examination techniques— all combine to reach a closer approximation to social truth by balancing partial and conflicting perspectives.[21]

The available evidence on commissions in the United States, however, indicates that conflict between commissioners is minimal and that every effort is made to facilitate cooperation and harmony *before* commissioners evaluate evidence and sign their final report. This is not to suggest that there are no disagreements among commissioners but rather that disagreements occur only around a small range of issues. With the notable exception of the 1935 Harlem Commission, whose internal conflicts were in part responsible for the shelving of their final report, minority reports and divisiveness are rare in riot commissions.

A black member of the 1965 McCone Commission, Reverend James Edward Jones, filed a modest two-page minority report criticizing two points in the final report, while concurring with the remainder of the commission's conservative conclusions. There were some disagreements also on the Kerner Commission between the followers of John Lindsay, representing a liberal position, and those of Charles Thornton, following a more conservative line. But even these disagreements, as Andrew Kopkind observed, revolved around petty and largely symbolical issues, such as whether to emphasize or underplay the role of the "criminal element" in riots.[22] Occasionally, there is a public display of conflict, as in the memorable televised exchange between Eric Hoffer and Judge Higginbotham during the Violence Commission's public hearings in 1969. The Violence Commission later issued a report which was virtually unanimous, with the exception of some minor issues and the question of civil disobedience in which a majority adopted a resolution condemning non-violent civil disobedience. But even in his dissent, Judge Higginbotham was gracious and conciliatory:

There is no disagreement among any of the commissioners in our unanimous condemnation of civil disobedience accompanied by violence. I sincerely regret that due to the pressure of our adjournment time, we were not able to have an additional Commission meeting wherein my present separate statement could be presented and considered. For I know that by their *deeds*, some members of this Commission's majority, such as Congressman William M. McCulloch, have been great profiles in courage to all men interested in equal justice under the law.[23]

From the perspective of commissioners, differences of personality, opinion, and ideology may appear to pose a major threat to a commission's solidarity and effectiveness. And there is no doubt that there is often considerable conflict among commissioners as to the appropriate tone and interpretation of their findings. Nevertheless, commissioners generally demonstrate a high degree of cohesiveness and unanimity. This is partly explained, as Michael Lipsky and David Olson have noted, by the fact that commissioners are motivated by a sense of urgency to suspend their partisan differences on behalf of the "national interest" and to avoid conflicts which might jeopardize the authority of their findings.[24] Since commissioners are genuinely concerned about influencing government policy and public opinion, they appreciate the importance of producing a unanimous report. A seriously divided commission, as in the case of the recent Commission on Obscenity and Pornography, cannot expect its findings to win political or public support.

Another explanation of solidarity of commissions may be found in the congruence of ideology and interchangeability of interests among commissioners.[25] Many commissioners "represent" more than one interest group, many are often personally familiar with and sympathetic to representatives of other groups, and most commissioners share a similar class and educational background. For example, the overwhelming majority of "political" commissioners are also trained lawyers who not only share a common frame of reference with commissioners from other professions, particularly law enforcement, but are especially likely to be unsympathetic to "lawlessness" and "violence." Also, representatives from business and industry, such as John McCone from the Watts Commission and Charles Thornton from the Kerner Commission, are so active in politics that some of their business and government interests are inseparable. McCone owns shipping companies, is on the boards of several major corporations, and is a former chairman of the Atomic Energy Commission and former chief of the Central Intelligence Agency. Thornton has served on numerous governmental committees relating to defense and military matters; he is also chairman of the board of Litton Industries. Conversely, many commissioners selected for their political affiliations have a variety of business interests: for example, Alderman Ralph Metcalfe of the 1968 Chicago Commission owns an insurance company; former Kentucky Commissioner of Commerce Katherine Peden, a member of the Kerner Commission, owns a radio station; and former Governor William Scranton, appointed by President Nixon in 1970 to head the Commission on Campus Unrest, has various business interests. Finally, the fact that some commissioners, such as Hale Boggs, Leon Jaworski, Albert Jenner and William McCulloch, are appointed to more than one commission may indicate that their selection partly depends on their proven ability to work harmoniously with other commissioners.[26]

To summarize, three basic inconsistencies have been noted between the pluralistic rhetoric and actual composition of riot commissions. (1) Commissions appear to be composed of and balanced by elite representatives from all established interest groups. In fact, representatives of politics, industry, and law predominate the composition of commissions. (2) Commissions appear to be composed of persons who unequivocally represent established interest groups. In fact, their representativeness is often disputed by their alleged constituencies. (3) Commissions appear to operate on the basis of an adversary system of conflict resolution. In fact, commissioners generally work harmoniously and cooperatively as a result of their similar class backgrounds, interchangeability of interests, and mutual ideology.

Beyond Pluralism

In addition to the objections that government officials do not act in ways which are consistent with their political rhetoric, more fundamental criticisms can be raised about the basic fairness and impartiality of the pluralist concept of riot commissions. First, the theory of pluralism is intrinsically conservative and selective in that, to quote Robert Wolff, it "always favors the groups in existence against those in the process of formation."[27] According to Wolff:

> . . . pluralism is not explicitly a philosophy of privilege or injustice—it is a philosophy of equality and justice whose *concrete application* supports inequality by ignoring the existence of certain legitimate groups.
>
> This ideological function of pluralism helps to explain one of the peculiarities of American politics. There is a very sharp distinction in the public domain between legitimate interests and those which are absolutely beyond the pale. If a group or interest is within the framework of acceptability, then it can be sure of winning some measure of what it seeks, for the process of national politics is distributive and compromising. On the other hand, if an interest falls *outside* the circle of the acceptable, it receives no attention whatsoever

and its proponents are treated as crackpots, extremists, or foreign agents.[28]

This means in practice that government officials will select the members of riot commissions from established political organizations, established religions, and established economic groups. Republicans and Democrats will be favored over independents and radicals; Catholics, Protestants, and Jews will be favored over members of the Nation of Islam, agnostics, and atheists; representatives of big business and organized labor will be favored over small businessmen, non-unionized workers, and consumers. In this sense, riot commissions are inherently conservative, protective of existing institutions and not disposed to propose radical changes which will diminish the power of established groups. We can not find, therefore, nor expect to find official riot commissions which are critical of the two-party political system, of organized religion, or of corporate capitalism.

Although government officials try dramatically to publicize and communicate the representative and impartial qualities of riot commissions—and thus to monopolize the legitimacy of their inquiry—it is often the case that groups without established power will contest this monopoly and create counter-commissions. For example, a number of black politicians and intellectuals were critical of the composition of Mayor Daley's 1968 riot commission and formed the "Greater Chicago Citizens' Riot Probe Commission" to conduct an independent investigation. Similarly, the 1968 New Jersey commission's report prompted the New Jersey State Patrolmen's Benevolent Association to create its own "Riot Study Commission." More recently, both the American Civil Liberties Union and the American Association of University Professors established independent commissions to investigate the shootings at Kent State University and Jackson State College,[29] despite the existence of a blue-ribbon presidential commission. While these counter-commissions serve to publicize the ideological bias of established commissions, they clearly lack the economic and political resources to successfully compete with commissions that can hire large research staffs, employ sophisticated public relations experts, and enjoy virtually unlimited access to the mass media.[30]

A second major criticism of pluralist imagery concerns the failure of government officials to appoint to commissions persons who are most intimately concerned with and affected by rioting. Rioters are predominantly youthful, commissioners are predominantly middle-aged; rioters are predominantly black, commissioners are predominantly white; rioters are predominantly members of the working and lower classes, commissioners are predominantly middle-class professionals and politicians; rioters include a significant number of women, commissioners are almost exclusively males; rioters typically live in areas affected by rioting, commissioners almost always live outside areas affected by rioting. Thus, the main participants in riots—lower-class blacks and whites, and the police—are ineffectively represented in the composition of commissions. Writing about the 1919 Chicago commission, Arthur Waskow noted that:

> Since the commission's financial support came not from the public but from the voluntary contributions of the wealthiest citizens of Chicago, the commission was more dependent than it might otherwise have been on their basic outlook on racial policy. . . . The Negroes had a voice on the commission, though a much weaker one than that of the wealthy whites who sponsored it; the less comfortable, more angry whites had not even a voice.[31]

Waskow's observation about the 1919 commission holds true also for public- and government-sponsored commissions: participants in and victims of riots are not represented in the membership of commissions.

The preceding analysis attempts to challenge seriously the propositions that riot commissioners are (1) representatives of either the total population or established interest groups and (2) capable of objective and impartial investigations. When establishing commissions, government officials justify their selection of commissioners by noting that "riots" are controversial issues and easily subject to emotional and political bias. It is important, they note, that commissions should be properly balanced so that all possible views and interpretations are included. This rhetoric is not consistent with their actions, for they then proceed to appoint to commissions men and women drawn from the ranks of the most successful and powerful interest groups in American society, interest groups which derive much of their power and success from those economic and political institutions which generate the conditions for riots—namely the unequal distribution of wealth, institutional racism, and inadequate political representation. As Robert Wolff has observed, "any vision of the national interest which emerges from such a group will inevitably be a standard pluralist picture of a harmonious, cooperative, distributively just, *tolerant* America. One could hardly expect a committee of group representatives to decide that the pluralist system of social groups is an obstacle to the general good!"[32]

ORGANIZATION OF COMMISSIONS

The Executive Staff

Although commissions are appointed to study riots and make policy recommendations, it is rare for commissioners themselves to conduct such studies. Most commissioners, having neither the time nor expertise to conduct research and evalute evidence, limit themselves to appearing at public hearings, conducting occasional field visits, meeting with other commissioners to discuss the progress and policies of research, and signing the final report. Commissions are typically organized in three levels—the commissioners, the executive staff, and the research staff. With the exception of the 1917 East St. Louis Commission and the 1943 Detroit Commission, which were more limited in the scope of their inquiry, the remaining commissions adopted this tripartite form of organization. In the case of the 1919 Chicago Commission and the 1935 Harlem Commission, the executive staff positions were filled by commissioners—Francis Shepardson in the former and Eunice Hunton Carter in the latter. In every major riot commission since 1965, the executive staffs were composed of lawyers hired by the commissions to organize and supervise the research staff.

Commissioners rarely concern themselves with administrative or research tasks. The notable exceptions are Shepardson and Carter. Francis Shepardson, Illinois Director of Registration and Education, was "loaned" by Governor Lowden to the 1919 Chicago Commission in which he played an important role in the formulation and execution of research policies. Shepardson in a sense "represented" the governor's interests and also served as an intermediary between the commissioners and research staff.[33] Eunice Hunton Carter, a lawyer and future Assistant District Attorney, was both a commissioner and executive secretary for the 1935 Harlem Commission. She was responsible for administering and supervising the commission's policies —handling correspondence and public relations, scheduling public hearings, arranging policy and research meetings, etc.—and for facilitating communications between commissioners and researchers. Since commissioners are usually involved in full-time occupations beyond their obligations as commissioners, it is rare for them to perform executive functions. In fact, many commissioners do not even find the time to attend all the public hearings associated with their commission.

Commissions hold public hearings for the purpose of hearing testimony from citizens and public officials, receiving reports from experts, and making a commission visible to the public and the mass media. Although such hearings are quasi-legal (proceedings are recorded, witnesses are cross-examined, etc.) in the style of a legislative investigation, their purpose is largely ceremonial and symbolic. Public hearings communicate an appearance of impartiality and authority; they serve to dramatize the legitimacy of the commission and its inquiry. But they are rarely taken seriously by persons responsible for a commission's final report.[34] The 1965 McCone Commission, according to Robert Fogelson, systematically ignored and repudiated most of its expert testimony.[35] Similarly, the design and tone of the Kerner Report was decided before the commission held public hearings.[36] According to Lipsky and Olson, the Kerner Commission "took the testimony of many black militants whose names appear on the witness list at a period when many chapters in the report already had been approved in relatively final form."[37] The same may be said of the Violence Commission's final report which bears little resemblance to the testimony of its expert witnesses, especially those experts speaking on behalf of blacks and students.

The responsibility for supervising the progress of a commission's report is invariably left to the executive staff. Since 1965, the key positions on the executive staff have been filled by prominent business lawyers with previous experience in governmental affairs. The McCone Commission hired as its Executive Director Thomas Sheridan "whose entire legal career had been as a prosecuting attorney" before he entered private practice.[38] The Executive Director of the Kerner Commission, David Ginsburg, was appointed by President Johnson to serve in part as liaison between the Commission and the White House. Ginsburg is a partner in a major Washington law firm and has extensive governmental connections. Mayor Daley followed this precedent and appointed Charles Bane, a prominent corporation lawyer, as Chief Counsel to the 1968 Riot Study Committee. Bane in turn recruited two more attorneys from his own firm to serve as assistant executives. Finally, in 1969, President Johnson recruited Lloyd Cutler from a prominent Washington law firm to serve as Executive Director of the Violence Commission. Cutler is perhaps best known for his lobbying activities on behalf of automobile companies during the 1966 auto safety debates in Congress.

In all of these cases, the lawyers are "loaned" without charge by their firms to the commissions. But as Ralph Nader has observed, this type of altruism brings its own rewards:

> [A]ll of these nonremunerative "public services," of course, have an implicit *quid pro quo*. The lawyer is repaid with special early access to Government information that will be of use to his corporate clients on rulings, regulations, licensing or quotas; or the Government will take a stand favorably disposed to a particular economic interest represented by such a lawyer; or a Federal agency will delay in acting contrary to that economic interest.[39]

The executive staff of commissions, therefore, is usually composed of persons who by their professional training and economic self-interest regard themselves as advocates for their clients (commissioners) rather than as neutral mediators between commissioners and researchers. It is one task of the executive staff to decide the tone of the final report, a tone which will be acceptable to all the commissioners, and to guarantee that the researchers produce supporting evidence for their position. James Short, who was Co-Director of Research for the Violence Commission, summarizes the issue as follows:

> The tendency of the law is to adopt a position and then seek evidence to support that position, to play the role of advocate, arguing as to the rightness or wrongness of a course of action. The social scientists found themselves at times in the position of having to argue the case for taking a systematic, objective view, looking at alternative hypotheses, and bringing the weight of evidence upon alternatives.[40]

The executive staff play an essentially conservative role in commissions, for it is their job to screen research findings and to protect commissioners from interpretations of data which may be ideologically or politically controversial. Thus, a number of social scientists were fired from the Kerner Commission when they produced a document, "The Harvest of American Racism," which "defied the categories that the top officials had established for the 'social science input.' "[41] Hans Mattick, a sociologist and consultant for the Kerner Commission, commented that:

> Just as the commission displayed a tacit circumspection about the hard realities of war and money in relation to the President and the Congress, the upper staff levels displayed a cautionary sense for the presumed tolerance limits of the ideological spectrum comprising the commission. The upper staff levels, all bright, knowledgeable and ambitious young men, organized the working drafts from materials supplied by the lower staff levels and more than two hundred "consultants, contractors, and advisors." It was the upper staff levels who decided what materials would be allowed to survive in the final drafts submitted to the commission for review, acceptance, or rejection. Whether the upper staff levels were any more accurate in their perceptions about the commission than the latter were about the President and the Congress is a question that is unanswerable, but this entire process of anticipations and the exercise of restrained sensibilities underlines the conservative nature of the *Report*.[42]

The Research Staff

Social scientists have participated in the research programs of most riot commissions. Under the direction of Graham Romeyn Taylor, a white writer-reformer, and Charles S. Johnson, a black sociologist and student of Robert Park at the University of Chicago, social scientists played an active and important role in the 1919 Chicago Commission. The 1935 Harlem Commission hired as research director E. Franklin Frazier who, even at the time of his appointment, had already distinguished himself as a leading scholar and black intellectual. Social scientists served as consultants to the McCone Commission in 1965, as staff members on the Kerner Commission, and as members of the executive staff on the 1969 Violence Commission.

Research for riot commissions is not always delegated to persons with academic qualifications. The 1943 Detroit Commission conducted its investigation with the exclusive cooperation of the FBI, Navy Intelligence, Army Intelligence, and the State Police. Similarly, the research staff of the McCone Commission was for the most part composed of lawyers and legally oriented investigators. Of the eleven staff attorneys hired by this commission, only two had experience in the area of race relations; of the ten investigators, four were former FBI agents, two were former agents of the Federal Narcotics Bureau, one had been a deputy sheriff, and the remaining three were private detectives. According to Paul Jacobs, "the full-time staff did not include a single professional working in the field of social sciences. . . . The social scientists were always downgraded by McCone and Sheridan, who viewed them as dreamers and visionaries."[43]

The 1968 Chicago Commission's research staff also relied on lawyers rather than social scientists. The "researchers" were donated by some of the city's leading law firms. Testimony was given in closed hearings; there were no social scientists on the staff; one corporate law firm provided the three white directors of the research staff; and the remaining lawyers-investigators had minimal experience in research and race relations. It is not surprising, therefore, that many black leaders in Chicago refused to cooperate with the commission on the grounds that it was intrinsically incapable of objective and impartial research.

When social scientists are hired as part of the research team, as in the commissions of 1919, 1935, 1968, and 1969, they invariably find that they are expected to work under extraordinary conditions and time pressures. The 1919 Commission was first suggested "on the fourth day of the Chicago riot, while men were still dying on the streets and before the militia had gone on active duty."[44] Mayor LaGuardia appointed the 1935 Harlem Commission only two days after the violence had subsided and received an initial research report within ten weeks. The 1965 McCone Commission, appointed on the same day that the riot curfew was lifted, took only one hundred days to study the riot and formulate policy recommendations. The massive Kerner Report was completed within eight months. "We were working around the clock," said one staff member. "We slept in our offices—they brought in cots—and we never left. It was crazy. We'd be found in our underwear darting across the hall in the mornings, just before people came to work."[45] Much of the research for the 1969 Violence Commission was done under similar conditions. The first draft of *The Politics of Protest*, a task force report for the Violence Commission, was completed after four months of intensive research and writing, with staff members regularly working late into the night and even on national holidays. These extraordinary time pressures are inherently incompatible with rational and proper research procedures:

It is uncertain whether any riot commission could adequately fulfill the research goals with which they are charged. Almost as soon as commissions are convened, their directors find themselves confronted by critical deadlines. They must hire staff quickly without the luxury of fully assessing their qualifications and before the research agenda has even been completed. . . . [O]ther talents, perhaps antithetical to those of the researcher, are demanded of the staff. These are the ability to work all day and night, the capacity to absorb endless criticism without taking personal affront, and the ability to synthesize the sentiments of the commissioners, or to anticipate their sentiments regarding various issues. These qualities are those of lawyers, of advocates who work under pressure for clients regardless of personal interests or allegiance to material.[46]

With the exception of the Skolnick Task Force to the Violence Commission (which was contractually guaranteed complete freedom of inquiry and publication), social scientists are hired as part of the research staff which in theory prepares reports and evaluations for commissioners. In fact, they are usually hired by and responsible to the executive staff who are ultimately responsible for integrating the commission's organization and final report. The social scientist's role in commissions is carefully defined and regulated: he is typically regarded and treated as a "technician," a "hired hand," and a "data-collector."

The formulation of a commission's research problems is often completed before a research staff is hired. By the time that E. Franklin Frazier was hired by the 1935 Harlem Commission, Mayor La-Guardia had already received a tentative outline of the final report from the Secretary of the NAACP and appointed a commission sympathetic to its perspective.[47] Similarly, President Johnson set the tone for the Kerner Commission's cautious liberalism by both condemning the violence of rioters and calling for long-range solutions to the "conditions that breed despair and violence."[48]

Riot commission scholarship is a good example of what Herbert Blumer calls "agency-determined research."[49] It imposes restrictions on the freedom of scientific inquiry by predetermining the problems which are to be studied and by inhibiting social scientists from examining distasteful or controversial possibilities. Secondly, it encourages elitism and a disrespect of the rights of the persons being studied.

"Agency-determined research," notes Blumer, "is prone to treat lightly the interests and claims of people who are the objects of study or whose lives are to be changed by applying the results of the study. The interests and needs of the agency on whose behalf the research is to be undertaken have priority in governing the research enterprise."[50] And finally, such research may have a corrupting effect on social scientists through the lure of research grants, prestige, travel, and other fringe benefits. Blumer summarizes the central problem as follows:

> One may appropriately ask why this attractiveness of agency determined research should be regarded as a source of corruption to social scientists. The answer, put simple and baldly, is that the participating social scientist who responds to the attraction is likely to subordinate his commitment to the genuine ideals and precepts of scientific endeavor. To enter into agency-determined research requires an acceptance of the terms and conditions of that research. In a general sense, this means fitting into a web of premises, perspectives, expectations, demands, and controls. To accommodate to this web, the participant may be easily led at differing points to sacrifice full observance of the precepts of science. One may get an initial understanding of this matter by thinking of the position of the social scientist who is engaged in his own independent research. Such a person is not beholden to an agency. He does not have to tailor his research to meet the interests and perspectives of the agency. He is free to carve out his own problem and to set his own objective. He is free to modify his problem and to redirect his research as he proceeds. He is not under pressure to produce "results" within a specified time period. He does not have to put on a front, pretending a knowledge or expertise that he does not possess in order to maintain status in the eyes of project directors or colleagues on the project. He does not have to contend with opportunities to make a showing on the basis of qualities other than the merit of his scientific work. He is free from the entanglements of the reward-system that are likely to attend agency-determined projects.[51]

Another consequence of "agency-determined research" is that social scientists tend to be regarded as glorified technicians, skilled collectors, and interpreters of data, rather than as scientists interested in the formulation and testing of theories. It was not by accident that E. Franklin Frazier was designated the role of "technical expert" in the Harlem Commission. This role resembles that of a "hired hand" in a production organization.[52] "The product is not 'his'," notes Julius Roth. "The production process gives him little or no opportunity to express any intrinsic interest he may have in the product. . . . It means that we are relying for an important part of our research operation on people who have no concern for the outcome of the study."[53] And if they are concerned about the outcome of their study, they are too far removed from the centers of power and decision-making to act upon their concerns. This creates a further danger that the researcher "will sooner or later fall into a pattern of carrying out his work with a minimum of effort, inconvenience, and embarrassment—doing just enough so that his product will get by."[54] This may be especially true of the lower levels of a commission's research staff.

While it is true that riot commissions often misuse and exploit social scientists, it should be recognized that social scientists have often been willing, even enthusiastic, "victims" of this kind of relationship. The image of social scientists as value-free technical experts ready for hire is one which social scientists have themselves helped to build. Academics are not forced to work for government commissions; they are free to negotiate the terms of their work; they can resign if they feel that their intellectual freedom is restricted; they can publicly criticize a commission for dishonest or inadequate research; and they can write dissents and minority reports. Unfortunately, too many social scientists sacrifice their intellectual obligations for prestige and narrow self-interest.[55] Moreover, there are a large number of academics who are not only willing to do "agency-determined" research but who also share the "agency's" perspective on the problem to be studied. As the following analysis suggests, there are remarkable similarities in official and academic explanations of rioting.

THEORIES OF RIOTS[56]

The Meaning of Riots

Riot commissions are charged with the task of explaining the causes of civil disorders and suggesting policy recommendations for preventing their recurrence. In order to construct theories of rioting, commissions depend extensively on social scientific explanations of collective behavior. This dependency is not accidental, for there are many similarities between academic and official views on the nature, causes, and control of civil disorders.

Almost every official riot commission takes the position that riots are irrational, self-defeating, and immoderate:

> The problem will not be solved by methods of violence.[57]

> The avenue of violence and lawlessness leads to a dead end.[58]

> [There] can be no justification in our democratic society for a resort to violence as a means of seeking social justice.[59]

> [Unless] order is fully preserved, . . . no meaningful, orderly and rational physical, economic, or social progress can occur.[60]

> Violence cannot build a better society. Disruption and disorder nourish repression, not justice.[61]

This initial premise of riot commissions is generally supported by social scientific approaches to collective behavior which do not go very far beyond the "common sense" view of riots as threatening, irrational, and senseless. They are regarded as formless, malign, incoherent, and destructive; they seem to raise to the surface those darker elements of the human character which are ordinarily submerged.

Social scientists usually place riots under the heading of "collective behavior," a broad concept which includes a wide range of phenomena such as panics, crazes, disaster behavior, and organized social movements of various kinds.[62] Underlying this union of apparently diverse behavior is the idea that each in some sense departs from the more routine and stable aspects of social life. Collective behavior, in the words of a leading social psychology text, is not only "extraordinary" and "dramatic," but also "likely to be foolish, disgusting, or evil."[63] The crucial element of "collective behavior," according to this perspective, is not that it is collective—since all group interaction is collective—but that it is qualitatively different from the "normal" group processes of society.[64]

"Collective behavior" is thus often conceived as nonconforming and even deviant group behavior; its unstable and intemperate qualities are characteristic of those groups which are either experiencing "social strain" or acting in opposition to constituted authority—for example, "the unemployed, the recent migrant, the adolescent."[65] As such, "collective behavior" is characteristically the behavior of out-siders, the disadvantaged and disaffected.

Related to this conception of collective behavior as abnormal and deviant is an implicit notion that collective behavior is, particularly in its more "explosive" forms, inappropriate behavior. Just as many be-wildered observers tend to view a riot in the same terms as a temper tantrum, so a social scientist categorizes collective behavior as "the action of the impatient."[66] Implicit in this perspective is the idea that collective behavior is an inappropriate and immoderate solution to collective problems.

This perspective on the meaning of riots is open to challenge in three ways. First, social scientific and official explanations of riots make strong value judgements about the uselessness of collective vio-lence and often assert that riots are inherently destructive for both their participants and victims. This judgmental aspect of collective behavior is often left unexpressed and disguised by claims that it is "scientific" or "value-free." Moreover, many such treatments display an obvious bias on behalf of official authorities and take a managerial perspective on collective behavior.

Secondly, this perspective tends to manipulate the definition of "violence" for ideological purposes. It refers only to the domestic violence of disaffected groups, while ignoring the fact that systematic *official* violence for social ends is widely upheld in other spheres. Thus, the commissions of 1919, 1943, 1968 and 1969 do not even mention the possibility of a connection between World War I and World War II and the Vietnam War on the one hand, and domestic violence on the other. It is a matter of moral judgement, not scientific analysis, to attribute "normality" to one kind of violence—such as American foreign policy in Vietnam—but not to another.[67]

Furthermore, conventional theories of riots focus on the destructive behavior of disaffected groups while accepting the behavior of au-thorities as normal, instrumental, and rational. Yet established, thor-oughly institutionalized behavior may be equally destructive as, or considerably more so than, riots. No riot, for example, matches the destructiveness of military solutions to disputed political issues. Moreover, available evidence suggests that (a) armed officials often demonstrate a greater propensity to violence against persons than un-armed civilians; and (b) these actions often escalate the intensity of the disorder and comprise a good part of the "destructiveness" of riots, especially in terms of human deaths and injuries. It is both intellectually dishonest and misleading to ignore the part played by social control agencies in aggravating and sometimes initiating a riot, especially when commissions obtain evidence to this effect. It is not unusual, as the Harlem, Kerner and Walker commissions observed, for a riot to begin *and* end with police violence.[68]

Thirdly, whether or not violence is "useless" is a problem for historical analysis, not a certainty. Rioting is not a particularly novel or unusual technique for expressing grievances. Instances of such rioting by both the respectable and disreputable poor in eighteenth- and nineteenth-century Europe have been well documented by historians.[69] Eric Hobsbawm has noted, for example, that the preindustrial mob "did not merely riot as a protest, but because it expected to achieve something by its riot. It is assumed that the authorities would be sensitive to its movements, and probably also that they would make some sort of immediate concession." Like the modern riot, the classical mob was composed of a cross section of "the ordinary urban poor, and not simply of the scum."[70] Hobsbawm also gives the example of the Luddites, whose "collective bargaining by rioting was at least as effective as any other means of bringing trade union pressure, and probably *more* effective than any other means available before the era of national trade unions."[71] Another historian, George Rudé, has documented the various successes and failures of the preindustrial crowd, noting its long-term contributions:

> As society has changed, so the crowd has changed with it and, in changing, has left its legacy to succeeding generations. As the sans-culotte, small freeholder, and cottager have given way to the factory worker and farm laborer, so the machine wrecker, rick burner, and "Church and King" rioter have given way to the trade unionist, labor militant, and organized consumer of the new industrial society. New wine has certainly on occasion been poured into old bottles; but, in general, it is perhaps not unreasonable to see these earlier, immature, and often crude, trials of strength, even when doomed to failure, as the forerunners of later movements whose results and successes have been both significant and enduring.[72]

The view that riots are "useless" is unsupported and lacks any empirical foundation. The most notable exception to this argument are revolutions which are often prefaced by "riots" and other attacks on existing regimes. As Barrington Moore has pointed out:

All the major democracies, England, France, and the United States passed through a period of civil war or revolutionary violence (the difference is mainly one of terminology) which by destroying or crippling certain features of the old order—royal absolutism in England, the landed aristocracy in France, plantation slavery in the United States—made possible long periods of social struggle within the democratic framework.

Revolutionary violence, including dictatorship, has been the precursor of periods of extended freedom at several points in western history. It is simply impossible to put violence, dictatorship, and fanaticism in one category; freedom, constitutionalism, and civil liberties in another. The first has played a part in the development of the second. To deny the connection is no more than a partisan trick. It becomes a hollow partisan trick when in the name of democracy one condones saturation bombing against peasant revolutionaries; hollower still if one chooses to condone such violence and then criticize a Robespierre for shedding blood in the name of future liberty.[73]

Participants in Riots

Until recently, riots were regarded as the work of either outsiders or criminals. The "riffraff" theory, as it is known, has three assumptions—that a small minority of the black population engages in riot activity, that this minority is composed of the unattached, uprooted, and unskilled, and that the overwhelming majority of the black population deplores riots.[74] This "theory" may be traced to the seventeenth century at least when it was fashionable to label participants in popular disturbances as a "mob" or "rabble." According to Rudé, "rioters and other disturbers of the peace were generally dismissed by contemporaries as 'banditti', 'desperadoes', 'mob', 'convicts', or 'canaille'; and even a revolutionary democrat like Robespierre, though passionately devoted to 'the people,' was inclined to see food rioters . . . as agents of the English or aristocracy. . . . And the 'mob' in question, having no ideas or honorable impulses of its own, is liable to be presented as the 'passive' instrument of outside agents—'demagogues' or 'foreigners'—and as being prompted by motives of loot, lucre, free drinks, bloodlust, or merely the need to satisfy some lurking criminal instinct."[75]

In recent years, government officials have made wide use of the "riffraff" stereotype. The day after the Harlem riot of March 1935, Mayor LaGuardia announced that:

> The people of New York must know that the overwhelming majority of the Negro population of West Harlem are splendid, decent, law-abiding American citizens.
>
> The unfortunate incident of last night and early morning was instigated and artificially stimulated by a few irresponsible individuals. A very small fraction of one percent of the population took part in the demonstration and violence.[76]

Similarly, President Johnson, in his 1967 address to the nation on civil disorders, claimed that "the looting, arson, plunder and pillage which have occurred are not part of a civil rights protest. . . . The criminals who committed these acts of violence against the people deserve to be punished—and they must be punished. Explanations may be offered, but nothing can excuse what they have done."[77] These kinds of inference serve to dramatize the criminal character of riots, to undermine their political implications, and to uphold the argument that social change is only possible through lawful and peaceful means. If riots can be partly explained as the work of a few agitators or hoodlums, it is then much easier to engage wide support in repudiating violent methods of social protest.

Official investigations generally publicize the fact that normal, ordinary, law-abiding persons do not instigate riots. According to the FBI, riots are typically instigated by a "demagogue or professional agitator" or by "impulsive and uninhibited individuals who are the first in the mob to take violent action or to keep it going when it wanes."[78] Thus, "hoodlums" were responsible for the 1943 riot in Detroit, "marauding bands" of criminals in Watts, "a small fraction of the city's black population" in Chicago in 1968, and "self-appointed leaders, opportunists, and other types of activists" in Pittsburgh.[79] The recent Chicago Commission noted that the riot was an "excuse for lawlessness, destruction and violence" on the part of some "leaders and followers." They also suggested that "irresponsible advocates are encouraging the black youth of this city to join in a wholesale rejection of our national traditions, our public institutions, our common goals and way of life. Advocates of black racism encourage political rebellion in the place of political participation, violence in the stead of non-violence, and conflict rather than cooperation."[80] Implicit in the "riffraff" theory is the idea that riots are unilaterally violent, that public officials and agencies merely respond in defense against the violence of "irresponsible advocates," and that the riots have little wider meaning in the black community.

The "riffraff" theory has been challenged by various studies. As long ago as 1935, the Harlem Commission reported that "among all classes, there was a feeling that the outburst of the populace was justified and that it represented a protest against discrimination and aggravations resulting from unemployment."[81] More recently, a study of participants in the Watts riot suggests that 46 percent of the adult population in the curfew zone were either actively or passively supporting the riot. The riot had a "broad base" of support and was characterized by "widespread community involvement." Although participants in the Watts riot were predominantly male and youthful, support for rioting was as great from the better-educated, economically advantaged, and long-time residents as it was from the uneducated, poor, and recent migrants.[82]

The Kerner Report provided further evidence to contradict the "riffraff" theory, but its significance was lost in the mass of facts and figures. The most convincing attack on this theory came from Fogelson and Hill's study of participation in the 1967 riots which was published at the end of the Kerner Commission's supplemental studies. The authors found that (1) a substantial minority, ranging from 10 to 20 percent, participated in the riots, (2) one-half to three-quarters of the arrestees were employed in semiskilled or skilled occupations, three-fourths were employed, and three-tenths to six-tenths were born outside the South, and (3) individuals between the ages of fifteen and thirty-four and especially those between the ages of fifteen and twenty-four are most likely to participate in riots.[83]

Riots are generally viewed by blacks as a useful and legitimate form of protest. Survey data from Watts, Newark, and Detroit suggest that there is an increasing support, or at least sympathy, for riots in black communities. Over half the people interviewed in Los Angeles responded that the riot was a purposeful event which had a positive effect on their lives.[84] Thirty-eight percent of the population in the curfew area said that the riot would help the Negro cause. "While the majority expressed disapproval of the violence and destruction," writes Nathan Cohen in the Los Angeles Riot Study, "it was often coupled with an expression of empathy with those who participated, or sense of pride that the Negro has brought worldwide attention to his problem."[85]

That riots are seen by many as a legitimate and instrumental method of protest has drastic implications for the "riffraff" theory. Fogelson and Hill ask:

> Is it conceivable that . . . several hundred riots could have erupted in nearly every Negro ghetto in the United States over the past five years against the opposition of 98 or 99 percent of the black community? And is it conceivable that militant young Negroes would have ignored the customary restraints on rioting in the United States, including the commitment to orderly social change, unless they enjoyed the tacit support of at least a sizeable minority of the black community?[86]

Studies of riot participation suggest that "rioters" represent a cross section of the lower-class community. The young people who participate are not known to be psychologically impaired or especially suffering from problems of masculine identity. Juveniles arrested in the 1967 Detroit riot were found by a psychological team to be less emotionally disturbed and less delinquent than typical juvenile arrestees.[87] Furthermore, the recent riots have served to mobilize the younger segments of the black community and to educate them to the realities of their caste position in American society:

> Today it is the young men who are fighting the battles, and, for now, their elders, though they have given their approval, have not joined in. The time seems near, however, for the full range of the black masses to put down the broom and buckle on the sword. And it grows nearer day by day. Now we see skirmishes, sputtering erratically, evidence if you will that the young men are in a warlike mood. But evidence as well that the elders are watching closely and may soon join the battle.[88]

Riots and Political Protest

While commissions generally deplore the violence of "rioters" (but minimize or ignore the significance of official violence) and attribute rioting to the "riffraff" element, they are still faced with the problem of explaining why riots are participated in by a cross section of the ghetto communities, and given wide support by those communities. Given these facts, few serious official treatments of riots now attempt to explain the resulting violence purely in terms of a "riffraff" theory. With the exception of the 1943 Detroit Commission, staffed by law enforcement officials, commissions try to account for the popular support and participation in riots.

Most commissions resolve this dilemma by arguing that riots are invariably aggravated or instigated by the criminal activities of a small group of provocateurs who take advantage of human weakness and transform basically nonviolent individuals into an irrational mob. Thus, riots are widely characterized as outlets for pent-up frustrations and grievances sparked by a few. In Chicago, according to the 1919 commission, even "normal-minded Negroes" exhibited a "pathological attitude to society which sometimes expresses itself defensively in acts of violence and other lawlessness."[89] The 1935 Harlem riot also drew upon the participation of "normal" citizens:

> Neither the threats nor the reassurances of the police could restrain these spontaneous outbursts until the crowds had spent themselves in giving release to their pent-up emotions. . . . Negro crimes result from the fact that normal individual impulses and desires are often forced to express themselves in a lawless manner in a disorganized social environment.[90]

The Watts riot was characterized as an "insensate rage of destruction," a "spasm," and a "formless, quite senseless, all but hopeless violent protest." Even the conservative McCone Commission was well aware that it took more than criminal impulse for over 10,000 citizens to "escalate the routine arrest of a drunken driver into six days of violence."[91] Similarly, the 1968 commissions noted that riots were the product of a "sense of rage" and "years of frustration born and bred in poverty."[92]

Underlying most official conceptions of riots is the assumption that rioting is a pathological outburst and that "rioters" are irrationally compelled into violence by distorted perceptions of social reality. Though it may be granted that "rioters" have some objective justification for their unhappiness and anger, it is also argued that they tend to exaggerate the importance of underlying grievances:

> Some kind of provocation triggers the violence. This precipi- tating incident, *even though it might have been completely*

> *imaginary*, becomes exaggerated through rumor and magnified out of proportion to its actual importance.[93]

> [M]any Negroes have felt and *were encouraged to feel* that they had been affronted by the passage of Proposition 14— an initiative measure passed by two-thirds of the voters in November 1964 which repealed the Rumford Fair Housing Act. . . .[94]

> There is a conviction on the part of a clear majority of our black citizens that [political] representation is entirely unsatisfactory and must be improved. This conviction, *whether or not or to what extent it is true*, is of critical importance to the continued health of our city.[95]

This perspective on the popular participation in riots leads many theorists to examine the psychological dynamics of rioting. Rioters are "compelled" into violence; they are "frustrated" and "irrational"; they are "not responsible" for their actions. The essential problem with this analysis is that it neglects the intrinsically political and rational aspects of collective protest and fails to take seriously the grievances which motivate riots. The explanation of riots in terms of "frustration-aggression" is both analytically unsound and politically deceptive. It is unsound because it neglects the subjective meanings of rioting and too easily obscures the specificity of political grievances. As Allan Silver has noted, "men who engage in dangerous and desperate behavior— indeed, any behavior—have a certain claim to have taken seriously the meanings which they see in their own acts, and wish others to see in them."[96] The "frustration-aggression" approach is also deceptive because it focuses on the psychological motives of "rioters" and ignores the corresponding motives of officials.[97] This is not to suggest that individual participants in riots lack their share of psychological disturbance or ignorance. But the substitution of a psychological analysis for a political one is clearly motivated by ideological bias, for it implicitly serves to uphold the legitimacy of established authority and discredit the collective aspirations of disaffected groups.

To summarize, then, official theories of rioting are inadequate on a number of grounds. They tend to disguise normative and political evaluations in scientific terms; they manipulate definitions to suit ideological conveniences; they focus on the violence of "rioters" and generally neglect the at least equally serious problem of "official" violence; and they disparage the rational and political grievances which motivate many riots.

These misconceptions of riots correspond with the political assumptions and liberal ideology of commissioners and government officials who appoint commissions. "Violence" is condemned; the instigators of riots are branded as "demagogues" and "agitators"; sympathy is extended to the otherwise law-abiding persons who become involved in riots through a process of "contagion"; the general underlying causes of riots—poverty, misery, racism, etc.—are acknowledged as a contributing factor; and the legitimacy of the existing order is affirmed, especially its generous capacity to redress grievances and assimilate the disaffected.

Furthermore, these ideological convictions are for the most part shared by social scientists. As Rudé has observed, "the social psychologist, like the historian, continues to show reluctance to abandon the old concept of the crowd as 'mob,' with all its disparaging connotations."[98] At the same time, however, social scientists provide commissions with techniques and imagery for justifying liberal ideology:

> The American notables who made up these commissions— like those middle and upper-class liberals and professionals who form a sympathetic audience for their reports—have tended broadly to support some or many key aspirations of Negroes. At the same time, they are perhaps among those most likely to accord high priority to the vision of a pervasively pacific society. . . . What social science perspectives do for liberals is to make it possible for them to maintain broad political sympathy for the urban Negro "underclass" and simultaneously come to terms with popular unruliness, riot, and violence even though these things are especially disturbing to them. This function of social science perspectives also testifies to the remoteness of the relationship between the rioting classes and those officially designated to interpret their behavior.[99]

If official and academic conceptions of riots are distorted by ideological assumptions which seriously misconstrue the meaning of riots, it follows that riot control recommendations based on these conceptions may also be inadequate and self-defeating. The following section addresses this issue.

CONTROLLING RIOTS

Order and Reform

It is part of the mandate of commissions to recommend measures for the control of future riots; many social-scientific treatments of riots take up a similar task. Modern theories of riots usually focus on two sources of disorders: a condition of social "strain" or "tension," leading to frustration and hostility on the part of disaffected groups; and a breakdown of "normal" systems of social control, in the sense of both widespread social disorganization and the inability of local authorities to maintain order. Thus, a leading textbook suggests that the origins of collective disorders are to be found in a combination of "social disintegration" and the failure of social control agencies to adequately perform their functions.[100] Another contemporary theorist, while stressing the importance of "frustration" as one kind of strain leading to "hostile outbursts,"[101] also argues that firmness in the "agencies of social control" may play a role in preventing outbursts.[102] "A key element in the outbreak of riots," notes another sociologist, "is a weakness in the system of social control."[103]

Similarly, official theories of riots have usually been translated into recommendations combining a program for the reduction of social tensions with a call for the development of sophisticated strategies and technology to contain riots. Recommendations aimed at eliminating the underlying causes of riots have not varied much since 1919—more and better educational facilities, equal job opportunities, integrated recreation, more responsible news reporting, better police-community relations, more efficient transportation services, better political representation, more public housing, more federal funding for urban programs, etc., etc.

At the same time, riot commissions are concerned with stressing the importance of inhibiting the resort to violence as a means of resolving grievances and have consequently recommended improved methods of riot control. The 1919 Chicago Commission recommended enlargement of the police force and special training in the control of disorders. It noted a "marked contrast between the militia and the police"[104]—the former well-organized and disciplined, the latter largely ineffective—and noted the need to plan joint police-militia action in handling riots.[105] The 1943 Detroit Commission noted the numerical inadequacy of the police and the need for the formulation of special riot plans.[106] The 1965 McCone Commission also recommended the necessity for "massive force" in dealing with riots, stressing the need for early commitment of National Guard troops.[107] The Kerner Commission, in its "Supplement on Control of Disorder," urged elaborate contingency planning, involving the National Guard and Army, for controlling riots.[108] Finally, the 1969 Violence Commission recommended that police departments "improve their preparations for anticipating, preventing, and controlling group disorders. . . ."[109]

These recommendations stem from the conception of riots as irrational outbursts, reflecting a breakdown of social and personal controls, and aggravated by a process of contagion. For this reason, commissions generally view the control of rumor and other inflammatory information as useful in containing emergent disorders. The Kerner Commission, for example, recommended the establishment of "rumor collection centers" to gather and dispel "false and inflammatory reports."[110] Another expert, noting evidence for a "negative impact of the media on social values and on personal controls required to inhibit individual dispositions into aggressive actions," argues for reduction of riot coverage by the mass media, especially television, for "television images serve to spread the contagion pattern throughout urban areas and the nation."[111]

Once a riot has begun, however, the need for massive, immediate, and decisive action is recognized. A leading social-scientific work notes the dangerous consequences of a failure by auhorities to act quickly and decisively, suggesting as "a general principle" that "vacillation on the part of police authorities in deciding to use force tends to encourage the spread of disorder."[112] This applies also to the "weak governor who shilly-shallies in deciding to call in the National Guard to put down a dangerous riot."[113] Similarly, the FBI instructs police departments to quickly prevent the spread of riots by "rapid dispersal of the mob"[114] and an "impressive display of police power and resolve . . . to promptly overcome resistance."[115]

Commissions are also aware that social control agencies may aggravate riots and, in recent years, there has emerged a new concern for increasing the sophistication and technical efficiency of the police and National Guard.[116] Since the Army has been the most effective counter-riot force, it is generally used as a standard against which the performance of local units may be compared and towards which they should strive. As a 1968 Army memorandum noted, "the collocation of military and civil operational headquarters or command posts has become almost axiomatic" during the civil disorders.[117] *The Kerner Report* also adopted a similar militaristic perspective, noting the need for riot contingency plans, coordination with the National Guard and Army, and making riot training a standard procedure of police training.[118] The thrust toward the rationalization of social control agencies, therefore, has become in practice a demand for greater militarization of the official response. This means, for example, the replacement of anachronistic methods of riot control with more effective military procedures, such as "realistic training in sharpshooting and precision firing."[119] It also entails a search for technical solutions and a craftsmanlike distaste for administrative errors. Thus, a recent report from the Institute of Defense Analysis comments that:

> The National Guard . . . in response to the recent civil disorders has expanded its riot training into a thirty-two hour program of instruction. This is particularly focused at such problems as arson, looting, and sniping, the field intelligence problem, refresher aspects of tactical training and methods of detecting, neutralizing, and apprehending snipers, procedure for detention of suspects, area saturation, and cooperative activities with the civilian police. . . . As was nicely demonstrated in the Watts riot and since, incompatibilities of equipment, particularly communications equipment, between the various forces can impair the operational effectiveness of the collective forces.[120]

The Priority of Order

Riot commissions do not advocate purely repressive measures of control. Rather they adopt a seemingly moderate position, one which combines long-term recommendations aimed at reducing underlying tensions with the development of technical means of controlling riots. Although commissions recognize fundamental problems in the economic and political situation of urban blacks, they nevertheless maintain that the first priority is the restoration of public order. In the words of the Kerner Commission, "preserving civil peace is the first responsibility of government."[121]

Implicit in the "two-pronged approach" (reform and control) is the assumption that reform recommendations have about the same prospect of gaining executive and legislative support as control and firepower measures. Historical experience, however, suggests no such parity. On the contrary, riot commissions since 1919 have had minimal success in achieving the implementation of their reform recommendations. But they have had great success with their control recommendations. After the 1935 Harlem riot, for example, it was reported that "extra police stand guard on the corners and mounted patrolmen ride through the streets. . . . It offers no assurance that the legitimate demands of the community for work and decent living conditions will be heeded." And the Harlem Commission warned that riots would recur so long as basic grievances were not redressed.[122] Over thirty years later, the Kerner Commission similarly reported that "in several cities, the principal official response has been to train and equip the police with more sophisticated weapons."[123] Following the Kerner Commission, there has been considerable development of riot-control weaponry, police intelligence programs, and special riot-control "tactical squads."[124] There is no evidence of fundamental social, economic, and political reforms.

The two-pronged approach which gives equal weight to the desirability of control and reform fails to appreciate the dangerous consequences of escalated levels of force. As the Skolnick Task Force to the Violence Commission noted:

> We may suggest as a general rule that a society which must contemplate massive expenditures for social control is one which, virtually by definition, has not grappled with the necessity of massive social reform. . . . A democratic society cannot have it both ways: either it will carry through a firm commitment to massive and widespread political and social reform, or it will develop into a society of garrison cities where order is enforced without due process of law and without the consent of the governed.[125]

CONCLUSION

[If] the show seems familiar, it is because the show has been running a very long time, and most of the actors have had no choice but to speak the lines and make the moves assigned to them. There is a rumor—striking terror and chaos in the heart of the box office—that some people have become so weary of the spectacle that they have sent for a new show, which is presently on the road. But not until the wheels of those wagons are on our children's necks will we consider reading or revising or throwing away this script.

In the meantime, ladies and gentlemen, after a brief intermission—time out for one or two committee reports, time out for an anti-poverty pep talk, time out to make a Vietnamese child an orphan and then lovingly raise him to love all our works, time out for a White House conference, time out to brief and augment the police forces, time out to buy some Negroes, jail some, club some, kill some—after a brief intermission, ladies and gentlemen, the show begins again in the auction room. And you will hear the same old piano, playing the same blues.[126]

James Baldwin

Riot commissions, like other kinds of investigative commissions, have become a standard feature of governmental response to civil disorders. The riot commission seems familiar, to paraphrase James Baldwin, because it has been performing regularly since 1917. As the preceding analysis suggests, it is neither a crudely repressive nor conspiratorial performance. On the contrary, riot commissions are invariably benign and liberal, concerned about human misery and racism, and staffed by well-intentioned and educated persons. Despite the burden of time pressures and organizational problems, many riot commissions manage to make important public contributions: they assemble large quantities of demographic and statistical data; they provide a stimulus and forum for public debate about critical governmental issues;[127] they provide opportunities for intellectuals to influence public policies; and they occasionally effect the implementation of modest reforms.

Persons who work on and for commissions do not see themselves as advocates of racism or as defenders of inequality. Some regard themselves as "reformers" and "pragmatists," seeking ways of being effective and helpful in a difficult situation. Others genuinely believe that commissions can have a profound impact on government policies, "public opinion," and the mass media. The failures of riot commissions cannot be simply attributed to bad faith or malicious motivation.

Yet riot commissions have persistently failed to eliminate the miseries, persecution, and exploitation of black Americans. This failure stems partly from the fact that "there is a built-in tendency toward the whitewash, to the extent that riot commissions minimize criticism of the public officials to whom they must look for primary implementation of the report."[128] This is not to suggest that commissions are merely "lackeys" of their governmental sponsors. Some commissions go beyond the boundaries of their mandate, while others take a position that is considered too liberal by their sponsors.[129] Thus, the findings of the Scranton Commission, especially their criticism of law enforcement agencies, were at odds with the public position of President Nixon and many members of his cabinet. At the same time, however, there is considerable pressure on commissions to compromise findings and to avoid public criticism of government officials in the hope that their recommendations will be translated into public policy. Commissions which do not observe this lesson are vulnerable to political attacks on their motivation, impartiality, and intelligence.[130]

In summary, the failure of riot commissions is to be found in a combination of structural and organizational conditions: (a) Appointed by government officials who select commissioners and determine the parameters of their investigation, riot commissions are severely limited in the scope and quality of their inquiry. (b) Commissioners are selected from highly specialized and elitist interest groups which in no way reflect the full range of interests and opinion in American society. (c) Under considerable time and organizational pressures, commissions are usually incapable of reflective and careful scholarship. (d) The relationship of commissions with their research staff is typically exploitative and managerial. In turn, intellectuals have generally demonstrated a willingness to be misused, coopted, and exploited by commissions. (e) Riot commissions have produced theories and generalizations about "riots" which are for the most part based on insufficient data, inarticulated ideological preconceptions, and weak analysis. (f) And their recommendations for the control of riots are similarly based on inadequate theories, aggravated by inadequate consideration of the political consequences of their recommendations.

Finally, riot commissions fail in a much more fundamental sense. Riot commissions assume that (a) government is not a party to civil disorders, (b) changes in the conditions of blacks can be achieved by appealing to the good faith and reasonableness of government, and (c) fundamental changes in the conditions of blacks can be achieved without fundamental changes in existing political and economic institutions. These assumptions are implicit in and taken for granted by riot commissions. Their validity is *at least* open to question. The American government, from the days of slavery to the "war on poverty," is deeply implicated in the lives and suffering of blacks. To appeal to the "good will" of a government which has helped to enslave black Americans is both foolish and unreasonable. Also, since blacks are exploited economically and politically, as well as racially, we are unlikely to eliminate "racism" until there are fundamental changes in our political and economic institutions.[131]

Rioting is a serious and dramatic form of political protest. Potentially, it is the catalyst for organizing a radical movement aimed at the transformation of American institutions rather than inclusion into them.[132] This possibility does not escape the notice of political and economic elites. In this sense, riot commissions may be understood as an effort to coopt liberal reformers and professionals, to affirm the strength and flexibility of established institutional arrangements—to reduce any existing imperfections and facilitate their smooth management—to divide "radical" opposition and disparage socialist or "liberation" movements, and to inhibit the possibility of sudden and major change.[133]

NOTES

1. Herbert Aptheker, *American Negro Slave Revolts* (New York: International Publishers, 1969), p. 5.

2. For a general examination of these militant traditions, see "Black Militancy," *The Politics of Protest*, ed. Jerome Skolnick (New York: Simon and Schuster, 1969), chapter IV.

3. Ibid., p. 129.

4. Arna Bontemps, *Black Thunder* (Boston: Beacon Press, 1968), p. vii.

5. See, for example, The National Commission on the Causes and Prevention of Violence, *To Establish Justice, To Insure Domestic Tranquility* (Washington, D.C.: U.S. Government Printing Office, 1969); The Cox Commission, *Crisis at Columbia* (New York: Vintage Books, 1968); American Bar Association, Commission on Campus Government and Student Dissent, *Report* (Chicago: American Bar Foundation, 1970); and The Walker Report, *Rights in Conflict* (New York: Bantam Books, 1968).

6. For an analysis of this issue, see Elliott Currie's essay on p. 452.

7. See, especially, the final report of The National Commission, *To Establish Justice*.

8. Harold Cruse, *The Crisis of the Negro Intellectual* (New York: William Morrow, 1967), pp. 370-71.

9. For a discussion of these reports on the judicial system, see Skolnick, *Politics of Protest*, pp. 293-326.

10. The National Advisory Commission on Civil Disorders, *Kerner Report* (New York: Bantam Books, 1968), p. 29.

11. The National Commission, *To Establish Justice*, pp. 116-17.

12. Howard Zinn, *The Politics of History* (Boston: Beacon Press, 1970), p. 102.

13. According to Zinn, "we would see more clearly the limitations of government investigating committees set up to deal with deep-rooted social problems if we knew the history of such committees." Ibid., p. 44.

14. Chicago Commission on Race Relations, *The Negro in Chicago: A Study of Race Relations and a Race Riot* (Chicago: University of Chicago Press, 1922), p. xvi.

15. Governor's Committee to Investigate the Riot Occurring in Detroit, June 21, 1943, *Final Report* (Detroit: Ms., 1943), p. 2.

16. Governor's Commission on the Los Angeles Riots, *Violence in the City—An End or a Beginning?* (Los Angeles: College Book Store, 1965), p. i.

17. National Advisory Commission, *Report*, p. 537.

18. Robert Paul Wolff, "Beyond Tolerance," in *A Critique of Pure Tolerance* (Boston: Beacon Press), p. 51.

19. Reported in *Newsweek*, 10 August 1970, p. 21.

20. Murray Edelman, *The Symbolic Uses of Politics* (Urbana: University of Illinois Press, 1967), p. 193.

21. Charles J. Hanser, *Guide to Decision: The Royal Commission* (Totowa, N.J.: Bedminister Press, 1965), p. 148.

22. Andrew Kopkind, "White on Black: The Riot Commission and the Rhetoric of Reform," *Hard Times*, 15 September 1969, no. 44, pp. 15-22.

23. National Commission, *To Establish Justice*, p. 109. But another commissioner, Patricia Harris, was not so gracious: "Those who adopted the [majority opinion] have never belonged to a group required to sit in the back of a bus, or excluded from restaurants because of race, with the approval of legislatures, courts and administrators. I am a member of such a group, and I refused to obey those segregation laws. . . ." Ibid., p. 106.

24. Michael Lipsky and David J. Olson, "Riot Commission Politics," *Trans-action*, July–August, 1969, pp. 8-21.

25. This perspective is developed more fully by C. Wright Mills, *The Power Elite* (New York: Oxford University Press, 1966), especially chapter 12.

26. The following commissioners have served on more than one major commission: Bayless Manning, Leon Higginbotham, Hale Boggs, Leon Jaworski, Albert Jenner, William McCulloch, and Charles Thornton.

27. Wolff, "Beyond Tolerance," p. 41.

28. Ibid., pp. 43-44.

29. The ACLU study is reported in the *San Francisco Sunday Chronicle and Examiner*, 5 July 1970, Section A, p. 20 and the AAUP study is reported in *The San Francisco Chronicle*, 27 June 1970, p. 2.

30. The final report of the "Greater Chicago Citizen's Riot Probe Commission," for example, received much less press coverage and was printed much less competently than the report of Mayor Daley's commission.

31. Arthur I. Waskow, *From Race Riot to Sit-In, 1919 and the 1960s* (New York: Doubleday, 1966), p. 67.

32. Wolff, "Beyond Tolerance," p. 51.

33. Waskow, *From Race Riot*, pp. 60-104.

34. A notable exception is the 1935 Harlem Commission which included in its final report a chapter on the hearings and their results.

35. Robert M. Fogelson, "White on Black: A Critique of the Mc-

Cone Commission Report on the Los Angeles Riots," *Political Science Quarterly* 82, no. 3 (September 1967): 333-67.

36. Kopkind, "White on Black," p. 1.

37. Lipsky and Olson, "Riot Commission Politics," p. 16.

38. Paul Jacobs, *Prelude to Riot* (New York: Random House, 1967), p. 249.

39. Interview, "Ralph Nader," *Playboy* (October 1968), p. 108.

40. Stanley Friedman, "Dialogue with James F. Short," *Issues in Criminology* 5, no. 1 (Winter 1970): 30.

41. Kopkind, "White on Black," p. 3.

42. Hans W. Mattick, "The Form and Content of Recent Riots," *Midway* 9, no. 1 (Summer 1968): 4.

43. Jacobs, *Prelude to Riot*, p. 253.

44. Waskow, *From Race Riot*, p. 60.

45. Kopkind, "White on Black," p. 3.

46. Lipsky and Olson, "Riot Commission Politics," pp. 11-12.

47. See, for example, letter and memorandum from Walter White, Secretary of NAACP, to Mayor LaGuardia, dated March 26, 1935. Copy available in New York Municipal Archives.

48. National Advisory Commission, *Report*, p. 539.

49. Herbert Blumer, "Threats from Agency-Determined Research: The Case of Camelot," *The Rise and Fall of Project Camelot*, ed. Irving L. Horowitz (Cambridge: The M.I.T. Press, 1967), pp. 153-74.

50. Ibid., p. 165.

51. Ibid., pp. 169-70.

52. Julius A. Roth, "Hired Hand Research," *The American Sociologist* 1, no. 4 (August 1966): 190-96.

53. Ibid., pp. 192, 194.

54. Ibid., p. 192.

55. See, for example, Noam Chomsky, *American Power and the New Mandarins* (New York: Pantheon Books, 1967).

56. The remainder of this paper relies extensively on a report co-authored with Elliott Currie for the Task Force on Violent Aspects of Protest and Confrontation, National Commission on the Causes and Prevention of Violence. The following analysis has also benefited from a paper by Elliott Currie and Jerome Skolnick, "A Critical Note on Theories of Collective Behavior."

57. Chicago Commission, *The Negro in Chicago*, p. xiii.

58. Governor's Commission on the Los Angeles Riots, *Violence in the City*, p. 9.

59. Chicago Riot Study Committee, *Final Report* (Chicago, 1968), p. 3.

60. Mayor's Special Task Force, *Progress Report* (Pittsburgh, 1968), p. 5.

61. National Advisory Commission, *Report*, p. 2.

62. See, for example, Roger Brown, *Social Psychology* (New York: Free Press, 1965); Herbert Blumer, "Collective Behavior," *Review of Sociology: Analysis of a Decade*, ed. J. B. Gittler (New York: John Wiley, 1957); Neil J. Smelser, *Theory of Collective Behavior* (New York: Free Press, 1962), and R. H. Turner and L. M. Killian, *Collective Behavior* (Englewood Cliffs, N.J.: Prentice-Hall, 1957).

63. Brown, *Social Psychology*, p. 709.

64. For a critique of this perspective, see Carl J. Cough, "Collective Behavior: An Examination of Some Stereotypes," *Social Problems* 15, no. 3 (1968): 310-22.

65. Smelser, *Theory*, p. 1.

66. Ibid., p. 72.

67. As long ago as 1919, Carl Sandburg noted a relationship between war and "the race problem." During his assignment for the *Chicago Daily News*, he observed that there "are thousands of strong young men who have been talking to each other on topics more or less intimately related to the questions, 'What are we ready to die for? Why do we live? What is democracy? What is the meaning of freedom; of self-determination?' In barber shop windows and in cigar stores and haberdasheries are helmets, rifles, cartridges, canteens and haversacks and photographs of negro [sic] regiments that were sent to France." *The Chicago Race Riots, July 1919* (New York: Harcourt, Brace & World, 1969), pp. 8-9.

68. See, especially, The Walker Report, *Rights in Conflict*, pp. 1-11 and the Mayor's Commission on Conditions in Harlem, *The Negro in Harlem* (New York, 1936), chapter 1.

69. See, for example, George Rudé, *The Crowd in History: A Study of Popular Disturbances in France and England, 1730–1848* (New York: John Wiley, 1964); E. P. Thompson, *The Making of the English Working Class* (Middlesex, Eng.: Pelican Books, 1968), especially pp. 59-83; Eric Hobsbawm, *Primitive Rebels* (New York: W. W. Norton, 1959); and Charles Tilly, "Collective Violence in European Perspective," *The History of Violence in America: Historical and Comparative Perspectives*, eds. Hugh D. Graham and Ted R. Gurr (New York: Bantam Books, 1969), pp. 4-45.

70. Hobsbawn, *Primitive Rebels*, p. 114.

71. Eric Hobsbawn, *Laboring Men: Studies in the History of Labor* (New York: Basic Books, 1964), p. 16.

72. Rudé, *The Crowd in History*, p. 268.

73. Barrington Moore, Jr., "Tolerance and the Scientific Outlook," in *A Critique of Pure Tolerance*, p. 74.

74. The "riffraff" theory is fully described and criticized by T. M. Tomlinson and David O. Sears, *Los Angeles Riot Study: Negro Attitudes Toward the Riot* (Los Angeles: Institute of Government and Public Affairs, University of California, 1967); see also Robert M. Fogelson and Robert B. Hill, "Who Riots? A Study of Participation in the 1967 Riots," in *Supplemental Studies for the National Advisory Commission on Civil Disorders* (Washington, D.C.: U.S. Government Printing Office, 1968), pp. 221-43.

75. Rudé, *The Crowd in History*, pp. 7-8.

76. Mayor F. H. LaGuardia, "Statement on Harlem Situation" (March 20, 1935). Copy of press release available in New York Municipal Archives.

77. National Advisory Commission, *Report*, pp. 538-39.

78. Federal Bureau of Investigation, *Prevention and Control of Mobs and Riots* (U.S. Department of Justice: FBI, 1967), p. 31.

79. Governor's Committee to Investigate the Riot Occurring in Detroit, *Final Report*, Part II, pp. 1-3; Governor's Commission on the Los Angeles Riots, *Violence in the City*, p. 1; Chicago Riot Study Committee, *Final Report*, p. 3; and Mayor's Special Task Force, *Progress Report*, p. 3.

80. Chicago Riot Study Committee, *Final Report*, p. 28.

81. Mayor's Commission on Conditions in Harlem, *Negro in Harlem*, p. 11.

82. David O. Sears and John B. McConshan, *Los Angeles Riot Study: Riot Participation* (Los Angeles: Institute of Government and Public Affairs, University of California, 1967), pp. 20-21; see also Nathan E. Cohen, *Los Angeles Riot Study: Summary and Implications for Policy* (Los Angeles: Institute of Government and Public Affairs, University of California, 1967), pp. 20-21.

83. Fogelson and Hill, "Who Riots?".

84. Tomlinson and Sears, *Los Angeles Riot Study*, p. 33.

85. Cohen, *Los Angeles Riot Study*, p. 4.

86. Fogelson and Hill, "Who Riots?", p. 243.

87. Richard Komisaruk and Carol Pearson, "Children of the Detroit Riots," *Journal of Urban Law* 44 (Spring and Summer, 1968): 599-626.

88. William H. Grier and Price M. Cobbs, *Black Rage* (New York: Basic Books, 1968), p. 211.

89. Chicago Commission, *The Negro in Chicago*, p. 342.

90. Mayor's Commission on Conditions in Harlem, *Negro in Harlem*, pp. 7, 99.

91. Governor's Commission on the Los Angeles Riots, *Violence in the City*, pp. 1, 4-5, 6.

92. Chicago Riot Study Committee, *Final Report*, p. 3 and Mayor's Special Task Force, *Progress Report*, p. 4.

93. Federal Bureau of Investigation, *Prevention and Control*, p. 25. (Emphasis added.)

94. Governor's Commission on the Los Angeles Riots, *Violence in the City*, p. 4. (Emphasis added.)

95. Chicago Riot Study Committee, *Final Report*, p. 112. (Emphasis added.)

96. Allan A. Silver, "Official Interpretations of Racial Riots," *Proceedings of the Academy of Political Science*, 29, no. 1 (July 1968): 154.

97. For a comparable critique of theories of student protest, see John P. Spiegel, "Campus Conflict and Professional Egos," *Transaction*, October 1969, pp. 41-50.

98. Rudé, *The Crowd in History*, p. 10.

99. Silver, "Official Interpretations," pp. 149-51; for a more general critique of the relationship between social scientists and the federal government, see Alvin W. Gouldner, "The Sociologist as Partisan: Sociology and the Welfare State," *American Sociologist*, 3 (1968): 103-16.

100. Turner and Killian, *Collective Behavior*, pp. 20-21.

101. Smelser, *Theory*, p. 246.

102. Ibid., p. 261f.

103. Morris Janowitz, *Social Control of Escalated Riots* (Chicago: University of Chicago Center for Policy Study, 1968), p. 7.

104. Chicago Commission, *The Negro in Chicago*, p. 42.

105. Ibid., p. 640.

106. Governor's Committee to Investigate the Riot Occurring in Detroit, *Final Report*, p. 14.

107. Governor's Commission on the Los Angeles Riots, *Violence in the City*, p. 21.

108. National Advisory Commission, *Report*, pp. 484-527.

109. The National Commission, *To Establish Justice*, p. 487.

110. National Advisory Commission, *Report*, p. 487.

111. Janowitz, *Social Control*, p. 33.

112. Smelser, *Theory*, p. 262.

113. Ibid.

114. Federal Bureau of Investigation, *Prevention and Control*, p. 82.

115. Ibid., p. 87.

116. See, for example, Joseph F. Coates, *Some New Approaches to Riot, Mob, and Crowd Control* (Institute of Defense Analysis, 1968).

117. Department of the Army, *Operations Report—Lessons Learned, Civil Disturbances, April 1968* (Washington, D.C.: Office of the Adjutant General, 1968), p. 2.

118. National Advisory Commission, *Report*, p. 17.

119. Janowitz, *Social Control*, p. 24.

120. Coates, *New Approaches*, p. 14.

121. National Advisory Commission, *Report*, p. 17.

122. Mayor's Commission on Conditions in Harlem, *Negro in Harlem*, p. 109.

123. National Advisory Commission, *Report*, p. 18.

124. See, for example, Garry Wills, *The Second Civil War* (New York: New American Library, 1968).

125. Skolnick, *Politics of Protest*, pp. 344, 346.

126. From *The Negro in New York: An Informal Social History*, eds. Roi Ottely and William J. Weatherby (New York: Oceana Publications, 1967), p. xix.

127. Daniel Bell, "Government by Commission," *The Public Interest*, Spring 1966, pp. 3-9.

128. Lipsky and Olson, "Riot Commission Politics," p. 21.

129. The 1935 Harlem Commission is an example of the former and the Kerner Commission of the latter.

130. See, for example, the attacks on the Scranton Commission on Campus Unrest by Vice-President Agnew, Senator Gordon Allott, Senator Barry Goldwater, and other conservative Republicans.

131. For an example of the political exploitation of blacks, see Harold M. Baron, "Black Powerlessness in Chicago," *Trans-action*, November 1968, pp. 27-42; for a discussion of the relationship between economic and racial exploitation, see Paul A. Baran and Paul M. Sweezy, *Monopoly Capital* (New York: Modern Reader Paperbacks, 1966), especially chapter 9.

132. See, for example, Skolnick, *Politics of Protest*, chapter 4; and Stokely Carmichael and Charles V. Hamilton, *Black Power* (New York: Vintage Press, 1967).

133. For an analogous discussion of the United States Commission on Industrial Relations, see James Weinstein, *The Corporate Ideal in the Liberal State, 1900–1918* (Boston: Beacon Press, 1968), especially chapter 7.

II

East St. Louis, 1917

INTRODUCTION

There were some eighteen major interracial disturbances in the United States between 1915 and 1919. In 1917, serious incidents of racial violence occurred in East St. Louis, Chester (Pennsylvania), Philadelphia, and Houston. According to the sociologist Allen Grimshaw, "large-scale interracial violence became almost endemic in the United States toward the end of the first World War and during the months immediately following it."[1]

A congressional inquiry into the East St. Louis riots, in which at least thirty-nine blacks and nine whites were killed, culminated in the publication on July 15, 1918, of a short but incisive report on the nature of the riots and their underlying causes. The final report was based on four weeks of hearings (amounting to twenty-three volumes of transcript), official memoranda, and personal observations by committee members in East St. Louis.

The selections from Elliott Rudwick's *Race Riot at East St. Louis* include a detailed account of how local and national politicians, and the mass media responded to the riot. Also included is a discussion and analysis of the political decisions which led to the congressional inquiry. Rudwick documents how Congress persisted in its investigation despite presidential indifference and an uncooperative Department of Justice.

NOTES

1. Allen D. Grimshaw, *Racial Violence in the United States* (Chicago: Aldine, 1969), p. 60.

2.

BEN JOHNSON
JOHN E. RAKER
M. D. FOSTER, and
HENRY ALLEN COOPER

Report on the Special Committee Authorized by Congress to Investigate the East St. Louis Riots

Your committee appointed under House Resolution No. 128 for the purpose of making an investigation of the East St. Louis riots which occurred on May 28 and July 2, 1917, reports that as a result of unlawful conditions existing at that place, interstate commerce was not only openly and violently interrupted but was virtually suspended for a week or ten days during and following the riot of last July. For months after the July riot interstate commerce was interfered with and hindered, not, however, by open acts of violence, but by a subtle and effective intimidation of colored men who had been employed by the railroads to handle freight consigned from one state to another. So many of these men were driven out of East St. Louis as the result of the July riot that the railroads could not secure necessary help. After the worst effects of the riot had passed this class of labor remained so frightened and intimidated that it would not live in East St. Louis.

SOURCE: From House of Representatives, 35th Cong., 2d Sess., Document No. 1231 (July 15, 1918), pp. 1-24.

Some of them took up their residences across the river in St. Louis, and would go over to East St. Louis in the morning to work and would return to that place before nightfall. In order to get out of East St. Louis and back to St. Louis before night came on, the length of the day's work was reduced. The fright of these laborers went to such an extent—and it was fully justified by existing conditions—that special means of transportation had to be provided for them back and forth between St. Louis and East St. Louis in order to get them to work at all. Besides the killing of a number of these negro [sic] laborers, a very large number, indeed, fled from the work and never returned to it. In addition to this, 44 freight cars were burned and serious damage done to the railroad tracks, all of which will be referred to further along in this report.

Your committee made an earnest, nonpartisan effort to determine the basic cause of the riot. We endeavored to pursue every avenue of information to its source, searched the hearts and consciences of all witnesses, and sought the opinions of men in every walk of life. The officers of the mills and factories placed the blame at the door of organized labor; but the overwhelming weight of testimony, to which is added the convictions of the committee, ascribes the mob spirit and its murderous manifestations to the bitter race feeling that had grown up between the whites and the blacks.

The natural racial aversion, which finds expression in mob violence in the North as in the South, was augmented in East St. Louis by hundreds of petty conflicts between the whites and the blacks. During the year 1917 between 10,000 and 12,000 negroes came from the Southern states to seek work at promised high wages in the industries of St. Clair County. They swarmed into the railroad stations on every train, to be met by their friends who formed reception committees and welcomed them to the financial, political, and social liberty which they had been led to believe Illinois guaranteed. They seldom had more than enough money to exactly defray their transportation, and they arrived dirty and hungry. They stood around the street corners in homesick huddles, seeking shelter and hunting work.

How to deal with them soon became a municipal problem. Morning found them gathered at the gates of the manufactories, where often they were chosen in preference to the white men who also sought employment. But as rapidly as employment was found for those already there, fresh swarms arrived from the South, until the great number without employment menaced the prosperity and safety of the community.

The Aluminum Ore Co. brought hundreds and hundreds of them to the city as strike breakers to defeat organized labor, a precedent which aroused intense hatred and antagonism and caused countless tragedies in its aftermath. The feeling of resentment grew with each succeeding day. White men walked the streets in idleness, their families suffering for food and warmth and clothes, while their places as laborers were taken by strange negroes who were compelled to live in hovels and who were used to keep down wages.

It was proven conclusively that the various industries in St. Clair County were directly responsible for the importation of these negroes from the South. Advertisements were printed in various Southern newspapers urging the negroes to come to East St. Louis and promising them big wages. In many instances agents were sent through the South to urge the negroes to abandon profitable employment there and come to East St. Louis, where work was said to be plentiful and wages high.

One of the local railroads sent an agent to the Southern states, and on some trips he brought back with him as many as 30 to 40 negro men, all of them employed at their Southern homes, making from $2 to $2.50 a day. A number of these men testified before the committee that they were promised $2.40 a day and "board" if they would come to East St. Louis; but when they did come they were paid only $1.40 a day, with an allowance of 60 cents a day for board, and were fed on coffee, bread, and "lasses" and made to sleep on sacks in box cars, where they suffered keenly from the cold.

Responsibility for this influx of 10,000 or more negroes into East St. Louis rests on the railroads and the manufacturing establishments, and they must bear their share of the responsibility for the ensuing arson and murder that followed this unfortunate invasion.

It is a lamentable fact that the employers of labor paid too little heed to the comfort or welfare of their men. They saw them crowded into wretched cabins, without water or any of the conveniences of life; their wives and children condemned to live in the disreputable quarters of the town, and made no effort to lift them out of the mire.

The negroes gravitated to the unsanitary sections, existed in the squalor of filthy cabins, and made no complaint; but the white workmen had a higher outlook, and the failure to provide them with better homes added to their bitter dissatisfaction with the burdens placed upon them by having to compete with black labor. This resentment spread until it included thousands who did not have to work with their hands.

Ten thousand and more strange negroes added to the already large colored population soon made East St. Louis a center of lawlessness. Within less than a year before the riot over 800 "holdups" were committed in the city. More than 80 percent of the murders were committed by negroes. Highway robberies were nightly occurrences; rape was frequent; while a host of petty offences kept the law-abiding citizens in a state of terror.

White women were afraid to walk the streets at night; negroes sat in their laps on streetcars; black women crowded them from their seats; they were openly insulted by drunken negroes. The low saloons and gambling houses were crowded with idle vagabonds; the dance halls in the negro sections were filled with prostitutes, half clad, in some instances naked, performing lewd dances.

Negroes were induced to buy homes in white districts by unscrupulous real estate agents; and, as a consequence, the white people sold their homes at a sacrifice and moved elsewhere.

Owners of cheap property preferred negroes as tenants, charging them $15 a month rent for houses for which white workmen had paid only $10.

Corrupt politicians found the negro vote fitted to their foul purpose, and not only bought them on election day, but in the interval protected them in their dens of vice, their low saloons and barrel houses. They had immunity in the courts; crooked lawyers kept them out of jail; and a disorganized, grafting police force saw to it that they were not molested.

East St. Louis wallowed in a mire of lawlessness and unashamed corruption. Criminals from every quarter of the country gathered there, unmolested and safe from detection.

This was the condition of affairs on the night of July 1, 1917, when an automobile—some witnesses say there were two—went through a negro section of the city and fired promiscuously into their homes. No one was injured, but the act aroused a fierce spirit in the breasts of the negroes.

The ringing of a church bell at midnight, which was a prearranged signal, drew a crowd of negroes from that immediate section armed with guns and pistols. They marched through the streets ready to avenge the attack on their homes. They had not gone far until an automobile containing several policemen and a newspaper reporter crossed their path, having been notified by telephone that there was danger of an outbreak. The negroes cursed them and told them to drive on, although one of the detectives flashed his police badge and assured them that they had come to protect them.

For answer the negro mob fired a volley into the machine, which, at the first shot, drove rapidly away. The negroes continued to empty their guns and pistols, with the result that one of the officers was instantly killed and another so badly wounded that he died later.

The police automobile, riddled with bullets, stood in front of police headquarters next morning and thousands viewed it. The early editions of the papers gave full details of the tragedy of the night before. And, on July 2, East St. Louis awoke to a realization of the awful fact that the dread which had knocked at every heart for months could no longer be denied. Years of lawlessness had at last borne bloody fruit. As the day wore on negro mobs killed other white men, and shot at men and women who were offering them no wrong.

Dr. McQuillan, a well-known physician, and his wife were dragged from their machine and shamefully abused. The doctor was shot, his ribs were broken, and both he and his his wife were badly beaten. One of his assailants remarked, "Boys, this is Dr. McQuillan, the Aluminum Ore Co. doctor," and pleaded for his life. The would-be murderers, some of whom must have been employed by the Ore Co., helped the doctor and his wife into their machine and, cranking it for them, sent them on their way.

The news of these murders and fresh outrages spread rapidly, and the streets soon filled with excited people. Men and boys, girls and women of the town began to attack every negro in sight. All fared alike, young and old, women and children; none was spared. The crowd soon grew to riotous proportions, and for hours the manhunt continued, stabbing, clubbing, and shooting, not the guilty but unoffending negroes. One was hanged from a telephone pole, and another had a rope tied around his neck and was dragged through the streets, the maddened crowd kicking him and beating him as he lay prostrate and helpless.

The negroes were pursued into their homes, and the torch completed the work of destruction. As they fled from the flames they were shot down, although many of them came out with uplifted hands, pleading to be spared.

It was a day and night given over to arson and murder. Scenes of horror that would have shocked a savage were viewed with placid unconcern by hundreds whose hearts knew no pity, and who seemed to revel in the feast of blood and cruelty.

It is not possible to give accurately the number of dead. At least thirty-nine negroes and eight white people were killed outright, and hundreds of negroes were wounded and maimed. "The bodies of the dead negroes," testified an eyewitness, "were thrown into a morgue like so many dead hogs."

There were 312 buildings and 44 railroad freight cars and their contents destroyed by fire; a total loss of $393,600. Your committee cannot go into all the harrowing details of how the negroes—men, women, and children—were killed and burned during the riot, but there were so many flagrantly cruel cases that a bare recital of the facts concerning some of them will be given.

At Collinsville and Illinois Avenues a negro man and his wife and fourteen-year-old boy were assaulted. The man was beaten to death; his head was crushed as if by a blow from a stone, and the boy was shot and killed. The woman was very badly injured; her hair was torn out by the roots and her scalp was partly torn off by someone who took hold of the ragged edges of a wound and scalped her. After a time an ambulance drove up and the bodies of these three negroes were loaded into it. The father and the son were dead, and when the woman regained consciousness she found herself lying on the dead bodies of her husband and child. This family lived across the Mississippi River in St. Louis and were on their way home after having been on a fishing trip north of East St. Louis. They were innocent of any connection with the race feeling that brought about the riot and were victims of the savage brutality of the mob, who spared neither age nor sex in their blind lust for blood.

Another negro who was trying to escape from a mob of thirty or forty men was knocked down, kicked in the face, beaten into insensibility; and then a man stood over him and shot him five times as he lay helpless in the street.

A white man shot at a negro and killed another white man, his bad aim infuriating the mob that pursued the unoffending negro.

Two negroes were taken from a street car at Illinois and Collinsville Avenues. They were on their way to St. Louis to escape the fury of the mob. Both were killed.

Near the stockyards a white man knocked a negro senseless from a wagon, and when two reporters offered to take the wounded man to the hospital another white man threatened their lives and forced them to drive away and leave him.

At Collinsville and Division Avenues a mob of about 100 men

drove a negro into the street, knocked him down, stamped on his face, and one of the crowd drew a pistol and shot him through the head, the bullet coming out between his eyes.

An old negro, about seventy years old, stepped off a street car, having come from St. Louis on his way home. The mob immediately attacked him with such fury that he was left senseless after being stoned and beaten. A witness who described this particular case to your committee said, "This old man, his dinner bucket lying on the ground beside him, apparently was dead, although he had his arm arched up over his face as if to protect himself from blows. At about that time an ambulance driver came up and started to pick him up to put him into the ambulance. A white man standing over him said, 'If you pick up this negro, you'll get what he got.' I saw that same negro in the undertaking establishment the next day, dead, with his arm still arched over his face."

Around Third and Brady Avenues the mob was firing promiscuously into houses and sheds where the negroes had taken shelter. Every time one of them ran from these houses he was shot and killed.

The rioting continued all along Broadway, between Collinsville Avenue and Eighth Street; houses were burned and the poor wretches were driven from their homes or shot as they were trying to escape the flames. Two of them, with hands above their heads, were shot and killed.

A negro child two years old was shot and thrown into a doorway of a burning building, and nothing ever was found of the remains.

There was a crippled negro who took care of horses and mules for the Hill-Thomas Lime & Cement Co. He was a faithful, hard-working, loyal fellow. The day of the riot his employer's stable was in the path of the flames. He called up Mr. Thomas, on the telephone, and said: "I just called you up to tell you good-bye. I'm here in the barn, and I ain't goin' to leave; I've turned all the stock out; I'm going to stay here; I'm not going outside to be shot."

This faithful negro must have been consumed in the flames as no trace of him ever was found.

It is impossible to say how many people perished in the 312 houses that were burned by the mob, but many negroes who lived in those houses still are missing, and it is not possible to get an accurate report as to just how many found death in the flames.

East St. Louis for many years has been a plague spot; within its borders and throughout its environs every offense in the calendar of crime and every lapse in morals and public decency has been openly committed, each day increasing the terrors of the law-abiding. No terms of condemnation, applied to the men who were responsible for the appalling conditions revealed before your committee, can be too severe. No punishment that outraged justice may visit upon them will be adequate. In many cases they deserve the extreme penalty; in every case they merit the execration of a despoiled and disgraced community.

The purpose of the politicians of both political parties, who found East St. Louis respected and prosperous and in a few years robbed its treasury, gave away valuable franchises, sank it in the mire of pollution, and brought upon it national censure and disgrace, was deliberate. They united to elect men to high office who would further their schemes of spoliation even when they feared to share their plunder. It was a conspiracy as shameless as it was confident. They left nothing to chance. It took account of the executive; it provided for an unscrupulous legislative board; it made certain of police commissioners who would take orders and deliver the goods; it embraced the courts high and low; it went into partnership with every vile business; it protected every lawless saloon; it encouraged houses of prostitution in the very shadow of the city hall; it gave protection to gamblers, immunity to thieves and murderers.

The gang that took possession of East St. Louis harbored the offscourings of the earth. The vag, the safe-blower and the "stick-up man" flocked to its sheltering arms, safe from arrest or disturbance.

The good people of this sorely afflicted community were powerless. The chamber of commerce, which should have had the courage to rally the law-abiding and drive out the lawless, was ineffective. They actually "laid upon the table" a resolution of inquiry to investigate the conditions that made property unsafe and life perilous.

The owners of the great corporations whose plants were in and about East St. Louis lived in other cities. They pocketed their dividends without concern for the municipal dishonesty that wasted the taxes, and without a thought for the thousands of their own workmen, black and white, who lived in hovels, the victims of poverty and disease, of long hours and incessant labor.

The greed that made crooks of the politicians made money grabbers of the manufacturers, who pitted white labor against black, drove organized labor from their plants, brought thousands of inefficient negroes from the South, crowding the white men from their positions.

All this stirred the fires of race hatred until it finally culminated in bloody, pitiless riot, arson, and wanton murder.

Mayor Mollman surrounded himself with advisers who were familiar with the game of politics. They were not interested in securing an honest and economical administration. Their business first was to elect a man who would be subservient; one who possibly might not put his own hand into the public treasury, but would look the other way if a friend were so engaged. They needed a man who would stand between them and the indignant taxpayer; a fair promiser but a poor performer; personally honest, maybe, but so weak, so feeble, and so easily influenced that the conspirators were able to dictate his policies, and in the shadow of his stupidity loot the municipality. This was not the result of corruption in only one political party. It was brought about by a combination between the leaders of the worst elements in both parties. They pooled issues in the city election and declared regular dividends on their investment at the expense of honest people.

In the history of corrupt politics in this country there never has been a more shameless debauchery of the electorate nor a more vicious alliance between the agencies and beneficiaries of crime than for years existed in East St. Louis. It is a disgraceful chapter. It puts an ineffaceable brand on every man engaged in the conspiracy. Its contamination, spreading from a reservoir of corruption in the city hall, filtered through carefully laid conduits into every street and alley; into the hotels where girls, mere children of fifteen years of age, were violated; into the low dance halls where schoolgirls listened to lewd songs and engaged in lascivious dances, and in the interval retired to assignation rooms with the drunken brutes who frequented these resorts; into the gambling houses where poorly paid workmen were robbed of their daily earnings; into the 350 saloons which kept open on Sunday, many of them running without license; into the barrel houses, where the vilest of whiskey was sold in bottles, the resort of vagrants and drunkards, rendezvous of criminals and schools of crime.

This corruption palsied the hands of prominent officials whose duty it was to enforce the law. Lawyers became protectors of criminals; the courts were shields for the highwayman, the prostitute, the gambler, the sneak thief, and the murderer. The higher courts were not free from this baneful influence, which invaded all ranks and brought them to its low level.

Local judges were found who would take straw bonds that the

worst criminals might escape; exacting only costs, two-thirds going into the pockets of the judge and one-third into the waiting palm of the chief of police.

A police force is never better than the police commissioners; and the police commissioners, in turn, reflect the character and wishes of the mayor. If a city has a mayor of courage and ability, who is not the weak and willing prey of political crooks and grafters, he is certain to appoint a board of police commissioners who will name policemen intelligent enough to know the law and brave and honest enough to enforce it.

East St. Louis was doubly unfortunate. In the person of Mayor Mollman it had an executive who obeyed orders from a gang of conscienceless politicians of both political parties, who were exploiting the city for their own aggrandizement, careless alike of its good name, its security, or its prosperity. They were harpies who closed their eyes to the corruption that saturated every department of the public service and fattened on its festering carcass. Without conscience and without shame they led the mayor into devious paths, tempted him with assurances of political support for his future ambitions, packed the police force with men whose incompetency was only surpassed by their venality, and so circumscribed him with flattery and encouraged his cupidity that they were able to take the reins of government from his feeble hands and guide it to suit their own foul and selfish purposes.

The great majority of the police force appointed by Mayor Mollman's board of police commissioners had served an apprenticeship as connivers at corrupt elections; as protectors of lawless saloons, and hotels run openly as assignation houses. They turned criminals loose at the dictation of politicians, and divided with grafting justices of the peace the fines that should have gone into the treasury.

This was the general character of the police force of the city of East St. Louis on July 1, 1917, when the spirit of lawlessness, long smoldering, burst into flame.

When acts of violence were frequent on the night of May 28, after a largely attended public meeting in the city hall, at which Attorney Alexander Flannigan, by unmistakable implication, suggested mob violence, the police department failed to cope with the incipient mob.

When lawlessness began to assume serious proportions on July 2, the police instantly could have quelled and dispersed the crowds, then made up of small groups; but they either fled into the safety of cowardly seclusion, or listlessly watched the depredations of the mob, passively and in many instances actively sharing in its work.

The testimony of every witness who was free to tell the truth agreed in condemnation of the police for failure to even halfway do their duty. They fled the scene where murder and arson held full sway. They deserted the station house and could not be found when calls for help came from every quarter of the city. The organization broke down completely; and so great was the indifference of the few policemen who remained on duty that the conclusion is inevitable that they shared the lust of the mob for negro blood, and encouraged the rioters by their conduct, which was sympathetic when it was not cowardly.

Some specific instances will be given in proof of the above conclusions:

After a number of the rioters had been taken to jail by the soldiers under Colonel Clayton, the police deliberately turned hundreds of them loose without bond, failing to secure their names or to make any effort to identify them.

In one instance the mob jammed policemen against a building and held them there while other members of the gang were assaulting unoffending negroes. The police made no effort to free themselves, and seemed to regard the performance as highly humorous.

The police shot into a crowd of negroes who were huddled together, making no resistance. It was a particularly cowardly exhibition of savagery.

When the newspaper reporters were taking pictures of the mob, policemen charged them with their billies, broke their machines, destroyed the negatives, and threatened them with arrest if any further attempt was made to photograph the rioters who were making the streets run red with innocent blood, applying the torch to reach their victims who were cowering in their wretched homes.

A negro was brutally clubbed by a policeman who found him guilty of the heinous offense of hiding in an ice box to save his life.

Two policemen and three soldiers were involved in the shooting of Minneola McGee under circumstances of extreme brutality. This occurred, not at the scene of the riots, but as she was going from an outhouse to the kitchen of the residence where she was employed, when the police and the soldiers who accompanied them fired at her deliberately, without even the slightest provocation, and shot off her arm near the shoulder.

Minneola McGee is a negro girl about twenty years old. She was induced to leave one of the Southern states and go to East St. Louis by the many enticing but misleading advertisements scattered among Southern negroes. It is apparent that even before her injury she was a frail and rather delicate girl. When she appeared before your committee, with one arm off just below the shoulder, she was a physical wreck. She has no education whatever. It is not possible for her to earn a living in any other way than by manual labor. Now, as the result of as fiendish a piece of work as was ever perpetrated, she must, at least to some extent, be an object of charity. Because of her youth this sort of a life is before her. She was interrogated by your committee to ascertain whether it was possible for her to have been shot by accident. Her simple story removed all doubt upon that score, as she satisfied everyone who heard her that she was purposely and deliberately shot. In answer to questions put to her by your committee she said:

> I wuz in a outhouse in de garden. I hea'd de shootin' an' started fo' de house. When I got put'y nigh de house a soljer histed his gun and pinted it right at me and shot my arm off. Dar wuzn't nobody twixt me and de soljer fo' him to be shootin' at, an' dar wuzn't nobody on de udder side of me for him to be shootin' at. He jist histed his gun and pinted it at me an' shot my arm off when I hadn't done nothin'. When he shot me I fell on de ground an' didn't know nothin'.

Her pitiful recital of this piece of brutality toward her had the effect of stirring the indignation of everybody in the room where the hearing was being conducted, and at the same time to arouse the utmost sympathy for her.

Many other cases of police complicity in the riots could be cited. Instead of being guardians of the peace they became a part of the mob by countenancing the assaulting and shooting down of defenseless negroes and adding to the terrifying scenes of rapine and slaughter.

Their disgraceful conduct was the logical fruit of the notorious alliance between the City Hall and the criminal elements, aided by saloons, gambling houses and houses of prostitution. The city administration owed its election to their support and rewarded them for their fealty by permitting them to debauch the innocent, rob drunken victims, make assignation houses of the hotels, protect the gambler and the thief, and commit any act by which they might profit.

Mayor Mollman appointed the police commissioners. He was responsible for their failure to divorce the police from its partnership with crooked lawyers, corrupt justices of the peace, and notorious criminals. He knew full well what the conditions in the police department were. Prominent citizens had warned him repeatedly and had supplied convincing proof of their charges against the department. He paid no attention to their warnings and appeals. By his failure to remove the police commissioners he acquiesced in their misfeasance, and equally is responsible with them for the heartless crimes committed by an unrestrained mob, and for the lawlessness that was encouraged and fostered by his failure to enforce the law and to hold his subordinates responsible for the proper conduct of the police department.

Much of the energy, some of the brains, and nearly all of the audacity of the gang that in recent years has held East St. Louis in its merciless grasp were centered in Locke Tarlton, president of the East Side Levee Board. It was his cunning mind that helped devise the schemes by which he and his associates were enriched. It was his practiced hand that carried them out. He made Mayor Mollman believe that he was his creator; that he had elevated him to high station; and that his blind obedience to orders would mean rich political rewards in the future.

As president of the levee board, Tarlton deposited millions in a local bank and exacted no interest from it. The taxpayers suffered, while the bank lent the money and pocketed the proceeds. In further proof of the close relationship that existed between the levee board and the bank, Thomas Gillespie, brother of the bank's president, was elected attorney for the levee board.

Locke Tarlton knew how to handle the negro vote. He had an unanswerable argument to use with "floaters." He told them for whom he wanted them to vote, agreed on the price they were to get by casting their ballots, or rather having them marked for them by corrupt election officers, and always paid them promptly. Locke Tarlton was a man of honor when dealing with crooked voters. He always kept his word; he was sure pay. One of the picturesque sights in East St. Louis was to see Locke Tarlton with a stack of $5 bills in his hands publicly paying the negroes who helped him win an election. . . .

Hubert Schaumleffel is the States Attorney for St. Clair County, his authority extending over East St. Louis. It was his duty to prosecute the criminals that made an interstate playground of that city. No disorderly saloon, no gambling house, no house of prostitution could have existed if he had raised a threatening finger. He held in his hand the moral destiny of this city of 90,000 people. Had he been a man of average moral courage, prompted by high motives and responsive to his oath of office, East St. Louis and its border towns would have escaped the maelstrom of vice that all but engulfed them.

But Schaumleffel had no civic pride; he was devoid of character; he was the boon companion of the low and dissolute; the ready servant of scheming politicians; at heart a sympathizer with criminals whom he should have prosecuted relentlessly. A member of the Tarlton-Canavan corrupt machine, he rendered menial service to his masters. It is in evidence that before the city election, when Mollman was a candidate for mayor, with all the hopes and prospects of the gang centered on him, Schaumleffel called together the leaders among the negroes, those who controlled the vicious elements of their race, and were permitted to violate the law whenever they rendered proper service to his administration. He told them plainly that they had to vote for Mollman for mayor, and if they failed to support him he would close the gambling dens and the dance halls, the policy shops and the dice games, and the lid would be securely placed on an absolutely "tight town."

Many other instances could be given of Schaumleffel's alliance with the worst elements. Alexander Flannigan relied on and was emboldened by his friendship; the lottery sharks in St. Clair County escaped indictment by his inaction; countless criminals went unwhipped of justice, either because he neglected his duty, was blind to offenses committed by his political supporters, or was so benumbed by drink that he did not have the intelligence to realize the enormity of his official omissions.

Rev. Father Christopher Goelz testified that he went to see Schaumleffel in order to protest against the existence of a cockpit at Woodland Park, with its attendant scenes of beastly drunkenness and debauchery. He found the States Attorney, as he was on his way to St. Louis to attend a prize fight, so drunk that he could not talk to him intelligently.

The day of the riot, with the mob rushing through the streets, hundreds of houses in flames, and men, women, and children victims of the rifle, pistol, and the bludgeon, States Attorney Hubert Schaumleffel staggered drunken along the way, heedless of crimes that were being committed in his presence and callous to the cries of the injured and the dying.

It is his habit to drink to excess. His infirmity is known to all. His love for liquor seems to have stripped him of all moral courage and manhood, and left him naked and unashamed.

When will the authorities confront him with his official derelictions and his personal delinquencies, and take him from the high place which he has disgraced? . . .

Joseph B. Messick is the county judge of St. Clair County. As judge he appoints two members of the board of review which has power to increase or reduce all assessments made by the city assessor and county officials. He also appoints the election board, and that board made his son its secretary. This young man is a lawyer of limited capacity with an earning power of perhaps a hundred dollars a month, but his profound (?) knowledge of the law appealed to some of the great corporations of St. Clair County, and they at once employed him as attorney to appear before his father's board of review to secure for them a reduction in their assessments. Young Messick rapidly developed an insight into assessment values, and proved conclusively that from their standpoint his selection was wise.

The board of review was composed of William A. Swartztrauber, Frank M. Miller, with powerful political connections, and Charles F. Krebs.

It did not take the son of the county judge long to convince this board, appointed by his father, that the assessments made by the city assessor and increased by the county assessor were an unjust burden on some of these rich corporations.

Here are the assessments and reductions of the leading corporations:

St. Louis Bridge Co., assessed at $3,500,000, which included only the east half of Eads Bridge, was reduced to $2,500,000, although for the four years previous it had been assessed at $3,150,000.

The Aluminum Co. of America was assessed by Assessor O'Day at $699,990. Assessor Warning raised it to $799,990, and the board of review, perhaps after an eloquent appeal by young Messick, cut it to $200,000.

Ninety-four lots owned by the Wiggins Ferry Co. were assessed at $1,518,470. This assessment was cut by the board to $803,245. The assessment of these lots was cut virtually in half by the board; and in some other instances the board reduced the Wiggins properties but left unchanged the assessments on adjacent lots owned by others.

The plant of the Malleable Iron Co. was assessed at $465,000. It was raised by Warning, the county assessor, to $519,000 and was cut by the board to $132,000.

The American Steel Foundries' assessment was reduced about $38,000.

The Republic Iron and Steel Co.'s assessment was reduced from $63,990 to $16,788.

The Elliot Frog and Switch Co. was reduced from $24,420 to $9,000.

Lots owned by the Water Co. assessed at $9,600 were reduced by the board to $2,220.

These assessments held for four years, and during that period the St. Louis Bridge Co. would save $116,654 in taxes, the Wiggins Ferry Co. $84,140, the Aluminum Co. of America $69,952, and the Malleable Iron Co. $45,148.

Although the assessment of virtually every big corporation in and around East St. Louis was reduced, assessments of very many of the small householders were increased.

Your committee is not informed just what fee was paid to young Messick for appearing as attorney before the board appointed by his father.

The strike in the plant of the Aluminum Ore Co. was caused by a demand on the part of organized labor for an adjustment of wages, a reduction in hours and an improvement of conditions under which the men worked. The company refused to meet any of these demands, declined to discuss the matter with the workmen's committee, and added insult to injury by importing negro strike breakers and giving them the places of the white men.

It is not the purpose of your committee to discuss the merits of this controversy, although the bringing of negroes to break a strike which was being peaceably conducted by organized labor sowed the dragon's teeth of race hatred that afterwards grew into the riot which plunged East St. Louis into blood and flame.

But there grew out of this strike a violation of the law of such a reckless and defiant nature that it calls for the severest condemnation.

One E. M. Sorrels was a secretary of an alleged rifle club which never had maintained more than a desultory organization. The members virtually had ceased to use a temporary range; and there were stored in the club house a number of rifles and thousands of rounds of ammunition, the property of the United States. Sorrels, either on his own initiative or at the suggestion of an officer of the Aluminum

Ore Co., entered the storeroom of the rifle club at midnight and secretly transferred to the plant of the Aluminum Co. between thirty and forty rifles and hundreds of rounds of ammunition; the purpose being to arm the strike breakers and turn guns of the United States against the forces of organized labor and shoot down the strikers should this be necessary to break the strike.

Sorrels violated the law by burglarizing the house containing these rifles; but the Aluminum Ore Co. recognized the risk he had taken; and, grateful for the unlawful service he had rendered, promptly took him into its employ at a salary of $175 a month.

The War Department should not be blamed when United States rifles and ammunition are stolen and turned over to a private corporation to be put to unlawful uses; but the attention of the Secretary of War is invited to Sorrels's criminal act, and he should request the United States district attorney to have him indicted and prosecuted to conviction.

The character of the police force and its utter demoralization was strikingly shown in the murder of H.B. Trafton, head of the "morality squad" of the police force, by Assistant Chief of Detectives Frank Florence. The murder grew out of the fact that Trafton, acting under orders and in the line of his duty, raided a house of prostitution which, to the astonishment of the community, turned out to be owned by Florence. When they met, Florence drew his weapon; Trafton threw both hands up above his head; but nevertheless, Florence shot and killed him in cold blood. Florence was indicted and tried, but being one of the "gang" was, of course, acquitted. . . .

The looting of the city and county treasury has grown into a habit in East St. Louis. More than $250,000 has been stolen by various defaulting officials in the last five years. In one instance the school fund was robbed of $45,000, but the prosecution of the thief has gone on listlessly for several years without any real effort to convict him. He was not arraigned for trial until after your committee had left East St. Louis. He then pleaded guilty. Everybody knows who were protecting him, but so many similar thefts have been overlooked that there is but little public sentiment against him.

After one of the defalcations, the thieves took everything in the vault but the metal hinges of a loose-leaf ledger, and the fire they started to destroy the evidence of their guilt left that as the only souvenir for the taxpayers.

The names of the saloons in and about East St. Louis were typical of the wildest West in the mining-camp days; and, while picturesque in their nomenclature, they breathe a spirit of lawless defiance. Prominent among them were "The Bucket of Blood," "The Monkey Cage," "The Yellow Dog," "Uncle John's Pleasure Palace," with the seductive appeal, "Come in and be suited," and "Aunt Kate's Honkytonk," with "Something doing every hour."

In the latter part of 1912 or the first part of 1913 a hod carrier living in East St. Louis died. It was not known that he had any near relatives, although he carried $1,600 life insurance. The county took charge and the funeral was assigned to William Degen, an undertaker, who was a member of the city council. A relative of the deceased appeared later and claimed the insurance. It was found that all the money had been paid to Degen except about $200. Degen supplied an itemized bill, containing such items as $800 for a casket, $100 for a suit of clothes, $20 for shoes, $5 for shaving the dead man, and other similar extravagant items.

The whole matter was exposed in the *St. Louis Post-Dispatch*, and such a scandal resulted that the authorities exhumed the body. It was found to have been buried in a rough pine box, with scarcely enough clothing to cover it. The whole outfit cost less than $50.

It was reported at about the same time that the bodies of women were not safe from the degeneracy of an employee of another prominent undertaker. Another employee of this establishment reported one such instance to his employer and was discharged, while the man against whom the accusation was made was retained in the employ of the undertaker.

On the night of July 1, Mayor Mollman telephoned the acting adjutant general of Illinois that the mob spirit was rampant; that the police were unable to cope with the situation; and that it would take the strong hand of the militia to preserve order.

At 8 o'clock the next morning Colonel S.O. Tripp, assistant quartermaster general, arrived under orders from the office of the adjutant general of the state. After an unnecessary journey to St. Louis he came to the city hall of East St. Louis and reported for duty to the mayor, who described the situation to him and gave him entire charge to deal with the condition as the necessities of the case might arise.

It may be well at this point to describe Colonel Tripp, because he fills an important role in this tragedy, and responsibility for much that was done and left undone must rest on him.

When the adjutant general's office summoned Colonel Tripp in the early hours of the morning, he answered the call to duty arrayed in a seersucker suit and a dainty straw hat, after having, as he informed your committee, hastily packed his hand bag with a lot of toilet articles. Thus ready for any emergency he took the first train for East St. Louis. He brought no uniform with him and although it was his duty to face and quell a riotous mob, at no time was he garbed as a soldier.

Evidently it was his intention to secure some bullet-proof coign of vantage from which he could view the turbulent scenes in perfect safety; while, with a megaphone, he could command and dispose of his troops. After hours of consultation with his companion in timidity and inefficiency, the mayor, he ventured in the direction of the mob, and according to his own testimony, saw a helpless negro with a rope around his neck being dragged to his death.

He described, with a great show of courage, how he grabbed a gun from a soldier and, facing this terrible mob, pressed back 1,500 people by his own unaided effort. Your committee was unable to find any evidence to confirm this valiant deed of the redoubtable Colonel, where he practically mastered hundreds of infuriated rioters; but, as he states it to be a fact, it must be true.

It is the unanimous opinion of every witness who saw Colonel Tripp on that fateful day that he was a hindrance instead of a help to the troops; that he was ignorant of his duties, blind to his responsibilities and deaf to every intelligent appeal that was made to him. His presence in East St. Louis was a reproach to the assistant adjutant general who sent him there and a reflection on the judgment of the governor for burdening his staff with so hopeless an incompetent. Instead of putting himself at the head of his troops, uniformed as a soldier, and going boldly into the mob, dispersing them, and, if necessary, risking his own life to rescue the poor wretches who were dragged through the streets by the neck, shot, and mutilated, he remained in the city hall from 8 A.M. until 12 o'clock, when he calmly repaired to a restaurant outside the danger zone, secured a delightful lunch which took him more than an hour to order and masticate, and at 1:30 he resumed his survey of the situation from the safe shelter of the city hall.

When Colonel Tripp was asked why he spent four hours in the city hall, with East St. Louis in the hands of a murderous mob, and failed to go to the scenes of conflict and take charge of his troops who were sorely in need of a commander, he absolved himself of all responsibility by answering, "The President never goes out of his office"; and so, by comparing himself to the Commander-in-Chief of the Army and Navy of the United States, he was perfectly satisfied with his conduct. "Me and the President" was, in his opinion, a complete defense.

The mayor called the governor on the long-distance telephone and urged that additional troops be sent, saying that the lives and property of the citizens were endangered. But Colonel Tripp assured the governor that he "had the situation well in hand," and that there was no need for more troops. His judgment in this matter was no better than his ability and courage as a soldier; qualities which he totally lacked.

Your committee desires to speak a special word in commendation of the conduct, bravery, and skill of Colonel C.B. Clayton, of the Fourth Infantry, next in command to Colonel Tripp. Had it not been for his promptness and determination the mob certainly would have committed many more atrocities.

Colonel Tripp, in his testimony before your committee, undertook to defend his blunders; but he failed utterly. If he had taken hold of the situation upon his arrival, inspired his soldiers with respect for him, gone to the center of the disturbance, and turned loaded guns against the mob, he would have spared East St. Louis much of the ignominy from which it now suffers and saved the lives of many innocent men, women, and children.

Your committee invites attention of the Secretary of War to the record of this officer as set forth under oath by himself and many other witnesses.

The conduct of the soldiers who were sent to East St. Louis to protect life and property puts a blot on that part of the Illinois militia that served under Colonel Tripp. They were scattered over the city, many of them being without officers to direct or control them. In only a few cases did they do their duty. They seemed moved by the same spirit of indifference or cowardice that marked the conduct of the police force. As a rule they fraternized with the mob, joked with them, and made no serious effort to restrain them.

Following are a few of the many instances testified to by responsible witnesses:

A negro, unarmed, making no resistance, and trying to escape the fury of the mob, was knocked down and cruelly kicked and beaten. His condition was so pitiable that a soldier said to the rioters, "Boys, he has suffered enough; let him alone." For answer one of the mob drew his pistol and shot the negro five times, one bullet plowing through his brain. The soldier then put his gun on his shoulder and calmly walked away, making no arrests.

A number of soldiers openly stated that "they didn't like niggers" and would not disturb a white man for killing them.

Three soldiers and two policemen were ordered to close a negro saloon. On their approach two negro men ran, and the soldiers and policemen shot and killed both, although neither had committed any offense.

The same crowd shot off the arm of the negro servant girl, Minneola McGee, already mentioned. They had no warrant for her; she had not committed any offense; she was not even running away; she was cruelly maimed for life by these official murderers. This unoffending girl was wantonly shot by the soldiers as testified to by the policemen who have been prosecuted. Your committee was unable to secure the names of these militiamen. They must be known to the military authorities. It is the duty of the governor and the adjutant general of Illinois to find these men and to punish them for their brutal crime. It was one of the most flagrant cases of cruelty revealed to your committee.

Paul Y. Anderson, reporter for the *St. Louis Post-Dispatch*, testified that he heard a soldier tell a white man who was loading a revolver to "kill all the negroes he could, that he didn't like them, either."

A member of the Sixth Illinois Infantry boasted that he had fired his gun seventeen times during the riot and every time at a "black target." Your committee was unable to secure the name of this soldier.

It was a common expression among the soldiers: "Have you got your nigger yet?"

A militiaman in uniform, said to have been on furlough, led a section of the mob that was killing negroes.

A soldier stabbed a white boy with a bayonet, and the boy bled to death. The boy was carrying a pair of pantaloons across his arm. That was his sole offense. The soldier was drinking and murderously assaulted him. After a full hearing, the coroner's jury unanimously held him on a charge of murder. But, later, at a secret trial by the military authorities, he was released.

Soldiers deliberately shot into a house where seven negroes had taken shelter.

G.E. Popkess, a reporter for the *St. Louis Times*, testified that he saw two inoffensive negroes, while fleeing for their lives from a burning building, shot down by soldiers.

The governor of Illinois has a responsibility in this matter that he can not evade. The militia of the state are under his control. He can arraign militiamen for misconduct; he can remove officers for inefficiency; he can institute a thorough inquiry that will expose the criminal and the incompetent.

A prominent merchant of East St. Louis testified that within twenty-four hours after the occurrence he notified the governor of the case of a militiaman who deliberately shot a negro without provocation, a crime committed in cold blood. He did not know the militiaman's name, but it was possible for the governor to learn who he was and to visit proper punishment upon him.

The governor must be familiar with the wanton stabbing of the boy by a drunken soldier. The facts were reported at the time in all the newspapers as they were testified to before your committee. They are within the reach of the governor in the records of the court-martial which is said to have tried and released this murderer.

Has any official effort been made to apprehend the three militiamen who next morning after the riot, in company with two policemen, shot off the arm of the negro girl, Minneola McGee? These men were state militiamen, were in regular uniform, and subject to the authorities of the great State of Illinois. At that time it would have been an easy matter to identify them and turn them over to the authorities to be tried for their crimes. It is evident that no military inquiry conducted by such courts-martial as sat in similar cases growing out of the East St. Louis riots would have given them their deserts.

What was to hinder the proper state authorities from making an investigation of this murderous assault? They had the power to search the roster of the companies present at East St. Louis. These men were known to their companions, who could have identified them easily.

Special commendation is due Attorney General Brundage and Assistant Attorney General Middlekauf. The Attorney General answered every appeal made to him by the good people of East St. Louis and St. Clair County and, virtually without assistance from the local authorities, remedied many evils. It was due entirely to his efforts that lawless resorts were closed, and wherever there had been a violation of the state law he was quick to order the arrest and prosecution of the offender.

Assistant Attorney General Middlekauf had active charge of the prosecutions growing out of the riot, and he showed neither fear nor favor. Capable, determined, and courageous, he allowed neither political influence nor personal appeals to swerve him from the strict line of duty.

As a result of these prosecutions by the Attorney General's office, eleven Negroes and eight white men are in the state penitentiary; two additional white men have been sentenced to prison terms; fourteen white men have been given jail sentences; twenty-seven white men, including the former night chief of police and three policemen, have pleaded guilty to rioting and have been punished.

These convictions were obtained in the face of organized, determined effort, backed with abundant funds, to head off the prosecutions and convictions. In the case of Mayor Mollman there seems to have been an open, paid advertising campaign to slander and intimidate the Attorney General.

The State of Illinois is fortunate in having men of ability and character at the head of its law department.

Your committee wishes to commend the work of Rev. George W. Allison, pastor of the First Baptist Church of East St. Louis, and to express thanks to him for much information which was of vital assistance in bringing out the criminal life of the city and the political influence that encouraged lawlessness. The Rev. Allison is a man of courage, capacity, and determination. Conspiracies against his character and threats against his life did not deter him; the constant danger of bodily harm did not prevent him from continuing his investigations and fighting with all his splendid power the organized forces of evil. If there had been others on the "committee of one hundred" with even half his moral force, the example might have leavened that whole lot of selfish incompetents.

Paul Y. Anderson, reporter of the *St. Louis Post-Dispatch*, was assigned during the past three years to duty in East St. Louis, and was to your committee an inexhaustible source of valuable information. In serving his newspaper fearlessly he rendered the public a more important service by laying bare the story of faithless officials who could not be lashed, even by exposure, to do their duty. He personally laid before the Mayor positive evidence of the guilt and incompetency of his police force, and demanded that he close the gambling houses and the lawless and unlicensed saloons. His investigations, thwarted on every hand, were thorough and trustworthy. He saw everything; reported what he saw without fear of consequences; defied the indignant officials whom he charged with criminal neglect of duty; ran a daily risk of assassination, and rendered an invaluable public service by his exposures. His testimony before your committee was most interesting and illuminating; his harrowing experiences before and during the riot threw a flood of light on conditions.

Your committee is indebted to Rev. Father Christopher Goelz, pastor of St. Phillips Church, at Edgemont, for much valuable information. He was a power for good in his community, and the fact that it escaped much of the contamination of the greater city was due to his vigilance and the publicity he gave the low characters that attempted to gain a foothold in Edgemont.

Your committee has not adjourned *sine die* for the reason that it is possible, at least, that a supplementary report may be made showing the beneficial results of the exposures brought about by the investigation and also by the vigorous prosecutions hereinbefore referred to.

3.

ELLIOTT M. RUDWICK

Race Riot at East St. Louis, July 2, 1917

THE CALL FOR FEDERAL INTERVENTION

In the wake of the July riot, Washington received innumerable appeals for intervention. After the Executive branch of the national government responded with silence and equivocation, the United States Congress made the East St. Louis race riot its responsibility.

On July 3, 1917, Woodrow Wilson's secretary, Joseph Tumulty, told the press that the details of the riot were so sickening that he found it difficult to read about them.[1] Despite these sentiments of a national figure close to the President, no help came from Wilson. Several Northern white editors criticized the President's silence. The *Christian Register* considered it imperative that Wilson tell the country what he thought about race violence, and the *New York Evening Post* recognized that his failure to condemn the riot was part of a pattern indicating an unsympathetic attitude toward Negroes. The

SOURCE: From Elliott M. Rudwick, *Race Riot at East St. Louis, July 2, 1917* (Carbondale: Southern Illinois University Press, 1964), chapter 10. Reprinted with the permission of the author and publisher.

Syracuse Post-Standard saw little difference between the President's views toward Negroes and those expressed by such Southern racists as Senators Tillman and Vardaman.[2]

In contrast to Wilson, Theodore Roosevelt was incensed by the "appalling brutality" of East St. Louis. His remarks prefaced a Carnegie Hall speech honoring Russia. Samuel Gompers also shared the platform, and interpreting the former President's angry comments as hostile to organized labor, he declared that the racial violence, while deplorable, had occurred because employers imported Negroes to East St. Louis. When Gompers sat down, Roosevelt crossed the stage and shook his fist in the AFofL leader's face: "I am not willing that a meeting called to commemorate the birth of democracy in Russia shall even seem to have expressed or to have accepted apologies for the brutal infamies imposed on colored people. . . . Let there be the fullest investigation into these murders."[3]

The Negro press was stirred and although some editors, such as Du Bois, had previously condemned Roosevelt for racism, the former President received unanimous praise.[4] The Negro reaction to Roosevelt's statement emphasized the growing bitterness that they felt toward Wilson, and the fear that his silence indicated federal consent of mob violence.[5] A Baltimore Negro delegation seeking to persuade Wilson to issue a proclamation was unable to obtain a White House appointment. Replying that he wished to conserve his time, the President sidestepped the interview because it was obvious what the group really wanted—recognition by the national government of a responsibility to intervene and protect Negroes from local lawlessness.[6] Articulate Negroes across the country observed that despite an avowed belief in the states rights doctrine, American Presidents had intervened in capital-labor struggles when Caucasian lives or property seemed seriously threatened (e.g., Cleveland interceded in the Haymarket Riot, Roosevelt in the anthracite coal fields, and Wilson sent federal troops during the Colorado coal strike of 1914).[7]

The N.A.A.C.P. and other Negro organizations tried to exert pressure on Wilson by sponsoring a "Silent Parade" in New York and other cities. The marchers sought to use the East St. Louis riot to arouse the public conscience and gain support for federal legislation or a Constitutional amendment outlawing lynching and other forms of mob violence. On New York's Fifth Avenue, thousands marched to the beat of muffled drums draped with black handkerchiefs, petitioning for action on their grievances. The placards and banners told their story: "We Are Maligned As Lazy And Murdered When We Work"; "We Have Fought For The Liberty Of White Americans In 6 Wars, Our Reward Is East St. Louis"; "Pray For The Lady Macbeths Of East St. Louis."[8] After the parade a committee led by N.A.A.C.P.'s James Weldon Johnson called at the White House. Mr. Tumulty assured them that although no Presidential interview could be arranged, their aspirations were understood by Wilson. The delegation left after listening to "general and platitudinous phrases."[9]

Other Negro groups participated in a concerted public campaign blanketing Wilson with "Protest and Petition" forms which announced that, after East St. Louis, Americans of Negro descent were "restless and were feeling unsafe." The Negro press published many "open letters" to the President. After an anti-Wilson letter was printed in the *Norfolk Journal and Guide*, a Richmond postmaster refused to allow it in the mails. The *Journal and Guide*'s editor engaged a Washington lawyer who had the ban lifted. The offending letter was written by a youth announcing his refusal to join the military service unless Wilson and the U.S. Department of Justice eschewed hypocrisy and insincerity and guaranteed to protect Negroes from mobs like those in East St. Louis.[10]

Washington also received requests for another kind of intervention —a federally sponsored investigation of the East St. Louis riot—and like previous proposals for an anti-lynching and anti-riot law, this one also represented a demand for federal responsibility to protect Negroes when state or local governments failed to do so. The earliest appeals for a federal inquiry came from the "outraged public sentiment" of East St. Louis business leaders, who considered it the only measure which would force the city to prevent another race riot after Illinois national guardsmen were recalled.[11] This position was echoed by the *Post-Dispatch*, which doubted the willingness of state investigative and judicial agencies to conduct a fair investigation.[12]

Within two weeks after the riot the appeals crystalized into a plan for calling a federal grand jury under the direction of Judge Kenesaw Mountain Landis. Landis, who later became famous as Commissioner for the American and National Leagues of Professional Baseball Clubs, had been United States District Judge for the Northern District of Illinois since 1905. In December 1916, he had gained prestige with the "church people" of East St. Louis when he forced Mayor Mollman and Chief of Police Payne to confess publicly that they had allowed saloons to remain open on Sundays in violation of state law.

Among those favoring a Landis investigation were Illinois Senators
Sherman and Lewis, Congressman Rodenberg, U.S. Attorney Karch,
and the Committee of One Hundred.[13]

Since the assignment of Landis required the authorization of President Wilson and his Attorney General, Thomas W. Gregory, the latter
asked U.S. Department of Justice lawyers to examine the legal basis
for intervention by the federal judiciary. They advised Gregory that
appropriate jurisdiction lay in Section Nineteen of the U.S. Penal
Code and the 1866 Civil Rights Act. Section Nineteen made it possible to prosecute persons conspiring to violate rights and privileges
guaranteed by the Constitution and federal law; under the Civil
Rights Act, Negroes possessed the right to equal benefit of all laws
protecting the security of persons and property. A Justice Department
attorney informed Gregory "that, if evidence can be procured showing
that either the State, the county, or the municipal authorities failed to
perform the duties required of them by the Illinois law in relation to
these people because they were Negroes, there is a basis for a [fed-
eral] grand jury investigation and such an investigation should be
had."[14]

From East St. Louis, U.S. Attorney Charles Karch notified Gregory
that "the violence against the negroes and the consequent denial of
their constitutional prerogatives and immunities, were directly due to
State action," i.e., East St. Louis, St. Clair County, and Illinois officials had acquiesced in the violence because of sympathies with racist
mobs. In Karch's opinion, Section Nineteen also supplied the basis for
taking action, and he favored the appointment of Judge Landis with
whom he had recently conferred at the request of the Department of
Justice.[15] A few days after Karch's letter was written, a local newspaper quoted him as saying that although the United States Government might not have explicit legal grounds for a grand jury investigation, "the fact that federal troops [the Illinois National Guard was
federalized on July 25, 1917] are now being held on duty [in East St.
Louis] and unable to go to Europe, if needed, probably would afford
the basis for federal jurisdiction."[16] However, despite a *New York
Times* announcement that the Department of Justice had decided to
go ahead with an investigation,[17] neither Virginia-born Woodrow
Wilson nor Texas-born Thomas W. Gregory were disposed to permit
a federal inquiry. In their view jurisdiction to intervene did not exist
since no evidence was uncovered indicating the violation of federal
statutes during the race riot.[18] The Wilson Administration, strongly
backed by Southerners who barred Negroes from ballot boxes, had no

desire to use federal powers to investigate the denial by state officials of constitutional prerogatives.

Even if the national government had decided to send a judge to conduct the riot inquiry, there was never any real possibility of obtaining Landis's services. In a confidential letter to the Attorney General, Karch reported that the jurist had incurred the animosity of Illinois's Joe Cannon, former Speaker of the U.S. House of Representatives. Cannon was determined that Landis would never again handle cases in the judicial district of which East St. Louis was a part.[19] Although Landis had privately told Karch that Section Nineteen afforded ample basis for an inquiry at least, after Wilson and Gregory ruled against convening the grand jury, a story appeared in the *New York Times* showing that the jurist changed his mind or had it changed for him: "Landis . . . took the view that it was questionable whether as an infraction of state law, the riot was a proper subject of [federal] judicial inquiry."[20]

Even while Gregory's attorneys were involved in deliberations, L. C. Dyer, St. Louis's Representative in Congress, introduced a joint resolution requesting the Senate and House Committees on the Judiciary to sponsor the riot investigation.[21] Dyer maintained that a Congressional inquiry was justified because the riot had interfered with interstate commerce.[22] Illinois's Senator Sherman supported a similar resolution, and two weeks after the riot he told the United States Senate that East St. Louis contained all the ingredients for an even greater racial explosion.[23]

Negro groups, of course, supported the Dyer resolution, and among those who exerted pressures were the National Association of Colored Women and the N.A.A.C.P.[24] Race papers such as the *St. Louis Argus* wanted to avoid disappointment and seemed cautious in regard to the expected accomplishments of a Congressional inquiry.[25] The *New York Age* was somewhat pessimistic, fearing that the only result might be a recommendation for a federal law preventing Negroes from migrating to the North.[26]

In August there was a modification of the plan for a joint House-Senate subcommittee to investigate the riot, with the House passing a resolution establishing its own subcommittee composed of five members.[27] (Rep. John E. Raker, California; Rep. Martin D. Foster, Illinois; Rep. Henry A. Cooper, Wisconsin; Rep. George E. Foss, Illinois; and Rep. Ben Johnson of Kentucky, who acted as chairman.) Hearings were conducted in East St. Louis from mid-October until mid-November of 1917 following the summer violence, and nearly five thousand pages of testimony were taken. During the opening days, committee members established a reason to legitimize their presence and meet the objections of those Americans who felt that a branch of the national government was capriciously interfering in a local problem. The Congressmen presented several witnesses who testified that the riot had obstructed the flow of interstate commerce between Illinois and Missouri.[28] For example, Phillip W. Coyle, traffic manager of the St. Louis Chamber of Commerce stated that from May 28 to July 10, there had been an interruption of over one hundred thousand tons of material which was normally sent between St. Louis and East St. Louis.[29] Furthermore, St. Louis shipping companies found it difficult to employ Negroes, who feared to unload goods in East St. Louis.[30] Packing plant superintendents reported that the riot delayed fulfillment of wartime government contracts.[31] The Armour Company noted that during the week after the riot, when Negroes refused to work, there had been a fifty percent drop in the number of cows killed and a seventy-five percent reduction in the number of hogs slaughtered.[32] As late as October and November, many companies allowed colored laborers to leave work one hour earlier because the men were afraid to be on the streets when darkness came.[33]

After the obstruction of interstate commerce was inserted into the record, the Committee turned its attention to the background of the riot. The legislators requested and received transcripts of testimony taken by the Illinois National Guard Military Board of Inquiry and the Labor Committee of the Illinois State Council of Defense. However, the U.S. Department of Justice refused to grant access to its records on the race riot, since in the opinion of Attorney General Gregory, "it would not be in the public interest."[34]

During the four weeks of hearings scores of witnesses from all strata of the East St. Louis community were given an opportunity to testify—from bank presidents to labor organizers, from bailbondsmen to influential political leaders, from newly arrived Negro migrants to colored professional men who had lived in the city for a large part of their lives. A great deal of the testimony was based on verifiable facts, but a substantial portion was hearsay evidence requiring further investigation. Unfortunately, several factual errors appeared in the final report because some leads were not adequately explored by the Congressmen, e.g., the charge of importation, estimates of Negro crime, and the size of the Negro population in East St. Louis.

After a month of listening to accounts of graft, corruption, prostitution, murder, race prejudice, and community apathy, one legislator told the press, "I had never dreamed that such a condition existed in this country—or on the face of the earth."[35] On the eve of the Committee's departure local newspapers had only praise for the tireless, dedicated performance of the members. The editor of the *Globe-Democrat* recalled that when the possibility of the investigation was first discussed, he had opposed it, believing that Illinois was able to put its own house in order. However, after observing the diligence of the Committee, he concluded that the inquiry cleared the air, bringing an awareness that "there is no depth to which prostituted politics, in a long tolerant or indifferent community will not descend."[36] Other newspapers similarly commended the Committee.[37]

The Congressmen returned to Washington, spending several months sifting through all the data which had been collected. Despite the expectations of some East St. Louisans, no indictments or courts-martial resulted from the hearings. Nevertheless, the report presented to Congress was a stinging condemnation of the community's mores, clearly showing how the activities of employers, labor organizers, and politicians created a milieu which made the race riot possible. . . .

NOTES

1. *St. Louis Globe-Democrat*, July 4, 1917.

2. Reprinted in *Crisis* 14 (1917): 305.

3. *St. Louis Post-Dispatch*, July 7, 1917. See also *New York Times*, July 7, 1917. "Riots in East St. Louis," *Pan-American Magazine* 25 (1917): 173-74.

4. *Crisis* 14 (1917): 164. *New York Age*, July 12, 1917.

5. *New York Age*, July 12 and 19, 1917. *St. Louis Argus*, July 27, 1917.

6. *Cleveland Gazette*, July 21, 1917.

7. *Norfolk Journal and Guide*, July 21, 1917. *California Eagle*, July 21, 1917. See also Arthur S. Link, *The New Freedom* (Princeton: Princeton University Press, 1956), pp. 457-59.

8. "Minutes of the N.A.A.C.P. Board of Directors," (September 17, 1917). See also *Norfolk Journal and Guide*, August 11, 1917. *New York Age*, July 26 and August 2, 1917. *St. Louis Argus*, August 10, 1917. *Cleveland Gazette*, August 18, 1917. *Chicago Defender*, July 28, 1917. *New York Times*, July 29, 1917. *Crisis* 14 (1917): 241, 244.

9. *New York Age*, August 9, 1917.

10. *Norfolk Journal and Guide*, July 21 and August 18, 1917. See

also Kelly Miller's open letter to Woodrow Wilson, August 4, 1917, reprinted in *Congressional Record*, 65th Cong. 55 (1917): 6990-93.

11. "Congressional Hearings," p. 2639. See also letter from Charles Karch to Thomas W. Gregory, July 8, 1917, in unsigned memorandum to Gregory, July 20, 1917. (In United States Department of Justice files on East St. Louis riots, National Archives, Washington, D.C. Hereafter referred to as Department of Justice Files.)

12. *St. Louis Post-Dispatch*, July 8 and 10, 1917.

13. Telegram from Citizens Committee of One Hundred to Congressman Rodenberg, July 19, 1917. See also following communications—Congressman Rodenberg to Thomas W. Gregory, July 20, 1917. Charles Karch to Gregory, July 6, 1917. Congressman Dyer to Woodrow Wilson, July 20, 1917, Department of Justice Files.

14. Memorandum for Mr. Fitts from "Herron," July 20, 1917, Department of Justice Files.

15. Charles Karch to Thomas W. Gregory, July 23, 1917, Department of Justice Files.

16. *Belleville News-Democrat*, July 28, 1917.

17. *New York Times*, July 17, 1917.

18. See the following communications, Woodrow Wilson to Thomas W. Gregory, July 23, 1917. Thomas W. Gregory to Woodrow Wilson, July 27, 1917. Thomas W. Gregory to Charles Karch, July 27, 1917, Department of Justice Files.

19. Charles Karch to Thomas W. Gregory, July 23, 1917, Department of Justice Files.

20. *New York Times*, August 4, 1917. See also *St. Louis Globe-Democrat*, August 4, 1917.

21. The St. Louis Congressman did not want the public to be confused between his city and the Illinois community across the Mississippi River. Out of apparent seriousness and an undoubted desire for publicity, he asked East St. Louis to change its name. Postmaster-General Burleson was requested to take charge of the renaming rites. (*St. Louis Globe-Democrat*, July 12, 1917.)

22. H. R. Resolution #118, 65th Cong., 1st Sess., House of Representatives, July 9, 1917. See also *St. Louis Post-Dispatch*, July 9, 1917. *St. Louis Globe-Democrat*, July 10, 1917.

23. *Congressional Record* 55 (1917): 5150-51. See also *St. Louis Post-Dispatch*, July 15, 1917. *St. Louis Globe-Democrat*, July 17, 1917. *Cleveland Gazette*, July 21, 1917.

24. The N.A.A.C.P. took the position that there were no legal barriers to a federal investigation because the race riots had interfered

with the U.S. mails. Furthermore, because Negro males fled East St. Louis after the violence, their registration under the conscription law was "confused and aborted." *N.A.A.C.P. Branch Bulletin* 1 (1917): 57.

25. *St. Louis Argus*, October 26, 1917.

26. *New York Age*, July 19, 1917.

27. House Resolution #128, 65th Cong., 1st Sess., 1917.

28. "Congressional Hearings," pp. 64, 429-31.

29. Ibid., p. 7.

30. Ibid., pp. 19-20, 28-30.

31. Ibid., p. 72.

32. Ibid., p. 129.

33. Ibid., pp. 31, 105, 570.

34. Letter from Thomas W. Gregory to Congressman Ben Johnson, October 10, 1917, Department of Justice Files.

35. *East St. Louis Daily Journal*, November 19, 1917.

36. *St. Louis Globe-Democrat*, November 19, 1917.

37. *Belleville News-Democrat*, November 17, 1917. *East St. Louis Daily Journal*, November 20, 1917.

III

Chicago, 1919

INTRODUCTION

Three weeks before the eruption of Chicago's violent race riots in 1919, in which some 38 persons were killed and over 500 injured, Carl Sandburg was assigned by the *Chicago Daily News* to write a series of feature articles on the city's race relations. During the course of his research, the young reporter and writer interviewed Joel Spingarn, a former chairman of the NAACP, who suggested that "a commission, consisting of men and women from both races, should be appointed to investigate and make recommendations. Such a commission, if it has the right people on it, takes the thought of people away from violence."*

Spingarn's advice came too late. After the riot, however, a biracial commission was established with private funds and public support from city and state officials. The following selection from *The Negro in Chicago* represents only a small part of a very lengthy and comprehensive report which took nearly two years to complete and became a model for future riot commissions, notably the 1935 Mayor's Commission on Conditions in Harlem and the 1968 Kerner Commission.

Arthur Waskow's analysis of the politics and ideology of *The Negro in Chicago* has in turn become a model for social scientists interested in riot commissions. Its influence is clearly visible in the studies of Robert Fogelson, Paul Jacobs, Michael Lipsky, and David Olson. Waskow's critique, combining thorough historical research with sociological analysis, provides both insight into a unique event and theoretical generalizations for assessing the political role and processes of riot commissions.

NOTES
1. Carl Sandburg, *The Chicago Race Riots, July 1919* (New York: Harcourt, Brace & World, Inc., 1969), pp. 81-2.

4.

THE CHICAGO COMMISSION
ON RACE RELATIONS

The Negro in Chicago:
A Study of Race Relations
and a Race Riot

SUMMARY OF THE REPORT AND RECOMMENDATIONS
OF THE COMMISSION

The Summary
> The Chicago Riot

BACKGROUND

In July, 1919, a race riot involving whites and Negroes occurred in Chicago. For some time thoughtful citizens, white and Negro, had sensed increasing tension, but, having no local precedent of riot and wholesale bloodshed, had neither prepared themselves for it nor taken steps to prevent it. The collecting of arms by members of both races was known to the authorities, and it was evident that this was in preparation for aggression as well as for self-defense.

Several minor clashes preceded the riot. On July 3, 1917, a white saloon-keeper who, according to the coroner's physician, died of heart trouble, was incorrectly reported in the press to have been killed by a Negro. That evening a party of young white men riding in an automobile fired upon a group of Negroes at Fifty-third and Federal

SOURCE: From The Chicago Commission on Race Relations, *The Negro in Chicago: A Study of Race Relations and a Race Riot* (Chicago: University of Chicago Press, 1922), pp. 595-651. Reprinted with permission of the publisher.

streets. In July and August of the same year recruits from the Great Lakes Naval Training Station clashed frequently with Negroes, each side accusing the other of being the aggressor.

Gangs of white "toughs," made up largely of the membership of so-called "athletic clubs" from the neighborhood between Roosevelt Road and Sixty-third Street, Wentworth Avenue and the city limits—a district contiguous to the neighborhood of the largest Negro settlement —were a constant menace to Negroes who traversed sections of the territory going to and returning from work. The activities of these gangs and "athletic clubs" became bolder in the spring of 1919, and on the night of June 21, five weeks before the riot, two wanton murders of Negroes occurred, those of Sanford Harris and Joseph Robinson. Harris returning to his home on Dearborn Street, about 11:30 at night, passed a group of young white men. They threatened him and he ran. He had gone but a short distance when one of the group shot him. He died soon afterward. Policemen who came on the scene made no arrests, even when the assailant was pointed out by a white woman witness of the murder. On the same evening Robinson, a Negro laborer, forty-seven years of age, was attacked while returning from work by a gang of white "toughs" at Fifty-fifth Street and Princeton Avenue, apparently without provocation, and stabbed to death.

Negroes were greatly incensed over these murders, but their leaders, joined by many friendly whites, tried to allay their fears and counseled patience.

After the killing of Harris and Robinson notices were conspicuously posted on the South Side that an effort would be made to "get all the niggers on July 4th." The notices called for help from sympathizers. Negroes in turn whispered around the warning to prepare for a riot; and they did prepare.

Since the riot in East St. Louis, July 4, 1917, there had been others in different parts of the country which evidenced a widespread lack of restraint in mutual antipathies and suggested further resorts to lawlessness. Riots and race clashes occurred in Chester, Pennsylvania; Longview, Texas; Coatesville, Pennsylvania; Washington, D.C.; and Norfolk, Virginia, before the Chicago riot.

Aside from general lawlessness and disastrous riots that preceded the riot here discussed, there were other factors which may be mentioned briefly here. In Chicago considerable unrest had been occasioned in industry by increasing competition between white and Negro laborers following a sudden increase in the Negro population due to the migration of Negroes from the South. This increase developed a housing crisis. The Negroes overran the hitherto recognized area of Negro residence, and when they took houses in adjoining neighborhoods friction ensued. In the two years just preceding the riot, twenty-seven Negro dwellings were wrecked by bombs thrown by unidentified persons.

STORY OF THE RIOT

Sunday afternoon, July 27, 1919, hundreds of white and Negro bathers crowded the lake-front beaches at Twenty-sixth and Twenty-ninth streets. This is the eastern boundary of the thickest Negro residence area. At Twenty-sixth Street Negroes were in great majority; at Twenty-ninth Street there were more whites. An imaginary line in the water separating the two beaches had been generally observed by the two races. Under the prevailing relations, aided by wild rumors and reports, this line served virtually as a challenge to either side to cross it. Four Negroes who attempted to enter the water from the "white" side were driven away by the whites. They returned with more Negroes, and there followed a series of attacks with stones, first one side gaining the advantage, then the other.

Eugene Williams, a Negro boy of seventeen, entered the water from the side used by Negroes and drifted across the line supported by a railroad tie. He was observed by the crowd on the beach and promptly became a target for stones. He suddenly released the tie, went down and was drowned. Guilt was immediately placed on Stauber, a young white man, by Negro witnesses who declared that he threw the fatal stone.[1]

White and Negro men dived for the boy without result. Negroes demanded that the policeman present arrest Stauber. He refused; and at this crucial moment arrested a Negro on a white man's complaint. Negroes then attacked the officer. These two facts, the drowning and the refusal of the policeman to arrest Stauber, together marked the beginning of the riot.

Two hours after the drowning, a Negro, James Crawford, fired into a group of officers summoned by the policeman at the beach and was killed by a Negro policeman. Reports and rumors circulated rapidly, and new crowds began to gather. Five white men were injured in clashes near the beach. As darkness came Negroes in white districts to the west suffered severely. Between 9:00 P.M. and 3:00 A.M. twenty-seven Negroes were beaten, seven stabbed, and four shot. Monday morning was quiet, and Negroes went to work as usual.

Returning from work in the afternoon many Negroes were attacked by white ruffians. Street-car routes, especially at transfer points, were the centers of lawlessness. Trolleys were pulled from the wires, and Negro passengers were dragged into the street, beaten, stabbed, and shot. The police were powerless to cope with these numerous assaults. During Monday, four Negro men and one white assailant were killed, and thirty Negroes were severely beaten in street-car clashes. Four white men were killed, six stabbed, five shot, and nine severely beaten. It was rumored that the white occupants of the Angelus Building at Thirty-fifth Street and Wabash Avenue had shot a Negro. Negroes gathered about the building. The white tenants sought police protection, and one hundred policemen, mounted and on foot, responded. In a clash with the mob the police killed four Negroes and injured many.

Raids into the Negro residence area then began. Automobiles sped through the streets, the occupants shooting at random. Negroes retaliated by "sniping" from ambush. At midnight surface and elevated car service was discontinued because of a strike for wage increases, and thousands of employees were cut off from work.

On Tuesday, July 29, Negro men en route on foot to their jobs through hostile territory were killed. White soldiers and sailors in uniform, aided by civilians, raided the "Loop" business section, killing two Negroes and beating and robbing several others. Negroes living among white neighbors in Englewood, far to the south, were driven from their homes, their household goods were stolen, and their houses were burned or wrecked. On the West Side an Italian mob, excited by a false rumor that an Italian girl had been shot by a Negro, killed Joseph Lovings, a Negro.

Wednesday night at 10:30 Mayor Thompson yielded to pressure and asked the help of the three regiments of militia which had been stationed in nearby armories during the most severe rioting, awaiting the call. They immediately took up positions throughout the South Side. A rainfall Wednesday night and Thursday kept many people in their homes, and by Friday the rioting had abated. On Saturday incendiary fires burned forty-nine houses in the immigrant neighborhood west of the Stock Yards. Nine hundred and forty-eight people, mostly Lithuanians, were made homeless, and the property loss was about $250,000. Responsibility for the fires was never fixed.

The total casualties of this reign of terror were thirty-eight deaths—fifteen white, twenty-three Negro—and 537 people injured. Forty-one per cent of the reported clashes occurred in the white neighborhood near the Stock Yards between the south branch of the Chicago River and Fifty-fifth Street, Wentworth Avenue and the city limits, and 34 per cent in the "Black Belt" between Twenty-second and Thirty-ninth streets, Wentworth Avenue and Lake Michigan. Others were scattered.

Responsibility for many attacks was definitely placed by many witnesses upon the "athletic clubs," including "Ragen's Colts," the "Hamburgers," "Aylwards," "Our Flag," the "Standard," the "Sparklers," and several others. The mobs were made up for the most part of boys between fifteen and twenty-two. Older persons participated, but the youth of the rioters was conspicuous in every clash. Little children witnessed the brutalities and frequently pointed out the injured when the police arrived.

RUMORS AND THE RIOT

Wild rumors were in circulation by word of mouth and in the press throughout the riot and provoked many clashes. These included stories of atrocities committed by one race against the other. Reports of the numbers of white and Negro dead tended to produce a feeling that the score must be kept even. Newspaper reports, for example, showed 6 per cent more whites injured than Negroes. As a matter of fact there were 28 per cent more Negroes injured than whites. The *Chicago Tribune* on July 29 reported twenty persons killed, of whom thirteen were white and seven colored. The true figures were exactly the opposite.

Among the rumors provoking fear were numerous references to the arming of Negroes. In the *Daily News* of July 30, for example, appeared the sub-headline: "Alderman Jos. McDonough tells how he was shot at on South Side visit. Says enough ammunition in section to last for years of guerrilla warfare." In the article following, the reference to ammunition was repeated but not elaborated or explained.

The alderman was quoted as saying that the mayor contemplated opening up Thirty-Fifth and Forty-seventh streets in order that colored people might get to their work. He thought this would be most unwise for, he stated, "They are armed and white people are not. We must defend ourselves if the city authorities won't protect us." Continuing his story, he described bombs going off: "I saw white men and women running through the streets dragging children by the hands and carrying babies in their arms. Frightened white men told me the police captains had just rushed through the district crying, 'For God's sake, arm; they are coming; we cannot hold them.'"

Whether or not the alderman was correctly quoted, the effect of such statements on the public was the same. There is no record in any of the riot testimony in the coroner's office or state's attorney's office of any bombs going off during the riot, nor of police captains warning the white people to arm, nor of any fear by whites of a Negro invasion. In the Berger Odman case before a coroner's jury there was a statement to the effect that a sergeant of police warned the Negroes of Ogden Park to arm and to shoot at the feet of rioters if they attempted to invade the few blocks marked off for Negroes by the police. Negroes were warned, not whites.

CONDUCT OF THE POLICE

Chief of Police John J. Garrity, in explaining the inability of the police to curb the rioters, said that there was not a sufficient force to police one-third of the city. Aside from this, Negroes distrusted the white police officers, and it was implied by the chief and stated by State's Attorney Hoyne, that many of the police were "grossly unfair in making arrests." There were instances of actual police participation in the rioting as well as neglect of duty. Of 229 persons arrested and accused of various criminal activities during the riot, 154 were Negroes and seventy-five were whites. Of those indicted, eighty-one were Negroes and forty-seven were whites. Although this, on its face, would indicate great riot activity on the part of Negroes, further reports of clashes show that of 520 persons injured, 342 were Negroes and 178 were whites. The fact that twice as many Negroes appeared as defendants and twice as many Negroes as whites were injured, leads to the conclusion that whites were not apprehended as readily as Negroes.

Many of the depredations outside the "Black Belt" were encouraged by the absence of policemen. Out of a force of 3,000 police, 2,800 were massed in the "Black Belt" during the height of the rioting. In the "Loop" district, where two Negroes were killed and several others wounded, there were only three policemen and one sergeant. The Stock Yards district, where the greatest number of injuries occurred, was also weakly protected.

THE MILITIA

Although Governor Lowden had ordered the militia into the city promptly and they were on hand on the second day of the rioting, their services were not requested by the mayor and chief of police until the evening of the fourth day. The reason expressed by the chief for this delay was a belief that inexperienced militiamen would add to the deaths and disorder. But the troops, when called, proved to be clearly of high character, and their discipline was good, not a case of breach of discipline being reported during their occupation. They were distributed more proportionately through all the riotous areas than the police and, although they reported some hostility from members of "athletic clubs," the rioting soon ceased.

RESTORATION OF ORDER

Throughout the rioting various social organizations and many citizens were at work trying to hold hostilities in check and to restore order. The Chicago Urban League, Wabash Avenue Y.M.C.A., American Red Cross, and various other social organizations and the churches of the Negro community gave attention to caring for stranded Negroes, advising them of dangers, keeping them off the streets and, in such ways as were possible, co-operating with the police. The packing companies took their pay to Negro employees, and various banks made loans. Local newspapers in their editorial columns insistently condemned the disorder and counseled calmness.

THE AFTERMATH

Of the thirty-eight persons killed in the riot:

Fifteen met death at the hands of mobs. Coroner's juries recommended that the members of the unknown mobs be apprehended. They were never found.

Six were killed in circumstances fixing no criminal responsibility: three white men were killed by Negroes in self-defense, and three Negroes were shot by policemen in the discharge of their duty.

Four Negroes were killed in the Angelus riot. The coroner made no recommendations, and the cases were not carried farther.

Four cases, two Negro and two white, resulted in recommendations from coroner's juries for further investigation of certain persons. Sufficient evidence was lacking for indictments against them.

Nine cases led to indictments. Of this number four cases resulted in convictions.

Thus in only four cases of death was criminal responsibility fixed and punishment meted out.

Indictments and convictions, divided according to the race of the persons criminally involved, were as follows:

	NEGRO		WHITE	
	Cases	Persons	Cases	Persons
Indictments	6	17	3	4
Convictions	2	3	2	2

Despite the community's failure to deal firmly with those who disturbed its peace and contributed to the reign of lawlessness that shamed Chicago before the world, there is evidence that the riot aroused many citizens of both races to a quickened sense of the suffering and disgrace which had come and might again come to the city, and developed a determination to prevent a recurrence of so disastrous an outbreak of race hatred. This was manifest on at least three occasions in 1920 when, confronted suddenly with events out of which serious riots might easily have grown, people of both races acted with such courage and promptness as to end the trouble early. One of these was the murder of two innocent white men and the wounding of a Negro policeman by a band of Negro fanatics who styled themselves "Abyssinians"; another was the killing of a white man by a Negro whom he had attacked while returning from work; and still another was the riotous attacks of sailors from the Great Lakes Naval Training Station on Negroes in Waukegan, Illinois.

OUTSTANDING FEATURES OF THE RIOT

This study of the facts of the riot of 1919, the events as they happened hour by hour, the neighborhoods involved, the movements of mobs, the part played by rumors, and the handling of the emergency by the various authorities, shows certain outstanding features which may be listed as follows:

a) The riot violence was not continuous hour by hour, but was intermittent.

b) The greatest number of injuries occurred in the district west and inclusive of Wentworth Avenue, and south of the south branch of the Chicago River to Fifty-fifth Street, or in the Stock Yards district. The next greatest number occurred in the so-called "Black Belt": Twenty-second to Thirty-ninth streets, inclusive, and Wentworth Avenue to the lake, exclusive of Wentworth Avenue; Thirty-ninth to Fifty-fifth streets, inclusive, and Clark Street to Michigan Avenue, exclusive of Michigan Avenue.

c) Organized raids occurred only after a period of sporadic clashes and spontaneous mob outbreaks.

d) Main thoroughfares witnessed 76 per cent of the injuries on the South Side. The streets which suffered most severely were State, Halsted, Thirty-first, Thirty-fifth, and Forty-seventh. Transfer corners were always centers of disturbances.

e) Most of the rioting occurred after work hours among idle crowds on the streets. This was particularly true after the street-car strike began.

f) Gangs, particularly of young whites, formed definite nuclei for crowd and mob formation. "Athletic clubs" supplied the leaders of many gangs.

g) Crowds and mobs engaged in rioting were generally composed of a small nucleus of leaders and an acquiescing mass of spectators. The leaders were mostly young men, usually between the ages of sixteen and twenty-one. Dispersal was most effectively accomplished by sudden, unexpected gun fire.

h) Rumor kept the crowds in an excited, potential mob state. The press was responsible for giving wide dissemination to much of the inflammatory matter in spoken rumors, though editorials calculated to allay race hatred and help the forces of order were factors in the restoration of peace.

i) The police lacked sufficient forces for handling the riot; they were hampered by the Negroes' distrust of them; routing orders and records were not handled with proper care; certain officers were undoubtedly unsuited to police or riot duty.

j) The militiamen employed in this riot were of an unusually high type. This unquestionably accounts for the confidence placed in them by both races. Riot training, definite orders, and good staff work contributed to their efficiency.

k) There was a lack of energetic co-operation between the police department and the state's attorney's office in the discovery and conviction of rioters.

The riot was merely a symptom of serious and profound disorders lying beneath the surface of race relations in Chicago. The study of the riot, therefore, as to its interlocking provocations and causes, required a study of general race relations that made possible so serious and sudden an outbreak. Thus to understand the riot and guard against another, the Commission probed systematically into the principal phases of race contact and sought accurate information on

matters which in the past have been influenced by dangerous specula-
tion; and on the basis of its discoveries certain suggestions to the
community are made. . . .

The Recommendations of the Commission

Many of our citizens who were appalled by the rioting and murders
of 1919, feeling the need of a solution of the problem dealt with in
this investigation, have hoped that this Commission might suggest
some ready remedy, some quick means of assuring harmony between
the races.

Careful consideration of the facts set forth in this report shows that
no such suggestion is possible. No one, white or Negro, is wholly free
from an inheritance of prejudice in feeling and in thinking as to these
questions. Mutual understanding and sympathy between the races will
be followed by harmony and co-operation. But these can come completely only after the disappearance of prejudice. Thus the remedy is
necessarily slow; and it is all the more important that the civic conscience of the community should be aroused, and that progress should
begin in a direction steadily away from the disgrace of 1919.

Each member of this Commission feels that he has more understanding and less prejudice than before its work began. Therefore we
recommend the thoughtful examination of the body of this report, so
that all who read our recommendations may weigh for themselves the
evidence upon which they are based.

Having in mind the basic facts in the problem of race relations and
the conclusions from a careful study of the various phases of these
relations in Chicago, the Commission presents for the consideration
and action of state and local authorities, and of the social agencies
and citizens of Chicago, the following recommendations and suggestions.

To the Police, Militia, State's Attorney, and Courts:

HANDLING OF RIOTS

1. We recommend that the police and militia work out, at the
earliest possible date, a detailed plan for joint action in the control of
race riots.

2. In accordance with such a plan, and in the event of race rioting, we specifically recommend: (*a*) that the militia, white and
Negro, be promptly mobilized at the beginning of the outbreak; (*b*)
that police and deputy sheriffs and militia, white and Negro, be so

distributed as adequately to protect both races in white and Negro neighborhoods and to avoid the gross inequalities of protection which, in the riot of 1919, permitted widespread depredations, including murder, against Negroes in white neighborhoods, and attacks in Negro neighborhoods by invading white hoodlums; (c) that the police and militia be stationed with special reference to main street-car lines and transfer points used by Negroes in getting to and from work; (d) that substantial assurance be given of adequate and equal protection by all agencies of law enforcement, thus removing the incentive to arm in self-defense; (e) that in the appointment of special peace officers there shall be no discrimination against Negroes; (f) that all rioters, white and Negro, be arrested without race discrimination; (g) that all reports and complaints of neglect of duty or participation in rioting by police, deputy sheriffs, or militia be promptly investigated and the offenders promptly punished; (h) that all persons arrested in connection with rioting be systematically booked on distinct charges showing such connection, in order to avoid the confusion and eva-sions of justice following the riot of 1919.

3. We recommend that, without regard to color, all persons ar-rested in connection with rioting be promptly tried and the guilty speedily punished.

BOMBINGS

4. We recommend prompt and vigorous action by the police, state's attorney, and courts to suppress the bombings of Negro and white houses, these acts being criminal and likely to provoke race rioting.

5. The testimony of court officials before the Commission and its investigations indicate that Negroes are more commonly arrested, sub-jected to police identification, and convicted than white offenders, that on similar evidence they are generally held and convicted on more serious charges, and that they are given longer sentences. We point out that these practices and tendencies are not only unfair to Negroes, but weaken the machinery of justice and, when taken with the greater inability of Negroes to pay fines in addition to or in lieu of terms in jail, produce misleading statistics of Negro crime. We recognize that these practices and tendencies are in a large degree the unconscious results of traditional race prejudice. We recommend to the police, state's attorney, judges, and juries that they consider these conditions in the effort to deal fairly (and without discrimination) with all persons charged with crime.

6. We recommend that, in order to encourage respect for law by both Negroes and whites, the courts discountenance the facetiousness which is too common in dealing with cases in which Negroes are involved.

VICIOUS ENVIRONMENT

7. We recommend that the police, state's attorney, and other authorities promptly rid the Negro residence areas of vice resorts, whose present exceptional prevalence in such areas is due to official laxity.

POLICING OF PARKS AND BEACHES

8. We recommend better co-operation between the city and park police in and near parks, bathing-beaches, and other public recreation places, especially where there has been or is likely to be race friction; and in the speedy punishment of persons guilty of stoning houses, molesting individuals, or committing other depredations calculated to arouse race antagonism.

"ATHLETIC CLUBS"

9. We recommend that the police pay particular and continuous attention to the so-called "athletic clubs" on the South Side, which we have found to be a fruitful source of race conflict, and that when race conflict arises or is imminent the members and meeting places of such clubs be searched for arms and that, if deemed necessary, such clubs be closed.

THE BARRETT MURDER

10. We commend the police for the prompt and effective action in the Barrett murder case, September 20, 1920, which allayed public alarm and averted a serious clash.

To the City Council and Administrative Boards, the Park Boards and the Municipal Bureau of Parks, Playgrounds, and Bathing-Beaches:

CONTROL OF FIREARMS

11. We recommend that the most stringent means possible be applied to control the importation, sale, and possession of firearms and other deadly weapons.

SUPERVISION OF "ATHLETIC CLUBS"

12. In order to facilitate police supervision of so-called "athletic clubs," we recommend that all such clubs be required to file with the city clerk statements of their purposes and, at stated intervals, lists of their members and officers, with their addresses.

SANITATION

13. We recommend that the authorities exercise their powers to condemn and raze all houses unfit for human habitation, many of which the Commission has found to exist in the Negro residence areas on the South and West sides.

14. We recommend better enforcement of health and sanitary laws and regulations in the care, repair, and upkeep of streets and alleys and the collection and disposal of rubbish and garbage in areas of Negro residence, where the Commission has found these matters to be shamefully neglected.

RECREATION CENTERS

15. We recommend that the park and other proper authorities (a) put an end to the present gross discrimination by white persons which practically bars Negroes out of certain recreation centers near their own congested residence area; and (b) that a recreation center of adequate size and facilities be established for the use of both whites and Negroes in the principal Negro residence area of the South Side; and (c) that steps be taken to secure more adequately trained, competent, and intelligent playground and recreation-center directors, white and Negro, who shall be held responsible for racial clashes arising in places under their direction and shall be required to interest themselves in reducing and avoiding racial friction in their neighborhoods; and (d) that proper equipment and supervision be provided at the Twenty-sixth Street Bathing-Beach, where they are now almost wholly lacking; and (e) that, in co-operation with the city police, the park police adequately protect all citizens, without regard to color, in going to and from parks, recreation centers, and playgrounds.

To the Board of Education:

MORE SCHOOLS IN NEGRO AREAS

16. We recommend that in the areas where the main part of the Negro population lives, and where elementary-school accommoda-

tions are notably deficient, buildings, equipment, and teaching forces be provided which shall be at least equal to the average standard for the city, in order that the present conditions of overcrowding, arrangement of pupils in shifts, and the assignment of too large classes to teachers may be remedied.

NIGHT SCHOOLS AND COMMUNITY CENTERS

17. We recommend the establishment of night schools and community centers in sections of the city not now adequately provided with such facilities.

COMPULSORY EDUCATION

18. Having found that many Negro children who quit school at an early age, as in the case of similar white children, appear later as criminals and delinquents, we urge strict enforcement of regulations as to working permits for such children, and we especially recommend that truant officers give attention to school attendance by the children of Negro families migrating here from the South.

ATTITUDE OF PRINCIPALS AND TEACHERS

19. Since the attitude of principals and teachers vitally influences the relations of white and Negro children in the public schools, we recommend that special care be exercised in appointing principals and teachers who have a sympathetic and intelligent interest in promoting good race relations in the schools.

STUDENT ACTIVITIES

20. We recommend that public-school principals and teachers encourage participation by children of both races in student activities as a means of promoting mutual understanding and good race relations in such schools and in the community.

To Social and Civic Organizations, Labor Unions, and Churches:

PROMOTION OF RACE HARMONY

21. Being convinced by our inquiry that much of the antagonism evinced in the areas of marked hostility toward Negroes is founded upon tradition which is itself without foundation in fact or justice, we recommend to schools, social centers and agencies, churches, labor unions, and other organizations in these areas, and to public-spirited citizens, white and Negro, that they endeavor to dispel the false no-

tions of each race about the other and promote mutual tolerance and friendliness between them.

22. We recommend that both white and Negro churches seek and use means to improve race relations, and that these means include the finding of frequent occasion for having their congregations addressed by representatives of both races on the subject of race sympathy and tolerance.

SOCIAL AGENCIES IN NEGRO COMMUNITIES

23. We commend the course of such agencies as the United Charities, Illinois Children's Home and Aid Society, and American Red Cross in extending their work to the Negro community, and recommend that other agencies whose work is similarly useful extend their work in like manner.

24. Recognizing and commending the practical efforts of the Interracial Committee of the Woman's City Club, the Public Affairs Committee of the Union League Club, and the Chicago Urban League, in promoting better race relations, especially in the summer of 1920, when racial friction was deemed imminent, we recommend that other organizations of the same kind undertake like activities.

25. We recommend that the appropriate social agencies give needed attention to dealing extra-judicially with cases of Negroes coming before the morals and juvenile courts; also to cases of Negro children dropping out of school too early in age.

OPPORTUNITY FOR RECREATION TRAINING

26. We recommend that Negroes, as well as whites, be given opportunity for training for service in the city's public recreation facilities.

To the Public:

INTERRACIAL TOLERANCE

27. We are convinced by our inquiry: (*a*) that measures involving or approaching deportation or segregation are illegal, impracticable and would not solve, but would accentuate, the race problem and postpone its just and orderly solution by the process of adjustment; (*b*) that the moral responsibility for race rioting does not rest upon hoodlums alone, but also upon all citizens, white or black, who sanction force or violence in interracial relations or who do not condemn and combat the spirit of racial hatred thus expressed; (*c*) that race

friction and antagonism are largely due to the fact that each race too readily misunderstands and misinterprets the other's conduct and aspirations.

We therefore urge upon all citizens, white and Negro, active opposition to the employment of force or violence in interracial relations and to the spirit of antagonism and hatred. We recommend dispassionate, intelligent, and sympathetic consideration by each race of the other's needs and aims; we also recommend the dissemination of proved or trustworthy information about all phases of race relations as a useful means for effecting peaceful racial adjustment.

28. Since rumor, usually groundless, is a prolific source of racial bitterness and strife, we warn both whites and Negroes against the acceptance or circulation by either of reports about the other whose truth has not been fully established. We urge all citizens, white and Negro, vigorously to oppose all propaganda of malicious or selfish origin which would tend to excite race prejudice.

29. We commend race contacts in cultural and co-operative efforts as tending strongly to mutual understanding and the promotion of good race relations.

30. We condemn the provocation or fostering of race antagonism by associations or organizations ostensibly founded or conducted for purposes of patriotism or local improvements or the like.

PERMANENT RACE-RELATIONS BODY

31. We recommend as of special importance that a permanent local body representing both races be charged with investigating situations likely to produce clashes, with collecting and disseminating information tending to preserve the peace and allay unfounded fears, with bringing sound public sentiment to bear upon the settlement of racial disputes, and with promoting the spirit of interracial tolerance and co-operation.

To the White Members of the Public:

RACE ADJUSTMENT IN MIXED NEIGHBORHOODS

32. We call to public attention the fact that intensity of racial feeling is not necessarily due to the presence of Negroes in a neighborhood, either in the majority or minority, and that such feeling is not the rule but the exception; and we cite as a conspicuous example the peaceful conditions that have long obtained in the area between

Roosevelt Road and Thirty-ninth Street from Wentworth Avenue to Lake Michigan, in which the Negro population in 1920 numbered 54,906 and the white population 42,797.

BETTER NEGRO HOUSING WITHOUT SEGREGATION

33. Our inquiry has shown that insufficiency in amount and quality of housing is an all-important factor in Chicago's race problem; there must be more and better housing to accommodate the great increase in Negro population which was at the rate of 148 per cent from 1910 to 1920. This situation will be made worse by methods tending toward forcible segregation or exclusion of Negroes, such as the circulation of threatening statements and propaganda by organizations or persons to prevent Negroes from living in certain areas, and the lawless and perilous bombing of houses occupied by Negroes or by whites suspected of encouraging Negro residence in the district.

We therefore recommend that all white citizens energetically discourage these futile, pernicious, and lawless practices, and either cooperate in or start movements to solve the housing problem by constructive and not destructive methods.

DEPRECIATION AND PROPERTY RISKS

34. Testimony before the Commission and investigations made by it show two important facts: (a) that depreciation of residence property generally charged exclusively to the presence of Negroes in a neighborhood is often largely due to other factors; (b) that many Negroes of this city meet their obligations in such a manner as to make their home-building and home-owning investments seem a more desirable risk than has been generally supposed. We therefore recommend that these facts be taken into consideration in connection with loans on Negro property.

ADVANCED RENTS FOR NEGROES CONDEMNED

35. We condemn and urge the discontinuance of the practice of property owners who arbitrarily advance rents merely because Negroes become tenants.

INFORMATION ABOUT NEGROES

36. We recommend that white persons seek information from responsible and representative Negroes as the basis of their judgments about Negro traits, characteristics, and tendencies, and thereby coun-

teract the common disposition, arising from erroneous tradition and literature, to regard all Negroes as belonging to one homogeneous group and as being inferior in mentality and morality, given to emotionalism, and having an innate tendency toward crime, especially sex crime.

To the Negro Members of the Public:

RACIAL DOCTRINES

37. We recommend to Negroes the promulgation of sound racial doctrines among the uneducated members of their group, and the discouragement of propaganda and agitators seeking to inflame racial animosity and incite Negroes to violence.

SUPPORT OF SOCIAL AGENCIES

38. We urge Negroes to contribute more freely of their money and personal effort to the social agencies developed by public-spirited members of their group; also to contribute to the general social agencies of the community.

SPECIAL PROBLEMS

39. We recommend that the Negro community, through the extension or establishment of the necessary social agencies, undertake to supply means and encouragement for leisure activities, and undertake work among Negro boys and girls along the lines of prevention of vice and crime; also that it provide institutional care of dependent Negro children.

40. We particularly urge that Negroes vigorously and continuously protest against the presence in their residence areas of any vicious resort, and that they join in and support all efforts to suppress such places.

ADJUSTMENT OF MIGRANTS

41. We commend the important work done by the Chicago Urban League, the Negro churches, and other organizations in facilitating the adjustment of migrant Negroes from the South to the conditions of living in Chicago and urge its extension. We also commend the work already done by Negroes through community associations in bettering the appearance and sanitary condition of housing and recommend its further extension.

RACE PRIDE

42. While we recognize the propriety and social values of race pride among Negroes, we warn them that thinking and talking too much in terms of race alone are calculated to promote separation of race interests and thereby to interfere with racial adjustment.

To Employers and Labor Organizations:

ATTITUDE TOWARD NEGRO WORKERS

43. We have found that in struggles between capital and labor Negro workers are in a position dangerous to themselves and to peaceful relations between the races, whether the issues involve their use by employers to undermine wage standards or break strikes, or efforts by organized labor to keep them out of certain trades while refusing to admit them to membership in the unions in such trades. We feel that unnecessary racial bitterness is provoked by such treatment of Negro workers, that racial prejudice is played upon by both parties, and that through such practices injury comes, not alone to Negroes, but to employers and labor organizations as well.

We therefore recommend to employers that they deal with Negroes as workmen on the same plane as white workers; and to labor unions that they admit Negroes to full membership whenever they apply for it and possess the qualifications required of white workers.

NEGRO AND WHITE WORKERS

44. We commend to the attention of employers who fear clashes or loss of white workers by taking on Negro workers the fact that in 89 per cent of the industries investigated by this Commission, Negroes were found working in close association with white employees, and that friction between these elements had rarely been manifested.

INDUSTRIAL AND BUSINESS OPPORTUNITIES FOR NEGROES

45. In view of the limited field of employment within which Negroes are restricted we recommend that employers in all lines enlarge that field and permit Negroes an equal chance with whites to enter all positions for which they are qualified by efficiency and merit. In this connection especial attention is called to the fact that opportunity is generally denied to Negroes for gaining experience in business methods through service in responsible positions in business houses. Such opportunities, if made available for them, would not only be of benefit to Negroes in the development of sounder business methods among

them and the building up of their resources, but would also be a gain to the business establishments and the community at large.

46. We have found that Negroes are denied equal opportunity with whites for advancement and promotion where they are employed. As a measure of justice we urge that Negroes be employed, advanced, and promoted according to their capacities and proved merit. We call to the attention of those concerned the high qualifications of many Negro workers in sleeping-car and dining-car service, and recommend that when they deserve it and the opportunity offers, they be made eligible for promotion to positions as conductors and stewards.

TEMPORARY EMPLOYMENT OF NEGROES AS STRIKE BREAKERS

47. We point out as an injustice and a cause of racial antagonism the practice of some employers who having hired Negroes as strike breakers discharge them when the strike is settled to make places for former white employees.

NEGRO WOMEN WORKERS

48. We find that employment of Negro girls at a smaller wage than white girls and the denial to them of apprenticeship opportunities are a cause of racial antagonism. We therefore recommend that the employment of Negro girls be based on merit, with equality of wages, piece rates, and apprenticeship opportunities with white girls; we also recommend that Negroes in domestic employment rendering the same quality of service as whites be paid at the same rate as white domestics.

RACIAL PEACE IN INDUSTRY

49. Realizing that the common welfare is involved in the employment or non-employment of Negro workers, and seeking means to preserve racial peace in industry, we recommend: (a) that where Negro employees are dismissed for unsatisfactory service other Negroes, recommended by reliable Negro organizations, be given an opportunity to replace them; (b) that in times of industrial depression, employers reduce their forces in such a manner that the hardships of unemployment may not be disproportionately severe on Negro workers; (c) that where Negroes are employed with whites at the same tasks they be given equal pay for equal work and equal opportunity for piecework and overtime work; (d) that Negro workers be given opportunity for advancement and promotion according to merit and efficiency and without race discrimination; (e) that Negro

workers be afforded the opportunity to learn and engage in the skilled processes of their employment; (f) that superintendents closely supervise the relations of foremen with Negro workers and see that there is no racial injustice or discrimination; (g) that employers generally deal with Negroes, whether engaged in, or seeking opportunity to engage in, manual labor or clerical work, without discrimination as to race, and apply to them the same tests and conditions as to white employees.

SEPARATE LABOR UNIONS

50. We strongly condemn the efforts of self-seeking agitators, Negro or white, who use race sentiment to establish separate unions in trades where existing unions admit Negroes to equal membership with whites.

To Negro Workers:

RELATIONS WITH UNIONS

51. We recommend that qualified Negro workers desiring membership in labor organizations join unions which admit both races equally, instead of organizing separate Negro labor unions.

RELATIONS WITH EMPLOYERS

52. We recommend that Negroes completely abandon the practice of seeking petty advance payments on wages and the practice of laying off work without good cause.

LEARNING TRADES

53. We recommend that Negroes avail themselves wherever possible of opportunities in apprentice schools and classes.

54. We recommend to all Negroes dependent on manual labor the learning of some skilled trade even though there is no present opportunity to engage in it.

To the Street-Car Companies:

PROTECTION OF PASSENGERS

55. In view of the large number of racial assaults on persons riding in street cars, we recommend that conductors and motormen be specially instructed concerning protection of passengers, white and Negro, and be rigidly held to the discharge of this duty.

OVERCROWDING

56. We recommend that at all loading-points where whites and Negroes board cars in large numbers, starters be employed and over-crowding be prevented as far as possible.

To Restaurants, Theaters, Stores, and Other Places of Public Accommodation:

EQUAL RIGHTS IN PUBLIC PLACES

57. We point out that Negroes are entitled by law to the same treatment as other persons in restaurants, theaters, stores, and other places of public accommodation, and we urge that owners and managers of such places govern their policies and actions and their employees accordingly.

To the Press:

HANDLING OF NEWS INVOLVING NEGROES

58. In view of the recognized responsibility of the press in its general influence upon public opinion concerning Negroes—especially important as related to the suppression of race rioting—we recommend: (*a*) that the newspapers generally, including the foreign-language press, apply the same standards of accuracy, fairness, and sense of proportion, with avoidance of exaggeration, in publishing news about Negroes as about whites; in this connection special attention is called to the fact that emphasis, greatly out of proportion to that given their creditable acts, is frequently placed on the crimes and misdeeds of Negroes, who, unlike other groups, are identified with each incident and thus constantly associated with discreditable conduct; (*b*) that the manner of news treatment be no different in the case of Negroes than in that of whites, to the end that there shall always be the unwritten assumption that the same responsibility for equal consideration of the rights of the one by the other rests on whites and Negroes alike, in respect of the matter involved in the publication; (*c*) that, in consideration of the great ease with which the public is influenced against the whole Negro group by sensational articles and headlines, the press should exercise great caution in dealing with unverified reports of crimes of Negroes against white women, and should avoid the designation of trivial fights as race riots; (*d*) that in recognition of the dangers of racial antagonism on the part of the ignorant, the unthinking, and the prejudiced of both races, publi-

cation be made, as opportunities offer, of such matters as shall in their character tend to dispel prejudice and promote mutual respect and good will.

We specially recommend more frequent publications concerning: (1) creditable achievements of consequence by Negroes; (2) their efforts toward a higher cultural and social life, and (3) their improvement of the physical conditions of their own communities; (4) the common obligation of all citizens of all races to recognize in their interrelations the supreme duty of strict obedience to the law, in spirit as well as in deed; (5) verification, so far as practicable, of all news concerning Negroes and their activities by reference to recognized Negro agencies or responsible representative Negroes. . . .

HANDLING OF NEWS INVOLVING NEGROES AND WHITES

59. To the Negro press we recommend greater care and accuracy in reporting incidents involving whites and Negroes, the abandonment of sensational headlines and articles on racial questions, and more attention to educating Negro readers as to the available means and opportunities of adjusting themselves and their fellows into more harmonious relations with their white neighbors and fellow-citizens, and as to the lines of individual conduct and collective effort which will tend to minimize interracial friction, promote their own social and economic development, and hasten interracial adjustment.

NOTES

1. The coroner's jury found that Williams had drowned from fear of stone-throwing which kept him from the shore.

5.

ARTHUR I. WASKOW

Chicago: The Riot Studied*

On the fourth day of the Chicago riot, while men were still dying in the streets and before the militia had gone on active duty, the governor of Illinois was asked to appoint a commission "to study troubles & formulate definite programme of race relations for state." That request came from a committee hastily assembled by the NAACP.[1] Two days later, a much more powerful group of Chicagoans asked Governor Frank Lowden to create "an emergency state committee to study the psychological, social, and economic causes underlying the present race riot and to make such recommendations as will tend to prevent a recurrence of such conditions in the future."[2] Out of these two appeals came the Chicago Commission on Race Relations.

The first call for a commission was suggested by Major Joel E.

* From Arthur I. Waskow, *From Race Riot to Sit-In, 1919 and the 1960's: A Study in the Connections Between Conflict and Violence* (New York: Doubleday, 1966), pp. 60-104. Reprinted with permission of the author and publisher.

Spingarn, an NAACP director who had been visiting Chicago when the riot broke out. Spingarn wrote Mary White Ovington, the NAACP's national chairman, that the committee that waited upon Governor Frank Lowden included former judges Robert McMurdy and Edward Osgood Brown (a former president of the Chicago NAACP); judges Orrin Carter and Henry Homer; Dr. Charles E. Bentley, a Negro physician; Carl Sandburg, then a reporter on the *Chicago Daily News*; Robert S. Abbott, publisher of the leading Chicago Negro newspaper, the *Defender*; Father E. A. Kelly, a "Catholic priest in the black district"; Col. Franklin A. Denison, commander of a Negro regiment in the Illinois National Guard; Marcus A. Hirschl, secretary of the Chicago NAACP; and Clarence Darrow, the renowned lawyer. This group suggested to Governor Lowden a commission of five or eight members, and Lowden replied that he would consult with Francis W. Shepardson, the state Director of Registration and Education, a former professor of history at the University of Chicago and Lowden's house expert on race relations.[3]

Despite Governor Lowden's promise of July 30 to consult with Shepardson, he was probably more powerfully influenced by the second call for a commission. For the power behind this second appeal was much greater than could have been wielded by a committee including a Negro publisher, a minor Catholic priest, and a heterodox lawyer like Clarence Darrow. The second appeal was issued on August 1 by a meeting at the Union League Club in Chicago. Among the signers were Cyrus Hall McCormick, Mary McDowell, Graham Taylor, and Harriet Vittum—pillars of the community all; and among the organizations represented were the Armour and Swift meat-packing houses, the Chicago Association of Commerce, the Chicago Federation of Settlements, the City Club, the Joint Committee on Americanization, the Real Estate Board, and the Medical and Bar associations.[4] The meeting had been called by the Joint Commission on Americanization, "representing the twenty-two leading clubs in Chicago." It was chaired by Charles W. Folds, president of the Union League Club, and led by Taylor, who headed the Chicago Commons, one of the city's best-known settlement houses, and who wrote frequent columns for the *Chicago Daily News*.[5] Certainly the Chicago Commission on Race Relations itself later believed that this appeal from some of the most influential citizens of Chicago was what moved the governor to announce he would appoint a mixed commission.[6]

Governor Lowden turned the problem over to Francis Shepardson, his cabinet member for education, who had been involved before the riot in an attempt to create by legislative act an official state commission on race relations and who would have been chairman of that commission if the bill had passed.[7] Shepardson later reported that the governor had followed this bill carefully, had been disappointed in its failure, and was thus mentally prepared for the possibility of an interracial commission when the riots came. Lowden was especially anxious for the commission to start work quickly because of the rash of riots across the country. He hoped the Chicago Commission might act as a model for other American cities.[8]

Most of the job of choosing members for the commission was left to Shepardson. At once he began to receive unsolicited nominations from white real estate interests and from Negro small businessmen, minor politicians, and church and lodge leaders, but these he ignored.[9] Out of his own knowledge of Illinois affairs, he decided on white members of the commission. When it came to Negroes, however, he had to seek advice concerning suitable leaders of the Negro community. On this question Shepardson talked with Julius Rosenwald of Sears, Roebuck and Company, who had long been involved in philanthropy for Negroes in Chicago and throughout the nation. From this beginning Shepardson built a relationship with Rosenwald that drew heavily upon his help for the commission and that later provided Shepardson with a profession in race relations as director of the Julius Rosenwald Fund. At Rosenwald's suggestion, Shepardson called upon A. L. Jackson, executive secretary of the Wabash Avenue YMCA (the Negro branch, which had benefited heavily from Rosenwald's philanthropies). He also corresponded with several social workers and with Father E. A. Kelly of Saint Anne's Rectory, that "Catholic priest in the black district" who had seen the governor on July 30.[10]

There are only two surviving indications of the bases on which Shepardson made his judgments from the various recommendations he received. One is an explanation that despite the ability of T. Arnold Hill, executive secretary of the Chicago chapter of the Urban League, he could not be appointed because "leading colored citizens of Chicago feel quite strongly that in a Commission composed only of six negroes, there are others whose claims to consideration are superior to those of one who has been in Chicago only three or four years and who is not widely known among the negro citizens."[11] The other is a fragment of Shepardson's handwritten notes on two Negroes he did name to the commission: Adelbert H. Roberts whom he described to himself (or to the governor) as "member of the Illinois legislature and sponsor . . . for a bill proposing a commission to consider race relationships," and Dr. George Cleveland Hall, "a physician long identified with all movements looking toward the betterment of the conditions of the colored people."[12] These notations suggest (as does the actual list of appointments) that Shepardson was seeking persons prominent and powerful in the white and Negro communities who had also in some way concerned themselves with race relations, rather than scholars or professional experts in race relations. The image of a permanent race commission able to sway public opinion and adjust issues in conflict seems to have been as much in his mind as the image of a special commission to study the causes of a particular riot.

The final report of the commission identified those members whom Governor Lowden appointed on August 20 as follows (the starred members being Negroes):[13]

*Robert S. Abbott, Editor.
Born, Savannah, Georgia; graduate, Hampton Institute; graduate, Kent College of Law; owner and publisher, the *Chicago Defender.*

Edgar Addison Bancroft, Chairman, Lawyer.
Born, Galesburg, Illinois; graduate, Knox College; graduate, Columbia Law School; ex-president, Chicago Bar Association, Illinois State Bar Association; trustee, Knox College, Carnegie Endowment for International Peace, and Tuskegee Institute; Senator of Phi Beta Kappa.

William Scott Bond, Real Estate Dealer.
Born, Chicago, Illinois; graduate, University of Chicago; graduate, Kent College of Law; member, real estate firm William A. Bond & Company; trustee, University of Chicago.

Edward Osgood Brown, Lawyer.
Born, Salem, Massachusetts; graduate, Brown University; graduate, Harvard Law School; for ten years judge of the Illinois Appellate Court, First District; for some years president, Chicago Branch of National Association for the Advancement of Colored People.

*George Cleveland Hall, Physician and Surgeon.
Born, Ypsilanti, Michigan; graduate, Lincoln University; graduate, Bennett Medical College; trustee, Provident Hospital; vice-president, Chicago Urban League; orator at

dedication of Booker T. Washington memorial monument at Tuskegee, 1922.

°George H. Jackson, Real Estate Dealer.

Born in Canada; graduate, Cincinnati Law School; former member, Ohio Legislature; president, Pyramid Building and Loan Association.

Harry Eugene Kelly, Lawyer.

Born, Des Moines, Iowa; graduate State University of Iowa; former member, Colorado Legislature; for some years United States district attorney for Colorado; former president, Denver Bar Association; attorney for Interstate Commerce Commission; regional counsel at Chicago for Director General of Railroads.

Victor F. Lawson, Editor.

Born, Chicago, Illinois; graduate, Phillips Academy, Andover, Massachusetts; owner, editor, and publisher, *Chicago Daily News* since 1876; ex-president and now a director, Associated Press; founder, Daily News Fresh Air Fund and Daily News Free Lectures; called "father of postal savings bank in America."

°Edward H. Morris, Lawyer.

Born in Kentucky; for two terms representative in Illinois General Assembly; member of Illinois Constitutional Convention, 1920-21; for eleven years Grand Master of the Colored Odd Fellows of America.

°Adelbert H. Roberts, Lawyer.

Born in Michigan; student, University of Michigan; graduate, Northwestern University Law School; for two terms representative in Illinois General Assembly.

Julius Rosenwald, Merchant.

Born, Springfield, Illinois; president, Sears, Roebuck & Company; philanthropist, stimulated construction and contributed $325,000 toward total cost of Y.M.C.A. buildings for Negroes in thirteen cities; contributed over $1,000,000 toward rural schools for Negroes in fourteen southern states; trustee, Tuskegee Institute, University of Chicago, Rockefeller Foundation.

°Lacey Kirk Williams, Minister.

Born, Eufaula, Alabama; graduate, Arkansas Baptist College; pastor, Olivet Baptist Church, Chicago, since 1916 (largest Protestant Church in America); president, Illinois

General Baptist State Convention; vice-president, Colored National Baptist Convention.

Shepardson himself was not initially named; but during a long illness of Bancroft, the designated chairman, Shepardson acted as chairman and was later formally added to the roster of members.[14] His was the energy that carried the commission through to the completion of its work. Of the other members, Shepardson leaned most heavily on Rosenwald with his great influence in the business and philanthropic worlds.

Once the members of the commission had been appointed, they had to face in several different ways the problem of building an identity for the commission. The two simplest possible roles were that of a political body which could mediate, manage, and "accommodate" new racial disputes as they arose; and that of a purely scholarly body which could study, analyze, and explain the one historical event of the 1919 Chicago riot. There was a third possibility, less obvious and more difficult: to unite the functions of scholarship and politics, by applying an analysis of past racial clashes like the Chicago riot to the control of continuing racial conflict. Governor Lowden evidently hoped that the Commission would take on the political role, for he wrote its members that his purpose was "to secure harmonious co-operation where there is friction, . . . [by getting] representatives of the interests affected together, to talk things over and settle mooted points in free and friendly discussion."[15] But the financial problems the commission faced and the decisions it made concerning staff led it in the direction of more scholarly concerns. Ultimately, the commission essayed the third role, that of the expert in policy who bases his recommendations for change in the future upon his scholarly analysis of the past.

The commission's status as a private rather than an official state agency helped to direct its energies away from politics toward scholarship and expertise. For the absence of state funds meant, first, that the finances of the commission were always so precarious and its life so clearly temporary that it had to focus upon studying an event in the past, upon a scholarly project whose end could be seen in advance, rather than upon the open-ended, continuing problem of assuaging future racial unrest. Moreover, since the commission's financial support came not from the public but from the voluntary contributions of the wealthiest citizens of Chicago, the commission was more dependent than it might otherwise have been on their basic outlook on racial policy. To operate as an effective political instrument, the commission would have had to be more closely attuned to demands of both the Negro community and those less well established whites who had been most hostile to Negroes. The Negroes had a voice on the commission, though a much weaker one than that of the wealthy whites who sponsored it; the less comfortable, more angry whites had not even a voice. Thus at least one of the "interests affected," in the governor's terms, was not even present "to talk things over and settle mooted points." They would probably have been present if the commission had been a public body; but without them the commission found study of the problem and recommendations of new policy an easier task than the actual politics of managing conflict.

Anxiety over its precarious finances plagued the commission throughout its life. The question arose almost at once when William C. Graves, Rosenwald's secretary and the man who was to be his alter ego in the actual workings of the commission, asked Shepardson "whether any of the Governor's emergency fund or any other state fund is available for expenses of this commission and if so in what maximum sum."[16] Shepardson explained that no state money was available, but that he had been told by the Chicagoans he had talked with "that there would be no difficulty in raising the necessary funds in Chicago."[17] Although Shepardson did not mention it at the time— at least on paper—he had also been told by the governor that if all else failed, Lowden himself would see that the commission had money for its work.[18] The commission was ultimately to find the governor's help necessary to speed up collection of funds from the upper class of Chicago.

Indeed, the commission tried to turn the governor's promise to some immediate use. In their first meeting, the members asked Lowden to appoint a fund-raising committee so that their own independence need not be compromised. When he refused, the commission had to turn to its own myriad acquaintanceships among wealthy Chicagoans. It asked the Chicago Association of Commerce, the Union League Club, and the City Club to co-operate as a finance committee for the commission.[19] And Shepardson got James B. Forgan of the First National Bank of Chicago to set up a fund-raising committee of prominent white citizens, after assuring Forgan that the entire commission approved of his choice to do the job.[20]

Not until months later was an attempt made to raise money from Chicago's Negro community, and then chiefly because trouble was at hand in meeting the budget. At that point, a Negro Finance Committee was set up with considerable direct help from Negro members of the commission's staff (despite the stated hopes of the commission that neither members nor staff would be compromised in this way). The 300 Negroes to whom an appeal was sent were asked to contribute enough so that Negroes would provide about one third of the commission's treasury—that is, approximately $8,000. By November 23, total Negro contributions were $349.[21]

Estimates of the commission's needs fluctuated during its work. Its own budget committee reported on October 20, 1919, that $20,000 would be necessary. Shepardson himself thought one month later that $12,000 to $14,000 would be enough. By March 1920, the commission thought that $30,000 would be necessary, and in November and December 1920 hiked its estimate first to $34,000 and then to $36,000.[22]

This succession of reassessments imposed a series of financial crises on the commission. At the very beginning of its work, before any contributions had been made, Julius Rosenwald lent it enough money to start, but that was repaid within a month.[23] In March 1920, Shepardson began to worry over the rate of contributions. He cautioned the staff that cutbacks in the proposed research might be necessary, nor was he wholly calmed by their proposal that the indicated shortage of $5,000 might be raised from Negro contributors, from sale of the commission's furniture and typewriters, and by slight reductions in staff.[24] Through the spring and summer of 1920, the commission kept only one month ahead of its bills, and by late August its executive secretary was urging that Shepardson consider cashing in the governor's promise to make sure money was available.[25] In October, a loan from Rosenwald again met the payroll. Almost all pretense of non-involvement by staff and members of the commission in money-raising was dropped, as all hands turned to public speaking, and as possible contributors were invited to observe operations at commission headquarters.[26] Emergency conferences with the staff of the Association of Commerce indicated that banker Forgan's special finance committee had already milked that source dry. It was pointed out, however, that eight or ten individuals who had not responded to letters from the finance committee might be expected to give a total of about $8,000 if they were more directly solicited. And Shepardson was specifically requested to ask the governor to appeal to the few wealthy men who might provide the needed cash.[27]

Before turning to this last resort, however, Shepardson tried using

Forgan's finance committee once more. The Union League Club itself gave $1,000. Edgar Bancroft, the commission's chairman-designate, who had returned in June after an illness but had not spent enough time in the commission office to understand the staff's work and had not taken over the real direction of the commission from Shepardson, was brought into the financial campaign. Forgan, although he was not optimistic about the prospects, asked for second contributions from those who had already given.[28]

But this attempt by Shepardson and the commission to make ends meet without the governor's help was a failure. Not until after the staff had completed almost all the work on the report and Lowden had left the governorship did the commission meet its bills, and then only with Lowden's help. In April 1921, a luncheon was arranged by Lowden for a number of wealthy Chicagoans in order to raise the commission's remaining deficit. Rosenwald withheld the announcement of his planned second $1,000 gift until the luncheon, and Lowden himself gave $1,000. He later wrote sixteen Chicago businessmen to thank them for their gifts. So the Chicago Commission on Race Relations ended, as it had begun, in the hands and with the support of the most substantial, powerful, and honored men of the city.[29]

When in October 1919 the commission began its substantive work with the search for an executive secretary, the members had not yet decided between being a politics-oriented organization, resolving racial tensions, or a research-oriented organization, studying only the past. Nor had they begun to work out the role with which they concluded: that of an organization oriented to the study and invention, but not the implementation of new policy. Even before the commission met for the first time, Rosenwald—with Shepardson's blessing—had begun to canvas such leading white scholars as the sociologist Edward A. Ross of the University of Wisconsin and such leading Negro educators as Robert R. Moton of Tuskegee Institute for names of possible secretaries. The suggestions ranged from Robert E. Park, an eminent sociologist at the University of Chicago, to Will W. Alexander, then with the YMCA's War Work Council and later director of the Commission on Interracial Cooperation, to Mordecai Johnson, then a clergyman in Charleston, West Virginia, and later the President of Howard University, to Charles S. Johnson, director of research of the Chicago branch of the Urban League. Some of these men were scholars; some were interracial "accommodators" who could have directed the commission's work toward semi-private coping with racial conflict.[30]

A considerable discussion arose at once over whether the executive secretary should be white or Negro, or whether there should be two secretaries. The commission generally agreed that a Chicago man would be best for the job. Rosenwald, Hall, Jackson, and Shepardson were designated to seek out a secretary, and by October 20 had narrowed the field to seven men. One of these, Charles S. Johnson, a Negro, had already filed a proposed outline on how to go about studying the Chicago riot. He was a graduate student in social science at the University of Chicago, under Robert E. Park, as well as a researcher for the Urban League. Another, Graham Romeyn Taylor, a white man, was the son of the Graham Taylor who had helped initiate the commission. He had just returned from several years abroad, doing social service work in Russia and East Asia and acting as a special assistant to the American ambassador to Russia during and after the 1917 revolutions. He had written a book and a number of articles on urban problems, and was reported by an editor for whom he had written to have made an extraordinarily fair study of the great Calumet strike.[31]

Taylor and Johnson were approached by the commission—Taylor by Rosenwald's secretary, William Graves, and Johnson by the commission's senior Negro member, George Cleveland Hall. Both were interested. Still the commission was unsure how to equalize racial status in its staff. In November, five of the members "favored two secretaries with equal rank, and three, while recognizing the importance of having investigations made both by whites and colored people, favored but one secretary." One suggestion that won considerable approval was to have the chairman of an executive committee of the commission act as staff director over two equal secretaries; but no decision was made until both Taylor and Johnson had appeared before the commission. The latter was reported to have "made a favorable impression . . . in a brief talk in which he called attention to the available material for study already gathered by other agencies and to the machinery through which investigations might be made." The commission then decided to hire both men, Taylor as executive secretary at a salary of $5,000 and Johnson as associate executive secretary at $3,500.[32] The decision to hire two men whose chief work had been in research and writing rather than in actual politics or racial conciliation clearly bespoke the commission's choice of the role of policy expert rather than that of active politician.

A lingering unpleasantness over the staff problem—what Graves called "the clash of authority which threatened a few weeks ago"—was dissolved when Taylor and Johnson presented on December 11 a joint outline of the way in which they proposed to study race relations in Chicago as they bore upon the riot. Graves himself thought the outline a "marvel," and Shepardson said it was "the finest thing of the kind" he had ever seen.[33] Most of this outline can be attributed to Johnson, who according to Taylor's widow "set up the study" and was the researcher of the two men. Taylor, she recalled, was "skilled in writing but not in research." In addition to her testimony, there is the evidence of the two outlines—one formally submitted by Taylor and Johnson on December 12 and one sent by Johnson to Shepardson on October 5 as part of his application for a job with the commission. The two outlines show a close resemblance, and the commission's final report is clearly the direct offspring of the second outline, which is itself a direct offspring of the first.[34]

From this point on, the efforts of the commission were more and more directed at supporting, reviewing, and supervising the research work of the staff, and at keeping the commission's money in balance with its needs. With the staff organized, the commission also began to meet less often as a unit; from October 8 to December 18, 1919, it met ten times, and only another eight times in all of 1920. The burden of research and writing was turned over to the staff.[35]

To oversee this work, the commission divided into six committees: on racial clashes, housing, industry, crime and police, racial contact, and public opinion. Each committee kept in touch with the staff research going on in its own area. Each of the six areas had been set forth in the Taylor-Johnson outline and each developed into a major section of the commission's final report. Two areas that had been suggested in the original Johnson outline were dropped in the second outline and in the final report: the politics of the Black Belt, and the extent and causes of racial segregation (as distinguished from inequality).[36]

In addition to the six sub-committees, the commission appointed an executive committee made up of Brown, Hall, Kelly, Morris, Rosenwald, and Shepardson *ex officio*.[37] This group—but chiefly Shepardson, and Graves acting for Rosenwald—effectively managed most of the over-all work for the rest of the commission's history.

Before we enter upon a discussion of the commission's research efforts, however, it should be noted that the role as racial adjuster and accommodator early envisioned for the commission was not wholly abandoned. On four occasions, the commission felt it necessary to concern itself with current racial unrest.

The first came in late October 1919, when the commission issued press releases to all the Chicago newspapers, white and Negro, saying that it had heard reports of "a continued state of unrest in neighborhoods where white and black people live," and urging calmness, patience, and tolerance.[38] In December, Shepardson told the commission he had had a reporter attend and take notes on the Kenwood and Hyde Park Property Owners Association meeting at which threats were made against Negroes who "invaded" those residential areas; and the commission staff expressed its concern with the meeting and the "inflammatory" newspaper of the association, but did not recommend any action.[39]

In February 1920, an increase in bombings of Negro property and in hostile statements by white real estate dealers prompted Governor Lowden to ask that Shepardson have the commission look into the problem. Shepardson agreed, writing the governor, "There seems to be no authority interested in the protection of Americans whose skins are black." Considering that he was writing the fountainhead of police authority in the state of Illinois, Shepardson's comment seems full of irony—probably unconscious. When Shepardson talked the problem over with the commission's executive committee, they voted to send committees to the mayor of Chicago and the state's attorney to see what they had done to investigate the bombings. These committees were to report back to the commission, but no record exists of their having done so.[40]

Shepardson himself, however, spoke publicly of existing troubles as evidence of an approaching volcanic eruption, which would occur unless terrorism and bomb-throwing ceased. Shepardson added, "The negro does not desire to scatter himself over the entire city . . . We have no intelligent segregation that will permit the negro to live among those of his own kind whom he prefers, but a segregation that throws all negroes into one vicious neighborhood."[41] Shepardson did not make clear that this acceptance of a racially segregated city (albeit "intelligently" segregated) was his own, not the commission's. He probably thereby contributed to the belief, later reported by Johnson to be held by many Negroes, that the commission would propose a scheme for compulsory segregation.[42] Shepardson's concern to keep the peace may thus have backfired and stirred new resentments in the city.

In June 1920, another flurry of concern by the commission over immediate problems was stirred by a clash in which two whites were killed by members of the Star Order of Ethiopia. These men had been publicly burning an American flag in order to demonstrate their loyalty to the King of Ethiopia. When several Negro and white passersby objected, the "Ethiopians" shot them. Shepardson, reading of this incident in the newspapers, hastened to ask Taylor to investigate it, although he said he gathered "this was a sporadic outbreak not blameable on Chicago negroes at all but upon that special company of people." Taylor replied that he and Johnson (who had been very near the scene of the clash and was investigating it within twenty minutes) had found that all was now quiet on the South Side.[43]

Taylor did warn, however, that the *Chicago Tribune's* attempt to connect the Star Order of Ethiopia with the NAACP and W.E.B. Du Bois would anger the very Negro leaders who had condemned the "Ethiopians." Shepardson answered that he too was sorry to see the NAACP confused in the press with the "Ethiopians," adding that he found the writings of Du Bois impressive but disturbing. Then Shepardson wrote the governor that no further racial clashes were likely and added the somewhat puzzling comment that his "advices from Chicago" suggested that the affair might "be helpful rather than hurtful to the general cause for which we have been working."[44]

That the degree of involvement of the commission in easing current racial tensions was being reduced can be seen from the way in which it disengaged itself as a body from even those efforts that were undertaken. Thus, in October 1919, the full commission was publicly involved; in February 1920, only its chairman was speaking publicly; by June, the chairman and staff were acting in private. After June 1920, the commission did not again take action as a racial accommodator or adjuster and instead focused upon the role of investigator and researcher. An estimate of the relative importance of these roles to the commission can be made from its reaction to a suggestion that it ask newspapers to stop labeling criminals as Negroes. It was pointed out that such requests might give the impression of complaint or special pleading, and might thereby interfere with the readiness of newspaper editors to co-operate in the commission's research into public opinion. For this reason, the commission decided not to urge changes in newspaper habits until it had completed its study and was ready to adopt final recommendations.[45]

On two matters of investigation, the commission itself took a considerable hand. One of these was the question of radical and seditious incitement of Negroes as a factor in causing the riot.

The commission's attention was first drawn to the possible involvement of "bolshevists," "radicals," or the Industrial Workers of the World (IWW) by a syndicated column by David Lawrence in the *Chicago Daily News* of November 5, 1919. Lawrence reported that the United States Government had evidence of sedition among some Negro leaders, in the form of such attitudes as "an ill-governed reaction toward race rioting; . . . the threat of retaliatory measures in connection with lynching; . . . demand for social equality; . . . advocacy of the bolshevist or soviet doctrine." The *Daily News* also published on the same day a local story reporting the presence of an IWW organizer in Chicago and an increased amount of radical propaganda among Negroes but cautioned that there was no widespread interest in radicalism among Chicago Negroes. The *News* also quoted Dr. George Cleveland Hall, calling him "one of the leaders of the colored race in Chicago and a member of the state's Race Relationships Committee," to the effect that there was far more sedition in the southern whites' attack on the Negro than in the Negro's defense organizations.[46]

The day these stories appeared, Rosenwald had his secretary write David Lawrence to ask for references to the reports on which the story was based. Lawrence answered that he had been given access to an unpublished report and could not disclose who had given him the story; but he suggested that Francis Garvan, the Assistant Attorney-General in whose jurisdiction fell the Federal Bureau of Investigation, could help Rosenwald out.[47]

Shepardson then took the matter up. On behalf of the commission, he wrote Garvan to ask for any information that could help determine whether the Chicago riot was in any part due to radical propaganda among the Negroes. Shortly afterward, a lodge brother of Shepardson's, who happened also to be an army intelligence agent, wrote Shepardson of an army intelligence report on "Radicalism and Race Riots" and explained how Shepardson could get a copy for the commission's use.[48]

Shepardson did so, and on December 4 read the commission parts of "a confidential report from the Department Intelligence Office of the United States Army located at Chicago." The report claimed that IWW propaganda among Negroes had a major role in inciting the 1919 riot. Some of the "facts" adduced, however, made the commission dubious of the entire report. It listed the National Urban League and the NAACP as organizations engaged in spreading IWW propaganda, and commission members knew from their own memberships in these organizations that they had no interest in the IWW's program; indeed, much the reverse.[49]

The commission's minutes report its reactions this way:

> Some of the items were not considered significant because it happened that members of the Commission had attended some of the meetings referred to and were able to report personally the entire absence of any of the features described in the report. In other cases, members of the Commission had knowledge of facts which seemed to cast doubt upon the conclusion of the report, but it was felt that the Commission should have the benefit of all information in the hands of the government and it was voted that the officer in charge be thanked for his courtesy in permitting the Commission to see the confidential material and be asked to furnish the Commission any material which might be helpful to it and its study.

A much more disapproving assessment was ultimately made in the commission's report, which remarked, "These reports were founded upon scarcely anything more than suspicion due to lack of information and acquaintance with the Negro group." That the commission felt strongly is made clear in Shepardson's letter thanking his friend in the intelligence service, for Shepardson mentioned a "lively discussion" and "sharp expression of dissent" from the army report.[50]

The other research problem in which the commission itself took a major hand grew out of difficulties made by the Pullman Company for staff researchers seeking data on the Negro's place in industry. When the staff and the commission members found they were unable to get the Pullman Company to co-operate (or even to be polite), Shepardson wrote the governor. The chief difficulty had been with the president of Pullman, John S. Runnells, both a personal and a business associate of the governor; so Shepardson asked the governor to drop a word that would secure the company's co-operation.[51]

Lowden was obviously reluctant to act. The original request came in June 1920. In August, Taylor reminded Shepardson of the problem and added that Pullman had not only refused to give any information to the research staff, but was also the only large industry that had refused to contribute any money. In December Shepardson reported that he had talked with Lowden again; but not till February 1921 did Lowden telegraph Runnells asking him to see Edgar Bancroft, the commission's chairman, in order to learn about its work. By that time the research work of the commission was complete.[52]

Aside from these two incidents, the commission allowed the staff to carry out the research work with considerable independence and to make its own arrangements with sources of information. The research job began with the commission's approval of the Taylor-Johnson outline in December, although the hiring of more than a dozen full-time and half-time staff investigators took much of January and February.[53] The work program outlined by Taylor and Johnson was to begin with the study of a mass of data on hand, including all the testimony on the riot given to the coroner's jury, six studies of Negro housing in Chicago done by various scholars or social agencies, the Urban League's collection of 3000 letters of migrating southern Negroes, and a file of white and Negro press clippings on the riots and on racial matters in Chicago. From this material, the research work would move on to the collection of new data from police court records, from interviews with industrialists, teachers, and labor leaders, and from other such sources of information.[54]

To gather this material, Johnson and Taylor hired eighteen staff researchers, about equally divided between whites and Negroes and between half-time and full-time workers. Most of them had been social workers in such institutions as the Red Cross, the Urban League, the Federal Children's Bureau, and the Juvenile Protective Association; three were, like Johnson himself, students of Robert E. Park at the University of Chicago.[55] Seven other persons were hired later to compile the collected data and write drafts of sections of the commission's report. Of these, three had studied under Park.

Park had not only studied race relations and the process of acculturation in Negroes and immigrants but during 1917 and 1918 had been president of the Chicago Urban League. Before the riot, he had predicted an exacerbation of racial conflict resulting from the great Negro migration North and from the unsettling effects of the exposure of Negro troops to new ideas and conditions. Park had also espoused the Urban League's distinctive approach to Negro betterment through industrial employment and social welfare agencies. Park thus joined in himself the dominant orientations of the commission, both in its approach to racial policy and its research program.

He was able to impress these orientations on the work of the commission staff even more strongly than many of the commission members themselves could have. For he influenced the research process not only indirectly through what he had previously taught his students, but directly, through constant consultation during both the investigation and writing periods of the staff's work. An internal memorandum from Taylor and Johnson to the commission's executive committee noted that Park had "given seriously of his time," had "more familiarity than anyone else" except the commission and the staff with the data collected, and was prepared to help organize the report. In these ways, he colored the research work with his interests in great popular migrations, in the city as a confluence of various cultures, in the impact of urban industrialism on the rurally bred, and in the growth of popular stereotypes and their influence on public opinion.[56]

When the investigators started work, they organized their efforts around the six areas that Taylor and Johnson had spelled out: race clashes, housing, industry, crime and police, racial contacts, and public opinion. Some of their work was semi-formal observation of interracial behavior on streetcars, in factory areas, etc., and door-to-door interviews in white and Negro homes. But most of it centered around the distribution of formal questionnaires to various leadership groups in the schools, labor unions, social-service agencies, industries, and other segments of society, and in the organization of thirty conferences or informal hearings at which members of the staff and the relevant subcommittee of the commission interviewed community leaders.[57]

These conferences provided much of the richest and meatiest material in the commission's final report. A sampling of them will indicate the sorts of problems examined and sources used. One conference, on Negro housing in outlying areas, brought together members of the Chicago Planning Commission and the Park Board, the secretary of the Lower North Community Council, real estate men on the west side, and an official of the West Englewood Savings Bank. Another, on the Negro in industry, had in attendance the managers of industrial relations at International Harvester and Armour and Company, the superintendent of Argo Corn Products, a labor administrator at the Yellow Cab Company, and the industrial secretary of the Chicago Urban League. The investigation of public opinion brought editors and reporters from the white and Negro press but separately—at the suggestion of Victor Lawson, commission member who was publisher of the *Chicago Daily News*.[58] Other conferences assembled similar community spokesmen and leaders to review the state of race relations in their own bailiwicks.

It would be enlightening to review the research methods used by the commission in these interviews and in its other work. But unfortunately, the data that were turned up by the commission's researchers—conference transcripts, door-to-door interviews, maps, questionnaires—were destroyed in a fire at the offices of the Chicago Urban League, where the research files were deposited after the commission had completed its work.[59] Aside from the final report itself, only a few items remain—some blank questionnaires, fragments of conference transcripts, some reports in commission minutes of staff activities.

Nevertheless, a review of these fragments sheds some light on the commission's approach in the six different sub-studies.

The first sub-study, "racial clashes," covered both the Chicago riot and a number of smaller events, including two other major Illinois riots, one at Springfield in 1908 and one at East St. Louis in 1917. Not much effort was put into research on these older riots, because East St. Louis had been carefully examined by a congressional committee and Springfield seemed to Taylor not indicative of the kind of racial conflict "in which economic, industrial and housing factors, resulting from the migration, played an important part." Instead, Taylor thought, the Springfield riot was "a sudden racial outbreak of passion, following two terrible crimes," and therefore relatively unimportant.[60]

In the only other indication of the approach with which the commission came to the "racial clashes" part of its research, Shepardson expressed considerable interest in a conference to be held with some of the militia who had helped quell the Chicago riot, because "quite a number of them who were college boys . . . might be able to say a few things worth knowing."[61] This statement of the superior value of elite perceptions and definitions of racial problems was unusual in its explicitness; but the very structure of the conferences was a silent endorsement of the value of testimony from a number of different leadership groups rather than from randomly selected residents of Chicago, or from a representative sample of the entire population.

A partial attempt to redress the balance and reach out to a broader population was made in the studies of Negro housing and employment. The "housing" sub-study did examine census data and got out into the neighborhoods, in order to map out the boundaries of the Negro population and to look at the sort of housing available to Negroes. The study included two-hour interviews with 274 Negro families living in all sections of Chicago.[62] But even this sub-study did not attempt to search out the opinions or situations of ordinary whites living in or near "negro neighborhoods," in any fashion similar to its interviews of Negro families. And the housing study turned to leadership groups like "real estate companies, various organizations on the south side and key people" to learn what the impact of the expiration of yearly leases was on the Negro population.[63] It was of the home builders and real estate managers, not of the white or Negro residents, that the commission asked, "What accounts for the run-down appearance of many homes in negro communities? . . . What types of the negro population are most in need of homes? . . . Do you know of cases in which 'accommodation' that is, total or partial absence of friction, has followed the moving of a negro family into a white neighborhood? . . . Do you believe that any agencies, real estate firms or Associations have exploited or attempted to exploit negroes in search of homes?"[64]

In the study of the Negro in industry, researchers conducted interviews with 865 Negro workers. Again, they did not parallel these with a series of interviews of white workers. And once again, the study placed great emphasis on several conferences with leaders of Chicago industry and labor unions.[65] In the industrial sub-study there occurred the only case for which evidence has survived of the commission's ordering the staff to drop a question it had proposed to ask during its research. That was a question to be asked of all industrial concerns in Chicago employing 500 persons or more: "Is your plant an open or closed shop?" The commission ordered this omitted, "it being felt that some managers might not wish, for various reasons, to answer this question, and that sufficient information for the purposes of the commission could be secured by subsequent intensive study of typical industries by the commission's investigators."[66]

For the sub-study of "crime and the police," the commission's staff contemplated administering to prisoners a questionnaire asking their life histories, the nature of the crimes for which they were convicted, former arrests, the treatment accorded them by officers of the law, etc.[67] But no report of results from this questionnaire is presented in the relevant pages of the commission's final report,[68] nor is it mentioned anywhere in the minutes of commission meetings. It seems, therefore, not to have been given; and almost all the information reported on Negro crime and the treatment of Negroes accused of crime is taken from conferences in which municipal judges, police officials, or social workers answered such questions as, "Is the hearing of colored cases as serious and dignified in manner as the hearing of white cases, or is it likely to be more on the comedy order . . . Please discuss the relative place of gangs or criminal bands in crimes committed by white and colored boys."[69]

The "racial contacts" sub-study is the only one in which even a fragment survives of the transcript of one of the investigatory conferences. This fragment is of particular interest because direct quotations from the commission members present are included. The conference was concerned with high schools, and three school principals were present in addition to both Taylor and Johnson, and commission members Williams, Brown, Jackson, and Rosenwald. In this conference, one of the principals mentioned that he had abandoned the notion of a racially mixed glee club because white children would not take part. He had proposed setting up two racially separate glee clubs, and explained how shocked he was the next day to have "two or three hundred white and colored gathered in the assembly hall, with both aldermen, wanting to know why I wanted to start segregation. I did not intend to start segregation."

Three commission members reacted to this statement. Edward Osgood Brown, the white lawyer who had for years been president of the Chicago branch of the NAACP, asked the principal, "You could not understand this . . . protest of what seemed segregation? Is there not danger that the colored parents feared that their children were put into a musical society by themselves with the idea that they were not good enough to be put in the other class's?" Julius Rosenwald, expressing more readiness to accept segregation under some circumstances, commented, "With the [racially mixed] system that exists, might not those on both sides be losing? White children are losing the advantage they would get under this arrangement of segregation, and both might have it if they were willing to say we find this way is not possible, we will try another way." But Lacey K. Williams, the Negro Baptist minister, at once replied, "Voluntary grouping represents the white pupil's idea, not the negro's. Segregation is the white children's notion; voluntary on the part of the whites and forced on the colored"; and Brown spoke again to back him up. In the commission's final report, the principal's action was described; but there was no hint of a description of the commission's reaction.[70]

The sixth sub-study, that on "public opinion," engaged more of the staff's interest and energy than any of the others. It was the only one in which Taylor urged that every member of the commission attend each of several research conferences,[71] and it takes more space than that allotted to any other of the six areas in the commission's final report.[72] Once again, Park's interest may have been responsible, since the chief researchers in the "public opinion" sub-study were students in his class on "The Crowd and the Public," chosen by Taylor for that reason.[73]

Despite the staff's emphasis on public opinion, no more of the research materials have survived in this field than in the others. One item is a list of questions prepared for the conference of white newspapermen, such as, "Are negroes of reliability used as information checks on serious matters regarding negroes?" and "Are there issues, items, or incidents involving negroes which stimulate an unusual public interest measurable by an increased sale of papers?"[74] Another surviving item is a memorandum on reactions of white newspapermen to being invited to this conference, in which it was noted that the *Chicago Tribune's* editor "could only be described as churlish, if not insolent," though men from the other newspapers and the Associated Press were wholly co-operative.[75]

Although most of the task of gathering data in the six sub-studies had been completed by September 15, 1920, additional research conferences were held into December. In September the commission replaced many of its data-gathering staff with new personnel equipped to digest and write up the data. Indexes to the conference reports were prepared, the statistics were tabulated, and maps were drawn during October, November, and December. As a draft version of each sub-study was completed by the staff, it was brought before the relevant committee of the commission for discussion and revision and then before the full commission for its approval.[76]

But it was not until January 1921, that the commission, with a finished text of the report before it, could begin to consider what conclusions and recommendations it would draw from the study.[77] (The staff had presumably avoided thinking about recommendations at all, "believing that the work of investigation and collection of data should not be even unconsciously influenced by preconceived ideas of what ought to be done.")[78] The recommendations were drafted by Taylor, Johnson, and Shepardson, and were circulated for the commission's approval.[79]

The rest of 1921 was used in completing and polishing the report, in raising money to meet the commission's deficit, and in seeking a publisher for the full report. Commission chairman Bancroft talked with Macmillan and with Harper and Brothers, only to find that the length of the manuscript and its comparatively restricted appeal made it an unlikely commercial venture. One publisher asked for a $5000 subsidy and the other suggested "distilling" the report into a short book. Neither approach was practicable, and so the commission turned to the University of Chicago Press, which agreed to publish the full book of almost 700 pages in September 1922.[80]

Former Governor Lowden gave the proofs a final look in order to write a foreword to the volume, and had one suggestion to make. Whereas in the proofs the commission called the notion "that Negroes have inferior mentality" a "prevailing misconception," Lowden explained that he was "not persuaded that the commission acted upon sufficient evidence." He argued that the intelligence tests used in the Army during the war found Negroes mentally inferior, and expressed the belief that although recent Negro progress had been great, Negroes were still inferior to "the race which furnished . . . [the world] with Aristotle more than 2000 years ago."[81]

Although Lowden made clear that he was not insisting on any change, the passage first was revised slightly to read that the "prevailing misconceptions" were that Negroes are "capable of mental and moral development only to an inferior degree."[82] In the end it was removed from the report. Where the comment probably originally stood, there appears this paragraph:[83]

> Much might be said of influences which have operated to counteract the opinion-making literature as to the utterly hopeless condition of Negroes. The object of this study, however, is not to attack these conclusions, but merely to cite them as indicating how certain attitudes detrimental to racial friendliness and understanding have had their rise.

One other last-minute hitch had to be resolved. Edward Morris, a Negro member of the commission, had refused to sign the preliminary report to the governor because the word "Negro" had been used instead of "colored person." In the final report he requested that his dissent be recorded, explaining that he disagreed with the summary and recommendations but not indicating any particular points of disagreement.[84] His dissent was recorded in the report, although Bancroft had hoped merely to omit his signature.[85]

These, then, were the final decisions of the Chicago Commission on Race Relations. In September 1922 the University of Chicago Press published *The Negro in Chicago: A Study of Race Relations and a Race Riot.* Copies of the book were distributed free to many influential Chicagoans, especially to those who had made financial contributions to the commission.[86] And so the work that had begun over three years before in the midst of the riot itself was completed in an atmosphere of scholarly calm. As the first call for the commission had asked, the racial troubles of Chicago had been studied; but had a "definite programme of race relations" been formulated?

* * *

Certainly a definite series of recommendations were made, but it is not at once clear whether these made up a program in the sense of a set of proposals that would actually change race relations in Chicago. It is necessary to examine closely these recommendations and the underlying logic and assumptions of the study, in order to come to some conclusions on whether or not a "definite programme" was formulated.

Without ever directly raising the issue of racial equality or inferiority, *The Negro in Chicago* makes clear in a number of places that it assumes the equality of Negroes and whites in their capabilities for life in an urban industrial society.

This assumption is made clear in the report's discussion of education, crime, employment, the press, and racial contacts. Thus in an examination of child retardation, it is noted that "of course . . . comparisons of Negro with white children are hardly fair, since Negro children have not had the same opportunities as whites to make normal progress."[87] An important distinction is made between Negroes born and bred in the North and in the South, a distinction based on the lack of general education and of training for urban life that was said to be characteristic in the South.[88] Thus economic and social causes, rather than biologically racial causes, were assumed to account for the difficulty that comparatively high proportions of Negroes had in coping with formal education.

The report on crime carefully points out that statistics indicating higher Negro than white crime rates are misleading because of "the disposition, conscious or unconscious, to arrest Negroes more freely than whites, to book them on more serious charges, to convict them more readily, and to give them longer sentences."[89] For these reasons, the commission decided not to use crime figures "which carried . . . clear evidence of their own inaccuracy and misrepresentation," in order to avoid giving such figures currency.[90] Responsibility for the existence of many houses of prostitution in the Negro residential districts is laid to laxity in law enforcement, rather than to Negro complacency, and instances are cited in which respectable Negroes have requested the closing of such places, only to find the police turning a deaf ear.[91] The report also points out that crimes of Negroes may have a special origin in "the traditional ostracism, exploitation, and petty daily insults" that have "doubtless provoked . . . a pathological attitude toward society which sometimes expresses itself defensively in acts of violence."[92]

The study of Negroes in industry emphasized that a great proportion of establishments employing five or more Negroes reported that their work had proved satisfactory. Simultaneously, however, there was cited the warning that a direct comparison of Negro and white workers was unfair because the Negro "was still a newcomer in manufacturing and could not be expected to be as efficient, reliable, and regular as the white worker."[93] Lack of "hope on the job" was also cited by *The Negro in Chicago* as an explanation for the faster turnover of Negro labor.[94] And the doubts held by white labor-unionists of Negroes' capacity for loyalty to unionism were explained by the commission in terms of the Negroes' antagonism to racially exclusive unions and their loyalty to employers who have, "sometimes at considerable risk, . . . opened . . . new opportunities."[95] The commission also cited cases in which white unionists who did have Negroes as co-members found them conscientious.[96] Again, in discussing contacts between the races in public transportation the commission examined claims that such contacts were made specially unpleasant by the dirt and unpleasant smell often attributed to Negroes as Negroes. First the commission reported finding that the difficulty was actually due to the sorts of work most Negroes did (for example, at the stockyards), and in many cases to the lack of enough facilities for cleaning up after such work. Then the report added that white workers often had the same difficulty and that complaints were made about them as well.[97] Indeed, this analysis is a paradigm of the way in which the commission took up claims of Negro inferiority, reported that in actuality Negroes were not so inferior as had been claimed, and argued further that what inferiority existed was caused by social and economic conditions, not by racial differences.

A second major assumption underlying *The Negro in Chicago* was that there is no instinctual hostility between whites and Negroes. The commission reported that friction existed in only a minority of shops between the races in which both were hired,[98] in only a minority of unions in which both were allowed equal membership rights,[99] in very few penal and correctional institutions,[100] in a minority of schools,[101] and in only those public parks where Negroes were newcomers, not in those where Negroes had long been present.[102] The commission suggested that the most important differences between those situations in which racial contacts were hostile and those where they were friendly were the attitude of authoritative figures in the particular setting, and the length of time that the racial confrontation had been occurring. The commission referred repeatedly to the attitudes of principals as governing race relations in the schools and those of employers as governing on the job.[103] In the field of housing, the commission distinguished two large areas of Chicago in which Negroes lived: one, the "adjusted neighborhoods" in which Negroes had been long established, represented a majority (but not an overwhelming one) of the residents, and got along amicably with whites; and the other, neighborhoods of sporadic or organized antagonism between the races, where few Negroes lived but the whites feared an "invasion."[104]

The two assumptions—that neither biological inequality of the races nor instinctual hostility between the races existed but rather social pressures and institutions that could either reinforce or eliminate inequality and hostility—run through and under the text of *The Negro in Chicago*. For that reason it is especially interesting that the one place in which one of these assumptions would have been explicitly stated (or at least its opposite described as "mistaken") was changed in accord with Governor Lowden's doubts. It is also interesting that the two assumptions seem not to have been made by the author of a two-page preface to the body of the report entitled "The Problem."[105]

In that prefatory note, the race problem is said to be based on "the instinct of each race to preserve its type." Phrases like "our Negro problem" and "old prejudices against the Negroes" are used in such a way as to give the impression that whites are discussing among themselves a problem somehow tied to "those others," thus creating an atmosphere quite different from that of the body of the report. In the report itself, the writing is so effectively detached that neither a Negro nor a white seems to be writing (and in a sense this was the case, since the writing was done by Negroes and whites in close collaboration). Again, the prefatory note refers to the need for "the Negro race" to "develop, as all races have developed, from lower to higher planes of living." No such acceptance of the notion that the Negro race is on a lower plane of living is apparent in the report itself. Training for Negroes in "industry, efficiency, and moral character" is called the fundamental need in the prefatory note, although the report itself does not single out either race in this way.

In short, the prefatory note called "The Problem" gives the impression of having been written by a white man, separately from the report, and of not having been reviewed by Negroes before printing. No signature is attached, and no records of the commission mention this note. It may well have been written, along with Lowden's "Foreword" and an "Introduction" describing the origin of the commission, for the published version of the report—long after the commission had disbanded. Perhaps Shepardson or Bancroft was responsible for it. In any case, its chief effect is to highlight by contrast the presence in the report itself of the two assumptions of equal racial capabilities and racial amity.

Several assumptions involving wise racial policy (rather than the nature of human psychology or biology) can be identified in *The Negro in Chicago*. The possible values of a "pluralist" or "separatist" racial-cultural structure for the United States are not seriously examined. The assumption of the commission seems to have been that a constant evolution of America in the direction of a "quasi-white" society, racially integrated and possessed of white middle-class values, would be best for whites, Negroes, and the nation.

This assumption can clearly be seen in the report's descriptions and recommendations. Both the political separatism that later came to be called Black Nationalism, and the cultural separatism that later made up the Harlem Renaissance, are dismissed by the commission.

Marcus Garvey's version of Black Nationalism is described with considerable neutrality—in part, the report makes clear, because its slogan is really "Back to Africa," not, as rumors had said, "Down with the United States."[106] But the Star Order of Ethiopia, quite aside from the deaths caused by its members, is described in hostile terms.[107] And the commission explicitly recommended that Negroes discourage "propaganda and agitators seeking to inflame racial animosity,"[108] and warned Negroes "that thinking and talking too much in terms of . . . race pride . . . and race alone are calculated to promote separation of race interests and thereby to interfere with racial adjustment."[109] The creation by Negroes of separate labor unions (in trades where Negroes were admitted to unions on an equal footing with whites) was strongly condemned.[110]

The commission rejected not only Negro nationalism and separatism, but the notion that a separate contribution was possible from Negro culture to American culture. This second rejection is the more surprising in that Taylor had expressed warm approval of a book by the ·NAACP's Herbert Seligmann, *The Negro Faces America*, which had argued that Negro jazz, the Negro's capacity to play, sing, and dance "for the love of what he is doing and experiencing," had "introduced human values into American civilization of a sort in which it has been found peculiarly lacking."[111] No hint of this view of the Negro as teacher and vivifying force comes through in *The Negro in Chicago*. For example, the report applauds Negroes who respectably opposed the "black and tan" cabarets in which racially mixed couples enjoyed "coarse and vulgar dancing," and these troublesome contacts were contrasted with the beneficial effects of interracial contacts under the auspices of "institutions of learning" such as libraries and universities.[112] The latter contacts were clearly those in which Negroes did the learning of white art and music, rather than the reverse. Again, the report directly recommended "that Negroes completely abandon the practice of seeking petty advance payments on wages and the practice of laying off work without good cause."[113] Seligmann's line of argument, that just such "Negro" habits might teach white America how to enjoy itself, was not examined.

Just as the commission's crucial assumption concerning wise racial policy was that the goal should be an integrated quasi-white society, so the crucial assumption on wise economic policy was that the goal should be a more effectively rationalized private-enterprise society. The rationalization of practices on hiring and on admission to labor unions was understood to require that all qualified personnel be treated equally, regardless of race, so that an indigestible mass of irrationally excluded persons would not clog the efficient processes of economic enterprise. The commission recommended that employers hire, train, pay, and promote their workers on grounds of merit alone (but not that the state intervene to enforce this recommendation). The commission also urged that labor unions admit Negroes on an equal standing "whenever they apply . . . and possess the qualifications required of white workers." The commission carefully avoided taking sides on the question whether Negro workers should seek protection by joining unions or by "loyalty" to the employer. It urged only that Negroes who did want to join unions choose integrated unions where they were available, rather than establish separate ones.[114]

In its only reference to a model of the future economy other than rationalized private enterprise, the commission reported on the IWW's attempts to appeal to Negro workers. There was no direct criticism of the IWW's argument for a joint effort by the working class of all races to abolish the capitalist system. Indeed, the commission's report presented almost two full pages of direct quotations from the IWW almost without comment.[115] But the commission's own view was clearly that race relations could and should be transformed within the capitalist system. The report referred to A. Philip Randolph and Chandler Owen's magazine, *The Messenger*, but did not explain their argument that racial equality—even equality with white working-men—could be achieved only under socialism, and that socialism could only be achieved if racial equality also were. Again, this omission is surprising in the light of Taylor's admiration for the parts of Seligmann's book which described *The Messenger's* position.[116]

Any close examination of *The Negro in Chicago* must confront the question of how the commission expected its recommendations to come into force. To fill adequately the role it had chosen to play of expert on policy and policy change, the commission needed to explain clearly what sort of power must be exerted in order to bring about changes in policy on race relations.

But except for a few scattered hints, *The Negro in Chicago* avoided the problem of power relations in the city. The report did say that part of the Negroes' difficulty in securing decent housing stemmed from their exclusion from most of the banking system that lent money to build or buy housing.[117] The report also made clear the one-sidedness of the police in protecting whites and arresting Negroes during the riot, the unreadiness of the police force to protect Negro homes from bombings, and the refusal of the police to enforce laws against prostitution and gambling in the Negro residential areas.[118] Again, the report pointed out that many of the violently anti-Negro teen-age "athletic clubs" had been founded by white politicians in order to reach young men before they had attained voting age.[119] Yet the commission did not examine in any systematic way the questions of why the police and politicians acted in these ways, or what ramifications grew out of the exclusion of Negroes from financial power. No study was made, in short, of the ways in which the pattern of race relations in Chicago fit into the political structure of the city, or the connections between the political system and various urban economic interests as they affected race relations. Johnson's first outlined suggestions for the study had proposed a section on just such questions, but by the time he had been hired and had worked out with Taylor the actual guide for the study, that section had been dropped.[120]

The omission of any section on politics and power probably contributed to the difficulty of finding in the commission's recommendations any clear indication of how they were to be put into effect. Many recommendations were made, for example, that the police act with far more energy and neutrality to protect Negroes, to eliminate vice in Negro districts, and to control the white adolescent "athletic clubs" that had proved a source of anti-Negro violence in sporadic race conflict and in the riot. No consideration was given, however, to the problem of what interests of their own the police would have to jettison, in order to act in these fashions. What might their own interests have been in protecting houses of prostitution? in looking the other way when white real estate dealers and property owners tried to force Negroes to move? in protecting and encouraging "athletic clubs" that were sponsored by particular white politicians? Simply because such questions were not asked, there is no way of telling what the commission thought would have to be done to get the police to act in accord with their recommendations.

From the absence of explicit discussion of levers of change, from the commission's emphasis on the importance of public opinion and the press as an instrument in forming public opinion, from the report's interest in the power of authoritative figures in particular institutions to affect race relations within those institutions, and from the way in which the commission distributed the report to "opinion leaders" in Chicago, it may be gathered that the commission expected its constituency of powerful and prestigious Chicagoans to act quietly to implement the recommendations. Such men could presumably reorient the newspapers, open the banks to Negro employment and order loans granted on Negro housing, insist that politicians allow the "athletic clubs" to be watched and order the police to protect Negroes and their property, and begin to hire and pay workers without regard to race. And presumably such men could do all this without making any public fuss.

This view of the commission's expectations would explain what is otherwise difficult to explain, the absence of any recommendations (other than "thrift" and "industry") to Negroes on how to *take* the progress that the commission was urging should be *given* them. Nor were there any suggestions to whites who wanted race relations altered but did not hold positions of power, on how to get neighborhood associations to change their attitudes or how to open labor unions to Negroes.

The question must then be raised, why did the commission expect its audience of the city's leaders to act in accord with its recommendations, when these would interfere with interests and attitudes long cherished? What new element in the situation was expected to stimulate leaders into changing their approach, in the absence of any pressure from below by Negroes or whites? Why should white bankers channel their loans to Negro home-builders, white newspapermen stop exaggerating Negro peculiarities and race conflict in order to build their circulation, white politicians transfer their protection from white to Negro interests? The only answer that can emerge from a study of *The Negro in Chicago* is: fear of future violence in the pattern of the 1919 race riot.

In other words, the commission was warning that more violence awaited Chicago unless many accommodations were made to Negro demands, many white myths about Negroes were exposed as untrue and eliminated from white minds, harmony between whites and Negroes was deliberately encouraged, and the city was set on the road toward being economically rationalized and racially integrated—a larger version of the best-organized, most "industrious" and "thrifty," and most highly respectable segments of white society. Frank Lowden, in his foreword to the report, explicitly pointed to the commission's recommendations as a means to make impossible a repetition of "the appalling tragedy which brought disgrace to Chicago in July of 1919."[121] And in this direct statement Lowden was only summarizing the intentions of the commission, referred to in a number of places in the report.[122]

A review of the origins, the work, and the recommendations of the Chicago Commission on Race Relations must emphasize the following important points:

That the commission was mostly instigated by, half made up of, and heavily financed by the prominent and powerful men of Chicago's white community;

That its research was heavily, but not wholly, oriented to the examination of facts known to and opinions held by a number of different leadership groups in the city;

That the commission's image of a future Chicago was one in which Negroes had joined—but not essentially changed—the existing white society, and had changed whichever of their own values and behavior were incompatible with that society;

That its view of the way in which this should be accomplished was that persons of power and prestige in the white community should influence that community to accept the entrance into it on an equal footing of Negroes who had learned how to behave in it;

That the commission expected the fear of future "disgraces to Chicago" like the riot of 1919 to move Chicago's leadership to implement the commission's recommendations, as a way of preventing future violence and thus of preventing the damage to its own interests and feelings that such violence would cause.

How can one measure the effects of the commission's work and recommendations? In part by looking at the verbal response of Chicago and the nation to the commission's efforts; in part by examining whether the recommendations were in fact adopted; and in part by assessing the impact of the commission's scholarship on later social science.

Many Negroes in Chicago made clear by word and deed that they were thoroughly suspicious of the commission's efforts. Although Walter White of the NAACP had responded favorably to the first announcement of the men who were to make up the commission,[123] one Negro newspaper, the *Broad Axe*, bitterly attacked the commission because one of its members, the white real estate dealer William Scott Bond, was listed as a member of the executive committee of the anti-Negro Kenwood and Hyde Park Property Owners Association.[124] Bond had already written to the association that his name had been used without his permission and demanded its removal from the list. At the request of the commission, Charles S. Johnson called on the editor of the *Broad Axe* to explain the misuse of Bond's name.[125] Yet the commission continued to be aware of the opposition of many Negroes.

The attempts of the commission to raise money from the Negro community involved constant efforts to overcome suspicion. The Negro Finance Committee went out of its way to explain that neither politics nor "preconceived opinions" had entered into the choice or the work of the commission and that its staff was biracial.[126] Yet still the belief persisted among some Negroes that the commission was planning to propose a scheme for compulsory segregation,[127] and Hall and Johnson finally told the commission that both "political struggles" among the Negroes (probably involving opposition to Lowden) and "misunderstanding of the function of the Commission" had damaged the prestige of the commission.[128]

Outside Chicago as well, the commission found some Negroes mistrustful. W.E.B. Du Bois, the editor of *The Crisis*, major militant Negro magazine published by the NAACP, denounced a questionnaire on racial matters that the commission had asked him, among other Negro leaders, to fill out. He called the questionnaire an insidious way of "pushing . . . a program of racial segregation."[129]

When the commission issued its report, responses were generally favorable. The *Daily News* and the *Defender*, as could have been expected from the involvement of their publisher-editors in the commission, supported the report vigorously. The *Chicago Post* echoed their approval, and the New York *Herald* and the *Times* placed great value on the commission's findings and recommendations.[130]

From a southern white man, however, came strong criticism of the report. Alexander Lawton, addressing the alumni of the University of Georgia, praised such efforts at betterment of race relations as those of the Southern Commission on Interracial Cooperation. But he cited the commission's findings as evidence that "race instinct and race prejudice in Chicago are at least as strong in proportion to contact as in Georgia." On that basis he ridiculed almost all the commission's recommendations as attempts to suppress rather than recognize "race instinct"—attempts that would be "impracticable, visionary, and impossible."[131]

By the second standard for measuring the commission's work, the extent to which its recommendations were adopted, the commission would not fare well. By the report of the leading historians of black Chicago, no major break was made in the racial lines around skilled jobs, union membership, residential areas, or public myth-making until long after 1922.[132] Even the commission's one institutional recommendation—that a permanent commission like itself be created —was not accomplished till the 1940s, when the mayor of Chicago (in fear of another riot) appointed a Committee on Race Relations that included Charles S. Johnson as one member.[133] A white expert on Chicago race relations, a Negro journalist, two former members of the commission's research staff, and a Negro lawyer who had pressed some damage suits on behalf of Negroes hurt in the 1919 riot all agree that *The Negro in Chicago* had little effect on racial practices.[134]

The report did have more effect upon social science. The commission's account of the riot itself and its description of the Negro's status in Chicago have been taken as major sources by sociologists and historians.

Theoretical examinations of rioting have drawn heavily upon the commission's account of the ways in which late-adolescent gangs formed nuclei for mobs; unneutral acts of the police both instigated the riot and exacerbated it; hot weather first assisted and then rainy weather discouraged and helped end the milling of crowds which turned into mobs; and the swift spread of fearful rumors fed the hatred that spawned violence.[135]

Similarly, the leading history of American Negroes cites *The Negro in Chicago* as a major source for understanding "the period of reaction."[136] Discussions of Chicago's juvenile gangs[137] and the Chicago Negro community[138] have drawn heavily upon the commission's report. Gunnar Myrdal's classic study of American racial patterns, *An American Dilemma*, cites *The Negro in Chicago* in discussing race riots, but does not use it for data on general Negro urbanization or Chicago in particular.[139]

The Negro in Chicago may thus be said to have exerted considerable influence among scholars as a study of the troubles that had brought on the 1919 riot and as a study of the riot itself. But in terms of its own choice of role, as the policy expert concerned with social change rather than as pure scholar concerned simply with social science, the commission accomplished little. Its unwillingness to give its recommendations a political cast and political relevance was probably the major factor in preventing its work from having a social effect. Its analysis stopped short of looking hard at the power structure of Chicago, by which change could be induced; and that was a crucial failing not only in the analysis but in any attempt to play a role in bringing change about.

NOTES

1. Joel E. Spingarn, "Hasty Notes in Chicago," July 30, 1919, NAACP MSS.

2. Chicago Commission on Race Relations, *The Negro in Chicago*, p. xv. (Hereafter cited as *Negro in Chicago*.)

3. Herbert J. Seligmann to Spingarn, telegram, July 28, 1919, Spingarn to Mary White Ovington, telegram, July 30, 1919, Spingarn, "Hasty Notes," NAACP MSS.

4. *Negro in Chicago*, p. xv; also see "Memorandum on meeting at Union League Club," Chicago Commission on Race Relations MSS., Illinois Archives. (Hereafter cited as CCRR MSS.)

5. Abraham Bowers to Francis W. Shepardson, Aug. 27, 1919 and Graham Taylor to .... [multiple letter], July 31, 1919, CCRR MSS.: Graham Taylor, "Diary," July 31 and Aug. 1, 1919, Taylor MSS., Newberry Library.

6. *Negro in Chicago*, p. xv.

7. Shepardson to John Cummings, April 15, 1919, CCRR MSS.

8. CCRR Minutes, Oct. 9, 1919, CCRR MSS.

9. Ivan O. Ackley to Shepardson, Aug. 4, 1919, Harve Budgerow to Shepardson and Shepardson to Budgerow, Aug. 5, 1919, L. Brackett to Shepardson, Aug. 5, 1919, Shepardson to James P. Hall, Aug. 9, 1919, William H. Huff to Everett C. Dodds, Aug. 1, 1919, Shepardson to Huff, Aug. 11, 1919, W. H. Riley to Frank O. Lowden, Aug. 15, 1919, CCRR MSS.; Hugh Reed to George E. Haynes, Aug. 8, 1919, Labor Dept. MSS., National Archives.

10. Alice H. Wood to Shepardson, Aug. 14, 1919, and Shepardson to Wood, Aug. 16, 1919, A. L. Jackson to Shepardson, telegram, Aug. 15, 1919, Shepardson to Julius Rosenwald, Aug. 21, 1919, Sophonisba P. Breckinridge to Shepardson, Aug. 19, 1919, and Shepardson to Breckinridge, Aug. 21, 1919, E. A. Kelly to Shepardson, Aug. 18, 1919, and Shepardson to E. A. Kelly, Aug. 18, 1919, CCRR MSS.

11. Shepardson to Wood, Aug. 6, 1919, CCRR MSS.

12. Undated memorandum in Shepardson's hand, CCRR MSS.

13. *Negro in Chicago*, pp. xvi and 652-53.

14. Ibid., p. xvi.

15. CCRR Minutes, Oct. 9, 1919, CCRR MSS.

16. William C. Graves to Shepardson, Sept. 5, 1919, CCRR MSS.

17. Shepardson to Graves, Sept. 15, 1919, CCRR MSS.

18. Graham Romeyn Taylor to Shepardson, Aug. 26, 1920, CCRR MSS. (Graham Romeyn Taylor, son of Graham Taylor, will hereafter be referred to as G. R. Taylor.)

19. CCRR Minutes, Oct. 9 and Oct. 20, 1919, CCRR MSS.

20. CCRR Minutes, Nov. 13 and Dec. 18, 1919, Shepardson to Charles W. Folds, Nov. 15 and Nov. 22, 1919, Folds to Shepardson, Nov. 20, 1919, Shepardson to Harry Eugene Kelly, Nov. 21, 1919, CCRR MSS.

21. CCRR Minutes, June 16 and Nov. 23, 1920, G. R. Taylor to Shepardson, July 8 and Aug. 10, 1920, Charles S. Johnson to Shepardson, Sept. 10, 1920, undated multigraphed letter "sent to 300 negroes," CCRR MSS.

22. CCRR Minutes, Oct. 20, 1919, Shepardson to Folds, Nov. 15, 1919, CCRR Minutes, March 19, 1920, CCRR Financial Statement, Nov. 1, 1920, Edgar A. Brancroft to James B. Forgan, Dec. 22, 1920, CCRR MSS.

23. Graves to G. R. Taylor, Dec. 31, 1919, and Jan. 30, 1920, G. R. Taylor to Rosenwald, Jan. 29, 1920, CCRR MSS.

24. CCRR Minutes, April 21 and June 16, 1920, Shepardson to G. R. Taylor, March 26 and July 28, 1920, CCRR MSS.

25. G. R. Taylor to Shepardson, Aug. 26, 1920, CCRR MSS.

26. M. E. Filer to Kelly, Oct. 4, 1920, G. R. Taylor to Shepardson, Nov. 11, 15, and 20, 1920, CCRR MSS.

27. CCRR Minutes, Nov. 23, 1920, CCRR MSS.

28. G. R. Taylor to Shepardson, Dec. 1, 3, and 16, 1920, Gen. Abel Davis to Shepardson, Dec. 8, 1920, CCRR Minutes, Dec. 28, 1920, CCRR MSS.

29. Rosenwald to Victor F. Lawson, April 7, 1921, and Graves to Davis, May 9, 1921, Rosenwald MSS., University of Chicago; Lowden to Folds, April 14, 1921, and Davis to Lowden [ca. April 30, 1921], Lowden MSS., University of Chicago.

30. CCRR Minutes, Oct. 9, 1919, CCRR MSS.

31. Paul V. Kellogg to Graves, Oct. 23, 1919, Rosenwald MSS.; CCRR Minutes, Oct. 9 and Oct. 20, 1919, CCRR MSS.; Negro in Chicago, p. 653; author's interview with Mrs. G. R. Taylor, 1959.

32. CCRR Minutes, Nov. 5, 13, 20, and 28, 1919, Graves to Rosenwald, Nov. 4, 1919, Shepardson to Johnson, Dec. 6, 1919, CCRR MSS.

33. Graves to Rosenwald, Dec. 12, 1919, Rosenwald MSS.

34. Author's interview with Mrs. G. R. Taylor, 1959; memo by Johnson to Shepardson, Oct. 5, 1919, memo by G. R. Taylor and Johnson to CCRR, Dec. 12, 1919, CCRR MSS.

35. CCRR Minutes, Oct. 8 and 20 (third meeting missing), Nov. 5, 13, 20, and 28, Dec. 4, 11, and 18, 1919 (eleventh meeting missing), Jan. 23, Feb. 6, March 12, April 21, June 16, Nov. 23, Dec. 28, 1920, CCRR MSS.

36. CCRR Minutes, Dec. 11, 1919, CCRR MSS.

37. CCRR Minutes, Dec. 4, 1919, CCRR MMS.

38. Chicago Tribune, Oct. 30, 1919, NAACP MSS.; CCRR Minutes, Nov. 5, 1919, CCRR MSS.

39. CCRR Minutes, Dec. 4, 11, and 18, 1919, CCRR MSS.

40. Lowden to Shepardson, Feb. 2, 1920, Shepardson to Lowden, Feb. 2, 1920, CCRR Executive Committee Minutes, Feb. 20, 1920, CCRR MSS.

41. Chicago Daily News, Feb. 25, 1920, NAACP MSS.

42. Johnson to Shepardson, Sept. 10, 1920, CCRR MSS.

43. Negro in Chicago, pp. 59-64; Shepardson to G. R. Taylor, June 21, 1920, G. R. Taylor to Shepardson, June 21, 1920, CCRR MSS.

44. G. R. Taylor to Shepardson, June 21, 1920, Shepardson to G. R.

Taylor, June 23, 1920, Shepardson to Lowden, June 23, 1920, CCRR MSS.

45. CCRR Minutes, March 12, 1920, CCRR MSS.

46. *Chicago Daily News*, Nov. 5, 1919, CCRR MSS.

47. Graves to David Lawrence, Nov. 5, 1919, Lawrence to Graves, Nov. 10, 1919, CCRR MSS.

48. Shepardson to Francis Garvan, Nov. 14, 1919, Castle M. Brown to Shepardson, Nov. 29, 1919, CCRR MSS.

49. CCRR Minutes, Dec. 4, 1919, CCRR MSS.

50. Ibid.; *Negro in Chicago*, p. 574; Shepardson to C. M. Brown, Dec. 8, 1919, CCRR MSS.

51. Shepardson to Lowden, June 4, 1920, CCRR MSS.

52. G. R. Taylor to Shepardson, Aug. 10, 1920, Shepardson to G. R. Taylor, Dec. 10, 1920, CCRR MSS.; Lowden to Runnells, telegram, Feb. 25, 1921, Lowden MSS.

53. CCRR Progress Report, Dec. 21, 1920, CCRR MSS.

54. Memo by G. R. Taylor and Johnson to CCRR, Dec. 12, 1919, CCRR MSS.

55. *Negro in Chicago*, pp. 653-55; undated memorandum of G. R. Taylor and Johnson to CCRR, CCRR MSS.

56. Memo by G. R. Taylor and Johnson, Sept. 15, 1920, CCRR MSS.; Chicago League on Urban Conditions among Negroes, *First Annual Report* (1917) and *Second Annual Report* (1918), pamphlets, University of Chicago. Park makes a special point in his introduction to these reports of Rosenwald's generosity to the Chicago Urban League. See also author's interview in 1959 with Esther Fulks Scott, former research worker for CCRR, for evidence of Park's constant help with research and analysis.

57. Author's interview with Esther Scott and Mrs. G. R. Taylor, 1959; CCRR Minutes, Jan. 23, 1920, Progress Reports, Dec. 21, 1920, CCRR MSS.

58. Undated memo by G. R. Taylor and Johnson to CCRR, CCRR Minutes, March 12, 1920, CCRR MSS.

59. Author's interview with Chicago Urban League officials, 1959. G. R. Taylor and Shepardson debated in 1921 where these files should be kept, both of them agreeing that the University of Chicago Library or the Crerar Library would be both safer and more accessible to scholars than the Urban League, which had requested them. Yet the Urban League got them. The correspondence files (out of which, Taylor reported, the confidential material had been destroyed) were

sent to the Illinois State Archives. G. R. Taylor to Shepardson, Sept. 12, 1921, Shepardson to G. R. Taylor, Sept. 20, 1921, Rosenwald MSS.

60. G. R. Taylor to Shepardson, Oct. 7, 1920, CCRR MSS.

61. Shepardson to G. R. Taylor, July 28, 1920, CCRR MSS.

62. CCRR Minutes, Jan. 23 and Feb. 6, 1920, CCRR MSS, *Negro in Chicago*, p. 152.

63. Undated memo from G. R. Taylor and Johnson to CCRR [*ca.* March 1, 1920], CCRR MSS.

64. Undated staff memo on "Suggested Questions for Conference on Negro Housing," CCRR MSS.

65. *Negro in Chicago*, pp. 360-61, 385; CCRR Minutes, Feb. 6, 1920, Executive Committee minutes, Sept. 15, 1920, G. R. Taylor to CCRR, Aug. 12, 1920, CCRR MSS., Report of CCRR Conference on the Negro in Industry, April 23, 1920, Rosenwald MSS.

66. CCRR Minutes, Feb. 6, 1920, undated staff memo, "Selected Questions for Persons in Industrial Conferences," CCRR MSS.

67. Questionnaire on "Intensive Court Study," CCRR MSS.

68. *Negro in Chicago*, pp. 327-56.

69. Undated staff memo on "Lines of Inquiry for Persons called into Conference on the Negro in the Courts," CCRR MSS.

70. Minutes of CCRR Committee on Racial Contact. March 11, 1920, CCRR MSS.; *Negro in Chicago*, p. 255.

71. Memo from G. R. Taylor to CCRR, Dec. 15, 1920, CCRR MSS.

72. *Negro in Chicago*, pp. 436-594.

73. G. R. Taylor to Rosenwald, Feb. 18, 1920, Rosenwald MSS.

74. Undated staff memo [*ca.* Dec. 1, 1920], CCRR MSS.

75. Undated memo from G. R. Taylor to CCRR [*ca.* Dec. 1, 1920], CCRR MSS.

76. Memo of CCRR executive committee meeting, Sept. 15, 1920. Progress Report, Dec. 21, 1920, CCRR MSS.

77. Progress Report, Dec. 21, 1920, CCRR MSS.

78. Memo of CCRR executive committee meeting, Sept. 15, 1920, CCRR MSS.

79. CCRR Minutes, Dec. 28, 1920, CCRR MSS.

80. Bancroft to Rosenwald, Jan. 10, 1922, Rosenwald MSS.

81. Lowden to Bancroft, Aug. 16, 1922, Lowden MSS.

82. Bancroft to Lowden, undated, Lowden MSS.

83. *Negro in Chicago*, p. 449.

84. Bancroft to Lowden, Aug. 7, 1922, Lowden MSS.

85. *Negro in Chicago*, p. xviii.

86. Bancroft to Joseph T. Ryerson, MS. letter pasted in author's copy of *Negro in Chicago*.

87. *Negro in Chicago*, p. 258.

88. Ibid., pp. 258-61, 267.

89. Ibid., p. 329.

90. Ibid., p. 330.

91. Ibid., pp. 323, 355-56, 622.

92. Ibid., p. 342.

93. Ibid., pp. 373-74.

94. Ibid., p. 390.

95. Ibid., p. 431.

96. Ibid., pp. 414-15.

97. Ibid., pp. 303-4.

98. Ibid., pp. 393-96.

99. Ibid., p. 415.

100. Ibid., p. 340.

101. Ibid., pp. 248-51, 253.

102. Ibid., p. 292.

103. Ibid., pp. 248-51, 397.

104. Ibid., pp. 113-21.

105. Ibid., pp. xxii-xxiv.

106. Ibid., p. 493, 540.

107. Ibid., p. 539.

108. Ibid., p. 646.

109. Ibid., p. 647.

110. Ibid., p. 649.

111. Herbert J. Seligmann, *The Negro Faces America*, pp. 279-80, 290; G. R. Taylor to Shepardson, Oct. 30, 1920, CCRR MSS.

112. *Negro in Chicago*, pp. 324-26.

113. Ibid., p. 649.

114. Ibid., pp. 647-49.

115. Ibid., pp. 587-89.

116. Ibid., pp. 476, 489-90; Seligmann, *op. cit.*, pp. 291-94.

117. *Negro in Chicago*, pp. 220, 229.

118. Ibid., pp. 35-39, 122-32, 199, 203, 344.

119. Ibid., pp. 12, 16-17, 55.

120. See above, p. 91.

121. *Negro in Chicago*, p. xiv.

122. Ibid., pp. xv, 2, 595, 602, 640.

123. Walter F. White to Ovington, Aug. 21, 1919, NAACP MSS.

124. *Chicago Broad Axe*, Jan. 24, 1920, CCRR MSS.

125. CCRR Minutes, Dec. 18, 1919, and Feb. 6, 1920, CCRR MSS.

126. G. R. Taylor to Shepardson, July 8 and Aug. 10, 1920, CCRR MSS.

127. Johnson to Shepardson, Sept. 10, 1920, CCRR MSS.

128. CCRR Minutes, Nov. 23, 1920.

129. *Negro in Chicago*, pp. 518-19, quoting *The Crisis* of January 1921.

130. Quoted in *Literary Digest*, Oct. 28, 1922, NAACP MSS.

131. Alexander R. Lawton, *The Negro in the South and Elsewhere* (Annual Address to University of Georgia Alumni, 1923: no publisher).

132. St. Clair Drake and Horace R. Cayton, *Black Metropolis*, pp. 78-83, 212.

133. *Negro in Chicago*, p. 645; Drake and Cayton, *op. cit.*, p. 92.

134. Author's interviews with Joseph D. Lohman, Roi Ottley, Esther Fulks Scott, Joseph D. Bibb, and Augustus L. Williams, 1959.

135. See, e.g., Hans H. Gerth and C. Wright Mills, *Character and Social Structure*, pp. 432-37; Robert E. L. Faris, *Social Disorganization*, pp. 393-97; Ralph Turner and Lewis M. Killan, *Collective Behavior*, pp. 83-161.

136. John Hope Franklin, *From Slavery to Freedom*, p. 616.

137. Frederic M. Thrasher, *The Gang*, pp. 54, 202, 453, 472.

138. Drake and Cayton, *op. cit.*, pp. 69-73, 99, 102, 212.

139. Gunnar Myrdal, *An American Dilemma*, pp. 567, 1126-27.

IV

New York,
1935

INTRODUCTION

Compared with the riots of 1917 and 1919 in East St. Louis and Chicago, the Harlem riot on March 19, 1935 was a brief and moderate outbreak. It was not a "race riot"; it lasted less than one full day; it required less than 100 arrests and caused only two deaths; and property damage and arson were quickly contained. Nevertheless, the riot was regarded by many citizens of Harlem and by city officials as an alarming sign of widespread frustration and protest among the black citizens of New York.

The day after the riot was controlled, Mayor Fiorello LaGuardia appointed a predominantly liberal, biracial commission composed of Charles Roberts, a black dentist and long-time resident of Harlem; Oswald Garrison Villard, a liberal publisher-editor and member of the NAACP; Eunice Hunton Carter, a black lawyer and social worker active in Harlem politics and civic affairs; Countée Cullen, a young black poet and writer; Hubert T. Delaney, a black city official and member of the NAACP; John G. Grimley, a former hospital administrator and army officer; Arthur Garfield Hays and Morris Ernst, lawyers and prominent civil libertarians; William McCann, a white priest representing Catholic interests; John W. Robinson, a black minister from the Interdenominational Ministers Alliance; A. Philip Randolph, the distinguished labor leader and president of the Sleeping Car Porters Union; William Jay Schieffelin, a trustee of Tuskegee Institute and philanthropist; and Charles E. Toney, one of the first black lawyers to be appointed to the Municipal Court in New York. This commission in turn hired as research director E. Franklin Frazier, a prominent black sociologist known in 1935 for his recently completed study of *The Negro Family*.

Nearly one year later, the Commission presented its final report to the Mayor. The political decisions concerning the publication, release and endorsement of the Commission's report are, to say the least, confusing and unclear.[1] The final report was not signed by at least three commissioners (Ernst, McCann, and Grimley) nor was it endorsed by the Mayor who was apparently embarrassed by some of its liberal findings, especially its criticism of institutional racism in New

York's police, hospitals, schools, and welfare agencies. Sections of the final report were leaked to the local press but the complete version was not made available to the public. The selections from the report of The Mayor's Commission on Conditions in Harlem are taken from an unpublished manuscript found in New York's Municipal Archives.

Alain Locke's article was commissioned for *Survey* by the journal's editor, Paul Kellogg, and with the explicit cooperation of Mayor LaGuardia. Kellogg wrote to the Mayor on April 22, 1936 asking permission to "carry a full length interpretation of the findings of the Commission. . . . Could you accord Dr. Locke's access to the complete filings with the understanding that we should not carry his article until the released date which may be set? I should like to add," continued Kellogg, "that we have tremendous confidence in Dr. Locke's insight and integrity, and you could rely on his not abusing this confidence in any way."[2] LaGuardia personally responded to Kellogg's letter, granting permission for Locke's story but also requesting the editor to "give the matter your personal attention."[3] In return for giving *Survey* access to confidential files and reports, Locke's story was submitted before publication to the Mayor's office and some city officials so that several deletions and additions could be made.[4]

Alain Locke's article should be read not as a critical and objective evaluation of *The Negro in Harlem* but rather as a politically biased (and censored) analysis written on behalf of the LaGuardia administration. LaGuardia's handling of the commission's final report had been severely criticized by the press. By May 1936, the Mayor still had not issued any comment on the report but had referred it to various department heads for "study and report."[5] As late as September 1936, there were complaints from one of the commissioners that "failure to publish this report is subjecting the Commission to widespread attacks—intimations that it has been called off and that the Mayor does not wish or is afraid to print the findings."[6]

Alain Locke's article in *Survey* was perhaps the most favorable publicity that the LaGuardia administration received for its response to the riot. But it is clear that the article did not fully represent the author's views, for in a confidential memo to the Mayor, Locke criticized the administration for withholding the report from the public, noting further that "it is significant and rather unfortunate that the very departments that take most serious issue with the findings of the report are those which, according to the Commission, refused to cooperate in its investigations. Their protest loses weight on this account. In addition," continued Locke, "it is poor strategy to correct many errors complained of and then claim the report contrary to the fact, even if recent improvements were hitherto and independently planned."[7]

NOTES

1. This issue will be treated more fully in a forthcoming book by this writer and Renetia Martin, to be published by The Macmillan Company in 1972.

2. Letter from Paul Kellogg to Mayor LaGuardia, April 22, 1936.

3. Letter from Mayor LaGuardia to Paul Kellogg, April 27, 1936.

4. This is evident from changes in Locke's original manuscript and from letters from Dr. Goldwater, Commissioner of Hospitals, to Alain Locke, June 23, 1936, and Charles Roberts to Mayor LaGuardia, July 12, 1936.

5. Letter from Mayor LaGuardia to Mayor's Commission on Conditions in Harlem, May 5, 1936.

6. Telegram from Oswald Garrison Villard to Mayor LaGuardia, September 26, 1936.

7. Confidential memo from Alain Locke to Mayor LaGuardia, June 12, 1936.

6.

THE MAYOR'S COMMISSION
ON CONDITIONS IN HARLEM

The Negro in Harlem: A Report on Social and Economic Conditions Responsible for the Outbreak of March 19, 1935

At about two-thirty on the afternoon of March 19, 1935, Lino Rivera, a sixteen-year-old colored boy, stole a knife from a counter in the rear of S. H. Kress and Company on 125th Street. He was seen by the manager of the store, Jackson Smith, and an assistant, Charles Hurley, who were on the balcony at the time. Mr. Hurley and another employee overtook the boy before he was able to make his escape through the front door. When the two men took the knife from Rivera's pocket and threatened him with punishment, the boy in his fright tried to cling to a pillar and bit the hands of his captors. Rivera was finally taken to the front entrance where Mounted Patrolman Donahue was called. The boy was then taken back into the store by the officer who asked the manager if an arrest were desired. While

SOURCE: From The Mayor's Commission on Conditions in Harlem, *The Negro in Harlem: A Report on Social and Economic Conditions Responsible for the Outbreak of March 19, 1935* (New York Municipal Archives, unpublished), chapters I and IX.

Mr. Smith, the manager, instructed the officer to let the culprit go free—as he had done in many cases before—an officer from the Crime Prevention Bureau was sent to the store.

This relatively unimportant case of juvenile pilfering would never have acquired the significance which it later took on, had not a fortuitous combination of subsequent events made it the spark that set aflame the smouldering resentments of the people of Harlem against racial discrimination and poverty in the midst of plenty. Patrolman Donahue, in order to avoid the curious and excited spectators, took the boy through the basement to the rear entrance on 124th Street. But his act only confirmed the outcry of a hysterical Negro woman that they had taken "the boy to the basement to beat him up." Likewise, the appearance of the ambulance which had been summoned to dress the wounded hands of the boy's captors not only seemed to substantiate her charge, but, when it left empty, gave color to another rumor that the boy was dead. By an odd trick of fate, still another incident furnished the final confirmation of the rumor of the boy's death to the excited throng of shoppers. A hearse which was usually kept in a garage opposite the store on 124th Street was parked in front of the store entrance while the driver entered the store to see his brother-in-law. The rumor of the death of the boy, which became now to the aroused Negro shoppers an established fact, awakened the deep-seated sense of wrongs and denials and even memories of injustices in the South. One woman was heard to cry out that the treatment was "just like down South where they lynch us." The deep sense of wrong expressed in this remark was echoed in the rising resentment which turned the hundred or more shoppers into an indignant crowd.

The sporadic attempts on the part of the police to assure the crowd within the store that no harm had been done the boy fell upon unbelieving ears, partly because no systematic attempt was made to let representatives of the crowd determine the truth for themselves, and partly because of the attitude of the policemen. According to the testimony of one policeman, a committee of women from among the shoppers was permitted to search the basement, but these women have never been located. On the other hand, when the crowd became too insistent about learning the fate of the boy, the police told them that it was none of their business and attempted to shove them towards the door. This only tended to infuriate the crowd and was interpreted by them as further evidence of the suppression of the wronged race. At 5:30 it became necessary to close the store.

The closing of the store did not stay the rumors that were current inside. With incredible swiftness the feelings and attitudes of the outraged crowd of shoppers was communicated to those on 125th Street and soon all of Harlem was repeating the rumor that a Negro boy had been murdered in the basement of Kress's store. The first sign of the reaction of the community appeared when a group of men attempted to start a public meeting at a nearby corner. When the police ordered the group to move from the corner, they set up a stand in front of the Kress store. A Negro who acted as chairman introduced a white speaker. Scarcely had the speaker uttered the first words of his address to the crowd when someone threw a missile through the window of Kress's store. This was the signal for the police to drag the speaker from the stand and disperse the crowd. Immediately, the crowd reassembled across the street and another speaker attempted to address the crowd from a perch on a lamppost. He was pulled down from his post and arrested along with the other speaker on a charge of "unlawful assemblage." These actions on the part of the police only tended to arouse resentment in the crowd which was increasing all the time along 125th Street. From 125th Street the crowds spread to Seventh Avenue and Lenox Avenue and the smashing of windows and looting of shops gathered momentum as the evening and the night came on.

During the late afternoon, the rumor that a Negro boy had been beaten and killed in Kress's store reached the headquarters of a group comprised mainly of Negroes and known as the "Young Liberators." The purpose of this organization is the protection of the rights of Negroes. Although it is not a Communist group, as has been rumored, it has Communists among its members, one being a member of its executive committee. According to Joseph Taylor, the president of the organization, upon hearing the story of the death of the Negro boy, he went to Kress's store in order to verify the rumor and, when he was refused entrance to the store, he went to the nearby police station from which he was also ordered away. Accepting the rumor as true (although Mr. Taylor denies that he was personally responsible), the Young Liberators printed and circulated the following leaflet.

CHILD BRUTALLY BEATEN—WOMAN ATTACKED BY BOSS AND COPS—CHILD NEAR DEATH.

One hour ago a twelve-year-old Negro boy was brutally beaten by the management of Kress Five and Ten cent store.

The boy is near death.

He was mercilessly beaten because they thought he had "stolen" a five cent knife.

A Negro woman who sprang to the defense of the boy had her arms broken by these thugs and was then arrested.

Workers: Negro and White. Protest against this lynch attack on innocent Negro people.

Demand the release of the boy and woman!

Demand the immediate arrest of the manager responsible for these lynch attacks.

DON'T BUY AT KRESS'S—STOP POLICE BRUTALITY IN NEGRO HARLEM—JOIN THE PICKET LINE

About the same time, the Young Communist League, without attempting to verify the rumor, issued a similar leaflet.

FOR UNITY OF NEGRO AND WHITE WORKERS:

Don't let the Bosses start Race Riots in Harlem!

The brutal beating of the 12-year-old boy, Riviera, by Kress's special guard, for taking a piece of candy, again proves the increasing terror against the Negro people of Harlem. Bosses, who deny the most immediate necessities from workers' children, who throw workers out of employment, who pay not even enough to live on, are protecting their so-called property rights by brutal beatings, as in the case of the boy, Riviera. They shoot both Negro and white workers in strikes all over the country. They lynch Negro people in the South on framed up charges.

The bosses and police are trying to bring lynch spirit right here to Harlem. The bosses would welcome nothing more than a fight between the White and Negro workers of our community, so that they may be able to continue to rule over both the Negro and White workers.

Our answer to the brutal beating of this boy, by one of the flunkies of Mr. Kress, must be an organized and determined resistance against the brutal attacks of the bosses and the police.

WORKERS NEGRO AND WHITE: DEMAND THE IMMEDIATE DISMISSAL AND ARREST AND PROSECUTION OF THE SPECIAL GUARD AND THE MANAGER OF THE STORE.

DEMAND THE RELEASE OF THE NEGRO AND WHITE WORKERS ARRESTED.

DEMAND THE HIRING OF NEGRO WORKERS IN ALL DE-
PARTMENT STORES IN HARLEM.
DON'T LET BOSSES START ANY RACE RIOTS IN HARLEM.
DON'T TRADE IN KRESSES.

Since neither of these leaflets, according to the testimony given to
the Commission, appeared on the streets before 7:30 P.M., the actions
of these two groups, though exhibiting a lack of due regard for the
possibly serious consequences of acting on mere rumors, were not
responsible for the disorders and attacks on property which were
already in full swing. Already a tabloid in screaming headlines was
telling the city that a race riot was going on in Harlem.

In fact, the Communists defend their part in the riot on the
grounds that they prevented the riot from becoming a clash between
whites and Negroes. While one, in view of the available facts, would
hesitate to give the Communists full credit for preventing the outbreak
from becoming a race riot, they deserve more credit than any other
element in Harlem for preventing a physical conflict between whites
and blacks. The young white men who mounted the ladder and lamppost on 125th Street and were beaten and arrested because they took
the part of the indignant Negro crowds certainly changed the complexion of the outbreak. It was probably due in some measure to the
activities of these radical leaders, both white and black, that the
crowds attacked property rather than persons.

In fact, the distinguishing feature of this outbreak was that it was
an attack upon property and not upon persons. In the beginning, to be
sure, the resentment was expressed against whites—but whites who
owned stores and who, while exploiting Negroes, denied them an
opportunity to work. Although the Jewish merchants in the Harlem
community naturally came in for their share of the attacks upon the
stores, there does not seem to be any foundation for the report circulated at first that these attacks were directed mainly at them. While of
course, many motives were responsible for the actions of these
crowds, it seems that as they grew more numerous and more active,
the personality or racial identity of the owners of the stores faded out
and the property itself became the object of their fury. Stores owned
by Negroes were not always spared if they happened to be in the path
of these roving crowds, bent upon the destruction and the confiscation
of property.

From its inception, as we have pointed out, the outbreak was a spontaneous and an unpremeditated action on the part, first, of women shoppers in Kress's store and, later, of the crowds on 125th Street that had been formed as the result of the rumor of a boy's death in the store. As the fever of excitement based upon this rumor spread to other sections of the community, other crowds formed by many unemployed standing about the streets and other onlookers sprang up spontaneously. At no time does it seem that these crowds were under the direction of any single individual or that they acted as a part of a conspiracy against law and order. The very susceptibility which the people in the community showed towards this rumor— which was more or less vague, depending upon the circumstances under which it was communicated—was due to the feeling of insecurity produced by years of unemployment and a deep-seated resentment against the many forms of discrimination which they had suffered as a racial minority.

While it is difficult to estimate the actual number of persons who participated in the outburst, it does not seem from available sources of information that more than a few thousand were involved. These were not concentrated at any time in one place. Crowds formed here and there as the rumor spread. When a crowd was dispersed by the police, it often re-formed again. These crowds constantly changed their make-up. When bricks thrown through store windows brought the police, the crowds would often dissolve, only to gather again and continue their assaults upon property. Looting often followed the smashing of store windows. The screaming of sirens, the sound of pistol shots and the crashing of glass created in many a mood for destruction and excitement. Rubbish, flower pots, or any object at hand were tossed from windows into the street. People seized property when there was no possible use which it would serve. They acted as if there were a chance to seize what rightfully belonged to them but had long been withheld. The crowds showed various moods and changed their mood from time to time. Some of the destruction was carried on in a playful spirit. Even the looting which had furnished many an amusing tale was sometimes done in the spirit of children taking preserves from a closet to which they have accidentally found the key. The mood of these crowds was determined in many cases by the attitude of the police towards their unruly conduct. But, in the end, neither the threats nor the reassurances of the police could restrain these spontaneous outbursts until the crowds had spent themselves in giving release to their pent-up emotions. The final dramatic attempt on the part of the police to placate the populace by having the

unharmed Lino Rivera photographed with the Negro police lieutenant, Samuel Battle, only furnished the basis for the rumor that
Rivera, who was on probation for having placed a slug in a subway
turnstile, was being used as a substitute to deceive the people.

Lack of confidence in the police and even hostility towards these
representatives of the law were evident at every stage of the riot. This
attitude of the people of Harlem has been built up over many years of
experience with the police in this section. During the early stages of
the excitement in the store when there was still time for the police to
prevent the spread of the rumor, they assumed, according to reliable
witnesses, the attitude which is reputed to be their general attitude
towards the citizens of the Harlem community. One witness described
the scene in the store around 4:30 or 5:00 o'clock in the afternoon as
follows:

> There were just a few policemen. They walked through the
> store to the back. Then something happened in the back.
> Some people say a woman screamed. All of the group surged
> to the back of the store. When I got back there, they were
> driven forward by the policeman who was in front of them
> and one woman particularly demanded that they produce the
> manager and the boy and the policeman told her it was none
> of her damned business. All of this time I heard no explana-
> tion, nothing except among the people themselves. Indigna-
> tion grew higher. In the meantime more policemen came
> into the store and they said, "Drive these people out," and
> became rather rough and pushed the people. I said to the
> policeman, "Can't you tell us what happened?" He said, "If
> you know what's good for you you better get on home."

Although Patrolman Timothy Shannon testified that he appointed a
committee of three women to go to the basement of the store to see
that no boy was there, he felt that a more effective procedure, namely,
to have shown the unharmed boy to the crowd "was up to my superiors." Nor was the action of the police towards those who attempted
to hold a street meeting more assuring when they broke up the meeting before anyone had spoken a word. Even if the police excuse such
action on the grounds that they were acting in an emergency, the
emergency did not require them to take two of the speakers to jail,
beat them up, leave them without food for almost twenty-four hours,
and refuse to permit them to get in touch with their attorneys. More-

over, the extreme barbarity was motivated by the fact that these police-men who made derogatory and threatening remarks concerning Ne-groes were outraged because white men dared to take the part of Negroes.

At the same time, it should be said in fairness to the police that many of them handled the situation with tact and understanding and even in their attempts to restrain the crowds showed neither animosity nor brutality. It is needless to say that in a trying situation like that of March nineteenth it was difficult at times for a policeman to carry out orders to protect property and restrain lawless conduct and at the same time show a humane regard for human life. Yet, after we have made allowances for all the difficulties involved in such a situation, the shooting of Lloyd Hobbs, a sixteen-year-old boy, on the night of the riot, was an inexcusable and brutal act on the part of the police. This was the one outstanding tragic event of the entire disorders.

Two high school boys, Lloyd and Russell Hobbs, brothers, on their way home from a motion picture house at 12:43 A.M., were attracted by a crowd in front of Greeneberg's automobile accessory shop on Seventh Avenue near 128th Street. They were standing there, accord-ing to the statement of Russell Hobbs and several witnesses, when a police car containing two policemen, one of whom was patrolman John McInerny, drove up. When McInerny alighted with a revolver in his hand, the crowd, including the Hobbs brothers, began to run. Lloyd, instead of running northward with the crowd, turned left at 128th Street and crossed the street diagonally. As he reached the further sidewalk, McInerny fired, the bullet passing through the boy's body and into his right hand. According to the testimony of several witnesses, the policeman fired without calling upon the boy to halt and struck him with his first and only shot. Lloyd Hobbs was taken to the Harlem Hospital where he died a few days later.

McInerny claimed that, when the police car reached 128th Street, he and his partner heard a window of the store crash and that during the time they came to a halt before the store, a distance of 175 feet from where they were when they heard the crash, Lloyd Hobbs had climbed into the window, passed some of the loot out to members of the crowd, and was in the act of jumping out. Moreover, McInerny claimed that he ordered Lloyd to halt and that, when the boy con-tinued to run with part of the loot in his hand, he fired the fatal shot.

Besides the testimony of witnesses, there are several facts which cast serious doubts on the statement of the police. Certain automobile accessories consisting of a wrench and part of a horn, which the boy was supposed to have dropped during his flight, were not turned over to the police department until eight days after the shooting. They were produced by McInerny and were seen for the first time by Detective O'Brien who was investigating the case in the office of the District Attorney on April first. Moreover, the original record of the arrest of Lloyd Hobbs made no mention of goods having been found.

The shooting of Lloyd Hobbs, a boy having a good record both in school and in the community, and being a member of a family of good standing and character, has left the impression upon the community that the life of a Negro is of little value in the eyes of the police. The circumstances surrounding this case exclude the excuse that the policeman was dealing with a dangerous criminal who threatened the safety and welfare of the community. In fact, it seems that many of the Negroes beaten and arrested on the night of the riot did not offer as great a threat to security of life and property as the alleged act of pilfering with which Hobbs was charged. It has been reported that only the hoodlum element and criminal class participated in the looting of stores. While it seems indisputable that the criminal element took advantage of the disorders, it seems equally true from the testimony of observers that many youngsters who could not be classed as criminals joined the looting crowds in the spirit of pure adventure. Even some grownup men and women who had probably never committed a criminal act before but had suffered years of privation seized the opportunity to express their resentment against discrimination in employment and the exclusive rights of property.

Of course, the respectable and secure members of the community refrained from joining the crowds and on the next morning some of them wanted to issue a statement to the effect that they condemned the actions of the mobs. But this was not the temper or attitude of all the respectable and law-abiding members of the community. Among all classes, there was a feeling that the outburst of the populace was justified and that it represented a protest against discrimination and privations resulting from unemployment. While they readily acknowledged that they would not use such violent means to register their protest, they were nevertheless in sympathy with those who had done so. As one professional man who has known discrimination and felt the pinch of the economic crisis through the unemployment of his clientele remarked, "Those poor ignorant and rough Negroes on 125th Street were fighting my battle." Such frank statements made in private bespeak more authentically the general mood and temper of the community than volumes of formal public statements by leaders.

What, then, was the deeper significance of the events of March nineteenth? Why should the mere detention of a boy for pilfering a knife have become the signal for a general alarm throughout the Harlem community? Why was the community so susceptible to an unfounded rumor which many continue to believe in spite of the sworn testimony of reliable witnesses? Why did large masses spring up spontaneously all over the community and spend their fury in the demolition of property? These are some of the questions which this report proposed to answer. The explosion of March nineteenth would never have been set off by the trifling incident described above, had not existing economic and social forces created a state of emotional tension which sought release upon the slightest provocation. As long as the economic and social forces which were responsible for the condition continue to operate, a state of tension will exist in Harlem and recurrent outbursts may occur. . . .

On March 19, 1935, several thousands of Harlem's citizens, after five years of the depression, which had made them feel more keenly than ever the injustices of discrimination in employment, the aggressions of the police, and racial segregation, engaged in a riot against these intolerable conditions. This spontaneous outbreak, the immediate cause of which was a mere rumor concerning the mistreatment of a Negro boy, was symptomatic of pent-up feelings of resentment and insecurity. Today, extra police stand guard on the corners and mounted patrolmen ride through the streets of Harlem. To the citizens of Harlem they symbolize the answer of the city authorities to their protest of March nineteenth. To Harlem this show of force simply signifies that property will be protected at any cost; but it offers no assurance that the legitimate demands of the citizens of the community for work and decent living conditions will be heeded. Hence, this show of force only tends to make the conditions which were responsible for the occurrence last March nineteenth more irritating. And so long as these conditions persist, no one knows when they will lead to a recurrence, with possibly graver consequences, of the happenings of that night. The Commission wishes therefore to present its conclusions relative to the data on these conditions presented in the preceding chapters and to offer such recommendations as seem proper to deal with them in order to allay much of the present unrest in Harlem.

The first and most fundamental problem of the Negro citizens of

Harlem is the economic problem. While it is true that the present economic crisis has been responsible for the appalling amount of unemployment and dependency in Harlem, the great mass of the workers in the community live even during normal times close to the subsistence level and many of them are forced to be supported by charitable agencies. The majority of Negro men are employed as unskilled workers and in domestic and personal service, while 85 percent of the women are engaged exclusively in the latter types of occupation. Negro workers, being newcomers to the city and the most recent entrants into industry, are on the whole marginal workers. But, in addition to the operation of the factors which are inherent in our economic system, there are certain social factors which keep the Negro worker in the ranks of unskilled laborers and in a state of perpetual dependency. The main social factor which is responsible for this condition is racial discrimination in employment. It is this factor more than any other factor that arouses so much resentment in the Negro worker. If the economic system through competition, he reasons, inevitably condemns many workers to a starvation level, then he demands the right to compete on equal terms with other workers for a decent standard of living. This, he is not permitted to do.

Racial discrimination as a factor in limiting the employment of Negroes is especially characteristic of the public utilities. These corporations upon which the community must depend for such necessities as heat, light, and the means of communication and transportation have maintained a strict color caste in regard to employment. Yet the Negro is forced by necessity to give up a relatively large part of his meager earnings to these corporations which remain adamant in their policy of excluding Negroes from employment. However, by their policies the corporations are teaching the Negro slowly but surely the lesson that only through collective or public ownership of the public utilities can he enforce his right to employment on the same basis as other races. The Independent Subway System in the beginning applied the caste principle to the employment of Negroes and allowed them to work only as porters. This system was later placed under Civil Service and a reclassification followed whereby Negroes were enabled to compete on the same basis as other people. While this reclassification gave to the Negro worker a more or less paper victory, it has nevertheless placed the City of New York in a position where it must either uphold the laws or follow the example of private employers in keeping the Negro in menial positions at starvation wages.

When employers exclude Negroes from employment or place the badge of inferior status upon them by keeping them in menial positions, they are only helping to make more acute the conflict between the employers and a large section of an urban proletariat which is coming to look more and more upon employers as mere exploiters. When the outbreak occurred last March, angry crowds attacked property which had become a symbol of racial discrimination and exploitation without even the compensating virtue of offering means of employment. However, we are fully aware that private employers often count upon competition between black and white workers as a means of holding the unemployed and dependent black and white masses in check. The attitude of many unions emphasized this, since, as we have shown above, they are among the chief obstacles to the employment of Negro workers. Yet these very craft unions, by their exclusion of Negro workers are driving them into the camp of those labor leaders, who claim that the craft organizations are ineffective as a means of securing the rights of labor. More specifically, labor unions that discriminate against black labor are not entitled to be recognized as the representatives of labor.

There is a certain retribution upon a community that discriminates against the Negro worker through the money which the community must spend upon him in the form of relief. Discrimination in employment is responsible at all times for a large number of Negroes who are supported by the relief agencies. The present economic crisis has simply accentuated the dependency of the Negro. Even in the relief set up as in other institutions in the community, Negro personnel was not employed upon the basis of individual merit but according to the prevailing conceptions concerning the Negro's proper place or status in relation to whites. For anyone to argue that Negroes were given positions in the personnel of the Home Relief Bureau solely on the basis of individual merit exposes him to the charge of being unbelievably naive or dishonest. To be sure, racial discrimination was not as open and brutal as in private employment, but it accomplished the same end. For example, Negroes were not put in such strategic positions as to see that work relief was given on an equitable basis. While naturally many mistakes were made in the classification of relief clients, mistakes do not explain the fact that most Negroes, no matter what their skill, were given the classification of laborers. It was only the standardization of relief budgets that prevented many southern-born white relief workers from giving Negro families a smaller allowance which would have conformed to their ideas of the needs of

Negroes. At any rate, it appears that only in the giving of home relief was the Negro treated on the whole as other citizens.

In view of the Negro's impoverished condition, it is not surprising to find him living in the often dilapidated and dangerous living quarters which whites have abandoned. Innumerable housing conferences, after having discussed the deplorable housing conditions of the Negro, have either passed resolutions or made known their desire that the Negro should have more wholesome housing. But nothing has resulted from these pious and sentimental expressions of humanitarian feelings. No doubt it is true, that, to give a new context to an old saw, if wishes were houses Negroes would live in palaces. Since building contractors do not find it profitable to construct homes for the low income groups among the whites, it is not surprising that Negro wage earners who live on the margin of subsistence cannot find decent homes. But here again color caste places an additional burden upon the Negro tenant. Crowded in a black ghetto, the Negro tenant is forced to pay exorbitant rentals because he can not escape. He is the veritable slave of the landlord, and because of the helplessness which his poverty and ignorance impose upon him, he can not persuade municipal authorities to see that he gets the minimum protection which the housing laws provide.

We must turn again to the economic factor for an explanation of the ravages of tuberculosis and infant mortality in the Harlem community. Ignorant and unsophisticated peasant people without experience with urban living would naturally find survival difficult in the city; but when poverty and inadequate health agencies are added to their burdens, they are doomed to extinction! Thus we find in Harlem that the Negro's battle against tuberculosis seemingly was bringing victory until, following the migrations from the South, the death rate ceased its downward trend about fifteen years ago. The health agencies, as in the case of housing, were designed for a community with a different pattern of life and a different set of problems. There has been no systematic and comprehensive effort to modify these agencies to serve the needs of the present community. Although Harlem Hospital, the chief health agency in the community, has taken on Negro physicians and offered training to Negro interns and nurses, this so-called partial victory, instead of opening the way for the appointment of Negro physicians and interns in the municipal hospitals, is turning out to be a policy of systematic racial discrimination with all the attendant evils. The lack of morale among the medical staff, the treatment accorded the patients, and the general management of the hospital have all indicated that standards are being set up to harmonize with the generally inferior status of the Negro as a distinct racial group.

As with the health agencies, so with the educational institutions which the Negro inherited when he took over a community which the whites had abandoned. The disgraceful physical condition of the schools of Harlem as well as the lack of recreational facilities and the vicious environments that surround the schools, all indicate the presence of a poverty stricken and therefore helpless group of people in the community. One can almost trace the limits of the Negro community through the character of the school buildings. That these conditions are due primarily to the fact that the Negro community is powerless to force the indifferent city authorities to afford adequate educational and recreational facilities was forcibly demonstrated by the fact that a recently proposed building program involving the expenditure of $120,747,000 included only $400,000 for an annex in Harlem, although most of the schools in this area were built before 1900.

Such an environment as Harlem is naturally a breeding place of juvenile and adult delinquency. What has been found in Harlem concerning juvenile delinquency only confirms the studies that have shown the decisive influence of community disorganization as a complex of causative factors no matter what racial group inhabits such a community. Yet in the case of Harlem we find few of the agencies that have an ameliorative influence upon juvenile delinquency. In regard to adult delinquency we find no organized criminal gangs, but a preponderance of such crimes as flourished among poverty stricken and disorganized people. Moreover, the fact should be stressed that the very economic impotence of the community and its subjection to exploitation by outside interests, such as the policy racket and the location of institutions in the community for the pleasure and vices of whites, who seek this means of escape from the censure of their own groups, encourages anti-social behavior and nullifies the efforts of responsible citizens to maintain social control. While one would not expect the policemen in Harlem to show any appreciation or understanding of the sociological factors responsible for crime in the community, the discipline of the Police Department should see to it that they do not become the persecutors and oppressors of the citizens of the community. Nevertheless, it is true that the police practice aggressions and brutalities upon the Harlem citizens not only because they are Negroes but because they are poor and therefore defenseless. But these attacks by the police upon the security of the home and the persons of the citizens are doing more than anything else to create a

disrespect for authority and to bring about mass resistance to the
injustices suffered by the community.

The Commission fully realizes that the economic and social ills of
Harlem, which are deeply rooted in the very nature of our economic
and social system, cannot be corrected forthwith. The process must of
necessity be gradual and patiently dealt with. Yet the Commission is
convinced that, if the administration machinery set itself to prevent
racial discrimination in such municipal institutions as the schools and
the city's subway system and impose, as far as possible, penalties upon
private concerns and individuals that practiced racial discrimination,
the people of Harlem would at least not feel that their economic and
social ills were forms of racial persecution. The Commission makes
the following recommendations:

First, in regard to discrimination in employment, the Commission
recommends:

1. That the City enact an ordinance to the effect that no future
   contracts may be given to any firm or corporation that directly
   or indirectly discriminates against workers on account of race,
   creed, or color.
2. That the City make provision in its contracts with public utilities
   that will prevent discrimination against workers on account of
   race, creed, or color.
3. That the wages of the porters in the Independent Subway System be increased to the maximum allowed under civil service
   regulations.
4. That officials in the Independent Subway System, who discriminate against employees on account of race, creed, or color,
   be dismissed from their positions.
5. That workers be permitted without police interference to carry
   on peaceful picketing of establishments refusing to employ
   workers because of race, creed, or color.

Second, in respect to the relief situation, the Commission recommends:

1. That a committee of persons representing the Harlem community
   be appointed for the purposes of conferring from time to time
   with the present head of the Home Relief Bureau with a view
   to clearing up the questions concerning the status of Negro personnel in the Bureau. There is a committee now functioning
   along these lines which would gain added authority if appointed
   by the mayor.

2. That this committee likewise inquire into conditions in the Work Relief Bureau and report to the mayor in the event of discrimination on account of race, creed, or color.

Third, in regard to housing, the Commission recommends:

1. That the New York City Housing Authority be empowered to plan a farsighted housing program for Harlem.

2. That the authorities of the City of New York enforce the housing code and condemn the dwellings unfit for habitation.

3. That an attempt be made to bring about coordination of all governmental agencies having to do with housing or planning.

4. That the City continue to support the legislation for improvement of housing conditions heretofore recommended by this Commission.

Fourth, in respect to education and recreation, the Commission recommends:

1. That P.S. 89 be condemned and torn down and a modern school building be erected on the site or on a more suitable site.

2. That the federal government be requested to provide the necessary funds for the immediate launching of an emergency school building program in Harlem.

3. That additional school quarters be secured forthwith—temporary in character if necessary—in order that classes may be reduced with all possible speed.

4. That every effort be made to secure additional playgrounds in cooperation with the churches, the park authorities, and welfare agencies; that the armory of the 369th Infantry be obtained for properly supervised recreation; that all existing school playgrounds be kept open under adequate supervision until 6 P.M., in term time, and all day long in the vacation period; that unemployed teachers be utilized for conducting groups of children to the more remote parks for play and games.

5. That the staff of teachers and especially of visiting teachers be adequately increased.

6. That the contract system of cleaning the schools be abandoned and that the work be done by city employees.

7. That the city direct particular attention, through social and governmental agencies, to the problem of deficient or delinquent children in Harlem.

Fifth, in respect to health and hospitalization, the Commission recommends:

1. That in accordance with the law which prohibits racial discrimi-

nation in tax supported hospitals, appointments be made to all
municipal hospitals without regard to race, creed, or color and
that the law be observed or enforced.

2. That the number of colored doctors on the medical staff of the
Harlem Hospital be increased with appointments based upon
merit.

3. That a new hospital equal in size to the present Harlem Hospital
be built or that the present hospital be enlarged to twice its
present capacity; that some arrangement should be made
whereby Harlem Hospital be relieved of the duty of acting as a
clearing house for the transfer of patients from other institutions.

4. That the number of nurses in the training school at Harlem Hospital be adequately increased to meet the needs of the hospital.

5. That Negro nurses of Harlem Hospital be given the identical
provisions for affiliate training in contagious diseases and psy-
chiatry that exist for all other nurses in training.

6. That a complete reorganization of Harlem Hospital, including
the medical staff and the Medical Board be immediately effected.

Sixth, in respect to crime and the police, the Commission recommends:

1. That the police in Harlem be instructed—and violation of these
instructions should be followed with disciplinary measures—that
it is not their duty to interfere with the association of white and
colored citizens.

2. That the commissioner of police arrange for the appointment of
a committee of from five to seven Harlem citizens of both races
to whom people may make complaint if mistreated by the police;
that this committee should sift all complaints and take up with
the commissioner, personally if necessary, such cases as merit
attention. We suggest that this committee might well also be an
advisory committee, so that the commissioner of police may
know how his men are regarded by the citizens and what can
be done to improve relations between citizens and their police
guardians.

3. That officers of the law who violate the law should not only be
subject to investigation and punishment by the Police Department, but that action should be taken by the district attorney,
where it is warranted, just as vigorously as where any other
person is charged with a crime. We recommend that in every
case of a shooting by the police a careful investigation should be

personally made by one of the highest officials in the department and the result of the investigation be communicated to the entire force, whether the result of the inquiry be censure or commendation.

4. That a system be devised by which, in the event of any happening likely to cause grave public disorder, the Police Department would be in a position to set forth the truth by distributing leaflets and placards giving the public authoritative information from high officials in the Department as soon as possible; that radio stations owned by private interests be asked to help in an emergency. In addition, we recommend use of the city station, WNYC.

7.

ALAIN LOCKE

Harlem: Dark Weather-Vane

Eleven brief years ago Harlem was full of the thrill and ferment of sudden progress and prosperity; and *Survey Graphic* sounded the tocsin of the emergence of a "new Negro" and the onset of a "Negro renaissance." Today, with that same Harlem prostrate in the grip of the depression and throes of social unrest, we confront the sobering facts of a serious relapse and premature setback; indeed, find it hard to believe that the rosy enthusiasms and hopes of 1925 were more than bright illusions or a cruelly deceptive mirage. Yet after all there was a renaissance, with its poetic spurt of cultural and spiritual advance, vital with significant but uneven accomplishments; what we face in Harlem today is the first scene of the next act—the prosy ordeal of the reformation with its stubborn tasks of economic reconstruction and social and civic reform.

Curtain-raiser to the reformation was the Harlem riot of March 19 and 20, 1935—variously diagnosed as a depression spasm, a ghetto

SOURCE: From Alain Locke, "Dark Weather-Vane," *Survey Graphic* 25: (August 1936), 457-62.

mutiny, a radical plot and dress rehearsal of proletarian revolution. Whichever it was, like a revealing flash of lightning it etched on the public mind another Harlem than the bright surface Harlem of the night clubs, cabaret tours, and arty magazines, a Harlem that the social worker knew all along but had not been able to dramatize, a Harlem, too, that the radical press and street-corner orator had been pointing out but in all too incredible exaggerations and none too convincing shouts.

In the perspective of time, especially if the situation is handled constructively, we shall be grateful for that lightning flash which brought the first vivid realization of the actual predicament of the mass life in Harlem and for the echoing after-peals of thunder that have since broken our placid silence and Pollyanna complacency about it. For no cultural advance is safe without some sound economic underpinning, the foundation of a decent and reasonably secure average standard of living; and no emerging élite—artistic, professional or mercantile—can suspend itself in thin air over the abyss of a mass of unemployed stranded in an over-expensive, disease- and crime-ridden slum. It is easier to dally over black Bohemia or revel in the hardy survivals of Negro art and culture than to contemplate this dark Harlem of semi-starvation, mass exploitation, and seething unrest. But turn we must. For there is no cure or saving magic in poetry and art, an emerging generation of talent, or in international prestige and interracial recognition, for unemployment or precarious marginal employment, for high rents, high mortality rates, civic neglect, capitalistic exploitation on the one hand and radical exploitation on the other. Yet for some years now Harlem has been subject to all this deep undertow as against the surface advance of the few bright years of prosperity. Today instead of applause and publicity, Harlem needs constructive social care, fundamental community development and planning, and above all statesman-like civic handling.

Immediately after the March riot, Mayor LaGuardia appointed a representative bi-racial Commission of Investigation, headed by an esteemed Negro citizen, Dr. Charles H. Roberts. After twenty-one public and four closed hearings conducted with strategic liberality by Arthur Garfield Hays, and nearly a year's investigation by subcommissions on Health and Hospitalization, Housing, Crime and Delinquency and Police, Schools, the Social Services and Relief Agencies, a general report has been assembled under the direction of E. Franklin Frazier, professor of sociology at Howard University, which was filed with the Mayor on March 31, 1936, just a few days after the first anniversary of the riots. A preliminary section on the causes of the riot has been published, and several other sections have found their way to publication, some regrettably in garbled form. The public awaits the full and official publication of what is, without doubt, an important document on the present state of Harlem. When published, the findings will shock the general public and all but the few social experts already familiar with the grave economic need and social adjustment in Harlem and the inadequacies of short-sighted provisions in basic civic facilities of schools, hospitals, health centers, housing control and the like—a legacy of neglect from the venal, happy-go-lucky days of Tammany-controlled city government. Now with a socially minded city and national government the prospects of Negro Harlem—and for that matter all handicapped sections—are infinitely brighter.

But there is evidence that the present city administration is losing no time in acting to improve the Harlem situation; partly no doubt upon the specific findings and recommendations of the recent investigation, but largely from previous plans, seriously delayed by lack of capital funds or féderal subsidies such as are now financing some of the major items of the reform program. Within recent months, in some cases weeks, Harlem's urgent community needs have been recognized in the reconditioning of its sorely inadequate and formerly over-crowded municipal hospital, the completion and equipment of a long delayed women's hospital pavilion approximately doubling the bed capacity of the Harlem Hospital, the remodelling of a temporary out-patient department, and the recommendation by the Commissioner of Hospitals of a new out-patient building and of plans for a new independent hospital plant. Similarly, in the school system's 1937 budget two new school plants for Harlem have been incorporated. On June 20, the Mayor and the Secretary of the Interior spoke at the dedication of the foundations of the new Harlem River housing project, which will afford model housing for 574 low income families with also a nursery school, community playground, model recreation and health clinic facilities—a $4,700,000 WPA project. On June 24, the Mayor drove the last foundation piling for another WPA project, the $240,000 district health clinic for the badly congested Central Harlem section, where the incidence of turberculosis, social disease, and infant mortality is alarmingly high, and announced the appointment of an experienced Negro physician as head officer. It has been announced that a stipulation had been incorporated in the contract specifications for these new public works that Negro skilled labor was to have its fair share of consideration.

All this indicates a new and praiseworthy civic regard for Harlem welfare, contrasting sharply with previous long-standing neglect. The Commission, in complaining of present conditions, is careful to make plain that the present city administration has inherited most of them and that, therefore, they are not to be laid at its door. Yet they are on its doorstep, waiting immediate attention and all possible relief. The conditions are a reproach not only to previous politically minded municipal administrations but also to the apathy and lack of public-mindedness on the part of Harlem's Negro politicians and many professional leaders who either did not know or care about the condition of the masses.

Recent improvements will make some sections of the Commission's report contrary to present fact when it appears, but few will care to cavil about that. Yet, both for the record and for the sake of comparison, the situation as the Commission found it should be known. Harlem may not be disposed to look gift horses in the mouth, though a few professional agitators may. Clearly the present administration is now aware of Harlem's objective needs and is taking steps to meet some of them. Mayor LaGuardia, speaking at the housing ceremony, said: "We cannot be expected to correct in a day the mistakes and omissions of the past fifty years. But we are going places and carrying out a definite program. While the critics have been throwing stones, I have been laying bricks." But admittedly the situation is still inadequately provided for, even when present plans and immediate prospects are carried out; compounding the actual need is a swelling sense of grievance over past civic neglect and proscription. A long-range plan of civic improvements in low-cost housing, and slum clearance, in further hospital and health clinic facilities, recreation, library and adult education centers, and auxiliary school agencies is imperatively necessary. And in certain city departments a clearer policy of fair play is needed, not so much with regard to the inclusion of Negroes in municipal posts—though that too is important—as in their consideration for executive and advisory appointments where they can constructively influence municipal policies and remedial measures for the Harlem constituency. One of the fatal gaps between good intentions and good performance is in this matter of local administrators, where often an executive policy officially promulgated gets short circuited into discrimination at the point of practical application. Negroes are often accused of race chauvinism in their almost fanatical insistence upon race representatives on executive boards and in councils of policy, but the principle of this vital safeguard is of manifest importance. Especially in situations of accumulated wrong and distrust, mere practical expediency requires public assurance and reassurance.

The riot itself might never have occurred had such imponderables been taken into consideration. Its immediate causes were trivial—the theft of a ten-cent pocket-knife by a Negro lad of sixteen in Kress's department store on 125th Street. It was rumored that the boy had been beaten in the basement by store detectives and was gravely injured or dead; by tragic coincidence an ambulance called to treat one of the Kress employees, whose hand the boy had bitten, seemed to confirm the rumor and a hearse left temporarily outside its garage in an alley at the rear of the store to corroborate this. As a matter of fact the boy had given back the stolen knife and had been released through the basement door. But it must be remembered that this store, though the bulk of its trade was with Negroes, has always discriminated against Negroes in employment. Shortly before the riot it had been the objective of a picketing campaign for the employment of Negro store clerks, had grudgingly made the concession of a few such jobs and then transferred the so-called "clerks" to service at the lunch counter. While the original culprit slept peacefully at home, a community of 200,000 was suddenly in the throes of serious riots through the night, with actual loss of life, many injuries to police and citizens, destruction of property, and a serious aftermath of public grievance and anger. The careful report of the Commission on this occurrence correctly places the blame far beyond the immediate precipitating incidents. It was not the unfortunate rumors, but the state of mind on which they fell; not the inflammatory leaflets issued several hours after the rioting had begun by the Young Liberators, a radical Negro defense organization, or the other broadside distributed a little later by the Young Communist League, but the sense of grievance and injustice that they could depend on touching to the quick by any recital of fresh wrong and injustice.

The report finds that the outbreak was spontaneous and unpremeditated; that it was not a race riot in the sense of physical conflict between white and colored groups; that it was not instigated by Communists, though they sought to profit by it and circulated a false and misleading leaflet after the riots were well underway; that the work of the police was by no means beyond criticism; and that this sudden breach of the public order was the result of a highly emotional situation among the colored people of Harlem, due in part to the nervous strain of years of unemployment and insecurity. ". . . Its distinguishing feature was an attack upon property rather than persons, and resentment against whites who, while exploiting Negroes, denied them an opportunity to work." The report warns of possible future recurrences, offering as the only safe remedy the definite betterment of economic and civic conditions which, until improved, make Harlem a "fertile field for radical and other propaganda."

It is futile [the report continues] to condemn the propagandists or to denounce them for fishing in troubled waters. The only answer is to eliminate the evils upon which they base their arguments. The blame belongs to a society that tolerates inadequate and often wretched housing, inadequate and inefficient schools and other public facilities, unemployment, unduly high rents, the lack of recreation grounds, discrimination in industry and the public utilities in the employment of colored people, brutality and lack of courtesy by police. As long as these conditions remain, the public order cannot and will not be safe.

Despite this clear diagnosis, there are those even in official circles who insist upon a more direct connection between Harlem's restless temper and radical propaganda. To do so seriously misconstrues the situation by inverting the real order of cause and effect. Discrimination and injustice are the causes, not radicalism. But to neglect the symptoms, to ignore the grievances will be to spread radicalism. Violence will be an inevitable result. Eleven years ago, in the Harlem issue of *Survey Graphic*, the writer said:

Fundamentally, for the present, the Negro is radical only on race matters, in other words, a forced radical, a social protestant rather than a genuine radical. Yet under further pressure and injustice iconoclastic thought and motives will inevitably increase. Harlem's quixotic radicalisms call for their ounce of democracy today lest tomorrow they be beyond cure.

That statement needs underscoring today, when aspects of discrimination, chronic through the years, become acute under the extra pressure of the depression. At such a time special—perhaps even heroic—remedy becomes necessary where preventive long-term treatment should and could have been the scientific course. It follows that at this stage both the basic disease and its many complications as well must be treated. Obviously both long- and short-term measures are indicated, from the temporary palliative that allays inflamed public opinion to the long-range community planning which requires years for development and application. The Commission report spreads its recommendations over just such a wide range. It is particularly wise and sound, even at the risk of appearing doctrinaire, in pointing to the Negro's economic exploitation through the employment policy of the whole community as the basic economic disease, and to segregation as inducing the radical complications. Unlike many such reports this one does not overlook fundamentals and, in that respect, renders a service of truly scientific and permanent value.

It follows then that Harlem's most acute problem is employment. Not mere job occupancy, but rather a lifting of its economic earning power through less discriminatory job distribution. A careful analysis of job categories and employment trends makes this clear and is the basis for the rather startling suggestion that the municipality grapple with the traditionally non-governmental problem of the right to work according to ability. Knowing, of course, that the city cannot directly control the private labor market, the report nevertheless suggests, as a long-term policy, measures of indirect control. It suggests that the city enact an ordinance that no municipal contracts be given to firms or corporations that discriminate, racially or otherwise, against workers, and that in its contracts with the public utilities it make provisions and reservations which will prevent flagrant labor discrimination. It further suggests that the city itself as an employer set a good example, not merely by the number of Negroes employed but by widening the range of jobs filled by Negroes. This is a particularly pointed suggestion in view of the fact that the relatively small quota of Negroes in the New York city service, 2.2 percent in 1928 had fallen to 1.4 percent in 1930, the latest figure available. The WPA housing project for Harlem sets the proper but daring precedent of specifying that the employment of less than one-third skilled Negro labor will constitute *prima facie* evidence of discrimination and furnish grounds for disciplinary action against the contractor. Revolutionary as all this may seem, it goes to the economic roots of the race issue and boldly carries the principle of the Fourteenth Amendment into the economic field. Typical is the report of the New York Edison Company with 65

Negroes in its employ out of 10,000 and the Fifth Avenue Coach Company with 213 Negroes out of a total of 16,000 employees. It is such an industrial policy that brings, in the words of the report, "a certain retribution upon a community that discriminates against the Negro worker through the money it must spend upon him in the form of relief."

The common sense and logic of such a position become obvious when a community has to pay the indirect costs of labor discrimination in relief to the victims of insecure and marginal employment. Definite proof of this economic inequality is seen in the disproportionate number of Negroes on New York City relief rolls. Ten percent of the Negro population is on relief, over double its relative population of 4 percent. It has been further evidenced in the difficulties encountered by Negro workers with skilled vocational training and experience in securing work relief assignments except as unskilled laborers. Negroes did not receive their proportionate share of work relief jobs even in sections predominantly Negro, and, in sections predominantly white, Negro home relief clients were not given their proportional share of referral assignments to work relief jobs. Many skilled Negro workers had either to accept places in the unskilled ranks or go back to the home relief rolls as "unemployables." Of the employables in New York city on relief the year preceding the riot, 14 percent or 58,950 were Negroes.

Most of the complaints of discrimination in the relief services have occurred in the work relief sections, where finally an advisory committee on Negro problems was appointed, and in the matter of personal policies of the Emergency Relief Bureau itself. In home relief, the investigation found substantial fairness and little or no justifiable complaint. Negroes have been employed in the relief services at a ratio almost double their percentage in the city's population, incidentally affording indirect evidence of the disproportionate amount of unemployment among Negroes with relatively high grade qualifications. There was some complaint, according to the report, about their slow admission to higher administration grades, especially the strategic positions of occupational clerks, a type of position vital for initiating any broader policy of labor classification for Negro eligibles. Recently, Mayor La Guardia announced the appointment of Dr. John H. Johnson, rector of St. Martin's Episcopal Church, as the sixth member of the Emergency Relief Bureau.

Housing is the most serious special community problem of Harlem. The Negro's labor short dollar is further clipped by the exorbitant rentals characteristic of the segregated areas where most Negroes must reside. Whereas rents should approximate 20 percent of family income, and generally tend to do so, in Harlem they average nearly double or 40 percent. Model housing does not begin to touch the real mass need either as slum clearance or low-cost housing until it brings the average rental down to $5 to $7 per room per month. The Dunbar Apartments, erected some years back with Rockefeller subsidy, could not meet this need although at the time it gave middle-class Harlem a real lift in the direction of decent housing and neighborhood conditions. The new Harlem River Houses, to be erected with federal subsidy, will be the first model housing to reach the class that needs it most. The New York Housing Authority deserves great credit for initiation and for the principle of local Negro advice and promised Negro management which it has adopted. Harlem's appreciative response was clearly evident at the recent cornerstone-laying when Secretary Ickes, Mayor La Guardia and Commissioner Langdon Post of the Tenement House Department endorsed the principle of bringing modern housing to the congested sections of Harlem. Secretary Ickes said: "The record of American housing is proof positive of one thing. Private initiative cannot, unaided, properly house our low income families. It is simply not in the cards. It can mulct unenviable profits by housing our people badly; it cannot make money by housing them well." That holds *a fortiori* for the Negro. But when the federally aided scheme has demonstrated its social and humane objectives, cut the cost of crime and juvenile delinquency, exerted its remedial influence on other negative social forces, including racial discontent, the subsidizing of still larger scale projects by the state and municipality will be wisely charged off to their proper balances in the saner bookkeeping of an intelligently social-minded community. The Commission's subcommission on housing under Morris L. Ernst was very active in its advocacy of progressive housing legislation before the state legislature, and considerable progress in condemning old-law tenements and in slum clearance projects is contemplated under the progressive state legislation for which the Harlem investigation housing commission was directly responsible.

Health is the second great problem and disease the second grim link in the ghetto chain which fetters Harlem life. Central Harlem's rate of infant mortality, tuberculosis, and venereal disease is expectedly high and in direct proportion to areas of congestion and poverty. Harlem's hospital and health facilities were handicapped over a period of years, directly by antiquated equipment, indirectly by political and racial feuds. Regrettable differences often brought the two professional organizations of Negro physicians in Harlem into conflict. Although these differences were often over divergent views as to the gains and losses of segregation, or of this or that tactic in securing the admission of Negroes to staff and interns' positions in the municipal hospitals, they were anything but conducive to the morale of Harlem Hospital or to any clear policy of the hospital authorities. It took years of agitation to get any Negroes on the staff and the governing medical board, and Negro interns were admitted to Harlem Hospital only within the last ten years. Until recently there was only one Negro on the Harlem Hospital Board, and one Negro physician of full staff rank. The situation both as to hospital facilities and staff personnel has shown material improvement recently under what promises to be a new and liberalized policy instituted by the present Commissioner of Hospitals, Dr. Goldwater. But that change was too recent to spare the Commissioner or his immediate subordinate in charge of the Harlem Hospital from adverse criticism by the Commission. Recent improvements offset some of the shocking and inadequate conditions that had existed for years.

On January 2 the opening of the new women's wing to Harlem Hospital increased its capacity from 325 to 665 beds. This pavilion, almost completed four years ago, had stood unfinished chiefly because of legal complications growing out of the failure of contractors. This relief from overcrowding, no doubt the basis for the most serious complaints as to previous maladministration, clears the way for remodelling and modernizing the older parts of the hospital, which is now proceeding under WPA grants. A new nurses' home has recently opened; plans for a new $1,500,000 outpatient department have been drawn, and an additional entirely new hospital has been recommended as an urgent item in the impending capital outlay for city hospitals. In the meantime, the Department of Hospitals has, with the assistance of the WPA, modernized a two-story building on the Harlem Hospital block, which will provide more than four times the space of the old clinic. These last projects are made necessary by the fact that the recently enlarged facilities of Harlem Hospital already are approaching a crowded condition at times.

Only incessant agitation brought staff appointments in municipal hospitals to Negro physicians. Recently, by a laudable departure in the direction of fairer play, five Negroes were given staff appointments to Queens' General Hospital and one to Sea View; and in the first six months of 1936 seven Negro physicians have been promoted from assistant to associate visiting rank, five from clinical assistants to assistant visiting rank, and seven new clinical appointments have been made. This, with three members of full attending rank and an increase of two members on the Medical Board of Harlem Hospital, represents a spectacular gain in comparison with the slow progress of former years. The Commission report, however, recommends "the admission of Negro physicians, interns, and nurses to all city hospitals on merit in accordance with law, and the withholding of municipal financial aid from any institution refusing equal treatment to Negroes."

With the completion of the new health unit, there will no longer be grounds for the present complaint that in the two health areas where Negroes are concentrated there is "conspicuous absence of the very agencies which deal with the major problems of Negro health—infant mortality and tuberculosis."

Similarly, the announcement of two new school buildings for Harlem in the 1937 Board of Education program corrects in prospect the major plant deficiencies complained of in the Commission's school report. It leaves for further consideration the plea for some special provisions to offset the effects of demoralized home and neighborhood conditions upon a considerable section of the Harlem school population. Primarily this is not a school function or responsibility, even though it gravely affects its work. Classes for deficient and delinquent children, special vocational guidance, and supervised play are recommended, and also greater protection of school children from the demoralized elements of the adjacent neighborhoods by the police department. Logically and practically, however, it is obvious that only wide-scale slum clearance will reach the roots of such conditions.

One of the rare bright spots in the situation is the fine policy of the New York City school system of entirely disregarding race in the appointment and assignment of Negro school teachers, which policy should point a convincing precedent to other city departments and, for that matter, to other great municipalities.

No field of municipal government is more tied in with a problem such as underlies the Harlem riots than the police department. Even at that time a spirit of general antagonism toward the police was evident, and the fatal shooting of a sixteen-year-old high school student, Lloyd Hobbs, whom the police charge with looting during the riot (a charge which several witnesses dispute), did much to aggravate the bitterness. As the report aptly says, "A policeman who kills is prosecutor, judge, and executioner." In fact a series of police shootings in Harlem, continuing down to two quite recent killings of children in the police pursuit of suspected criminals, has brought the community to the point of dangerous resentment toward the police. The frequent heavy mobilization of police forces in Harlem, however well based the fear or probability of public disorder and the recurrence of rioting, has the practical effect of stimulating the very thing it is meant to avert—abnormal tension, resentment, and disrespect for proper police authority. Every close student of the situation sympathizes with the police authorities in their difficult responsibilities, especially during the strenuous campaign against the vice and small-time racketeering which are all too prevalent in Harlem. But respect for and confidence in police authority are primary assets in such a housecleaning campaign, and the good-will and cooperation of the law-abiding, better class element are essential. Restored confidence and good-will are particularly vital in the situation fraught with possible racial antagonisms.

A surprising and convincing reason for suspecting police brutality and intimidation is the fact that many in the Harlem community feel as much resentment toward Negro police as toward white police, and even toward the Negro police lieutenant, who sometime back was a popular hero and a proud community symbol. The Commission's recommendations, therefore, that the police be given instructions to use greater caution and tact in emergencies and show the strictest regard for citizens' rights, and that a bi-racial Citizens' Public Safety Committee be appointed as an advisory body to the Police Commissioner and to hear possible complaints and grievances against undue use of police power or claims of police brutality and intimidation, are of crucial and constructive importance in a somewhat critical situation. For without restored confidence and unbroken public order, Harlem's wound will not heal.

Dark as the Harlem situation has been, and in a lesser degree still is, the depression in general and the riot in particular have served a diagnostic purpose which, if heeded and turned into a program of constructive civic reform, will give us improvement and progress instead of revolution and anarchy. After all, in these days of economic crisis and reconstruction the Negro has more than racial import. As the man farthest down, he tests the pressure and explores the depths of the social and economic problem. In that sense he is not merely the man who should not be forgotten; he is the man who cannot safely be ignored.

Yet, in addition, Harlem is racially significant as the Negro's greatest and formerly most favorable urban concentration in America. The same logic by which Harlem led the Negro renaissance dictates that it must lead the economic reconstruction and social reformation which we have been considering. There are some favorable signs from within and without that it will: from without, in terms of the promise of the new concern and constructive policy of the Mayor and a few progressive city authorities; from within, in terms of a new type and objective of Negro civic leadership. The latter is evidenced in part by the Mayor's Harlem Commission and its sustained activities, by the ever-increasing advisory committees of leading and disinterested citizens, and recently, quite significantly, by the organization of the biracial All Peoples' Party in Harlem for independent political action to "rid Harlem of the corrupt political control of the two major parties and end the tyranny of political bosses." Recently 209 delegates from 89 social, civic, and religious organizations organized with this objective of substituting civic organization and community welfare for political support and party spoils. A Harlem community-conscious and progressively cooperative is infinitely to be preferred to a Harlem racially belligerent and distempered. Contrast the Harlem of the recent WPA art festival, gaily and hopefully celebrating in a festival of music, art, and adult education, dancing in Dorrance Brooks Square, with the Harlem of the riot, a bedlam of missiles, shattered plate glass, whacking nightsticks, mounted patrols, police sirens and police bullets; and one can visualize the alternatives. It is to be hoped that Harlem's dark weather-vane of warning can be turned round to become a high index of constructive civic leadership and reform.

V

Detroit, 1943

INTRODUCTION

Following the bloody Detroit race riot of 1943, in which 34 persons were killed and over 1,000 injured, Governor Kelly appointed a "fact-finding committee" composed of three law enforcement officials to investigate the causes of the riot. The committee was instructed to answer the following questions: "Was the riot a 'planned outbreak'? Was it inspired by 'subversive enemy influence', or was it a spontaneous uprising resulting from long-neglected and side-tracked social problems?" Within two months, the committee completed its investigation and submitted a twenty-two page report, supported by hundreds of police documents and miscellaneous data.

Unlike the earlier commissions of 1917, 1919, and 1935, Governor Kelly's Committee adopted a strictly legalistic interpretation of their mandate and did not analyze the political and economic conditions which might have caused the riot. While the committee found no evidence of "subversive enemy influence" or conspiracy, they attributed the riot to "irresponsible" hoodlums and especially to the "rebellious attitude" of "some self-designated responsible Negro leaders." The committee also absolved the police and federal troops from all alleged improprieties.

The "findings" of the committee that (1) law enforcement agencies behaved lawfully and competently and (2) blacks were primarily responsible for the riot have been challenged by a number of authorities. Thurgood Marshall, writing for *Crisis* in 1943,[1] reported that the police "enforced the law with an unequal hand. They used 'persuasion' rather than firm action with white rioters, while against Negroes they used the ultimate in force: nightsticks, revolvers, riot guns, submachine guns, and deer guns. As a result, 25 of the 34 persons killed were Negroes. Of the latter, 17 were killed by the police. . . . This record by the Detroit police," concluded Marshall, "demonstrates once more what all Negroes know only too well: that nearly all police departments limit their conception of checking racial disorders to surrounding, arresting, maltreating, and shooting Negroes. Little attempt is made to check the activities of whites."

The selections from *Race Riot* by Alfred McClung Lee and Norman D. Humphrey further suggest that law enforcement agencies failed to protect blacks and were themselves responsible for violations of law. *Race Riot*, written and published shortly after the riot, also documents the extensive role played by whites in the riot, thus seriously discrediting the committee's finding that blacks were incited to riot only by their "militant" leaders.

NOTES

1. Thurgood Marshall, "The Gestapo in Detroit," *Crisis* (1943), 50: 232-33.

8.

HERBERT I. RUSHTON
WILLIAM E. DOWLING
OSCAR OLANDER, and
JOHN H. WITHERSPOON

Final Report of Governor's Committee to Investigate Riot Occurring in Detroit, June 21, 1943

Part I

In the early evening of June 20, 1943, there began in Detroit's Belle
Isle Park a series of incidents between whites and Negroes which
finally culminated in a serious riot. Acts riotous in character continued from that time until approximately 11 P.M., June 21, 1943.
For several days thereafter isolated acts of violence occurred, but the
rioting had been effectively ended with the arrival of federal troops in
Detroit on the night of June 21.

Belle Isle Park, Detroit's principal recreational center, is located in
the Detroit River and is connected with the mainland by a large
bridge at the intersection of E. Grand Boulevard and Jefferson Avenue. The Detroit Street Railway system furnishes bus transportation
to the island. Recreational facilities provided at the island include
picnic grounds, swimming beaches, swings, playgrounds, refreshment
stands, and the customary pavilions. The park has long been famous

SOURCE: From Governor's Committee to Investigate Riot Occurring in
Detroit, June 21, 1943, *Final Report* (August 11, 1943).

because of its size, natural beauty, and its many recreational facilities. On that warm Sunday afternoon and evening, June 20, there were nearly 100,000 people on the Isle, the majority of whom were Negroes.

While the disturbance began at Belle Isle, the nearest portion of the area principally affected by the rioting is located approximately three miles from the park. Its boundaries commence at Maple and Rivard Streets, extend directly north to Leicester, west to Woodward Avenue, Detroit's main thoroughfare, south to Adams, thence east to Rivard. This area consists of 2.26 square miles, inhabited overwhelmingly by Negroes. During the course of the rioting, disturbances were reported in all but one of the fifteen Detroit police precincts, but the brunt was born in the first, third, ninth, and thirteenth precincts, all of which enter or traverse the area described.

The incidents occurring on Belle Isle were little different in character than those which had occurred elsewhere in and about Detroit for some time preceding June 20.[1] On June 15, only five days before, there had been a disturbance at Eastwood Park, an amusement center located in Macomb County, just outside Detroit. On that occasion a group of colored boys was met by a stone attack by a number of white youths as the former were about to leave a street car in front of the park. The white boys prevented the colored youths from entering the park.[2]

Aaron Fox,[3] colored, 17, went to Belle Isle with Raymond Thomas, 17, colored, on Sunday noon, June 20. Fox intended to go swimming, but the line waiting for admission was too long. He spent considerable time wandering about the island. Later in the day these boys met Frank and Fred Neal, twins, 17, colored, and Kelly Lately,[4] 14, colored, who had gone to the Isle with LeRoy Howell,[5] 13, colored, at 3:30 in the afternoon. These six boys wandered to the playground where a number of colored youths were shooting dice. There they met Charles (Little Willie) Lyons,[6] 20, colored, who had come to the Island with H. D. (Handsome Harry) Minnifield, 17, colored. Aaron Fox and Charles Lyons talked of the Eastwood Park episode in which they had been involved. They agreed it would be a good idea to: "Go fight and do like they done us at Eastwood Park." Lyons suggested to the crowd of colored boys there at the playground that they: "Take care of the Hunkies." At the time there were several white people using the swings at the playground. The first incident occurred when Lyons, arming himself with a stick wrapped in paper, approached a white boy, struck him, and ordered him to leave the island. The white boy ran. There were at the time several white men seated on the grass. Lyons struck the feet of one of these white men, telling him: "Time to go home. Get going." The white men left. This colored group then began canvassing the island for white boys. Walking through a path they sighted Fred McClelland,[7] 16, colored, who had gone to the island at three o'clock with two colored youths and a colored girl. McClelland with John Wilson, 18, one of the colored boys who had come to the Isle with him, had left the girl and her friend who were selling a case of beer they had brought along. McClelland and Wilson were at first believed by the group previously mentioned to be white, and were about to be attacked when their color was noticed by Kelly Lately, who recognized McClelland. Fox and Lyons then told McClelland and Wilson that they were looking for white boys to beat up, to even the score of the Eastwood Park incident. McClelland and Wilson joined the group. Coming upon several white picknickers, Fox and Lyons ordered them to leave, and took their food from them. Several of the colored boys ate the melons taken from these picknickers. Fox then armed himself with two pop bottles.

Mattie Mae (Redcap) Byndon, 16, colored, went to the island about six o'clock with her sister and another colored girl. They went to the Casino, where she was seen by Alfred Peterson,[8] 16, colored.

Peterson witnessed an incident at eight o'clock at the skating pavilion near the Casino involving Earl Blayock, 16, white. Blayock had gone to Belle Isle alone at 4 o'clock that afternoon. Because of the size of the crowds Blayock was unsuccessful in his attempts to rent either a bicycle or a horse. He sat down near the lighthouse where there was no crowd, watching freighters passing in the Canadian channel until about eight o'clock, when he went to the Casino to purchase some hot dogs. After making his purchases he walked out the back door, where there were three lines of people waiting to get to the beverage stand, most of whom were Negroes. Crossing through the lines, he was stopped by a colored man, who told him he had: "Pushed through the line kind of close," and who insisted Blayock go back and apologize. Blayock replied that he had done nothing requiring an apology. The colored man threatened that he would make him apologize and struck him on the jaw. Blayock reeled backwards toward the water and was immediately struck again over the left eye. As this incident occurred, a colored and a white officer approached. They led Blayock through the building, and being assured by Blayock that he did not need medical attention, advised him to catch a bus and leave the island. As he walked from the building to the bus stop, he was attacked by a colored man who struck him on the head with a bottle. The white officer immediately returned, summoned a scout car, and with Blayock drove about the island in an unsuccessful effort to locate and identify the assailant. Blayock was thereafter taken to Detroit Receiving Hospital, where he received treatment for lacerations and contusions of the head, the first victim of the rioting to be hospitalized.

Another incident occurred at the bus stop just beyond the Casino a few moments later. Mrs. Anna Peterson, white, accompanied by a ten-year-old boy, was about to board a bus when James Wilson, colored, 18, pushed or was pushed against the child. Just before this, a group of 15 to 25 colored people had rushed to board the bus. The whites present formed a protective line to permit two elderly women to board. When Mrs. Peterson saw the boy pushed, she reached out to place him on the bus, pushing Wilson away. Wilson says he tried to jump on the bus to get out of the way of the crowd. Wilson's brother Ernest and their girl friends, Ruth and Doris Horton, colored, were already on the bus. When Wilson got on the bus, he went to Mrs. Peterson, struck her on the shoulder, and called her a "mother-fucking son of a bitch." Wilson claims that after he struck the woman, but before he made the indecent statement, Mrs. Peterson called him a "God-damned nigger." Mrs. Peterson denies this. Wilson attempted to strike Mrs. Peterson again, but was prevented from so doing by Mr. Peterson and an unidentified colored man, who assisted in maintaining order until the police arrived and placed Wilson under arrest.[9]

Shortly before nine o'clock there was a disturbance at the ferry dock when a group of colored boys tried to prevent some white people from boarding the ferry boat. There was considerable pushing and jostling of the crowd. The attendant closed the gate, stating to the crowd, both white and colored: "There is plenty of room for everybody, and when you can get on the boat properly, I will let you on."

Mattie Mae (Redcap) Byndon left the Casino at about 9:15 P.M. and walked over to the playground, opposite the swings. There she recognized several of a number of colored boys. She recognized Charles (Little Willie) Lyons, James Peterson, H. D. (Handsome Harry) Minnifield. Present also were Aaron Fox, Raymond Thomas, Fred and Frank Neal, and Fred McClelland. On her approach, she saw this group of colored boys beating Gus Niarhos, 14, and Clyde Fields, both white. The two white boys had been strolling near the swings when the colored group approached and asked: "Where are you going?" and immediately attacked them. After knocking Niarhos down and kicking him, Charles (Little Willie) Lyons asked Niarhos for his money, stating: "I ain't got no car fare. Give me some money." Niarhos gave him two dollars. The colored boys then ran off. At 9:30 the police arrived, removed Niarhos to the police station where he was given first aid, and then proceeded to drive the boys across the bridge so that they might catch a bus to go home. In the meantime the colored mob, led by Aaron Fox and Charles (Little Willie) Lyons had reassembled and headed toward the bridge. At the bus stop they hailed an approaching bus, but it would not stop for them. Continuing, they came upon a white boy, chased him through the woods, but he eluded them. As they approached the bridge, they were joined by several other colored girls and boys. Part way across the bridge Charles (Little Willie) Lyons brushed against Joseph B. Joseph, white, 38, who was walking alone close to the rail of the bridge. Lyons belligerently demanded to know: "Where do you think you are going, you white mother-fucking son of a bitch?" Lyons then struck Joseph and knocked him to the ground. Others in the mob kicked him. One suggested, "Let's throw him over the bridge." Managing to rise Joseph started running. Others of the mob shouted: "Hold him; hold him." Two white sailors approached with women companions and witnessed the attack. One of them blew a whistle and other sailors approached.

At that instant the police car carrying Gus Niarhos and Clyde Field across the bridge arrived and picked up Joseph. The police continued across the bridge to Jefferson Avenue where Joseph pointed out four colored boys who were then running as among his assailants. All concerned returned to Belle Isle Police Station in a police car, and there, following Joseph's uncertainty of identification, the four boys were released. At the station Joseph received first aid treatment for an injury to his eye.

The crowd of Negroes, including Mattie Mae (Redcap) Byndon, had continued in the meantime toward the Jefferson Avenue terminus of the bridge. Eleanor Giusto, white, her sister, Stella Redko, 18, and Margaret Hart, 17, attracted by the excitement, had started across the bridge. They were met by three white sailors who informed them that there had been trouble between whites and Negroes at the swings on the playground. One of the sailors told the girls that a colored man had been involved in a fight with a white sailor and his girl friend, and that the Negro had cut the white sailor. After talking for a few minutes, the girls decided to return to Jefferson Avenue. There was momentary quiet until the Byndon girl, walking with her friends, pushed against Eleanor Giusto. The Negress says that Margaret Hart called her a "black bitch," which provoked her to exclaim: "You mother-fucking bastard," and to strike Miss Hart. Margaret Hart denies the statement, but admits returning the blow, striking Miss Byndon with her fist. The colored boys with the Negress attacked Miss Hart, knocking her down and kicking her. This colored group then ran to Jefferson Avenue, the three sailors who had spoken to the girls remaining aloof from the disturbance. Suddenly, Stella Redko heard a scream coming from the bushes near the approach to the bridge. A crowd of white people ran toward the bushes.[10] Separate fights broke out the length of the bridge and along Jefferson Avenue.

When Aaron Fox reached Jefferson Avenue, he suggested to the crowd that they return to Belle Isle. He told them that a colored woman and her baby had been drowned.[11] Police reinforcements had arrived, however, and this group of boys refused to go back.[12]

Meantime, the traffic leading from Belle Isle was heavy, and crowds of people were in and about the intersection of E. Jefferson and E. Grand Boulevard, and there was heavy traffic on those two arteries. Numerous whites returning home via E. Jefferson Avenue stopped, many joining in the melee that had developed. The Negroes at the bridge approach were at the time outnumbered by whites. By 11:20 P.M., the crowd at the bridge approach had increased to more than 5,000, and the street fighting had spread west to Helen Avenue, east to Field, and north to Lafayette East.

Additional police reinforcements, dispatched to the intersection, struggled to keep the crowds under control. Some whites, who while waiting for bus transportation were menacingly approached by Negroes, took refuge in houses located in the vicinity. Some fifty to sixty Negroes were seen with knives. At one point, some Negroes who had been chased north of Jefferson Avenue were seen to reassemble and charge back toward Jefferson where police officers were stationed. Seeing, however, that they were outnumbered, they retreated.

The police in the meantime had blocked off the Belle Isle approach,[13] preventing anyone entering the island. By two o'clock in the morning of June 21, the augmented police force had succeeded, without firing a single shot, in dispersing the crowds and placing the situation under complete control.[14] The casualties resulting from disturbances at Belle Isle and the bridge approach from eight o'clock in the evening of June 20, until two o'clock the following morning numbered thirteen, of which eight were white and five were colored. There were no riot casualties in the Fifth Precinct after that hour.[15] None of the casualties occurring in this area, resulting from the initial disturbance, was serious. There is no record of the use of any firearms by any troublemakers during this period in this area. Weapons employed by either whites or Negroes there were stones, sticks, and knives.

Had the disturbance ended with the incidents at Belle Isle and the bridge approach, none of the deaths occurring in the riot would have resulted. More than 98 percent of the injuries would have been avoided; upwards of 95 percent of the reported property damage resulting from the rioting would never have been suffered; less than 3 percent of the reported law violations would have existed; less than 3 percent of the arrests made incident to the rioting would have been made.

But rioting was started by an episode which occurred at the Forest Club, 700 E. Forest, in the heart of the Negro section some five miles from Belle Isle. This occurrence excited passions and must be cited as the principal cause of the tragedy which followed.

The Forest Club is one of the larger recreational centers located in the Negro section of Detroit, commonly referred to as Paradise Valley. The Club consists of a dance hall, a roller skating rink, and a bowling alley at the above address. Patrons, all Negroes, estimated at 700 in number,[16] attended a dance there on Sunday evening, June 20. Shortly after midnight, Leo Tipton,[17] an employee of the Forest Club Ballroom, assigned to the checkroom that night, appeared on the stage, and seizing the microphone in front of the orchestra leader, aroused the dancers with the following announcement: "This is Sergeant Fuller.[18] There's a riot at Belle Isle. The whites have killed a colored lady and baby. Thrown them over the bridge. Everybody get their hat and coat and come on. There is free transportation outside."[19] Pandemonium broke loose! Some of the dancers dashed out of the building; others jumped out of the windows. Tamble Whitworth, a special officer working at the ballroom, attempted to dissuade the people from leaving, but to no avail. The crowd milled about the intersection of E. Forest and Hastings Streets. The transportation Leo Tipton had announced was available was not there to transport all of the mob. Automobiles operated by whites, stopping at the traffic signal at the intersection, were opened by members of the Negro mob, the whites taken from behind the wheel, and the vehicles appropriated.[20]

Simultaneously, the crowd commenced to throw stones at the passing vehicles and street cars. A white motorcyclist traveling east on Forest was struck by a stone. He fell off the motorcycle. Another stone struck the motor causing gasoline to spurt, setting fire to the cycle. At about 12:10 A.M., Tamble Whitworth called the police reporting the first rioting outside the Belle Isle area. Three cruisers had been dispatched by the Canfield station by 12:40 A.M. to Hastings and Forest, but the officers were unable to cope with the situation. Thereafter, numerous police arrived, but the rioting was by then out of control.

The Negro crowd, surging from the ballroom, incited by the announcement, spurred on by the rocks thrown by some, excited by the burning motorcycle, moved up and down Hastings Street, indiscriminately stoning white-operated automobiles and white-owned business places. The rioters moved west to Beaubien and thence north to Ferry.[21]

The first reported stabbing occurred at 1:40 A.M., June 21, at Alfred and Hastings, when Paul Haaker, 39, white, was stabbed by an unknown Negro. The first injury to a police officer, requiring hospitalization, was suffered by Patrolman Steward Marchant, Badge No. 2239, who was struck by a brick thrown by an unknown colored man at E. Forest and Hastings. Patrolman Marchant was injured at 1:45 A.M., June 21. He was hospitalized at Receiving Hospital, then transferred to Harper Hospital. The first homicide directly resulting from the riot occurred when Samuel Johnson, colored, 33, died at 6:15 A.M., June 21, at Edith K. Thomas Hospital.[22] The hospital attendants reported that this man was brought to the hospital by an unidentified colored man who stated Johnson had been seriously cut when a plate glass window in a store he was entering fell upon him. He died from loss of blood, resultant from severance of the large artery in his leg.

While struggling to restore order in the colored section, where the rioting had spread south to Adams and Hastings, and north to Oakland and Owen (but all east of Woodward Avenue), the Detroit Police Department in the early hours of June 21 took constructive action to prevent organized white retaliation. When, at about 4 A.M., June 21, whites were observed assaulting colored patrons leaving the Roxy and Colonial theatres on Woodward Avenue, in addition to arresting white persons, the police entered the theatres and instructed the colored folk to remain therein until adequate police protection could be assured them on leaving. Police officers were stationed at the exits to insure protection. Notwithstanding these measures, a group of whites began stoning colored-operated automobiles at Charlotte and Woodward shortly after 4 A.M., June 21.[23] Thereafter, numerous acts of violence were perpetrated by whites, until approximately eleven o'clock the following night. Most of the acts committed by whites took place on Woodward Avenue and immediately adjacent to Woodward Avenue. With the coming of daylight, June 21, and thereafter throughout the day varying youthful gangs of white "hoodlums" assembled, assaulted Negroes, and were dispersed, only to reassemble again and roam Woodward Avenue in search of additional colored victims.[24]

The enormity of the problem confronted by the Police Department after midnight, June 20, is perhaps most graphically illustrated by an appraisal of the damage resulting from the looting which took place in the affected Negro area. To afford the maximum possible protection within that area the Police Department assigned officers from the several precincts of the city to that district. At midnight, June 20, instructions were issued to retain on duty the one-third of the Detroit Police Personnel who would normally go off duty at that hour. This force augmented the platoon which came on duty at midnight. Shortly thereafter the entire police personnel was mobilized, and from that time all available personnel was kept on active duty twelve hours daily. It was, of course, impossible to divert all police to the affected area, as numerous police had to be retained in areas of potential trouble.[25]

This committee is of the firm conviction that both the white and Negro rioters lacked preconceived or premeditated organization. The riot incident tables disclose alternating periods of increased and abating violence by both white and colored rioters throughout June 21. The spontaneity with which incidents occurred at various locations, both within and outside the affected area, discloses the absence of planning on the part of either group.[26]

The only serious threat of whites toward any portion of the colored section existed between six and nine P.M., June 21, almost twenty-four hours after the initial disturbances at Belle Isle. At that time a large group of whites assembled at Woodward and Vernor Highway; coincidentally, a large group of Negroes assembled between John R [sic] and Brush on Vernor.[27] The efforts of the white group to enter the colored section at this point was readily prevented by the police, who were aided by reserves and tear gas squads.

The first contingent of federal troops arrived in Detroit at 9:45 P.M., following a proclamation issued by President Roosevelt.[28] The troops proceeded north on Woodward Avenue immediately upon arriving in Detroit. Within an hour following their arrival, rioting was effectively quelled.

The committee directs attention to the statistics made a part of this report, disclosing the ages of the participants. A fraction less than 35 percent of those detained in the rioting were 21 years of age or under. Almost 63 percent of those detained were under 31 years of age. Of the Negroes detained, less than 23 percent were 21 years old or under; whereas, of the white detained, almost 48 percent, or almost half of the whites, were 21 years old or under. While those under 31 years comprised over 66 percent of the whites detained, only a little over 60 percent of the Negroes detained were under 31 years of age. These statistics suggest that the riotous element among the whites was younger than the same element among the colored, and that among both white and colored, it was largely the youthful, irresponsible element which participated in this tragedy.

Based upon the statements herein contained, this committee finds:

1. The riot was not planned or premeditated.
2. The riot was not inspired by subversive enemy influence.
3. The riot resulted from a smouldering racial tension which was inflamed as the result of several disconnected incidents upon Belle Isle, provoked by a group of Negroes.
4. The looting and accompanying rioting followed the spreading of a false, inflammatory rumor by Leo Tipton, Negro, to the effect that whites had killed a colored woman and her child at Belle Isle.
5. Irresponsible white and Negro youths were responsible for most of the casualties and the damage resulting.
6. The ordinary law enforcement and judicial agencies have thus far adequately and properly dealt with the law violaters.

Part II

Frequent reference has been made in Part I of this report to the racial tension prevalent in certain Negro and white groups prior to the outbreak of June 20 and 21. This report would be incomplete without some reference to factors which have created and inflamed that tension.[29] There never was a time when people were not conscious of certain racial differences. Characteristics of color, stature, and speech have always marked off and distinguished one people from another. This, of course, is neither an argument for, nor a justification of any feeling of superiority on the part of any race. That certain misinformed people have relied upon their peculiar racial characteristics in asserting an alleged superiority over another race is unfortunate. But it must be recognized that only by education can this unwarranted assumption be dispelled. The animosity arising from this misinformation and want of education can be observed, not only in Detroit, but wherever different races are thrown together. Of present concern to this committee, however, is the increasing tendency among certain hoodlum elements in Detroit, both white and Negro, openly to flaunt the established social order in combatting this animosity.[30] Certainly no criticism is to be made of the honest efforts of responsible leaders, both Negro and white, who seek by lawful means the removal of unjust barriers between the races. But it is equally certain that vigorous criticism should be directed to those irresponsible leaders, who by their words and conduct, actively inspire among their followers a disregard for law, order, and judicial process, in seeking the racial equality to which they are entitled.

In studying the factors which created that state of mind which made whites and Negroes willing participants in a tragic riot, an answer has been sought to the questions: What particular factor is responsible for the uncontrolled belligerency prevalent in certain white and Negro groups in Detroit? Where have these young hoodlums been told they have a license to lawlessness in their "struggle to secure racial equality"? Who has told them it is proper themselves to redress actual and presumed grievances? Who has exhorted them violently to overthrow established social order to obtain "racial equality"? Who exaggerates and parades before these same elements sordid stories of sensational crime, giving an anti-social complexion to these incidents readily absorbed by the audience? Who constantly beats the drums of: "racial prejudice, inequality, intolerance, discrimination" and challenges these hoodlum elements "militantly" to rise against this alleged oppression? Who charges by their news stories and their editorials that all law enforcement agencies are anti-Negro, brutal, and vicious in the handling of Negroes, and bent upon their persecution?

Responsible Negro and white leaders alike will read with interest Dr. Warren Brown's article, "A Negro Looks at the Negro Press," first appearing in the December 19, 1942, issue of the *Saturday Review of Literature*, and reprinted in condensed form in the January, 1943, issue of the *Reader's Digest*. So important does this committee believe this article to be, written by the colored Director of Race Relations, Council for Democracy, that a copy of the article is appended to this report.[31]

The Negro newspapers of wide circulation in Detroit, the *Michigan Chronicle*, the *Pittsburgh Courier*, and the *Detroit Tribune*, are true counterparts of the newspapers described by Dr. Brown.

Typical of this press is the front page of the July 17, 1943 issue of the *Michigan Chronicle*. "DENIED BOY HANGS SELF, Eleven-Year-Old Boy Found Hanging by Neck from Tree"; "WIFE SLAYER PLEADS GUILTY, Let Her Kiss Baby Boy Before He Fired Fatal Shots"; "'GOOD-BYE DARLING' MAN TELLS WIFE" (with a detailed description of an attempted suicide following); "JILTED SUITOR STABBED WOMAN" are the headlines and sub-captions of some of the stories appearing on that page. Above the picture of a man wanted in Tennessee for murder appears the headline: "DON'T TAKE ME TO TENNESSEE." Another feature story appearing on the same page is entitled: "SOLDIER BEATEN BY MISSISSIPPI POLICE," under which is reported a strike at Flora, Mississippi. The second paragraph of that story reads:

> Immediate cause of the strike is said to have been the serious beatings of a colored soldier and the abuse of several of the soldiers' wives and women companions by Jackson Civilian police.

These stories are not isolated instances of inflammatory news reporting, but are characteristic of the news sheets mentioned.

A second theme, repeatedly emphasized by these papers, is that the struggle for Negro equality at home is an integral part of the present worldwide struggle for democracy. Editorially and otherwise these papers repeatedly charge that there is no more democracy here than in Hitler's Europe, or in Japan, and loudly proclaim that a victory over the Axis will be meaningless unless there is a corresponding overthrow in this country of the forces which these papers charge prevent true racial equality.

The topic is developed by numerous references to alleged "Jim-Crowism" practiced in our own Army and Navy. The refusal of certain Negroes to report for induction into the Army is reportorially justified by charging racial discrimination. Frequently recurring through these papers is the statement: "This nation cannot exist half free and half slave," the obvious purpose of which is to drive home to the Negro readers the alleged fact of their servitude, and to arouse a belligerent reaction.

The papers discuss a "Civil Disobedience Campaign" and condemn the leaders of the March on Washington Movement[32] for failing to authorize such a program at their convention held in Chicago June 30 to July 4, 1943.

Every instance of actual or presumed discrimination is reported with exaggeration,[33] and statements of charges made by Negro people, for which there is no support in fact, are worded to leave an impression of conviction of truth with the reader.[34]

While these papers consistently charge discrimination and plead for absolute equality between all races, at least some Negro organizations would disclaim all responsibility for the crimes committed by Negroes, and would conceal from the public the racial identity of law violators. A portion of the NAACP Conference Statement, adopted in Detroit on June 5, 1943 reads:

> The Associated Press, United Press and local editors should eliminate the designation of "Negro" in reporting crime news.

This committee feels that the fact that the Negroes in Detroit, who constitute less than 10 percent of the population, commit more than 71 percent of the major crimes[35] is one the public should know, that this circumstance may receive the public attention and constructive social measures it deserves.

Perhaps most significant in precipitating the racial tension existing in Detroit is the positive exhortation by many so-called responsible Negro leaders to be "militant" in the struggle for racial equality. A. Philip Randolph's statement appearing in the January 2, 1943, issue of the *Detroit Tribune* charging that:

> Justice is never granted, it is exacted. It is written in the stars that the darker races will never be free until they make themselves free. This is the task of the coming year.

clearly constitutes an appeal to extract "justice" by violence.

Such appeals unfortunately have been commonplace in the Negro newspapers. Can it be doubted that they played an important part in exciting the Negro people to the violence which resulted in Detroit on June 21?

Some self-designated responsible Negro leaders must share with the colored newspapers responsibility for the unfortunate attitude of certain Negro elements. Some of these leaders have themselves demonstrated an anti-social and factional outlook, which, if carried to their followers would account for the militantly rebellious attitude of those elements.[36]

The committee believes that positive action should be taken by both Negro and white leaders, and especially by the press, to avoid publication of those statements calculated to inflame and excite racial animosity, anti-social complexes, and disregard of legal process. The committee further concludes that both white and Negro leaders have refused responsibility in directing their respective followers toward a peaceful and lawful approach to this social problem. When these leaders teach their people that government is established for the good of all; that law enforcement agencies exist to punish all law violators; that the individual is subject to lawful authority; that those vested by democratic processes with civil authority are entitled to the respectful cooperation of all the people; and that redress of wrongdoing is by established judicial procedure, these leaders can approach the race problem assured that their efforts will produce a solid foundation for the harmonious association of all races.

NOTES

1. Race clashes of a minor character, but significant of local conditions had occurred in Detroit for upwards of a year. *Life* magazine in its August 17, 1942, issue attempted to portray conditions as they existed at that time. Every incident prior to the outbreak of June 20, 1943, had been handled by the local police authorities.

2. Of the eleven arrested, one pleaded guilty to a charge of disorderly conduct, and ten were found guilty on the same charge by the Mt. Clemens, Michigan, Justice of the Peace. All were sentenced to sixty days in the County Jail.

3. Now held on $2,000 bond on a charge of aggravated assault. Complaint filed June 20, 1943; examination waived; Detroit Recorder's Court File No. A-35069. Charged with Fox in the same case on the

complaint of Gus Niarhos are Fred Neal, Frank Neal, Raymond
Thomas, H. D. (Handsome Harry) Minnifield.

4. Delivered by Detroit Police Department to Wayne County Probate Court, Juvenile Division.

5. Delivered by Detroit Police Department to Wayne County Probate Court, Juvenile Division.

6. Convicted on July 22, 1943, of breaking and entering the store
of Sam Liederman, 5767 Hastings in the night time of June 21; sentenced to Jackson Prison to from two to five years.

7. Delivered by Detroit Police Department to Wayne County Probate Court, Juvenile Division.

8. Delivered by Detroit Police Department to Wayne County
Probate Court, Juvenile Division, where complaint charging felonious
assault is pending.

9. As a result of this incident, Wilson was arrested, charged with
disturbing the peace. He was found guilty by Judge Scallan of the
Recorder's Court for the City of Detroit on July 21, 1943, and placed
on six months' probation.

10. Some witnesses claim that this mob of whites was attacking a
colored man in the bushes.

11. This is the first reported statement of the rumor. It was this
rumor, afterwards discussed in the report, that immediately precipitated the riot in the Negro area.

12. The report of the Fifth Precinct Inspector Arthur J. Heidt of
June 24, 1943, to Senior Inspector Jesse Meade, Detroit Police Department, discloses that police reinforcements were sent to E. Jefferson
and E. Grand Boulevard as early as 10:45 P.M. Additional aid was
sent at 11:20 P.M., and still further reinforcements were added at 12
midnight. Seven lieutenants, ten sergeants, and 166 patrolmen, in
addition to one inspector, all from outside the Fifth Precinct, were
dispatched to that intersection.

13. All traffic to Belle Isle was stopped by 11:20 P.M. when a complete barricade was established by the Fifth Precinct police.

14. Inspector Heidt's report to Inspector Jesse Meade, previously
referred to, states: "At about 2 A.M. all rioting and fighting in the
Fifth Precinct was under control and had ceased." As a result of this
disturbance, twenty-seven colored prisoners were arrested for fighting;
nineteen whites for fighting; one colored woman for carrying a concealed weapon. From 2 A.M. to 6 P.M. June 21, the Fifth Precinct
arrested 49 for carrying concealed weapons and 31 for disorderly
conduct.

15. These figures clearly disclose that the rioting at Belle Isle was ended by 2 A.M. This finding is further supported by the statements of witnesses who tell of leaving the vicinity at that time because "everything was over."

16. A crowd attending this dance has been estimated by various witnesses as from 500 to 1,000. The figure 700 is taken from a statement made by William Henry Girard, manager of the Forest Club Ballroom, who has approximated this number by referring to a record of the tickets sold at the dance.

17. This man has a police record. He was picked up in February of 1929 for simple larceny, discharged; on June 5, 1929, suspected of robbery not armed, discharged; on September 12, 1929, investigated for robbery not armed, discharged; February 5, 1939, convicted of breaking and entering a building place in the night time, sentenced to from one and one half to fifteen years, Ionia State Reformatory; on July 20, 1933, investigated for larceny, discharged; on July 3, 1934, arrested for disturbing the peace, discharged; on August 29, 1934, arrested for frequenting a gambling place, dismissed; on August 31, 1934, arrested for frequenting a gambling place, dismissed; on May 30, 1935, fined $25 or thirty days for simple larceny; August 15, 1937, fined $5 or ten days for frequenting a gambling place; September 24, 1937, investigated for robbery not armed, discharged; on November 12, 1939, investigated for malicious destruction of property, discharged; on May 14, 1941, convicted of carrying concealed weapons, sent to Jackson Prison from five months to five years. He has been found guilty of violating his parole once. As a result of his statement at the Forest Club Ballroom, here reported, he has been charged with inciting a riot. When arraigned before Judge John V. Brennan in the Recorder's Court on August 5, 1943, he pleaded not guilty. He is held on bond awaiting trial.

18. Sergeant Fuller is a Negro police officer who at one time worked in the Thirteenth Precinct. There is no suggestion that this police sergeant is in any way connected with this announcement.

19. Tipton has had considerable experience with microphones. His principal employment by the Forest Club was in connection with the operation of a sound truck which is driven through the colored district advertising the dances held at the Forest Club Ballroom. He also has done work on the microphones at the Forest Club Ballroom, and on some instances has made announcements over the microphone. The quoted version of the announcement varies in some respect from the versions given by other witnesses. The quoted version is that of Joe

Wheeler Jamar, an employee of the Forest Club Ballroom, who was standing only a few feet from Tipton at the time. Other versions attribute to Tipton the statement: "Go home and get your guns."

20. The expression employed by some witnesses in describing this appropriation of automobiles is "snatched."

21. At this stage of the riot the violence was limited to the indiscriminate breaking of white-owned automobiles and business places. Witnesses are positive in their statements that there were no whites in this group. This mob left untouched many Negro-owned business places while completely destroying adjacent white-owned establishments. After the rioting, local papers carried pictures of such instances, showing the marking, "colored" on the Negro-owned undamaged premises.

22. Particular attention is directed to the fact that the first homicide in any way connected with the riot was the accidental death of John Bogan, white, who was run over by a cab at 2:20 A.M., June 21, on Brush Street between Willis and Canfield. Of the thirty-four homicides resulting from the riot, nine were white and twenty-five colored. The Police Department has classified them as follows: accidental two: one white, one colored; justifiable eighteen: no white, eighteen colored; murders ten: three colored, seven white; manslaughter one: no colored, one white; unclassified three: three colored, no white.

23. Other measures taken by the police to prevent the spread of rioting included instructions by Senior Inspector Edward Morgan of the Detroit Police Department at 10:30 A.M., June 21, to divert all northbound traffic at Vernor and Brush and all southbound traffic at Milwaukee and John R [sic] to prevent whites from entering the colored area. However, long prior to this, police officers stationed in the area had rerouted whites approaching the district and had exercised authority to forbid whites from going into that district. The [Detroit Street Railway] likewise, as early as 1:30 A.M., June 21, took measures to forestall riotous actions. At that hour, operation of the Oakland street car line was discontinued. Shortly thereafter the Charlevoix street car was rerouted so as to discontinue operation from Mack and McDougall to Cass and Stimson. Thereafter, changes were made in the Crosstown, Harper, and Baker street car lines, and John R [sic] bus.

24. In his report to the Common Council of June 28, 1943 Police Commissioner John H. Witherspoon stated: "From 12 o'clock noon to 6 P.M., the riot during this period was confined to smaller groups of from 25 to 100 which consisted of severe beatings by groups of

whites of one or two negroes and groups of negroes beating a few white residents. The rioting was still violent with store lootings, shootings, auto upsets, and resistance to officers continuing. A steady stream of wounded were admitted to Receiving Hospital. Since the beginning of the riot 257 store lootings were reported to the Canfield Precinct alone; eighteen cars owned by Negroes were upset on Woodward." The property damage reports (looting, malicious destruction of property) disclose the entire absence of looting by whites, and the arrest schedules and prosecution charts reveal that white rioting took the form principally of assaults upon the persons of Negroes, rather than the destruction of their property.

25. The actual decrease in number of police officers, notwithstanding the increase in population in Detroit of more than half a million since 1931, forcefully explains the tremendous problem confronted by the Department in this riot. [This] in itself does not disclose the true picture, because the Detroit Police Department is relied upon by suburban communities for some services; moreover, the Detroit police must handle the traffic coming from suburban communities, including Windsor, Hamtramck, Highland Park, and the out county districts. The newspapers have reported that in a disturbance in Harlem, New York City, on August 1, 1943, 6,000 police officers were rushed into the affected area, an impressive contrast with the personnel available to the Detroit Police Department in the disturbance of June 20 and 21. Notwithstanding the inadequate personnel, it was pointed out by General Henry S. Aurand, Commanding General, 6th Service Command, in charge of the troops sent here the night of June 21, that the Detroit police had the situation under control at the time the troops arrived.

26. An excellent illustration of this is found in two separate incidents both involving deliberate, premeditated crimes, one murder and the other arson. The murder of Moses Kiska, Negro, at 6:30, June 21, at Mack and Chene, by five white youths now awaiting trial in the Recorder's Court for the City of Detroit on a charge of first degree murder, was perpetrated without any instigation, other than the malignancy of these youths. The arson committed by eleven Negroes at the Federal Housing Project, 12169 S. Bassett in the extreme westerly part of the city was committed because: "We knew a riot was going on, and we just decided to set fire to this building."

27. The Negro newspaper contention that police officers indiscriminately machine-gunned a building at Vernor and John R [sic] arises out of this incident.

28. See Appendix A.

29. It is not intended that this report be a comprehensive study of the background of the racial problem in Detroit. The committee believes, however, that such a study should be made by the proper social agencies so that there can be a frank, straight-forward approach to this problem.

30. Reference is made to note 2, describing numerous incidents occurring on the Detroit Street Railway System since October, 1942, and to numerous incidents of resistance to lawful arrest, reported by Inspector Kennedy Lawrence of the Detroit Police Department Vice Squad. The June 17, 1943, issue of the *Detroit News* reported the following:

> In a threatening crowd of more than 100 persons, two policemen were injured today by four women. They were arrested near Hastings and Adelaide Streets. Walter Layman and David Harris, both of the Vice Squad, were treated at Harper Hospital. Harris was bitten on the arm, and Layman struck on the head with a brick. After Layman was injured, he fired his revolver and reserves from Canfield Station came to his aid.

The June 19, 1943, issue of the *Michigan Chronicle* reported an incident typical of the many recently encountered by members of the Police Department in effecting arrests:

> Charged with resisting arrest, Coltus Dunlop, 35, 710 Frederick Street, was held for trial Tuesday after an altercation with officers at Warren and Hastings, in which a large group threatened to take Dunlop from the police.

That this attitude among some elements persists is disclosed by events occurring on July 31, and August 1 and 2, 1943. At 1:25 A.M., July 31, 1943, Frank Hutchinson, white, was attacked and robbed by four colored men at St. Antoine and Hastings. One of the Negroes put a large knife to his throat as the others went through his pockets. On the same day, William Appleton, white, was assaulted by three Negroes, who struck him at W. Warren and McGraw Avenues, at 2:45 in the morning. One of the Negroes had a club. No effort was made to rob the man. At 3:30 in the morning of July 31, 1943, Edward Felske was brought to Receiving Hospital for treatment of lacerations of the forehead and nose suffered on Elizabeth Street between Fourth and Fifth Streets, when he was assaulted by three Negro men who struck him across the face with a club and took $8 from his trouser pocket.

On August 1 at 10:45 P.M., William T. Craft, white, operating a DSR bus on East Grand Boulevard, was struck in the back with a piece of concrete thrown by a Negro who had left the bus. This man was accompanied by three other Negroes. Shortly thereafter Craft fainted and was taken to Receiving Hospital where a diagnosis of possible fracture of the spine was made. There was no attempt to rob Craft.

On August 2, Charles Block, white, a conductor on a DSR streetcar, was stabbed in the back shortly before 8 A.M. by a Negro, who, when requested by the conductor to leave the exit clear, stated he wasn't: "Taking orders from any white ———."

31. See Appendix B.

32. The March on Washington Movement consists of a national body of local units throughout the country whose objectives as stated in Article IV of their constitution are:

> To awaken, teach, organize, mobilize, direct, and lead the Negro masses to struggle and fight for their own liberation, from racial discrimination, segregation, and Jim-Crowism, and achievement of complete recognition and enjoyment of Democratic citizenship, rights, freedom, justice, and equality, and to cooperate and colloborate with progressive movements, social, economic, political, and religious; to help build a free world for free men without regard to race, color, religion, or national origin.

The head of this organization is Dr. A. Philip Randolph, President of the Brotherhood of Sleeping Car Porters.

33. Frequently seen throughout colored papers are attacks on the policy prevailing in the Red Cross Blood Donor Stations, under which Negro plasma is separated from the white. The NAACP at their convention held in Detroit on June 5 distributed a pamphlet calling attention to its program, in which it is stated:

> that the American Red Cross should withdraw its insulting and unscientific rule, segregating the blood of Negro donors to blood plasma banks, from that of white donors.

34. Typical is the story reported in the *Michigan Chronicle* on July 17, 1943, of the burning of a building at 1971 Garfield Avenue. The article in part reads:

> Although police charged the fire was the result of defective wiring, Mrs. Ida D. Isaacs, founder and president of The Workers for Prosperity, is firmly convinced that the fire which did $2,000 worth of damage to the organization's home at 1971 E. Garfield was the work of white hoodlums.

35. These figures are taken from the permanent record maintained by the Bureau of Statistics, Detroit Police Department. The records disclose that of the murders and non-negligent homicides, rapes, robberies, aggravated assaults, burglaries, breaking and enterings, and concealed weapon cases prosecuted in Detroit in 1942, 71 percent were perpetrated by Negroes. These statistics further show that there has been a persistent increase in the percentage of crimes committed by Negroes from the years 1940 to 1942 inclusive. Other crimes predominantly Negro-committed are: violation of Narcotic Drug Laws, 88 percent; gambling, 65 percent; violation of liquor laws, 62 percent. Does this substantiate the boast of the local branch of the NAACP that for 33 years it has consistently advanced the best interests of the colored people?

36. Dr. James McClendon, President of the local branch of the NAACP, in August of 1942, threatened a Negro police officer, Joel Johnson, with proceedings before the Police Trial Board unless the police officer apologized to certain members of the NAACP for his action in arresting a Negro. While the arrested Negro was found not guilty of the charge of drunkenness by Recorder's Court Judge Joseph A. Gillis, the circumstances of the arrest disclose that Patrolman Johnson was acting within the boundaries of his police authority and duty in arresting the defendant, and that the threatened action by the NAACP President was entirely unjustified. The police officer did not apologize, nor did Dr. McClendon make application with the Police Trial Board for a hearing.

A Proclamation by the President of the United States

"WHEREAS, the Government of the State of Michigan has represented that domestic violence exists in said State, which the authorities of said State are unable to suppress; and

"WHEREAS, it is provided in the Constitution of the United States that the United States shall protect each State in this Union, on application of the legislature, or of the executive when the legislature can not be convened against domestic violence; and

"WHEREAS, by the law of the United States in pursuance of the above, it is provided that in all cases of insurrection in any State or of obstruction of the laws thereof, it shall be lawful for the President of the United States on application of the legislature of such State or of the executive when the legislature can not be convened, to call forth the militia of any other state or states or to employ such part of the land and naval forces of the United States as shall be judged necessary for the purpose of suppressing such insurrection and causing the laws to be duly executed; and

"WHEREAS, the legislature of the State of Michigan is not now in session and cannot be convened in time to meet the present emergency, and the executive of said State under Section 4 of Article 4 of the Constitution of the United States and the laws passed in pursuance thereof, has made application to me in the premises for such part of the military forces of the United States as may be necessary and adequate to protect the State of Michigan and the citizens thereof against domestic violence and to enforce the due execution of the laws; and

"WHEREAS, it is required that whenever it may be necessary, in the judgement of the President, to use the military forces of the United States for the purpose aforesaid, he shall forthwith by proclamation command such insurgents to disperse and retire peaceably to their respective homes within a limited time;

"NOW, THEREFORE, I, FRANKLIN D. ROOSEVELT, President of the United States, do hereby make proclamation, and I do hereby command all persons engaged in said unlawful and insurrectionary proceedings to disperse and retire peaceably to their respective abodes immediately and hereafter abandon said combinations and submit themselves to the laws and constituted authorities of said State; and

"I invoke the aid and cooperation of all good citizens thereof to uphold the laws and preserve the public peace.

"IN WITNESS WHEREOF, I have herewith set my hand and caused the seal of the United States to be affixed.

"Done at the City of Washington the 21st day of June, in the year of our Lord Nineteen Hundred and Forty Three, and of the independence of the United States the one hundred sixty seventh."

FRANKLIN D. ROOSEVELT,
President of the United States.

WARREN H. BROWN

A Negro Looks at the
Negro Press

My race in the United States can be divided into two groups: Negroes and sensation-mongering Negro leaders. So much is heard from some of the latter that the former are often ignored and more often misunderstood. That is bad for the Negro. It is bad for the white. It creates the impression that the Negro who speaks loudest and most is representative of most Negroes. That, happily for all of us, is not the case.

I was born in the South and raised in the Midwest. I taught in a Southern Negro college. I have now lived for twenty years in various Northern Negro communities. During that time I have come to know the Northern Negro, his problems, and his leaders.

The Negro that I know, North and South, is not what his agitator-leaders say that he is and want him to be. Despite the desperate times that he has lately been through and the all-out effort from certain quarters to turn his bad times to disruptive account, he has not been swept off his American balance. That is fortunate for America. Because it is fortunate for America, it is fortunate for the Negro. Despite his sometimes snail's pace progress, the Negro knows that in America—for the long pull—he can't lose.

But the drive to embitter and unbalance him, which began during the depression under Communist auspices, has gained momentum with American entrance into the war. Nowhere is that drive being so aggressively promoted as in the incendiary columns of the Negro press.

Most Negro newspapers are what they condemn the most prejudiced whites for being. They are Negro first and American second. They foster segregation by aiming to make all Negroes race-conscious before they are America-conscious. They feed and prosper by sensationally playing up the Negro at his worst. When they publish news of the white community, it is generally an account of the white man at his worst. Every incident that can be used to breed ill-will between the races is seized upon. If the incident is important, they play it up sensationally. If it is trivial, they inflate it until it seems important. In season and out, they present a distorted, dishonest picture of America —and of the progress, place, and opportunity of the Negro in it. Of course, there are some notable exceptions: Negro newspapers that are edited with exceptional skill and high ethical standards.

When a Negro runs seriously afoul of the law, the Negro press seldom stops to ask the facts. It goes to town in flaming headlines to turn the matter to race-rousing account.

Recently, in New York City, a demented Negro attempting to escape arrest was shot by a white policeman. *The People's Voice*—a Harlem newspaper—did not wait for an official investigation. It chose to ignore the fact that, under the Police Commissioner and courts of New York, a fair trial can be assured. Instead, this paper broke out its blackest type for a "police brutality" story. Behind the story was the editor of the paper, Adam Clayton Powell, Jr., a Baptist minister and New York City Councilman. The Rev. Mr. Powell called for "mass action." The kind of language he used made it plain that what he was asking for was mob action. He went further than that and—in a Negro parody of the Ku Klux Klan—cried out for the Negroes of Harlem to take the law in their own hands.

"We Won't Take It Any Longer," his editorial declared. "We refuse to be law-abiding citizens if there are to be special laws for Negro people.

"This is the final warning. If the officials of New York don't make the laws the same for all people, they must accept full blame for any consequences."

In August three Negro soldiers on guard duty near a Louisiana town were accused of making improper advances to a white girl. They allegedly confessed. The case went to court. A jury found the soldiers guilty. Southern juries in such cases would hardly be called unprejudiced. But statements made by the accused pointed out their own disregard for military regulations and serious indiscretion to the well-established Southern sex taboo. . . .

But the Negro press, from coast to coast, turned loose a typographical flood that left out nothing which might embitter and arouse the nation's Negroes.

"Southern Justice—Soldiers Found Guilty by White Jury," was the headline in the Los Angeles *Sentinel.*

"Torture Three Soldiers in Louisiana Scottsboro Case," ran the streamers in the Indianapolis *Recorder.*

"I Wanted to Serve My Country—They Wouldn't Let Me," was the played-up quote in the Houston, Texas, *Informer.*

"Parents Worry as Letters Tell of Possible Klan-Mob Violence," from the *Ohio State News.*

"Men Face All-White Jury in Frame-Up Case," from the San Antonio *Register.*

Recently reports were received in the United States of several incidents involving Negro troops in England. Some of the Negro weeklies without firsthand information twisted reports out of all proportions.

Just how the job was done can be gathered from the headlines in the *Amsterdam Star News* (New York City):

> U.S. Forces Britain to Jim Crow Troops.
> Churchill Puts Issue in Lap of Uncle Sam.
> Angry Parliament in Uproar over Vicious Treatment of Black Soldiers.
> Pacific Called "White Man's War."

It is true that the Negro does not yet, everywhere in the United States, receive adequate justice. It is true that American prejudices have been called forth among white troops in England. But the kind of justice for which the Negro strives is undoubtedly delayed by the Negro press. Its inflammatory attempts to indicate that the Negro never gets fair treatment, and its efforts—whether the Negro is right or wrong—to use his misfortunes, not to get justice but to arouse more violent racism, make the going more difficult for that great majority of white and black who are working for a more even-handed treatment of the Negro—not as a Negro, but as an American.

On no issue do the Negro papers get more quickly inflamed than the publication in white papers of Negro crime stories. Here, again, what the Negro press preaches it does not practice. Negro papers reek with stories of Negro violence and crime. These stories are not tucked away in the back pages. They are featured on the front pages.

> Bloody Wednesday—As Blazing Gunplay Drops Three on Avenue.
>
> Girl Roomer Kills Landlady.
>
> Stabbed 40 Times in Brooklyn Murder.
>
> Three-Cornered Love is Bad Medicine, She Finds, as Bullet Spoils Plan.
>
> Dope Ring Leader Dies in East Side Brawl: Slayer Shoots "Fat" in Heart after Knock-Down Stomping.
>
> Stabbing Victim Dies on Curb; Life Blood Oozes into Gutter as Girl-Slayer Flees.
>
> Five Wounded as Man Blasts Crowded Cafe in Old West Revival.

These are all Negro stories. They are not isolated headlines, but are a fair cross-section of "feature" news in numerous Negro papers. For giving a dishonest, discreditable picture of American Negro life, they are worse than the worst white newspaper. The average Negro newspaper portrays Negro life in burlesque.

No white community would any longer tolerate newspapers so blatantly sensational and hate-making. I do not believe that the Negro community can afford to continue to tolerate them. They give the lie to all that sane leaders of the race claim the Negro to be. They are a threat to what every honest, intelligent Negro wants to be.

In the larger centers of population, Negroes of high intelligence and skill are available to establish and publish newspapers that will be worthier representatives of the real mind and character of the American Negro. There is no greater opportunity before the Negro community than to undertake to establish such a press. Until it is established, every Negro—with any pride of race and any belief that his well-being and America's are inseparable—has a moral obligation, by protest and pressure, to demand less hate and sensationalism, more fairness and honesty in his press.

No one who has travelled, as I have recently, through the Negro communities in the great industrial centers of the North can fail to note with alarm the growing race tensions. Undoubtedly much of this tension is due to white prejudice against widening Negro employment. But the race clashes which in some places have already occurred, and the threats that remain in other places, are by no means wholly due to white prejudice. They are due also to an irresponsible Negro leadership which—living by agitation—aims to capitalize on the war.

The Negro newspapers are an effective media because they completely cover the Negro population. Relatively few whites read the Negro newspapers and the net result is a swelling up of emotional stress on the part of their audience. I am not advocating a muzzling of the Negro press, but it should not be encouraged to run at a venomous, hate-making pace.

(Note: This article is published under the auspices of the Council for Democracy. Mr. Brown is Director of Negro Relations for that organization.)

December 19, 1942
The Saturday Review

9.

ALFRED McCLUNG LEE and
NORMAN D. HUMPHREY

Race Riot (Detroit, 1943)

Thursday, June 24, 1943

On the third day after Bloody Monday, Governor Kelly decided to
ease curfew restrictions. He made midnight the street curfew; permitted alcoholic beverages to be sold between 7 A.M. and 10 P.M.;
allowed later closing hours for places of amusement; and reopened
Belle Isle to recreation seekers. He cancelled in addition all emergency
regulations as they affected the adjoining Counties of Oakland and
Macomb.

Several inquiries were started, and Congressman Dies threatened to
start one of his own. The Governor appointed a fact-finding committee of public officials and called for an early report from them. And
Dr. Lowell S. Selling, head of the Recorder's Court Psychiatric Clinic
of Detroit, assisted by his entire staff of twenty-three psychiatrists,

SOURCE: From Alfred McClung Lee and Norman D. Humphrey, *Race
Riot (Detroit, 1943)* (New York: Octagon Books, 1968), pp. 50-78. Reprinted with the permission of the copyright owners, Alfred McClung Lee
and Mrs. George Weible.

clinical assistants, and clerks, began an inquiry into the mental condition of 1,000 rioters. Announcing at the outset the kinds of "psychopathic failings" he expected to uncover, Dr. Selling said that "with 30 to 35 minutes to a person" he hoped to have a picture of the situation in "a few days at most." In addition to those two lines of inquiry, the Honorable Martin Dies of Texas, a Congressman from a district in which Negroes have traditionally "failed to qualify" to vote and the Chairman of the House Committee on Un-American Activities, threatened to descend upon Detroit and conduct a hearing into the causes of the race riots. As usual, Dies had an *a priori* basis for his investigations: He had the idea that the riots were fomented by Japanese-Americans who had been legally released from internment camps on the west coast after having been certified to the satisfaction of the U. S. Army as safely "pro-American." With the exception of the Rev. Gerald L. K. Smith and a few of his kind, Detroit newspapers and civic leaders joined in asking Dies to stay away from Detroit. They did not want a bad situation further confused with prejudiced and discredited investigating methods. . . .

The first meeting to form a permanent inter-racial citizens' body took place in the evening, at the Redeemer Presbyterian Church, in answer to a call by Dr. Benjamin J. Bush, President of the Detroit Council of Churches. This was later to be named the Greater Detroit Inter-Racial Fellowship, and was to embrace all possible race, religious, labor, nationality, and other groups. Plans for the creation of this body had been in the making ever since the Sojourner Truth Homes race riots, but it was not until the week before Bloody Monday that the June 24 meeting had been scheduled.

At this meeting, the body unanimously adopted the first seven of R. J. Thomas's eight points. The newly-formed organization refused to accept Thomas's eighth point, that an inter-racial committee be appointed by the Mayor, because—as someone at the meeting asserted—an official Mayor's committee would be hamstrung in its work by all kinds of political pressures and fears.

The Nazi-controlled Vichy radio hailed the Detroit riots as a "revolt" that would spread to other cities, a reflection of "the moral and social crisis in the United States." It piously added, "Today, on the morrow of the bloody incidents of Detroit, the French people, imbued with a sense of social justice, realize the dangers for European civilization inherent in the American aims of world domination." . . . Maximum misdemeanor penalties—90 days in the Detroit House of Correction—were meted out to several groups of rioters.

Friday, June 25, 1943

The Governor's fact-finding committee issued its first report. After several conferences with officers of law enforcing agencies, the committee concluded that sufficient evidence did not exist to indicate that the riots had resulted from organized instigation. It therefore arrived at the following startling *non-sequitur:* that the situation did not warrant a special grand jury. The grand jury, at any rate, was not ordered. . . .

Mayor Jeffries appointed a twelve-member inter-racial committee to study the race situation. As chairman, he appointed William J. Norton, Executive Vice-President of the Children's Fund of Michigan, and the members were five other whites and six Negroes. . . .

At the request of the Governor, Dr. C. F. Ramsey, Director of the State Department of Social Welfare, began what the newspapers called a "sociological inquiry" into the background of several hundred police prisoners picked up in the race riots. . . .

The Detroit Council of Churches, through its President, the Rev. Dr. Benjamin J. Bush, called upon the people of Detroit to observe the following Sunday as a day of humility and penitence. . . .

Funeral services were held for some of the riot victims. . . . Officials tried once more to quiet rumors that as many as 400 persons had died in the race clashes, but the unsubstantiated rumor persisted.

Saturday, June 26, 1943

Detroit remained "on probation" over the weekend. The Governor decided not to relax further the restrictions promulgated by him six days before. . . . The Inter-Racial Citizens' Committee, dating from the time of the Sojourner Truth race riots early in 1942 and headed by Pastor Hill, asked Mayor Jeffries to discourage the announced plan of Congressman Dies to come to Detroit for an inquiry. . . . Mayor Jeffries asked Police Commissioner Witherspoon to send a message over the police teletype to the effect that "the riot is over and the Police Department is to return to normal."

Sunday, June 27, 1943

The city was abnormally quiet that Sunday. Some 500 white and 200 Negro families visited Belle Isle where a week before estimates had placed the total at 100,000, of whom possibly 85 percent were colored. . . . Governor Kelly made this statement on the question of troop removal: "I must know that Detroit will be assured of adequate manpower at any further outbreak of racial trouble before I will ask for the troops withdrawal." . . . Ministers offered prayers for peace and harmony in hundreds of Detroit's churches. . . . Paradise Valley merchants sorted over materials police had recovered from looters.

Monday, June 28, 1943

Just short of one week after his declaration of a state of emergency, Governor Kelly lifted virtually all restrictions on civilians. Bottled liquor, however, was not to be sold. Federal troops were to remain for at least another week, and during this time they were to give training to the relatively green Michigan State Troops which had been organized to replace the National Guard units taken into the U. S. Army.

The Mayor's Inter-Racial Committee convened and agreed to center its efforts on the reduction of race frictions rather than to attempt to fix the blame for the riots.

The daily newspapers carried stories based upon a "Statement Unanimously Adopted by the Executive Board, Detroit Chapter, National Lawyers' Guild on the Recent Disorders in Detroit." This candid analysis of the situation concluded that the "charges of mismanagement laid at the door of the police commissioner plainly require investigation." It also called for the creation of "a commission on the development of inter-racial accord in Detroit to consist of three white and three Negro members," the endowment of "such a commission with authority to compel testimony by subpoena and to administer oaths," and the appropriation initially of a sum of $100,000 to subsidize its efforts.

Police Commissioner John H. Witherspoon himself made a report to City Council, a kind of "white paper," in which he not only vindicated the police, their policies, and their activities in connection with the riot, but praised the police as having shown "rare courage and efficiency" in handling the matter. The Commissioner pointed out that early violent rioting occurred in the Negro sections of the city's east side and that white "retaliatory action" had then speedily followed. He defended the so-called "kid gloves" policy enjoined by the Mayor upon the Police Department. As the Commissioner put it,

> We are at war—this was not believed to be a proper time, with a mailed-fist policy, to attempt to solve a racial conflict and a basic antagonism which has been growing and festering for years.

Such a policy could well have precipitated a race riot at a much earlier date and one of much more serious proportions. The fact remains that this department did not precipitate the riot.

Some have advocated a "shoot-to-kill" policy. Such a procedure might have terminated the riot at an earlier hour, but I am sure that it would have been with a far greater loss of life. . . .

If a "shoot-to-kill" policy was right, my judgment was wrong.

The alternatives were thus set in the Commissioner's mind between the alleged "kid gloves" policy his department was said to have followed and a "shoot-to-kill" policy. Many would see at least one other course.

City Councilman George C. Edwards tried to bring the discussions of his colleagues down to earth and into a somewhat more constructive and less apologetic vein by offering a practical six-point program. He proposed: (1) that the Governor call a twenty-three-man county grand jury, charged especially with inquiry into the fifteen unsolved murders; (2) that City Council help Mayor Jeffries keep the Dies Un-American Committee out of town; (3) that the possibility of subversive activities be investigated thoroughly; (4) that the Federal troops be kept as long as possible and arrangements made "for their speedy mobilization if needed again"; (5) that the Police Commissioner "appoint 200 Negro policemen for duty in Negro areas, if this is possible under the competitive examinations for policemen"; and (6) that the City Council set up a committee to work with the Mayor's Committee on Inter-Racial Relations, "with emphasis on added recreational and housing facilities for Negroes."

Tuesday, June 29, 1943

The City Council rejected nearly all of Councilman Edward's program. Council members joined with Police Commissioner Witherspoon in opposing the grand jury proposal. The Commissioner pointed out that all investigating agencies had searched the facts and that "none has one shred of proof now that the riot was planned or inspired." To this, he added these other protestations:

Possibly at some later date such evidence will develop and a grand jury could be called. . . . I have no objection to a grand jury. It would be an easy out for me. Don't get the impression I'm afraid of a grand jury. But it would be an unfair position to put any judge in.

This strange logic did not convince Councilman Edwards. To simplify matters, he withdrew all of his suggestions except the ones that a grand jury be called and that City Council appoint a committee on race relations. By a formal vote, City Council rejected the proposal for a twenty-three-man grand jury and approved that for a City Council committee. As a result, Council President John Lodge appointed a five-man committee charged with the responsibility for planning and financing new housing, recreation facilities, and other improvements to relieve pressure in the overcrowded sections of the city. . . .

The Detroit Branch of the National Association for the Advancement of Colored People sent a list of recommendations to Mayor Jeffries. They urged: (1) a grand jury investigation of the Police Department [an eventuality Commissioner Witherspoon apparently feared]; (2) extension of recreational facilities; (3) the hiring of more Negro school teachers; (4) removal of racial restrictions on all public housing units; (5) opening of summer camps to the children of all races.

Wednesday, June 30, 1943

Mayor Jeffries issued his "white paper," as the newspapers called it, to City Council on Wednesday, June 30. He explained in detail why it took so long for him to obtain the aid of State and Federal troops and admitted that much of the responsibility for bloodshed rested upon the long hours of delay in making final arrangements to get military aid. Here are some high points from the Mayor's statement:

It took us 24 hours to establish the peace after rioting broke out on the Belle Isle bridge the night of June 20. It took us 12 hours to get the Federal troops on the scene. . . .

It will not take us that long next time, and . . . you have my guarantee on that. . . .

We knew there was a full battalion of military police . . . stationed at Rouge Park. It was our understanding that it was ready to move instantly upon orders. . . .

That was our understanding because there had been many, many discussions over at least a period of a year on how to

get the regular Army troops here in any emergency situation.
. . .

But now you know that despite all of these discussions,
despite Col. Krech's practice tests with the troops, despite his
precautions, that the formula for getting the Army troops
here quickly broke down for one reason and for one reason
alone. We . . . could not get the necessary Army order to
pry the troops loose when we wanted it.

Mayor Jeffries covered his position on a crucial point when he said he
objected to outright martial law because "civil functions would be
completely abrogated and the Army commander in charge would rule
the area exclusively." He warmly praised the Police Department, saying that its "role in the riot needs no defense. On the whole it was
splendid and at times magnificent." He was "rapidly losing . . . patience with those Negro leaders who insisted that their people do not
and will not trust policemen and the Police Department. After what
happened I am certan that some of these leaders are more vocal in
their caustic criticism of the Police Department than they are in educating their own people to their responsibilities as citizens."

The Mayor's "was a fine statement," observed Councilman Comstock, "but it won't settle the racial question in Detroit. Nothing will
settle that. The racial conflict has been going on in this country since
our ancestors made the first mistake of bringing the Negroes to this
country." The Councilman bespoke the trend of sentiment among a
sizable segment of Detroit's white citizenry. Councilman Edwards,
with his insistence upon curative measures, represented another—
probably larger—segment.

Mayor Jeffries also assured the East Side Merchants Association
that they should re-open the rest of their stores, and that they could
expect "not only protection, but better police protection than you
have ever had." The association is composed of the white owners of
stores in the eastside Negro area. . . . The renewed disquietude of the
merchants had arisen from an episode in which four unidentified
hoodlums raced through the streets of northwest Detroit in a red
sedan hurling bricks through the windows of cars and houses.

Thursday, July 1, 1943

Editorial commendation for Mayor Jeffries' "white paper" was
somewhat offset by a letter of protest on it sent to the Mayor and the
newspapers by James J. McClendon, M.D., President of the Detroit

Chapter, National Association for the Advancement of Colored People.

> We do not condone the acts of hoodlums of our race [Dr. McClendon stated], any more than you condone those who overturned cars ... on Woodward avenue. ...
>
> It takes no crystal gazer to add the number of Negroes slain by the police or compare the lack of such "shoot to kill" policy on Woodward avenue. ...
>
> Killings, vile name-calling, wanton, unnecessary arrests of colored citizens, inspired no regard for a Police Department which spoke of some of our citizens as "niggers." ...
>
> In 1941, you appointed a Mayor's Committee after the Northwestern High School Riot. The committee . . . studied the conflict situation. Its recommendations were laid upon your desk where they lie, today, unheeded. ...
>
> Today we have a new committee. Its report can be written now. The question is whether you will do anything about it. ...

Patrolman Lawrence A. Adams, shot in the race rioting on June 21, died in Harper Hospital. ...

Police Commissioner Witherspoon told the Mayor's Bi-Racial Committee that new Negro policemen could be added to the force only through the usual competitive civil service examinations. He added that he would like to augment the Negro detail if it were possible. He tried to leave no doubt that he intended to punish any policeman found guilty of reviling Negroes, but he insisted that some of the names Negroes reserved for policemen were even nastier than those policemen were alleged to employ on Negroes.

The Mayor's Bi-Racial Committee also gave consideration to the housing problem and heard Brigadier General Thomas Colladay's defense of the conduct of the Michigan State Troops. "It was our first big mobilization," he pointed out. "Mobilization of volunteers takes more time than for soldiers." ...

With the tentative approval of Commissioner Witherspoon, Inspector John O. Whitman, head of the City Homicide Squad, sought through County Prosecutor Dowling and the Wayne County Board of Auditors to post rewards of $50 for information which would lead to the solution of thirteen unsolved riot deaths. . . . The Rev. Gerald L.

K. Smith, whom the late Huey Long praised as "a better rabble-rouser" than he was, made this disclaimer:

> The thought that I had anything to do with the Detroit race riot is almost too ridiculous to entertain, and the accusation is almost too extreme to answer.

Friday, July 2, 1943

The Rev. Horace White, Negro member of the Detroit Housing Commission, called for the inclusion of 1,000 new dwelling units in the Negro slum districts as a part of a project to erect 3,000 new dwellings with funds allocated to the National Housing Agency. The Commission adopted the proposal and ordered that it be carried out at sites in the Negro districts.

Sunday, July 4, 1943

Lieutenant Governor Eugene C. Keyes stated that the main reason State Troops had not assisted earlier in the race riots on June 21 was that they were not *properly* requested. . . . The County Board of Auditors was asked by Prosecutor Dowling to post rewards of $100 (rather than $50) for information leading to the conviction of persons guilty of each of thirteen unsolved riot deaths.

Monday, July 5, 1943

Governor Kelly announced that Federal troops would remain in Wayne County until at least August 2. This would have the advantage of providing a longer period in which to continue the training and organization of the Michigan State Troops. Federal troops, meanwhile, ceased their street patrols. On Monday evening, after marching in regimental formation up Woodward Avenue, Federal and State troops massed in solid phalanx in front of a reviewing stand before the Detroit Institute of Arts and heard warm words of praise for their efforts from Major General Henry S. Aurand, in command of the Federal soldiers.

Wednesday, July 7, 1943

In his first formal statement on the Detroit race riots, Governor Kelly explained that it was not until 11 P.M. on June 21 (Bloody Monday) that he became aware that a signed proclamation by President Roosevelt was necessary for the use of the Federal troops.

Upon arrival at Detroit [the Governor stated]: I . . . went to the 6th Army Corps Command at Detroit to confer in regard to Federal assistance. . . .

This conference was brought to a sudden . . . conclusion when the commanding Federal officer . . . received word from his superior officer . . . that the Federal assistance could not be given unless . . . I would declare the necessity for . . . Federal martial law. . . .

I informed the Federal authorities that the situation at that time did not make it possible for me to declare the necessity of such drastic action. . . .

About 8:30 that evening I received word from the District Command Office . . . that they had found out that my request could be granted without the necessity of a declaration of Federal martial law. . . .

It was approximately 9:00 o'clock that night . . . when I did sign the formal request . . . and I was there informed . . . that that was all that was necessary. . . .

I proceeded on an hour-and-a-half tour of the city, returning to the Police Headquarters shortly before 11 o'clock.

Upon my return I was informed . . . for the first time that . . . the commanding officers of Detroit and Chicago did not possess the power to move troops without a presidential proclamation. . . .

I immediately placed that call to the President.

He [the President] informed me that the proclamation had not yet reached him, but was on the way, and that he . . . wanted to be sure that the Federal troops would move into the Detroit area, assisting the constituted authorities, and without a declaration of Federal martial law.

When the Army moved in they did a mighty fine job.

Donald Van Zile, Presiding Judge of the Recorder's Court, denied blanket re-trials to those convicted of riot participation shortly after the cessation of overt hostilities. Pastor White had requested the re-trials on the ground that in the "heat of the tragedy" the judges had become "frightened like the rest of us" and had lost their sense of legal equilibrium. "I wish to say," replied Judge Van Zile, "that at no time were any of the judges frightened, nor did they lose their equilibrium."

Friday, July 9, 1943

The city had gone back to something that was being called "normalcy," a term reminiscent of President Warren G. Harding and of a similar era after another and much larger war. . . . Advised by James R. Walsh, Assistant City Corporation Counsel, that the City of Detroit had no legal liability for damages suffered by its citizens during the race riots, the City Council set a hearing for the following Thursday (July 15) on a claim by a white Brush Street grocer for $9,000, the value of his entire stock looted or destroyed during the riots. . . . Governor Kelly expressed thanks to the Detroit social workers who had conducted investigative interviews among the arrest rioters.

Saturday, July 10, 1943

Of the more than 4,000 soldiers who had been sent in to quell the race riots, only 1,400 soldiers in two Military Police Battalions remained in the city. Detroit was again designated as "in bounds" for Fort Custer soldiers.

Monday, July 12, 1943

John S. Bugas, Special Agent in charge of the Detroit F.B.I. office, spoke before the Michigan Association of Chiefs of Police who were holding a war conference at Charlevoix. He asserted that the Detroit police did a "magnificent and heroic job" in the race riots.

Tuesday, July 13, 1943

A white rioter, George Miller, 31, a convicted counterfeiter and larcenist, was sentenced to 90 days in the Detroit House of Correction. Miller was identified from a news photograph that showed two Detroit policemen holding a Negro victim and Miller brazenly slapping the Negro. Detective John J. Richard recognized Miller in the photograph and arrested him in a saloon hangout. Patrolman Paul Gyslvic, one of the officers in the picture, said that Miller was not arrested on the spot because he and his fellow officer had their hands full taking care of the mauled and stabbed Negro. . . .

Pastor White, the Negro leader, released a report compiled by Sheridan A. Bruseaux, a Chicago private investigator, which ascribed the riots largely to inadequate housing and poor recreational facilities.

Thursday, July 15, 1943

Attorney General Francis Biddle sent a letter to President Roosevelt on July 15 that was published in full August 10 in the *American Labor News*, supplement for shop papers issued by the United Automobile Workers (C.I.O.). Although the paper did not indicate how it had come by this confidential document, New York's *PM* also printed it.

In this letter, the Attorney General summarized the results of conferences by his personal representative with Governor Kelly, Mayor Jeffries, Police Commissioner Witherspoon, and other officials, the observations of Monsignor Haas of the Federal Fair Employment Practice Committee, and "daily reports from the Federal Bureau of Investigation." The letter contains these particularly significant passages:

> All of those familiar with the situation agree on the causes of the riot; briefly they may be summarized as follows:
> There is no evidence of any Axis, or Fascist, or Ku Klux Klan incitement. In fact there is no evidence of any concerted action to bring about the riots. From the enclosed report to me from Mr. Rhetts, who represented me in Detroit, it is evident that the trouble started on Belle Isle, where there was a crowd on Sunday night, June 20th, of approximately 100,000 persons, of which 90 percent were colored. The prevailing hostility between sailors and Negroes inflamed the Detroit riot in its first stages when sailors from the Navy Arsenal near the end of the Belle Isle bridge joined in the fights. Rioting spread late in the evening to the colored district along Hastings Street, known as Paradise Valley, where the overcrowding is very bad. Many Negroes were shot as a result of the looting. . . .
> The causes of the riots are apparent. During the past three years the population of Detroit has increased by 485,000 people, many of whom are colored. There are no subways or elevated trains in Detroit so that the transportation situation is particularly difficult causing great overcrowding in the buses. The housing situation, particularly among the colored sections, is deplorable. The same is true of the recreation situation, which is greatly overburdened and overcrowded.
> The Detroit Police Department is, in spite of the increase in population, actually 280 men short of budget allotment.

Moreover, many of the present policemen are not well trained on account of the number of men who have been drafted and whose places had to be filled from the only available and often inadequate personnel. These conditions prevail generally throughout the country.

Much of the violence could have been prevented had the troops arrived sooner. It is believed that there was a misunderstanding between the local officials and the military as to what steps should be taken to arrange for the troops to come in.

It is extremely interesting that there was no disorder WITHIN PLANTS, where colored and white men worked side by side, on account of efficient union discipline.

I believe that the riots in Detroit do not represent an isolated case but are typical of what may occur in other cities throughout the country. The situation in Los Angeles is extremely tense; I am also concerned with the racial unrest in Washington, D. C., Chicago, Ill., and elsewhere. The hot season up to Labor Day, when crowds seek outdoor relief, is the period of greatest danger.

As a result of such findings, Biddle believed "that certain steps could be taken which would, to a certain extent, ameliorate similar conditions elsewhere." He therefore recommended these six steps:

1. That you suggest to the Secretary of War that he work out a simple manual in co-operation with the Department of Justice which could be used by all local officials and by corps commanders to expedite the procedure of sending in troops.

2. That you suggest to Mr. McNutt that immediate arrangements be made to defer members of the city police forces. [In this connection he quoted F.B.I. Chief J. Edgar Hoover to the point that failure to make such deferments would lead to "a repetition of internal disorders such as the Los Angeles 'zoot suit' cases and the Detroit race riots."] . . .

3. That careful consideration be given to limiting, and in some instances putting an end to, Negro migrations into communities which cannot absorb them, either on account of their physical limitations or cultural background. This needs immediate and careful consideration. When postwar

readjustments begin, and jobs are scarcer, the situation will become far more acute. Witness the dislocations in cities caused by the migrations shortly after the last world war. It would seem pretty clear that no more Negroes should move to Detroit. Yet I know of no controls being considered or exercised. You might wish to have the recommendations of Mr. McNutt as to what could and should be done.

4. As to the general situation, I suggest that you direct the organization of an inter-departmental committee . . . to exchange information and discuss policies. Responsibility so far as possible should be fixed in the Committee to co-ordinate information work in this field and deal with delegations who have been coming to Washington to see you. . . .

5. I think it would be advisable that a national committee be formed to make a study of the whole situation and do an extended educational and publicity job chiefly in the local communities. Obviously this is something that the Government cannot do nor do I think you should appoint such a committee. . . .

6. It has been suggested that you should go on the radio to discuss the whole problem. This, I think, would be unwise. However, you might consider discussing it the next time you talk about the overall domestic situation as one of the problems to be considered.

When the third Biddle recommendation was challenged as contrary to the Federal Constitution by Lester B. Granger, Executive Secretary, National Urban League, the Attorney General replied that he could not comment on his "strictly confidential" letter to the President, but he did express his views on Negro migration. He pointed to the difficulty cities were having in absorbing large numbers of war workers, whether Negro or white, and said:

It seems to me advisable, therefore, that responsible officials should give careful consideration to the extent of required facilities before taking any steps to fill the particular manpower requirements.

º   º   º

For a time after the issuance of the Bruseaux report on July 13, nothing of significance took place locally that bore on the causes of the riots or on steps to prevent their recurrence. The general feeling of the white citizenry seemed to be that the less said about the whole affair the better off everyone would be.

One ex-felon, Robert Morgan, a convicted white slaver, easily identifiable in several news photos . . . in the act of assaulting a Negro, was momentarily freed because police could find no complainant to appear against him. One of the victims of his depredations subsequently came to the fore and made a formal complaint.

The Negro population still frankly lacked confidence in the police. This feeling was augmented by what it regarded as unwarranted arrests and the ruthless search of private homes for riot loot without due process of law.

The Mayor's Bi-Racial Committee, save for the recommendation by a sub-committee for a grand jury, continued to "muddle through" in much the same well-intentioned fashion that it had begun its work. The problems of housing and recreation mentioned by so many investigators as basic factors in the riot outbreaks, were receiving only desultory consideration by the agencies charged with taking definite steps to solve such problems. Detroit had largely gotten back to its "business as usual" method of ignoring its social problems when several new events again focused attention upon "doing something about it."

* * *

Gerald L. K. Smith continued his agitation of racial intolerance with an article on "Race Riots!" in the July number of his organ, *The Cross and the Flag*, published late in July. He gives his ideas on how to handle Negroes, as follows:

> I know of no self-respecting person in the City of Detroit who is opposed to Negroes having every modern facility necessary to make them comfortable and to assist them in their desire to be progressive. BUT . . . Most white people will not agree to any of the following suggestions:
> 1. Inter-marriage of blacks and whites.
> 2. Mixture of blacks and whites in hotels.
> 3. Mixture of blacks and whites in restaurants.
> 4. Intimate relationships between blacks and whites in the school system.
> 5. Wholesale mixture of blacks and whites in residential sections.
> 6. Promiscuous mixture of blacks and whites in street cars

and on trains, especially where black men are permitted to sit down and crowd in close to white women and vice versa. I have every reason to believe black women resent being crowded by white men on street cars and elsewhere.

7. Promiscuous mixture of blacks and whites in factories, especially where black men are mixed with white women closely in daily work.

Following the riots, fourteen national organizations had appealed to the Department of Justice to seek the indictment of Smith in connection with the outbreaks. His 100 percent white authoritarian point of view reminds one quite grimly of Nazi and Fascist ideology, of Southern Ku Klux Klanism at its worst.

Saturday, July 24, 1943

One event that may have joggled Detroit a bit was the "CBS Open Letter on Race Hatred" broadcast over the Columbia Broadcasting System's network at 7 to 7:30 P.M. this Saturday and repeated at 9 to 9:30 P.M. Particularly striking was the dramatized letter's "postscript" by Wendell L. Willkie in which he spoke of the "situation which flared so tragically in Detroit" and which "has its counterpart—actual or potential—in many American cities." He added that such "instances of mob-madness cannot be treated as single cases, because they are profound in their effect in this country and lasting in their impression throughout the world." He scored particularly the basic motivation of race rioters, "the same basic motivation as actuates the fascist mind when it seeks to dominate whole peoples and nations."

Sunday, July 25, 1943

An event that made a bigger impact upon white Detroit's "business as usual" policy because it took place at the State Fair Grounds, just north of the city, was the speech on Sunday, July 25, by Vice-President Henry A. Wallace. He told 15,000 whites and Negroes that we "cannot fight to crush Nazi brutality abroad and condone race riots at home."

Monday, July 26, 1943

Perhaps even more significant as omens of the immediate Detroit future were the statements the following Monday by Wayne County Prosecutor William E. Dowling and Detroit Police Commissioner John H. Witherspoon. Both of these gentlemen, with Willkie's and

Wallace's warnings echoing in some of their townsmen's ears, put the responsibility for the rioting of Bloody Week squarely on the Negro community and particularly on the Negro press. The Prosecutor again denied a petition to help create a grand jury to investigate the causes of the riots because he had "learned" from his own investigations who were to blame. Those to blame, he said, were a group of colored youths who committed depredations on Belle Isle on June 20 against white picnickers and then involved themselves in a fight on Belle Isle Bridge as people were leaving the island. He also placed responsibility on the broadcast of a false rumor over the public-address system of a Negro night club, to the effect that a Negro woman and her child had been thrown from the bridge.

Later in the day, Prosecutor Dowling denied having said that if a grand jury came into existence "I will guarantee the NAACP [National Association for the Advancement of Colored People] will be the first to be investigated." He viewed the statements, reported the Detroit *Times*, as "ingenious fabrications" rather than as his own words. "I do charge," Dowling asserted, "and so I told the committee, that the Negro press and Martin of the Detroit *Tribune* [Louis E. Martin is Editor of the *Michigan Chronicle*, and J. Edward McCall is Editor of the Detroit *Tribune*] had fomented dissension. I do charge Martin of the *Tribune* with being the principal instigator of dissension in this area."

Accusing the N.A.A.C.P. of being a trouble-making organization, the Prosecutor stated:

> They have been fomenting trouble with their crusades in the Negro neighborhoods from the start. If you want to do something constructive in this situation, you might try to control the Negro press.

The Prosecutor's accusations against the N.A.A.C.P. and the Negro press were particularly provoked, he said, by the Rev. George W. Baber, a Negro member of the Mayor's "peace board."

> Rev. Baber told me [the Detroit *News* quoted Prosecutor Dowling as saying] that there were a lot of facts that he could not disclose to me, that would justify a grand jury. I asked him what these facts were. He said that he was pledged to secrecy about them, but that he had turned them over to the NAACP.

Baber's version of this event, as set forth in a sworn affidavit, is as follows:

> I . . . stated that I knew persons who had information that they would present only to a Grand Jury. Mr. Dowling wanted to know what the Negroes were doing with their information. I stated that many were turning their information over to the National Association for the Advancement of Colored People to the end that proper protective measures might be pursued. Whereupon, Mr. Dowling pounded the table and jumped to his feet, saying, "Why do you turn your information over to the National Association for the Advancement of Colored People? They were the biggest instigators of the recent race riot. If a Grand Jury were called, they would be the first indicted."
>
> Continuing in the same vein, he charged, "You people have no confidence in the law enforcement agents but turn your information over to a trouble-making organization like that."

But, as Walter White of the N.A.A.C.P. adds, in a personal statement,

> Dowling . . . hastily disavowed [the extreme charge] when he found we were going to take him into court on libel.

Police Commissioner Witherspoon declared that the Prosecutor's statements conformed with the police view on the causes of the race riots. The Commissioner felt that the N.A.A.C.P. officers had been prone to listen to complaints of alleged improper conduct on the part of police officers, without attempting to investigate their correctness. "When the NAACP forwarded the unchecked claim to the department," he pointed out, "it had a tendency to encourage rather than discourage improper conduct on the part of Negroes." The Commissioner added that a study of white-Negro incidents on D.S.R. (City Department of Street Railways) vehicles in recent months showed a steady increase, with most of the trouble started by Negroes.

Tuesday, July 27, 1943

The immediate effect of these charges was to re-create tension. The Rev. Horace White warned of this in a talk before the Mayor's Inter-Racial Peace Board, thus:

I went down among the Negro people after those stories came out. It was as if a bomb had been dropped. The situation is what it was just before June 21.

R. J. Thomas of the U.A.W.-C.I.O. charged that the Police Commissioner's "statements are the most serious incitement to race riots that we have had since the riots themselves." Not only did these statements arouse discussion, but they finally led Mayor Jeffries to express the conclusion that there should be a grand jury investigation, but not by a 23-man grand jury such as Councilman Edwards had proposed almost a month earlier.

Thursday, July 29, 1943

Mayor Jeffries appeared before the City Council and proposed a one-man grand jury investigation into the causes and deaths of the riots. Asserting that he believed the grand jury would not accomplish anything more than had already been done by existing investigative bodies, he added that its value would lie in the "psychological reaction" it would bring. The Mayor was supported immediately by Councilman Edwards but opposed as quickly by Council President John Lodge. The latter insisted that Council await a report on the riots which Prosecutor Dowling was preparing for submission to the Governor and which was to be made public within a few days. Councilman Comstock, in opposing the grand jury proposal, said: *I don't like the idea of continuing this controversy by creating a grand jury to keep it alive.*

Friday, July 30, 1943

Prosecutor Dowling revealed that four white youths were being held by the police for the confessed slaying of the aged Negro, Moses Kiska, on the evening of June 21. The four youths, all under 21, had shot Kiska while they were roaming the streets in a car "hunting niggers." Leo Tipton, Negro social director and public relations executive of the Forest Social Club, Hastings Street at Forest Avenue, was also being held. Prosecutor Dowling said that Tipton was a "key figure" in the inception of the race riots. He claimed that this publicist had grabbed the microphone at the club and had broadcast the unfounded rumor on Sunday night, June 20, that had stampeded 500 Negro patrons into wanting to "get even" with the whites.

Sunday, August 1, 1943

Dr. James J. McClendon, Negro physician and President of the Detroit Chapter, National Association for the Advancement of Colored People, replied in the Sunday newspapers to Prosecutor Dowling's allegations that his organization had helped to foment the race riots. As Dr. McClendon put it,

> As for propaganda and the NAACP, and the local Negro press, when did it become a crime to ask that all citizens be treated fairly in a democracy? When did it become a crime to ask that loyal colored Americans be given jobs commensurate with their skill and training? . . .
>
> No amount of NAACP militancy and propaganda could make the average Negro more mindful of discrimination and inequality than acutal discrimination as practiced in the city. . . .
>
> The founding fathers did not make their decisions on fear. Neither do we. . . .
>
> We are fighting a war against race hatred, subjugation, and domination. Surely all Americans ought to be willing to rid our own country of these evils. If that is propaganda, . . . we are forced to plead guilty!

Yet on that Sunday night, a number of new inter-racial incidents dangerous to racial peace took place on the cars and buses of the City Department of Street Railways. A Negro blocked a bus entrance and precipitated an altercation with the white bus driver because of the trouble the Negro was giving other passengers who wished to alight from the vehicle. As a result, the Negro struck the driver on the back of the neck with a piece of concrete. Another Negro stabbed a white streetcar conductor in the chest, arm, and back in a similar situation. Other beatings were also reported, and city officials feared another major outbreak.

* * *

Over the August 1 weekend, public criticism of Prosecutor Dowling's statements issued from three distinct sources. The Executive Board of the Michigan C.I.O. Council called for a "fair, impartial grand jury investigation, under the direction of the court" and urged that Prosecutor Dowling dissociate himself from all prosecutions arising out of the race riots. The Detroit *Labor News*, organ of the Detroit and Wayne County Federation of Labor (A. F. of L.) de-

clared that "hopes for inter-racial harmony seem to be slipping farther
and farther into the background . . . with the Prosecutor and the
Police Commissioner making blanket allegations that irresponsible
leaders in Negro organizations were responsible for the race riot."
Father Malcolm M. Dade, Rector of St. Cyprian's Episcopal Church
(Negro), preached a sermon on "The Escapegoat," in which he replied to Prosecutor Dowling's accusations with the statement that the
100,000 "membership roll of the NAACP reads like a 'Who's Who' of
Negro life" and that "there are very few of you [his congregation]
that he doesn't include in his castigation." Since the N.A.A.C.P. also
includes whites in its membership, Father Dade added that "Wendell
Willkie and Col. Theodore Roosevelt are notable members of this
organization."

Wednesday, August 11, 1943

Governor Kelly's Fact-Finding Committee on the Detroit riots of
June 20-21 made public its 8,500-word report to the Governor on
August 11, nicely timed to coincide with a national convention of
chiefs of police meeting in Detroit. Since this committee consisted of
Wayne County Prosecutor Dowling, Detroit Police Commissioner
Witherspoon, State Attorney General Herbert J. Rushton, and State
Police Director Oscar C. Olander, much more than the general outlines of its report had already been set forth in previous "white papers" and other statements by the Governor, the Mayor, Dowling,
and Witherspoon. This treatise—called by the press the "Dowling
report"—stuck to the theory that racial tensions had been snapped
"by a group of young Negro hoodlums," and it claimed that the
"ordinary law enforcement and judicial agencies have thus far dealt
adequately and properly with the law violators." It blamed race tensions particularly on "the positive exhortation by many Negro leaders
to be 'militant' in the struggle for racial equality," and called a statement in the Detroit *Tribune* an "appeal to extract 'justice' by violence," adding:

> Such appeals unfortunately have been commonplace in the
> Negro newspapers; can it be doubted that they played an
> important part in exciting the Negro people to the violence
> which resulted in Detroit on June 21? . . .
> A theme repeatedly emphasized by these [Negro] papers
> is that the struggle for Negro equality at home is an integral
> part of the present worldwide struggle for democracy. These

papers loudly proclaim that a victory over the Axis will be
meaningless unless there is a corresponding overthrow in the
country of the forces which these papers charge prevent true
racial equality.

The report was not only singularly blind to the Federal Constitution and the Atlantic Charter; it also overlooked the responsibilities of
white individuals and groups for helping to start and carry on the race
riots. In this respect, Attorney General Biddle's confidential report of
July 15 had been much fairer, had placed the blame on the shoulders
of both whites and blacks, and had noted especially the part taken in
the Belle Isle Bridge battle by white sailors from the Naval Armory.

Thursday, August 12, 1943

The Detroit *Free Press* quoted the Mayor as commenting, "I would
say it's [the Fact-Finding Committee's] a very good report." Councilman Edwards noted pointedly that "there are still twelve unsolved
murders," and he continued to demand a grand jury investigation.
The *Free Press* itself called the report "wholly inadequate." Its editorial writer added, "Dowling merely shakes the tree instead of getting
at the roots."

In reply to the Fact-Finding Committee's attack on the Negro
press, the National Association for the Advancement of Colored People, and the Negro crime rate in Detroit, "Commentator" W. K.
Kelsey replied in the Detroit *News* that in doing so the committee had
"Directed its main attention to three factors, none of them basic."
Kelsey also pointed out that the Negro press is naturally more concerned with lynchings, race riots, and Jim-Crowism than the white
publications; that the N.A.A.C.P. "is of course a thorn in the flesh of
the peace authorities, as is the Civil Liberties Union and other organizations created for minority protection"; and that Negro crime cannot be understood and measured merely through reference to the
number of Negroes arrested. . . .

A white religious leader observed at the same time that a "series of
alleged assaults by Negroes on whites has been reported within the
past week in what looks like an attempt to smear the Negroes in such
a way as to prevent the thorough investigation that is being called for
by all reputable groups and individuals." This minister lamented the
Negro-smearing propagandas of so many city and state officials and
stressed the need for making "definite changes in public attitudes and
thought-life with regard to Negroes."

Sunday, August 15, 1943

Dr. William Allan Neilson, President-Emeritus of Smith College, and 137 other eminent Americans signed and released today an "appeal to the nation to create an atmosphere in which there can be no race riots such as that in Detroit." Here are some brief excerpts from this appeal:

> Every American who loves our nation and respects the principles upon which it was founded must have been shocked and dismayed by the recent race riot in Detroit. . . .
>
> The Detroit riot embodied many of the practices which have been associated with Nazi Germany and her partner, the Japanese Empire. . . .
>
> In a statement on July 20, President Roosevelt declared that the recent outbreaks of violence "endanger our national unity and comfort our enemies." . . .
>
> We call upon our people of every race, color, station and section to use all foresight in creating the atmosphere in which no battles between our people can occur.

Thursday, August 19, 1943

"Without even taking a formal vote," reported the Detroit *Times*, "common council today denied a new request from Mayor Jeffries for a grand jury to investigate the race riots."

Detroit's City Council thus apparently regarded the "incident" of the week of June 20 as being officially closed, except for whatever the Police Department might turn up concerning the ten or more unexplained riot deaths.

Grand jury investigations might unsettle things, and Detroit was determined to stay officially at "business as usual" as long as possible. . . .

Walter White found "a great difference" between the Harlem riots of early August, 1943, and "the conditions in Detroit" during the week of July 20. White, Secretary of the National Association for the Advancement of Colored People, told the New York *Post* after touring Harlem in the early hours of August 2, the high point of rioting, that in Detroit "the Mayor was weak and the police inefficient. Neither condition prevails here". . . .

To understand how the Detroit race riots were handled, it is first necessary to analyze a little more precisely how they were set in motion and how the authorities attempted to handle them at the outset. A Detroit police spokesman, as we have reported, told how "approximately 200 sailors were fighting with Negroes, and white men and Negroes were rushing into the fight," in speaking of the struggle at Belle Isle Bridge on Sunday night, June 20. A Negro co-ed of Wayne University pointed out, "We've really had trouble ever since that Naval Armory was erected there." A news photo showed sailors, in a line from curb to curb, clearing the streets near the bridge, for traffic. A sailor on a bus the next day told one of the authors, "We fixed those black bastards last night at Belle Isle." Attorney General Biddle confirmed these statements when he said that the "prevailing hostility between sailors and Negroes inflamed the Detroit riot in its first stages."

The inference to be drawn from these points is not that the riots began necessarily as a clash between Negroes and the Navy or that a Naval unit as such assumed any responsibility in stopping the race riots. It is rather that sailors off duty have much the same prejudices and compulsions that they had under similar circumstances before they joined the Navy. Therefore, as the police spokesman stated, the sailors were fighting *against the Negroes*, *not* against the rioters white or black in their capacity as instruments of the law to restore peace and order. In this sense, the start of the June 20 race riots resembled the "zoot-suit" war earlier the same month in Los Angeles. There, *Time* reports that "mobs of soldiers and sailors" beat zoot-suited Mexican-Americans and left their victims to be "arrested by the Los Angeles police for 'vagrancy' and 'rioting.'" In Detroit, however, the sailors were withdrawn, and the police played a somewhat less passive role than the Los Angeles police.

The attitude of the Detroit police toward the Negroes, even when on duty, resembled that of the Los Angeles soldiers and sailors towards the Mexican-Americans. As Detroit Police Commissioner John H. Witherspoon pointed out frankly in his "white paper" of June 28,

> For many years the Negroes in this and other communities have had an antagonistic attitude toward the police officer.
>
> This feeling has been such that the policy of the department for some time has been to treat all alike, to avoid discrimination, to attempt in every manner to gain respect and to avoid at all cost any incident which might provide the spark to set off a serious race riot.

The Detroit Chapter, National Association for the Advancement of Colored People (N.A.A.C.P.), agreed with Commissioner Witherspoon's generalization in effect when it took his position, as reported in the Detroit *Tribune* of July 3:

> There is overwhelming evidence that the riot could have been stopped in Detroit at its inception Sunday night had the police wanted to stop it. So inefficient is the police force and so many of its members are from the deep South, with all of their anti-Negro prejudices and Klan sympathies, that the trouble may break out again as soon as the troops leave.

This distrust of the civil authorities by Negroes even led to a "serious situation" at nearby Fort Custer Army Post when "a group of Negro soldiers in one of the quartermaster battalions . . . attempted to seize arms and trucks and start a pilgrimage to Detroit." Col. Ralph Wiltamuth, post commander said that the "men became restless over the disturbance in Detroit" and that they "wanted to go to Detroit to assist their families." He added: "Prompt action by military authorities restored order. Five men are confined in the post stockade awaiting investigation."

In other words, at the outset, the authorities of the State of Michigan and of the City of Detroit had two striking difficulties with which to cope in their efforts to restore nominal peace between whites and blacks. These difficulties were: (1) the Negroes regarded both the white sailors (although not the Federal soldiers) and the city police as anti-Negro, even as "natural enemies"; and (2) both the sailors and police demonstrated to the Negroes that they "had had enough" from the Negroes and that they would now like to "even things up."

Against this backdrop of police-Negro tension, how were the Mayor and his immediate associates equipped to handle the situation? As the attitudes and behavior of Mayor Edward J. Jeffries are summed up by an outsider, New York *PM* writer James A. Wechsler, the Mayor "wants to get a better break for minorities" but his "public record . . . is far from impressive. He has compromised, side-stepped, soft-pedalled." As Mr. Wechsler concluded, "What Detroit needs now is courageous and imaginative civic leadership." The Mayor, however, because of his indecisive role in so many race clashes, "is scorned by the 'pure whites,' distrusted by many Negroes."

The Wechsler story echoed an analysis of Detroit's race tensions

made fifteen months earlier by the Federal Office of Facts and Figures, an agency later merged with the Office of War Information. The
analysis was made shortly after the Sojourner Truth Homes race riots
of February 28, 1942, during which the police "pointed their horses,
guns, and tear gas at colored citizens" who had been accepted as
tenants and were attempting to move into their new homes. "It is
fairly obvious," this report indicated, "that Mayor Jeffries is not able
to handle this matter constructively." It added the sharp warning that
"unless some socially constructive steps are taken shortly, the tension
that is developing [in 1942] is very likely to burst forth into active
conflict." After fifteen more months of "nothing constructive," this
prophecy's fulfilment took the form of thirty-four deaths, untold
suffering, loss of morale, drop in war production, and property damage. The report also made a point of the way in which Detroit "Police
seem bent on suppressing the Negroes," a situation it dwelt upon as
follows:

> To assume that it is necessary to suppress one side or the
> other to keep the peace and that the choice is to be made
> from the fact that the Negro group is smaller, is not only
> unrealistic but at this point seems to point straight to civil
> warfare.

With such tensions brewing, with studies being made of them by
both Detroit and national agencies, one would expect the Mayor to
have benefitted from such planning. He did attempt to prepare for
emergencies—within the limits defined for him by his mode of operation and by the political and industrial characteristics of the "Arsenal
of Democracy." The Mayor had worked out a "formula" over a
period of a year for bringing in Federal troops, but it did not work.
This formula required the co-operation of the Governor but did not
contemplate the need for the Governor to declare martial law and to
obtain a Presidential proclamation. Both these technical details of
procedure, which one would have expected discussions with Army
officials to have brought out long before the actual riots, apparently
were unknown to Mayor Jeffries and Governor Kelly and created
costly delays in obtaining Federal troops.

Mayor Jeffries summed up the control situation himself in his
"white paper" of June 30 as follows:

It took us 24 hours to establish the peace after rioting
broke out on the Belle Isle Bridge the night of June 20. It
took us 12 hours to get the Federal troops on the scene. It
took 24 hours to mobilize the Michigan troops. It took hours
to clear a mob of 10,000 from Woodward Ave.

It will not take us that long next time, and again you have
my guarantee on that.

The responsible authorities at all three levels of government, City, State and Federal, were greenhorns in this area
of race riots, but we are greenhorns no longer. We are vet-
erans. I admit we made some mistakes, but we will not make
the same ones again.

He stressed the "tactical error" made at "about 6:30 A.M. on June 21
of thinking the race riots were under control. It was merely a lull in
hostilities." He praised the rapidity with which 150 state police were
rushed to the rioting scenes, adding, "If we had had 500 more of
them, we would not have needed the Army." The State troops took so
long to appear because they were a recent creation, relatively untrained.

Some took the position that the chief merit of the Mayor's report
was its political technique of taking the words out of the mouths of
his opposition. He admitted and described his own errors of omission
and commission, his own indecisiveness and inadequacy. Such fairness both disarms criticism and enlists sympathy. But the Negroes had
suffered, and they were not soothed by the Mayor's explanatory techniques. Dr. James J. McClendon, President of the Detroit N.A.A.C.P.
Chapter, admitted the Mayor's inadequacies, resented the way in
which he blamed Negro distrust of police upon Negro leaders, welcomed his newly-appointed twelve-man Inter-Racial Committee, and
then reminded the Mayor of another such committee which he had
appointed two years before to investigate another race riot, the one at
Northwestern High School in 1941. "Today we have a new committee," Dr. McClendon said. "Its report can be written now. The question is whether you [Mr. Mayor] will *do* anything after you receive
it."

Mayor Jeffries thus had with him at the top what he called "greenhorns." And neither he nor the "greenhorns" had put into operation
preventive measures urged by representative citizens' committees. Let
us see how well the Detroit Police Department prepared itself to

handle the race riot crisis of the week of June 20. In addition to those already highlighted in this chapter, these qualifying factors should be emphasized: (1) the department was 280 policemen short, owing to war conditions; (2) the police who were to have gone off duty at midnight Sunday night remained on their posts to see the fight through; (3) 175 police cars equipped with two-way radios enabled any trouble area "to be reached within two or three minutes"; (4) as various reports indicate, the Negroes were antagonistic to the police, regardless of the reasons for that situation; (5) race riots may require special techniques with which Detroit police were not acquainted; and (6) the police were deluged with false reports that made them move wastefully from place to place on false alarms. This last point made it necessary for the Police Department to utilize sixteen extra telephone operators on Bloody Monday.

On the other hand, in opposition to such qualifying factors, the following may also be said: (1) the police apparently regarded the race riots until late Monday afternoon as almost wholly Negro riots and thus permitted the gigantic Woodward Avenue mob of 10,000 whites to collect and to become menacing; (2) Philip A. Adler, columnist for the Detroit *News*, joined many citizens in wondering why fire hoses were not used on the mobs; (3) the police exceeded their legal prerogatives in some instances to "maintain order"; and (4) they failed to protect Negroes.

The last three of these points require additional comment: Walter Hardin, a Negro, International Representative of the U.A.W.-C.I.O., and a member of the Mayor's Bi-Racial Committee, said that a question existed as to why the police failed to move white mobs from Woodward Avenue during the heat of the rioting when he claimed he knew from "personal experience" how police handled such matters in industrial strikes. The following are examples of how police exceeded their rightful duties:

1. "Police brutality which reached a new high in Negro sections of the city during the race riot," the *Michigan Chronicle* charged on June 26, "was felt by news photographers as well as rioters and bystanders. Langford P. James had his arm broken by police early Monday morning while taking a picture in downtown Detroit. A policeman struck James across the arm with a club but did not interfere with white photographers making pictures of the same scene. . . . Frank Brown, an official *Michigan Chronicle* photographer,

had his camera confiscated Tuesday by police who said they were instructed to 'take all cameras to headquarters.' The camera was later released."

2. Social workers who were assigned to the interviewing of prisoners reported that the police refused to permit prisoners to telephone their families, sometimes for several days.

3. The police vilified innocent Negroes, as they did after the shooting of Julian Witherspoon at the St. Antoine (Negro) Y.M.C.A., an incident described in Chapter 3. The New York police during the August 2 riots furnished a pleasant contrast to this; in many cases, they had learned to take "Negro cussedness" smiling.

4. The police in general gave the impression of acting on the assumption that a person was guilty until proved innocent.

5. Looters were in many cases apparently shot on sight. As *The Nation* of July 3 put it, "When the white mob ran amok pulling Negroes from automobiles and streetcars, the police seem to have done little to interfere. But when the Negroes began to retaliate on white property, the police were quick to use both night sticks and guns." *The Nation* merely had the order wrong; it is probable that, so far as property destruction was concerned, the burning of cars came later after destruction and looting by Negroes.

6. On the other hand, police are also reported to have stood by and watched looting, as if unconcerned, and with no effort in such cases to stop it.

The statement that the police did not in many cases protect Negroes is well illustrated by these quotations from eye-witnesses:

Word got around awful fast. Those police are *murderers*, [said a husky Negro of 20]. They were just waiting for a chance to get us. We didn't stand a chance. I hate 'em. Oh, God, how I hate 'em. But the fellows who had guns were ready to go. They were saying, "If it gets tight, get two whites before they get you."

Dr. B. and I were on our way to City Hall to see the Mayor [recalled a prominent white minister]. We saw a crowd leading a young colored boy up the street. It was a crowd of about 500, made up of people under 20 with the exception of an older leader. I stopped the leader and asked where he was taking the boy. Several behind him answered, "They raped our sisters; they killed the sailors." I answered, "But this little fellow didn't do anything." We finally got him to the steps of the City Hall; he was only about 13; and several policemen (who had been standing there all the time) took him into the Hall. We tried to reason with the crowd but it was impossible. I think they would have been nasty to us if we hadn't gone in.

Police "standing there all the time" frequently were merely interested spectators at Negro beatings.

In all fairness, it must be admitted with Mayor Jeffries that "the police had a tough job. A lot of them have been beaten and stoned and shot." But the difficulty of the job and the injuries suffered by individual policemen are vastly overweighed by these unassailable facts: (1) the police force and the police officials had been warned severely and over a long period of time to prepare themselves for proper action in the event of a race outbreak; and (2) the police not only failed to afford Negroes the physical protection required by law; but (3) the police actually went beyond their prerogatives at the expense of the Negroes. These three facts of police misconduct must be borne in mind by police commissioners throughout the country, if race riots are to be superseded by inter-racial peace. And another fact must be remembered with it: the notably impartial behavior of the U. S. Army troops, which commanded immediate respect from both blacks and whites. The Detroit experience proved that impartial, rather than prejudiced, policing behavior is a crucial necessity in handling a riot situation, and the Harlem experience of August 1-2, 1943, offered additional verification of this point. . . .

VI

Los Angeles, 1965

INTRODUCTION

Watts, the south central ghetto of Los Angeles, was the scene of the first major civil disorder of the 1960s. The riots lasted for six days in August, 1965, resulting in the death of 34 persons, over 1,000 injured, and almost 4,000 arrests. Shortly after the riot was controlled, Governor Brown appointed a commission, under the chairmanship of John McCone, to "prepare an accurate chronology and description of the riots and attempt to draw any lessons which may be learned from retrospective study of these events." The commission was also instructed to "probe deeply the immediate and underlying causes of the riots" and to "develop recommendations for action designed to prevent a recurrence of these tragic disorders." The commission completed its brief report, *Violence in the City—An End or a Beginning?*, in just over three months after holding public hearings, consulting with a number of social scientists, and evaluating a variety of specially prepared data and reports.

The McCone Commission proved to be a disappointment on several grounds. Unlike the inquiries of 1919 and 1935, *Violence in the City* undermined the scholarship and findings of the commission's social science consultants by substituting ideology for analysis and ignoring evidence which contradicted ideological preconceptions. The final report of the McCone Commission was criticized by many scholars and policymakers for its conservative ideology, shoddy scholarship, and lack of political vision. Robert Blauner, a sociologist and consultant to the McCone Commission, called the report "sketchy and superficial. . . . The analytical perspective is overwhelmingly *riot control.* . . ."[1] Bayard Rustin, a moderate black spokesman, similarly found the report to be misinformed and politically irresponsible. "The Watts manifesto," wrote Rustin in 1966, "is a response to realities that the McCone Report is barely beginning to grasp."[2]

The selections from Paul Jacobs' *Prelude to Riot* are based on a first-hand evaluation of the staff and personnel of the McCone Commission. Jacobs' trenchant observations illuminate organizational relationships within the Commission as well as providing a unique assessment of the ideology and "working personality" of various commissioners and their executive staff.

Robert Fogelson's critique of the McCone Commission report is a scholarly and thorough analysis, influenced in general by Arthur Waskow's critique of *The Negro in Chicago* and more specifically by Robert Blauner's conception of the Watts riot as a "native uprising" against "colonial" oppression. Fogelson substantiates his arguments with solid evidence, mostly derived from the files and transcripts of the McCone Commission, and suggests that the McCone Commission report should be regarded as a proclamation of conservative political ideology rather than as a scholarly and impartial analysis of a serious social issue.

NOTES

1. Robert Blauner, "Whitewash Over Watts," *Trans-action*, March-April, 1966, pp. 3-10.

2. Bayard Rustin, "The Watts 'Manifesto' & The McCone Report," *Commentary*, March, 1966, pp. 29-35.

10.

GOVERNOR'S COMMISSION ON THE
LOS ANGELES RIOTS

Violence in the City—
An End or a Beginning?

THE CRISIS — AN OVERVIEW

The rioting in Los Angeles in the late hot summer of 1965 took six days to run its full grievous course. In hindsight, the tinder-igniting incident is seen to have been the arrest of a drunken Negro youth about whose dangerous driving another Negro had complained to the Caucasian motorcycle officer who made the arrest. The arrest occurred under rather ordinary circumstances, near but not in the district known as Watts, at seven o'clock on the evening of 11 August, a Wednesday. The crisis ended in the afternoon of 17 August, a Tuesday, on Governor Brown's order to lift the curfew which had been imposed the Saturday before in an extensive area just south of the heart of the City.

In the ugliest interval, which lasted from Thursday through Saturday, perhaps as many as 10,000 Negroes took to the streets in ma-

SOURCE: From Governor's Commission on the Los Angeles Riots, *Violence in the City—An End or a Beginning?* (Los Angeles: College Book Store, 1965), pp. 1-9, 22-25, 27-37, 81-86.

rauding bands. They looted stores, set fires, beat up white passersby whom they hauled from stopped cars, many of which were turned upside down and burned, exchanged shots with law enforcement officers, and stoned and shot at firemen. The rioters seemed to have been caught up in an insensate rage of destruction. By Friday, the disorder spread to adjoining areas, and ultimately an area covering 46.5 square miles had to be controlled with the aid of military authority before public order was restored.

The entire Negro population of Los Angeles County, about two thirds of whom live in this area, numbers more than 650,000. Observers estimate that only about two per cent were involved in the disorder. Nevertheless, this violent fraction, however minor, has given the face of community relations in Los Angeles a sinister cast.

When the spasm passed, thirty-four persons were dead, and the wounded and hurt numbered 1,032 more. Property damage was about $40,000,000. Arrested for one crime or another were 3,952 persons, women as well as men, including over 500 youths under eighteen. The lawlessness in this one segment of the metropolitan area had terrified the entire county and its 6,000,000 citizens.

Sowing the Wind

In the summer of 1964, Negro communities in seven eastern cities were stricken by riots.[1] Although in each situation there were unique contributing circumstances not existing elsewhere, the fundamental causes were largely the same:

> —Not enough jobs to go around, and within this scarcity not enough by a wide margin of a character which the untrained Negro could fill.
> —Not enough schooling designed to meet the special needs of the disadvantaged Negro child, whose environment from infancy onward places him under a serious handicap.
> —A resentment, even hatred, of the police, as the symbol of authority.

These riots were each a symptom of a sickness in the center of our cities. In almost every major city, Negroes pressing ever more densely into the central city and occupying areas from which Causasians have moved in their flight to the suburbs have developed an isolated existence with a feeling of separation from the community as a whole. Many have moved to the city only in the last generation and are totally unprepared to meet the conditions of modern city life. At the core of the cities where they cluster, law and order have only tenuous hold; the conditions of life itself are often marginal; idleness leads to despair and finally, mass violence supplies a momentary relief from the malaise.

Why Los Angeles?

In Los Angeles, before the summer's explosion, there was a tendency to believe, and with some reason, that the problems which caused the trouble elsewhere were not acute in this community. A "statistical portrait" drawn in 1964 by the Urban League which rated American cities in terms of ten basic aspects of Negro life—such as housing, employment, income—ranked Los Angeles first among the sixty-eight cities that were examined. ("There is no question about it, this is the best city in the world," a young Negro leader told us with respect to housing for Negroes.)

While the Negro districts of Los Angeles are not urban gems, neither are they slums. Watts, for example, is a community consisting mostly of one and two-story houses, a third of which are owned by the occupants. In the riot area, most streets are wide and usually quite clean; there are trees, parks, and playgrounds. A Negro in Los Angeles has long been able to sit where he wants in a bus or a movie house, to shop where he wishes, to vote, and to use public facilities without discrimination. The opportunity to succeed is probably unequaled in any other major American city.

Yet the riot did happen here, and there are special circumstances here which explain in part why it did. Perhaps the people of Los Angeles should have seen trouble gathering under the surface calm. In the last quarter century, the Negro population here has exploded. While the County's population has trebled, the Negro population has increased almost tenfold from 75,000 in 1940 to 650,000 in 1965. Much of the increase came through migration from Southern states and many arrived with the anticipation that this dynamic city would somehow spell the end of life's endless problems. To those who have come with high hopes and great expectations and see the success of others so close at hand, failure brings a special measure of frustration and disillusionment. Moreover, the fundamental problems, which are the same here as in the cities which were racked by the 1964 riots, are intensified by what may well be the least adequate network of public transportation in any major city in America.

Looking back, we can also see that there was a series of aggravating events in the twelve months prior to the riots.

—Publicity given to the glowing promise of the Federal poverty program was paralleled by reports of controversy and bickering over the mechanism to handle the program here in Los Angeles, and when the projects did arrive, they did not live up to their press notices.

—Throughout the nation, unpunished violence and disobedience to law were widely reported, and almost daily there were exhortations, here and elsewhere, to take the most extreme and even illegal remedies to right a wide variety of wrongs, real and supposed.

—In addition, many Negroes here felt and were encouraged to feel that they had been affronted by the passage of Proposition 14—an initiative measure passed by two-thirds of the voters in November 1964 which repealed the Rumford Fair Housing Act and unless modified by the voters or invalidated by the courts will bar any attempt by state or local governments to enact similar laws.

When the rioting came to Los Angeles, it was not a race riot in the usual sense. What happened was an explosion—a formless, quite senseless, all but hopeless violent protest—engaged in by a few but bringing great distress to all.

Nor was the rioting exclusively a projection of the Negro problem. It is part of an American problem which involves Negroes but which equally concerns other disadvantaged groups. In this report, our major conclusions and recommendations regarding the Negro problem in Los Angeles apply with equal force to the Mexican-Americans, a community which is almost equal in size to the Negro community and whose circumstances are similarly disadvantageous and demand equally urgent treatment. That the Mexican-American community did not riot is to its credit; it should not be to its disadvantage.

The Dull Devastating Spiral of Failure

In examining the sickness in the center of our city, what has depressed and stunned us most is the dull, devastating spiral of failure that awaits the average disadvantaged child in the urban core. His home life all too often fails to give him the incentive and the elementary experience with words and ideas which prepares most children for school. Unprepared and unready, he may not learn to read or write at all; and because he shares his problem with 30 or more in the same classroom, even the efforts of the most dedicated teachers are unavailing. Age, not achievement, passes him on to higher grades, but in most cases he is unable to cope with courses in the upper grades because they demand basic skills which he does not possess. ("Try," a teacher said to us, "to teach history to a child who cannot read.")

Frustrated and disillusioned, the child becomes a discipline problem. Often he leaves school, sometimes before the end of junior high school. (About two-thirds of those who enter the three high schools in the center of the curfew area do not graduate.) He slips into the ranks of the permanent jobless, illiterate and untrained, unemployed and unemployable. All the talk about the millions which the government is spending to aid him raise his expectations but the benefits seldom reach him.

Reflecting this spiral of failure, unemployment in the disadvantaged areas runs two to three times the county average, and the employment available is too often intermittent. A family whose breadwinner is chronically out of work is almost invariably a disintegrating family. Crime rates soar and welfare rolls increase, even faster than the population.

This spiral of failure has a most damaging side effect. Because of the low standard of achievement in the schools in the urban core and adjacent areas, parents of the better students from advantaged backgrounds remove them from these schools, either by changing the location of the family home or by sending the children to private school. In turn, the average achievement level of the schools in the disadvantaged area sinks lower and lower. The evidence is that this chain reaction is one of the principal factors in maintaining de facto school segregation in the urban core and producing it in the adjacent areas where the Negro population is expanding. From our study, we are persuaded that there is a reasonable possibility that raising the achievement levels of the disadvantaged Negro child will materially lessen the tendency towards de facto segregation in education, and that this might possibly also make a substantial contribution to ending all de facto segregation.

All Segments of Society

Perhaps for the first time our report will bring into clear focus, for all the citizens to see, the economic and sociological conditions in our city that underlay the gathering anger which impelled the rioters to escalate the routine arrest of a drunken driver into six days of violence. Yet, however powerful their grievances, the rioters had no legal or moral justification for the wounds they inflicted. Many crimes, a great many felonies, were committed. Even more dismaying, as we studied the record, was the large number of brutal exhortations to violence which were uttered by some Negroes. Rather than making proposals, they laid down ultimatums with the alternative being violence. All this nullified the admirable efforts of hundreds, if not thousands, both Negro and white, to quiet the situation and restore order.

What can be done to prevent a recurrence of the nightmare of August? It stands to reason that what we and other cities have been doing, costly as it all has been, is not enough. Improving the conditions of Negro life will demand adjustments on a scale unknown to any great society. The programs that we are recommending will be expensive and burdensome. And the burden, along with the expense, will fall on all segments of our society—on the public and private sectors, on industry and labor, on company presidents and hourly employees, and most indispensably, upon the members and leaders of the Negro community. For unless the disadvantaged are resolved to help themselves, whatever else is done by others is bound to fail.

The consequences of inaction, indifference, and inadequacy, we can all be sure now, would be far costlier in the long run than the cost of correction. If the city were to elect to stand aside, the walls of segregation would rise ever higher. The disadvantaged community would become more and more estranged and the risk of violence would rise. The cost of police protection would increase, and yet would never be adequate. Unemployment would climb; welfare costs would mount apace. And the preachers of divison and demogoguery would have a matchless opportunity to tear our nation asunder.

Of Fundamental and Durable Import

As a Commission, we are seriously concerned that the existing breach, if allowed to persist, could in time split our society irretrievably. So serious and so explosive is the situation that, unless it is checked, the August riots may seem by comparison to be only a curtain-raiser for what could blow up one day in the future.

Our recommendations will concern many areas where improvement can be made but three we consider to be of highest priority and greatest importance.

1. Because idleness brings a harvest of distressing problems, employment for those in the Negro community who are unemployed and able to work is a first priority. Our metropolitan area employs upwards of three millions of men and women in industry and in the service trades, and we face a shortage of skilled and semi-skilled workers as our economy expands. We recommend that our robust community take immediate steps to relieve the lack of job opportunity for Negroes by cooperative programs for employment and training, participated in by the Negro community, by governmental agencies, by employers and by organized labor.

2. In education, we recommend a new and costly approach to educating the Negro child who has been deprived of the early training that customarily starts at infancy and who because of early deficiencies advances through school on a basis of age rather than scholastic attainment. What is clearly needed and what we recommend is an emergency program designed to raise the level of scholastic attainment of those who would otherwise fall behind. This requires preschool education, intensive instruction in small classes, remedial courses and other special treatment. The cost will be great but until the level of scholastic achievement of the disadvantaged child is raised, we cannot expect to overcome the existing spiral of failure.

3. We recommend that law enforcement agencies place greater emphasis on their responsibilities for crime prevention as an essential element of the law enforcement task, and that they institute improved means for handling citizen complaints and community relationships.

The road to the improvement of the condition of the disadvantaged Negro which lies through education and employment is hard and long, but there is no shorter route. The avenue of violence and lawlessness leads to a dead end. To travel the long and difficult road will require courageous leadership and determined participation by all parts of our community, but no task in our times is more important. Of what shall it avail our nation if we can place a man on the moon but cannot cure the sickness in our cities? . . . .

Was There a Pre-established Plan?

After a thorough examination, the Commission has concluded that there is no reliable evidence of outside leadership or pre-established plans for the rioting. The testimony of law enforcement agencies and their respective intelligence officers supports this conclusion. The Attorney General, the District Attorney, and the Los Angeles police have all reached the conclusion that there is no evidence of a pre-plan or a pre-established central direction of the rioting activities. This finding was submitted to the Grand Jury by the District Attorney.

This is not to say that there was *no* agitation or promotion of the rioting by local groups or gangs which exist in pockets throughout the south central area. The sudden appearance of Molotov cocktails in quantity and the unexplained movement of men in cars through the areas of great destruction support the conclusion that there was organization and planning after the riots commenced. In addition, on that tense Thursday, inflammatory handbills suddenly appeared in Watts. But this cannot be identified as a master plan by one group; rather it appears to have been the work of several gangs, with membership of young men ranging in age from fourteen to thirty-five years. All of these activities intensified the rioting and caused it to spread with increased violence from one district to another in the curfew area.

The Grim Statistics

The final statistics are staggering. There were 34 persons killed and 1,032 reported injuries, including 90 Los Angeles police officers, 136 firemen, 10 national guardsmen, 23 persons from other governmental agencies, and 773 civilians. 118 of the injuries resulted from gunshot wounds. Of the 34 killed, one was a fireman, one was a deputy sheriff, and one a Long Beach policeman.

In the weeks following the riots, Coroner's Inquests were held regarding thirty-two of the deaths.[2] The Coroner's jury ruled that twenty-six of the deaths were justifiable homicide, five were homicidal, and one was accidental. Of those ruled justifiable homicide, the jury found that death was caused in sixteen instances by officers of the Los Angeles Police Department and in seven instances by the National Guard.[3]

It has been estimated that the loss of property attributable to the riots was over $40 million. More than 600 buildings were damaged by burning and looting. Of this number, more than 200 were totally destroyed by fire. The rioters concentrated primarily on food markets, liquor stores, furniture stores, clothing stores, department stores, and pawn shops. Arson arrests numbered 27 and 10 arson complaints were filed, a relatively small number considering that fire department officials say that all of the fires were incendiary in origin. Between 2,000 and 3,000 fire alarms were recorded during the riot, 1,000 of these between 7:00 A.M. on Friday and 7:00 A.M. on Saturday. We note with interest that no residences were deliberately burned, that damage to schools, libraries, churches and public buildings was minimal, and that certain types of business establishments, notably service stations and automobile dealers, were for the most part unharmed.

There were 3,438 adults arrested, 71 percent for burglary and theft. The number of juveniles arrested was 514, 81 percent for burglary and theft. Of the adults arrested, 1,232 had never been arrested before; 1,164 had a "minor" criminal record (arrest only or conviction with sentence of 90 days or less); 1,042 with "major" criminal record (convictions with sentence of more than 90 days). Of the juveniles arrested, 257 had never been arrested before; 212 had a "minor" criminal record; 43 had a "major" criminal record. Of the adults arrested, 2,057 were born in 16 Southern states whereas the comparable figure for juveniles was 131. Some of the juveniles arrested extensively damaged the top two floors of an auxiliary jail which had been opened on the Saturday of the riots.

Those involved in the administration of justice—judges, prosecutors, defense counsel, and others—merit commendation for the steps they took to cope with the extraordinary responsibility thrust on the judicial system by the riots. By reorganizing calendars and making special assignments, the Los Angeles Superior and Municipal Courts have been able to meet the statutory deadlines for processing the cases of those arrested. Court statistics indicate that by November 26, the following dispositions had been made of the 2278 felony cases filed against adults: 856 were found guilty; 155 acquitted; 641 were disposed of prior to trial, primarily by dismissal; 626 are awaiting trial. Of the 1133 misdemeanor cases filed, 733 were found guilty, 81 were acquitted, 184 dismissed and 135 are awaiting trial.

The police and Sheriff's Department have long known that many members of gangs, as well as others, in the south central area possessed weapons and knew how to use them. However, the extent to which pawn shops, each one of which possessed an inventory of weapons, were the immediate target of looters, leads to the conclusion that a substantial number of the weapons used were stolen from these shops. During the riots, law enforcement officers recovered 851 weapons. There is no evidence that the rioters made any attempt to steal narcotics from pharmacies in the riot area even though some pharmacies were looted and burned.

Overwhelming as are the grim statistics, the impact of the August rioting on the Los Angeles community has been even greater. The first weeks after the disorders brought a flood tide of charges and recriminations. Although this has now ebbed, the feeling of fear and tension persists, largely unabated, throughout the community. A certain slowness in the rebuilding of the fired structures has symbolized the difficulty in mending relationships in our community which were so severely fractured by the August nightmare. . . .

LAW ENFORCEMENT — THE THIN THREAD

As the patriots of seventy-six did to the support of the Declaration of Independence, so to the support of the Constitution and laws let every American pledge his life, his property, and his sacred honor—let every man remember that to violate the law is to trample on the blood of his father and to tear the charter of his own children's liberty. Let reverence for the laws . . . become the political religion of the nation; and let the old and the young, the rich and the poor, the grave and the gay of all sexes and tongues and colors and conditions, sacrifice unceasingly upon its altars.

Abraham Lincoln, January 27, 1837

Maintenance of law and order is a prerequisite to the enjoyment of freedom in our society. Law enforcement is a critical responsibility of government, and effective enforcement requires mutual respect and understanding between a law enforcement agency and the residents of the community which it serves.

The Problem—Deep and Serious

The conduct of law enforcement agencies, most particularly the Los Angeles Police Department, has been subject to severe criticism by many Negroes who have appeared before the Commission as witnesses. The bitter criticism we have heard evidences a deep and long-standing schism between a substantial portion of the Negro community and the Police Department. "Police brutality" has been the recurring charge. One witness after another has recounted instances in which, in their opinion, the police have used excessive force or have been disrespectful and abusive in their language or manner.[4]

On the other hand, the police have explained to us the extent to which the conduct of some Negroes when apprehended has required the use of force in making arrests. Example after example has been recited of arrestees, both men and women, becoming violent, struggling to resist arrest, and thus requiring removal by physical force. Other actions, each provocative to the police and each requiring more than normal action by the police in order to make an arrest or to perform other duties, have been described to us.

Chief of Police Parker appears to be the focal point of the criticism within the Negro community. He is a man distrusted by most Negroes and they carefully analyze for possible anti-Negro meaning almost every action he takes and every statement he makes. Many Negroes feel that he carries a deep hatred of the Negro community. However, Chief Parker's statements to us and collateral evidence such as his record of fairness to Negro officers are inconsistent with his having such an attitude. Despite the depth of the feeling against Chief Parker expressed to us by so many witnesses, he is recognized, even by many of his most vocal critics, as a capable Chief who directs an efficient police force that serves well this entire community.

With respect to the Los Angeles County Sheriff's Department, the situation is somewhat different. Generally speaking, the Negro community does not harbor the same angry feeling toward the Sheriff or his staff as it does toward the Los Angeles police. Nevertheless, witnesses recited to us instances of alleged brutality and excessive use of force by deputy sheriffs on duty.

The reasons for the feeling that law enforcement officers are the enemy of the Negro are manifold and it is well to reflect on them before they are accepted. An examination of seven riots in Northern cities of the United States in 1964 reveals that each one was started over a police incident, just as the Los Angeles riot started with the arrest of Marquette Frye. In each of the 1964 riots, "police brutality" was an issue, as it was here, and, indeed, as it has been in riots and insurrections elsewhere in the world. The fact that this charge is repeatedly made must not go unnoticed, for there is a real danger that persistent criticism will reduce and perhaps destroy the effectiveness of law enforcement.

Our society is held together by respect for law. A group of officers who represent a tiny fraction of one percent of the population is the thin thread that enforces observance of law by those few who would do otherwise. If police authority is destroyed, if their effectiveness is impaired, and if their determination to use the authority vested in them to preserve a law abiding community is frustrated, all of society will suffer because groups would feel free to disobey the law and inevitably their number would increase. Chaos might easily result. So, while we must examine carefully the claim of police brutality and must see that justice is done to all groups within our society, we must, at the same time, be sure that law enforcement agencies, upon which so much depends, are not rendered impotent.

Solution is Possible—But Action by Both Police and the Negro Community is Essential

Much can be done to correct the existing impressions and to promote an understanding between the police and the Negro community, and this, we believe, is essential in the interest of crime prevention. The steps that have been taken appear to us to be insufficient. Further action is indicated.

Basically, on the one hand, we call for a better understanding by the law enforcement agencies of Negro community attitudes and, on the other hand, a more widespread understanding within the Negro community of the value of the police and the extent to which the law enforcement agencies provide it with security. Although the criminal element among the Negroes is only a small fraction of the Negro population, over half of all crimes of violence committed in the City of Los Angeles are committed by Negroes, and the great majority of the victims of these crimes are Negroes. Thus, the police, in their effort to suppress crime, are doing so to protect the entire community, including the Negro community.

The Board of Police Commissioners— Strengthening Is Needed

The Board of Police Commissioners, as the civilian head of the Police Department, has a great responsibility. It is charged with establishing policies for the Department, supervising and managing the Department, and seeing to it that its policies are followed. In discharging its duties, the Board should have a major role in the improvement and maintenance of police-community relationships. In addition, the Board has extensive responsibilities for the issuance and revocation of permits for carrying on a large number of businesses.

The Commission believes that this Board, meeting one afternoon a week, with compensation of the members of the Board at $10.00 per meeting, cannot and does not exercise the control and direction of the Police Department which is prescribed by the City Charter. It is significant to us that the Board and its actions have not been drawn into the recent criticisms of police conduct in the predominantly Negro areas of the city. Almost without exception, the complaints that we have heard have been directed against Chief Parker and the police officers. No one, not a single witness, has criticized the Board for the conduct of the police, although the Board is the final authority in such matters. We interpret this as evidence that the Board of Police Commissioners is not visibly exercising the authority over the Department vested in it by the City Charter. Our own investigation and evaluation and the testimony of witnesses, confirm this.

Therefore, we urge that steps be taken immediately to arm the Board of Police Commissioners with all necessary tools to discharge its City Charter responsibilities. This will mean increased compensation for the Commissioners, more frequent meetings of the Board, a larger staff, and a revision of procedures that have been followed in the past. A Board, shouldering the responsibilities envisaged here, must be composed of capable and dedicated men, chosen by the Mayor and confirmed by the City Council, willing to devote the necessary time and thoughtful effort to the task.

Complaint Procedures—A New Approach to an Old Problem

A strained relationship such as we have observed as existing between the police and the Negro community can be relieved only if the citizen knows that he will be fairly and properly treated, that his complaints of police misconduct will be heard and investigated, and that, if justified, disciplinary action will be taken against the offending officer.

Under the present Police Department procedure, citizen complaints are received by the Police Department or by the Board of Police Commissioners. All investigations of citizen complaints, wherever received, are conducted under the overall supervision of the Internal Affairs Division of the Police Department. In the vast majority of cases, primary responsibility for investigating allegations of officer misconduct has in the past been placed with the division commander of the individual officer involved. After the investigation has been completed, the determination whether a complaint should be sustained is made either by the Chief of Police or by the Board of Police Commissioners, depending upon where the complaint was originally filed. Where a complaint is sustained, responsibility for discipline is vested in the Chief of Police and the Board of Rights, which provides a departmental hearing to an accused officer before serious sanctions can be imposed.

The Commission has concluded that there are several deficiencies in this existing procedure. We believe that division commanders and those in the command structure should not conduct investigations of complaints with respect to their own subordinate officers. Moreover, existing procedures are not sufficiently visible to or understood by the public. Finally, we do not think there should be a difference, as there now is, in the handling of a complaint depending solely upon whether it was filed with the Board or the Police Department.

Under the existing procedure, the impression is widespread that complaints by civilians go unnoticed, that police officers are free to conduct themselves as they will, and that the manner in which they handle the public is of little concern to the higher authorities. This impression is not consistent with fact. Departmental policies set high standards of conduct for police officers in their contacts with citizens, and these standards are conscientiously enforced. In 1964, 412 complaints of police misconduct were received from citizens. Forty-two complaints alleging police misconduct in contacts with citizens were sustained.[5] Despite these facts, the impression that citizen complaints are ignored continues because of deficiencies in the existing procedure. Thus, the clamor is raised from many sources for an independent civilian review board.

The Commission feels that a civilian review board, authorized to investigate, and perhaps to decide, complaints, but with no other law enforcement responsibilities, would endanger the effectiveness of law enforcement, which would be intolerable at a time when crime is on the increase throughout the country. Experience in two cities which have such boards—and in which alleged misconduct of police officers was a major issue in connection with riots which occurred in those cities in 1964—has not demonstrated the advantages of such a review board. From our observations and from testimony of knowledgeable law enforcement administrators, we are persuaded that the value of an independent board would not outweigh the likely deleterious effects on law enforcement. We, therefore, propose improvements in the existing procedure which will go far toward establishing the widest possible confidence in the handling of all complaints but which will not destroy the authority vested by the City Charter in the Board of Police Commissioners and the Chief of Police.

To insure independent investigation of complaints, we recommend that an "Inspector General" should be established in the Police Department, under the authority of the Chief of Police but outside the chain of command. Properly staffed with sworn officers and civilian personnel, the Inspector General would perform the functions of the present Internal Affairs Division and would be responsible for making investigations and recommendations on all citizen complaints, whether filed with the Board or the Department. An adequate hearing process for the complainant should be made available at some point in the procedure, and he should be informed of the action taken on his complaint. The "Inspector General" concept has proved, through years of experience, to be effective in the four military services, each of which has such an independent and objective agency under the Chief of Staff of the service. The Inspector General's investigations can be visible to the public. He would report to the Chief of Police, and his findings and recommendations on all complaints would be the basis for the Chief's report to the Board on all such complaints. The Board would act on all complaints as it now acts on some complaints initially presented to it; that is, it would pass on whether the complaint is or is not sustained. Under the procedure suggested here, responsibility for discipline would remain with the Chief of Police and the Board of Rights as provided by the City Charter.

These improvements, we believe, would provide a satisfactory procedure for processing citizen complaints both from the viewpoint of the Los Angeles Police Department and the community. We have focused our discussion on the existing procedure in the Police Department. We encourage the Los Angeles Sheriff's Department to adopt those aspects of our conclusions which may be applicable to its procedures for handling citizen complaints.

Community-Police Relations—
A Responsibility for Crime Prevention

In 1963, the Los Angeles Police Department issued an excellent statement of the need for and purpose of a community relations program. The order stated:

> The mutual advantages of a friendly relationship between the people of a community and their police force should be widely understood and more fully appreciated. The success of a police force in the performance of its duties is largely measured by the degree of support and cooperation it receives from the people it serves. It is of paramount importance, therefore, to secure for this department the confidence, respect, and approbation of the public. The cultivation of such desirable attitudes on the part of the public is dependent upon reciprocal attitudes on the part of this department.

Witness after witness, in discussing the question of police-community relations, emphasized the importance of "non-punitive contacts" as basic to the problem. But, from the statements of many witnesses it appears that the steps taken by the Los Angeles Police Department, although commendable, have been faltering. The worthwhile Deputy Auxiliary Police program, which was designed to bring youth into closer contact with police organizations, has been permitted to lapse and pass out of existence. The staff assigned to community relations activities is not large enough, and the range of community relations activities has been limited.

Moreover, little has been done in recent years to encourage the Negro youth's support of the police, or to implant in the youth's mind the true value of the Police Department with respect to the welfare of the youth. Productive programs can and must be developed in Los Angeles, as they have been developed elsewhere.

We commend the Board of Police Commissioners and the Chief of Police for the community relations activities which the Department has undertaken in 1965. These have included the appointment of a Coordinator of Community Relations Activity and a Community-Police Relations Advisory Committee, and an increase in the staff of the community relations unit. Visitation programs to elementary schools and command level seminars on community relations have also been useful steps. But, we believe, a greater effort is indicated.

We propose more intensive in-service human relations training programs for officer personnel; youth programs such as the Deputy Auxiliary Police program; periodic open forums and workshops in which the police and residents of the minority communities will engage in discussions of law enforcement; and frequent contact between the police and the students in junior and senior high schools.

Such programs are a basic responsibility of the Police Department. They serve to prevent crime, and, in the opinion of this Commission, crime prevention is a responsibility of the Police Department, equal in importance to law enforcement.

Programs of this nature, and the underlying philosophies that support them, can only be initiated through determined leadership at the top. If these actions are pursued energetically, we can expect a gratifying improvement in the relationship between the police and the community. Successful implementation of these programs will require additional personnel and funds and we believe that the City Council should authorize both without delay.

Again, while we have focused our discussion on the Police Department, we encourage the Los Angeles Sheriff's Department to introduce community relations activities of the character we have recommended for the Police Department.

More Negroes and Mexican-Americans Must Enter Careers in Law Enforcement

Finally, the Commission expresses its concern over the relatively few sworn officer personnel in the Police Department and the Sheriff's Department who are Negroes or Mexican-Americans. Only four percent of the sworn personnel of the Police Department and six percent of the Sheriff's Department are Negroes and an even smaller percentage are Mexican-American. Both of these departments recruit their personnel through the civil service agencies and selections are made on a basis of qualifications without regard for race, religion, or national origin. Despite efforts by the civil service agencies, the law enforcement departments, and some elected officials to encourage Negroes and Mexican-Americans to enter the law enforcement field, the results have been unsatisfactory.

We believe it essential that the number of sworn officers of each minority group should be increased substantially. To bring this about, more active recruitment by the Police and Sheriff's Departments and the civil service must be undertaken. Furthermore, educational and private institutions and organizations, and political leaders as well, should encourage members of the minority groups to enter careers in law enforcement. Finally, budget support for extensive efforts in recruitment, which should perhaps include pre-employment preparatory training, should be provided by both the City Council and the Board of Supervisors.

To implement our conclusions, we offer the following recommendations:

1) The Board of Police Commissioners should be strengthened.

2) Investigations of all citizen complaints should be conducted by an independent Inspector General under the authority of the Chief of Police in the implementation of procedures established by the Board of Police Commissioners.

3) The Police Department should institute expanded community relations programs.

4) The Sheriff's Department should effectuate these recommendations to the extent that they are applicable to it. . . .

A SUMMING UP — THE NEED FOR LEADERSHIP

The study of the Los Angeles riots which we have now completed brought us face to face with the deepening problems that confront America. They are the problems of transition created by three decades of change during which the historical pattern of urban and rural life—which for decades before existed side by side, each complementing and supporting the other—has been violently and irreversibly altered. Modern methods and mechanization of the farm have dramatically, and, in some regards, sadly reduced the need for the farm hand. With this, a drift to the city was the inevitable and necessary result. With respect to the Negro, the drift was first to the urban centers of the South and then, because scanty means of livelihood existed there, on northward and westward to the larger metropolitan centers. It was not the Negro alone who drifted; a substantial part of the entire farm labor force, white and Negro alike, was forced to move and did.

World War II and, to a lesser extent, the Korean War of the early 1950s, tended to accelerate the movement, particularly the drift of the Negro from the south to the north. Because job opportunities existed in the war plants located in our cities, the deep and provocative problem created by the movement was not at first appreciated by society. Since then, caught up in almost a decade of struggle with civil rights and its related problems, most of America focused its attention upon the problem of the South—and only a few turned their attention and thoughts to the explosive situation of our cities.

But the conditions of life in the urban north and west were sadly disappointing to the rural newcomer, particularly the Negro. Totally untrained, he was qualified only for jobs calling for the lesser skills and these he secured and held onto with great difficulty. Even the jobs he found in the city soon began to disappear as the mechanization of industry took over, as it has since the war, and wiped out one task after another—the only tasks the untrained Negro was equipped to fill.

Hence, equality of opportunity, a privilege he sought and expected, proved more of an illusion than a fact. The Negro found that he entered the competitive life of the city with very real handicaps: he lacked education, training, and experience, and his handicaps were aggravated by racial barriers which were more traditional than legal. He found himself, for reasons for which he had no responsibility and over which he had no control, in a situation in which providing a livelihood for himself and his family was most difficult and at times desperate. Thus, with the passage of time, altogether too often the rural Negro who has come to the city sinks into despair. And many of the younger generation, coming on in great numbers, inherit this feeling but seek release, not in apathy, but in ways which, if allowed to run unchecked, offer nothing but tragedy to America.

Realizing this, our Commission has made, in this report, many costly and extreme recommendations. We make them because we are convinced the Negro can no longer exist, as he has, with the disadvantages which separate him from the rest of society, deprive him of employment, and cause him to drift aimlessly through life.

This, we feel, represents a crisis in our country. In this report, we describe the reasons and recommend remedies, such as establishment of a special school program, creation of training courses, and correction of misunderstandings involving law enforcement. Yet to do all of these things and spend the sums involved will all be for naught unless the conscience of the community, the white and the Negro community together, directs a new and, we believe, revolutionary attitude towards the problems of our city.

This demands a form of leadership that we have not found. The time for bitter recriminations is past. It must be replaced by thoughtful efforts on the part of all to solve the deepening problems that threaten the foundations of our society.

Government

Government authorities have done much and have been generous in their efforts to help the Negro find his place in our society and in our economy. But what has been done is but a beginning and sadly has not always reached those for whom it was intended in time and in a meaningful way. Programs must not be oversold and exaggerated, on the one hand, or unnecessarily delayed on the other. What we urge is a submersion of personal ambition either political or bureaucratic, in the interest of doing the most good and creating the best results from each and every dollar spent in existing programs.

With particular respect to the City of Los Angeles, we urge the immediate creation of a City Human Relations Commission, endowed with clear cut responsibility, properly staffed and adequately funded. We envisage a commission composed of a chairman and six members with special competence in the fields of research, employment, housing, education, law, youth problems and community organizations. This City Commission should develop comprehensive educational programs designed to enlist the cooperation of all groups, both public

and private, in eliminating prejudice and discrimination in employment, housing, education, and public accommodations.

Business and Labor

Business leaders have their indispensable role. No longer can the
leaders of business discharge their responsibility by merely approving
a broadly worded executive order establishing a policy of non-discrimination and equality of opportunity as a basic directive to their
managers and personnel departments. They must insist that these
policies are carried out and they must keep records to see that they
are. Also, they must authorize the necessary facilities for employment
and training, properly designed to encourage the employment of
Negroes and Mexican-Americans, rather than follow a course which
all too often appears to place almost insurmountable hurdles in the
path of the Negro or Mexican-American seeking a job. Directly and
through the Chamber of Commerce, the Merchants and Manufacturers
Association, and other associations, the business leader can play a
most important role in helping to solve the crisis in our cities.

Labor unions have their very vital role. Union leaders must be
resolute in their determination to eliminate discrimination and provide
equality of opportunity for all within spheres of their jurisdiction and
influence. For one reason or another, the records of the ethnic mix of
the membership of many unions have not been furnished despite our
repeated requests. In labor, as in business, pronouncements of policy,
however well intended, are not enough. Unless a union conducts its
affairs on a basis of absolute equality of opportunity and non-discrimination, we believe there is reason to question its eligibility to represent employees at the bargaining table.

News Media

The press, television, and radio can play their part. Good reporting
of constructive efforts in the field of race relations will be a major
service to the community. We urge all media to report equally the
good and the bad—the accomplishments of Negroes as well as the
failures; the assistance offered to Negroes by the public and private
sectors as well as the rejections.

In our study of the chronology of the riots, we gave considerable
attention to the reporting of inflammatory incidents which occurred in
the initial stage of the Los Angeles riots. It is understandably easy to
report the dramatic and ignore the constructive; yet the highest traditions of a free press involve responsibility as well as drama. We urge

that members of all media meet and consider whether there might be wisdom in the establishment of guide lines, completely voluntary on their part, for reporting of such disasters. Without restricting their essential role of carrying the news to the public fairly and accurately, we believe news media may be able to find a voluntary basis for exercising restraint and prudence in reporting inflammatory incidents. This has been done successfully elsewhere.

The Negro and the Leader

Finally, we come to the role of the Negro leader and his responsibility to his own people and to the community in which he lives. The signing of the Voting Rights Act by President Johnson in the spring of 1965 climaxed a long and bitter fight over civil rights. To be sure, the civil rights controversy has never been the issue in our community that it has been in the South. However, the accusations of the leaders of the national movement have been picked up by many local voices and have been echoed throughout the Negro community here. As we have said in the opening chapter of this report, the angry exhortations and the resulting disobedience to law in many parts of our nation appear to have contributed importantly to the feeling of rage which made the Los Angeles riots possible. Although the Commission received much thoughtful and constructive testimony from Negro witnesses, we also heard statements of the most extreme and emotional nature. For the most part, our study fails to support—indeed the evidence disproves—most of the statements made by the extremists. We firmly believe that progress towards ameliorating the current wrongs is difficult in an atmosphere pervaded by these extreme statements.

If the recommendations we make are to succeed, the constructive assistance of all Negro leaders is absolutely essential. No amount of money, no amount of effort, no amount of training will raise the disadvantaged Negro to the position he seeks and should have within this community—a position of equality—unless he himself shoulders a full share of the responsibility for his own well being. The efforts of the Negro leaders, and there are many able and dedicated ones among us, should be directed toward urging and exhorting their followers to this end.

The Commission recognizes that much of what it has to say about causes and remedies is not new, although it is backed up by fresh additional evidence coming out of the investigation of the Los Angeles riots. At the same time, the Commission believes that there is an urgency in solving the problems, old or new, and that all Americans, whatever their color, must become aware of this urgency. Among the many steps which should be taken to improve the present situation, the Commission affirms again that the three fundamental issues in the urban problems of disadvantaged minorities are: employment, education and police-community relations. Accordingly, the Commission looks upon its recommendations in these three areas as the heart of its plea and the City's best hope.

As we have said earlier in this report, there is no immediate remedy for the problems of the Negro and other disadvantaged in our community. The problems are deep and the remedies are costly and will take time. However, through the implementation of the programs we propose, with the dedication we discuss, and with the leadership we call for from all, our Commission states without dissent, that the tragic violence that occurred during the six days of August will not be repeated.

NOTES

1. Summary of 1964 Riots

City	Date	Killed	Injured	Arrests	Stores Damaged
New York City	July 18-23	1	144	519	541
Rochester	July 24-25	4	350	976	204
Jersey City	August 2-4	0	46	52	71
Paterson	August 11-13	0	8	65	20
Elizabeth	August 11-13	0	6	18	17
Chicago (Dixmoor)	August 16-17	0	57	80	2
Philadelphia	August 28-30	0	341	774	225

2. The Coroner's Inquest into one of the deaths was cancelled at the request of the deceased's family. There was no inquest into the death of the deputy sheriff because of pending criminal proceedings.

3. A legal memorandum analyzing the procedures followed in the inquests, which was prepared at the request of the Commission, has been forwarded to the appropriate public officials for their consideration.

4. The more than seventy cases of alleged police brutality which were submitted to the Commission contributed to our understanding of the depths of the feelings of a segment of the Negro community toward the Police Department. Because our responsibility has been

to review the general policy and procedure for handling citizen complaints rather than to review individual cases, we have referred all of the cases to the appropriate and responsible agencies.

5. Of the forty-two complaints which were sustained, ten were for alleged excessive force, twenty-three were for alleged discourtesy or profanity, and nine were for alleged unlawful arrest or unreasonable search. In 1964, 470 officers, approximately 10 percent of the police force, were assessed disciplinary penalties of some type.

11.

PAUL JACOBS

The McCone Commission

"*What do you think is the most important bar to minority employ-ment that could be eliminated quickly?*" *the McCone Commission staff member asked me. We were sitting in the commission offices in downtown Los Angeles, and it was about the midpoint of the three-month investigation which was held before I began this book. Some members of the commission staff were friends of mine, and I had met with them and others on the staff a number of times to discuss some of their general problems. But now I was being questioned as an expert on employment.*

"The handicap that would be the easiest to wipe out is the arrest record," I answered. "*If arrest records weren't held against people, you could probably change the employment situation overnight and put a hell of a lot of people to work.*"

SOURCE: From Paul Jacobs, *Prelude to Riot: A View of Urban America from the Bottom* (New York: Random House, 1966), pp. 237-62. Reprinted with the permission of author and publisher.

The staff man looked at me, almost indignantly, and said, "I don't think a man who's got an arrest record should be employed in most businesses. I wouldn't hire anybody who had an arrest record for my family's business."

I sat there stunned. "What were you doing before you came to work for the commission?" I asked.

"I was a prosecuting attorney," he answered. "That's why I feel so strongly about people with arrest records."

At that moment I was convinced that the commission was going to fail. If a member of the commission staff had so little understanding of minority life, the investigation was doomed.

Months later I sat with McCone in his business office, talking with him for a long time about the commission's work. He was so sure of himself, so confident of his own correctness, that he never bothered to evade my questions or give me obscure answers as had some other people involved with the commission. He is the prototype of the American business and government success; on a table in the reception room of his financial empire is a large scrapbook with clippings attesting to his success as the head of the CIA. And he also is the prototype of the influential American who has failed to deal with the world in which we live.

Today, men exactly like him can be found on every commission appointed by governors and the President to investigate the wars in the cities. And those commissions will probably be of as little use in helping to end the wars as was the McCone Commission.

Perhaps Governor Edmund Brown might have made a worse choice than John A. McCone to serve as chairman of the governor's "Commission on the Los Angeles Riots." Perhaps. But in all of California it would be hard to find a man less qualified by training and attitude to investigate a social phenomenon like the one that shook Los Angeles in August 1965.

Yet the initial selection of McCone, the manner in which the other members of the commission were picked, the character of its staff, its methods of investigation, and the report it issued were all perfectly in character. The failure of government was a major cause of the terrible outbreak; it was almost inevitable, then, that in its investigation of the events government should also fail. And it did.

That failure was ordained from the moment the idea of an investigating commission was discussed in Los Angeles by Governor Brown and his staff, including two of his closest political advisors, Hale

Champion and Warren Christopher, a Los Angeles attorney, who is now Deputy Attorney General of the United States. The governor, who was vacationing in Greece when the social volcano erupted, had hurried back to California as soon as Champion telephoned the awful dimensions of the event to him. Christopher, on a holiday with his wife in the Bahamas when the first newspaper reports began to appear, had also cut short his holiday to rush back to Los Angeles.

The staff, shaken badly by what had been and still was happening, met in the governor's hotel suite in Los Angeles on Sunday, the day after his return to California. The city was growing quiet again and it seemed as if the worst was over; now it was time to assess what had occurred, find the causes, and make recommendations to avert any further outbreaks. The idea of the investigating commission was discussed, but neither the governor nor his associates had any clear idea of how such a commission would function. They did talk vaguely about patterning it after a British Royal Commission. As it turned out, no such comparisons can be made.

The initial failure of the commission was in the very limited conception the governor and his associates had of its function, a concept which led them inevitably to the choice of McCone as its head. "The governor was anxious to make a sound approach to the problem," states Christopher, "and he wanted to make a deep inquiry. But at the same time, he didn't want to do anything precipitous.

"He believed that what we needed to try and do was to move the total community to support the disadvantaged areas, and so he was instinctively drawn to a man with an impeccable reputation in the business community who would yet have enough experience with this kind of problem so that he could take a broad view of it."

In fact, neither the governor nor anyone on his staff understood what had happened in Los Angeles. Politically and psychologically they were unprepared to face the reality of the social cancer destroying the heart of the city and country. At a time when the city's future life depended upon making the most accurate diagnosis of its ills and perhaps prescribing drastic steps to help it survive, the liberal governor and his liberal staff still didn't want "to do anything precipitous."

Not only did they not want to do anything precipitous but in addition they sought a diagnosis of the city's sickness which would be acceptable to the very groups in the city which bore a heavy responsibility for creating the cancerous environment. Threatened by a real possibility of political defeat from the right, they gave the initiative to the right.

"The governor's basic purpose was to get a consideration of what had happened by some machinery that would be likely to have some persuasive effect with the establishment community down there," states Winslow Christian, then the governor's executive assistant. "The theory was that the Negroes themselves, living in those areas, perhaps had fairly realistic ideas of what was going on, and the liberal community likewise had ideas that from our point of view were fairly realistic . . . What we needed was to rub the noses of the establishment in some unpleasant facts in order to get their acquiescence in and understanding of the changes that were needed to deal realistically with the problems. And the notion was that McCone was personally a rather conservative sort of man, and we accepted that."

Certainly, McCone is the archetype conservative with "an impeccable reputation in the business community." A slender, rather short, wiry man with piercing eyes, McCone is a native Californian, a graduate in engineering from the University of California at Berkeley, and a very successful and wealthy businessman. During World War II he had operated engineering and shipyard enterprises engaged in overseas construction work and aircraft modification. He owns shipping companies that operate on a world scale and is on the boards of such corporations as Pacific Mutual Life Insurance Company, Western Banking, the First Western Bank, TWA, and Standard Oil. He is also a director of the Stanford Research Institute, a Trustee of the California Institute of Technology, a Regent of Loyola University in Los Angeles, and a founder of the Los Angeles World Affairs Council.

McCone's first experience with national government began in 1947, when President Truman appointed him to the President's Air Policy Committee. In 1948 he became a special deputy to Defense Secretary James Forrestal; in 1950 he was appointed Undersecretary of the Air Force, and served in that post until October 1951. Three years later he was appointed to the Dulles Public Committee on Personnel, which studied the personnel problems of the State Department. In July 1958 he became a member of the Atomic Energy Commission, moving into its chairmanship shortly afterwards; he remained on the AEC until January 1961.

Within the AEC, McCone was an advocate of the "Big Bomb" group, opposing those in the agency who favored developing limited nuclear weapons, test moratoriums, and controlled use of weapons. In

1956, when the issue of a moratorium on testing nuclear weapons became an issue in the Presidential campaign, McCone severely castigated ten Caltech professors who publicly supported Adlai Stevenson's position in favor of a moratorium. But he did more than attack them, according to Senator Eugene McCarthy, who claimed that McCone had attempted to get the ten scientists fired, a charge denied by McCone. At Caltech, however, many faculty members were convinced that McCone had called in the scientists and threatened them for their position.

In January 1962 John F. Kennedy, the liberal Democrat, appointed McCone as head of the CIA, a position he held until 1965. As the CIA chief McCone was also the chairman of the U.S. Intelligence Board, which coordinates the activities of all government intelligence agencies. Always a man supremely confident of the correctness of his views, McCone ran the CIA as if it were one of his business enterprises.

McCone's experience in the CIA was considered to be one of his potential assets as chairman of the commission, according to Christopher, who says, "His reputation in the CIA was a very good one. He went in at a time when it was easy to criticize him as a replacement for Allen Dulles, and I think the people in the CIA were initially quite skeptical about him. At least this is the story I'd heard and we discussed at the time. But over a couple of years he gained the complete confidence of most of the people in the CIA who were of an intellectual or academic type.

"And he demonstrated an open-mindedness to not dissimilar problems. The problems of developing countries, many of the intelligence problems have analogies here. How do you deal with minority groups in developing countries? I don't pretend to suggest any close parallels and I think the emphasis was more on his open-mindedness and his willingness to study an issue and to take a hard look at it.

"There was beyond that the very favorable things that were said about him by people who had obvious qualifications in this field, Bob Kennedy, for example. I think Bob McNamara thought very highly of him, too."

McCone was in New York attending a business meeting when he was called by the governor and asked to head the commission. He was somewhat reluctant to do so because he had only recently returned to California and was in the process of getting resettled both in his home and business life. But he didn't refuse the governor completely. "I told the governor I would give it thought," says McCone, "and see what my own commitments were, both with my business and with several government commissions on which I was working."

After this first conversation Brown called the White House, asking that President Johnson urge McCone to take the assignment. Johnson did contact McCone. "The President urged me to do it, if I possibly could," says McCone. "So on the basis of that and the conclusion that I could spare the time, I agreed that I would serve as chairman with the understanding that the governor and I would confer on the appointments to the commission, which we did." (McCone's conversation with Johnson was the first of a series of discussions between McCone and the White House about the commission, discussions which continued through the entire investigation and writing of the report.)

Like Brown and the members of his staff, McCone initially had no clear conception of the commission's mission. But he soon developed one, and it was his view of that mission, rather than the governor's, which became decisive. "There wasn't any model," he says, "and when I talked with the governor and his people on the telephone from New York and Washington over a period of two days, when we talked two or three times, I didn't really have a conception. Coming home on the plane, I gave it a good deal of thought and jotted down a few ideas, and then after I got here the first thing I had to give thought to was the frames of reference for the commission that the governor had to address to us. So Warren Christopher and I sat down and drafted a memorandum, a sort of frame of references, and this memorandum was transmitted and became, with such modifications as the governor's staff added, the directive to the commission from the governor."

Within the next few days proposed names for other members of the commission were discussed by Brown and McCone. Christopher was suggested immediately by the governor and was accepted by McCone along with the Very Rev. Charles S. Cassasa, President of Loyola University in Los Angeles. McCone then raised the question of putting Negroes on the commission, and Judge Earl S. Broady, a conservative Republican, was selected. Later another Negro, Rev. James Jones, a member of the Los Angeles City Board of Education, was added. Jones had been touring the Los Angeles area with Martin Luther King immediately after the upheaval and was at a meeting with King and the governor in the governor's hotel suite when Brown asked him if he would be willing to serve on the commission. Jones accepted and was approved by McCone.

"We wanted somebody that was in the field of medicine and health and also in the educational system," says McCone, "and the governor first raised the name of Chancellor Murphy at UCLA who was unable to serve because of other commitments. But he proposed Dr. Sherman Mellinkoff, who was not known to me at that time, but after one or two phone calls it was obvious that he would be an excellent man. There were two or three names that were brought up that the governor and I couldn't agree on, and so we dropped them." The seventh member of the group was Asa Call, like McCone a wealthy and conservative businessman, who had been president of a large insurance company for many years.

After the seven men had been chosen, McCone realized no woman was on the commission. "I believe I raised the question of putting a woman on the commission," recalls McCone, "and the governor brought up the name of Mrs. Neumann. She had been President of the League of Women Voters, and of course she was known to me, as was her husband. She was perfectly acceptable."

Only two of the eight commission members had any prior experience in the field of race relations. Father Cassasa had participated in such activities as teacher-training projects sponsored by groups like the American Jewish Committee, and Reverend Jones had been active in supporting Martin Luther King. The rest of the commission members had no special qualifications in this field: they were selected to give the impression of a broad community spectrum of the kind associated with community chest drives or anti-polio campaigns.

And so began the rapid transition from what had been called the "Governor's Commission" to what became known as the "McCone Commission." At the time McCone was appointed, some people believed that the governor and his staff had been looking primarily for a "good" name to head the commission, but that its actual work would be done by Christopher. If this version has any truth in it, McCone soon disabused everyone of the notion that he would play a purely passive role: not only had he insisted on veto power over the other members of the commission and, in addition, outlined the dimensions of its mission, but he also exercised a decisive voice on the appointment of key staff members, ran the commission with the same kind of discipline he had used in his CIA operations, dominated the commission hearings, and eventually made his personal stereotypes into the basic theme of the commission's report. Indeed, the commission was so much McCone's creature that its official secretary was Terence Lee, his longtime private secretary.

McCone settled another extremely important question: the short three-month period allocated to conduct the investigation and issue a report. Members of the governor's staff say that the reason for the three-month deadline was that the governor wanted some immediate remedial proposals to take to the state legislature; McCone says that he had his own considerations for setting the deadline: "I set it for several reasons. In the first place, I thought it was important to get the study done and get the recommendations in and get something on the rails to improve conditions. And secondly, this is a subject you can study forever and these were busy men; every one of them, including myself, had a full-time job, and we couldn't be expected to set aside a year of our life. And they worked very hard, day and night, seven days a week, to get the study done and the report out and I think it's just as good as if it took a year."

Evidently, no one gave serious consideration to such alternatives as issuing an interim report, at the end of the three-month period, with some recommendations for immediate action and following this up with a deeper analysis of the problems. . . .

[T]he governor's request that the "commission should probe deeply the immediate and underlying causes of the riots" was much less important to McCone than the more limited objective of ascertaining the facts about what had happened during the days of the rioting. So, too, McCone had, from the start, a very limited view of the kind of recommendations the commission should make in its final report.

"I felt," he says, "that those broad pronouncements so common in the writings of political sociologists would, if accepted by a commission such as ours, raise hopes, raise anticipations resulting in more frustrations, more anger, and finally more rage. Therefore we decided early on that we were going to be as pragmatic as possible about this and make recommendations that were defendable on the one hand and feasible on the other, and if followed would relieve a situation that concerned us. At the time I was reading deeply and intensively in the writings of a great many sociologists who had written on the whole question of the Negro and his place in our society, and while you can't disagree with what they say about a broad, humanitarian view, an official investigative body putting out such ideas in the form of recommendations was just impractical because the ideal of the goal of the complete extinguishing of any racial prejudice, to say nothing of barriers, is something that is going to go on for a long time. And therefore we as a commission felt that was not our responsibility nor our role. We weren't out to try to alter humanity by the printing of a little book but we were out to make some specific recommendations that would improve conditions in our community."

Christopher says he shared McCone's limited view of the commission's mission: "We felt that our mission or our role was to draw together the facts of the riots themselves and see if anything could be learned from the circumstances, the cops-and-robbers part of it. And then to look at what we thought were perhaps not the deepest underlying causes, but the ones that were susceptible of some immediate remedial efforts, some immediate improvements."

The commission began to function very quickly, although very chaotically, in offices provided in the State Office Building in downtown Los Angeles. An executive committee was appointed to make all the important decisions about the hiring of staff and the conduct of the investigation: the committee consisted of McCone, Asa Call, and Warren Christopher, and this small group made decisions on a day-to-day basis, generally without consulting the other commission members.

Very early, too, McCone established the role of his commission as the *sole* official governmental agency investigating the Los Angeles events. A White House task force, headed by Ramsey Clark, now the Attorney General of the United States, had come to Los Angeles to investigate the situation and make a report on it. But McCone, who states matter of factly, "Of course, I have a close relationship with the White House at every level," was able to head off any publication of the task force report.

He suggested to the White House that "it might be appropriate to wait until we came out with a report and recommendations before any White House pronouncement was made on what should be done in our city, and that was respected. And so, to the extent that there was a report, it was never published."

The three-man executive committee made the key decisions about the character of the commission's staff. The first person hired by the committee was the general counsel and executive director, Thomas Sheridan. The choice of Sheridan, and in turn the people he hired as members of his staff, very accurately reflected McCone's view of the commission's primary task and was another decisive element in determining the faulty character of the commission's investigation and ultimate report.

Sheridan, a fairly young man, was a former Assistant United States Attorney in Los Angeles, a member of the Robert Kennedy staff in the Justice Department, whose entire legal career had been as a prosecuting attorney. He had recently gone into private practice with a group of other men who had also been either with the Department of Justice or the FBI. None of the committee members knew him personally, although he was known, at least by reputation, to Christopher. Before hiring Sheridan, McCone discussed him with Nicholas de B. Katzenbach, who had succeeded Robert Kennedy as Attorney General. Katzenbach gave a favorable appraisal of Sheridan.

According to Sheridan, "I understand the basis for the recommendation from Nick to McCone was along the line that I had handled complicated, involved, fact-situation type things. He was going back to such cases as I was prosecutor for the Mickey Cohen case; I prosecuted the Sinatra kidnapping case. This sort of stuff."

The prosecutor of Mickey Cohen and the Sinatra kidnappers was interviewed initially by Christopher and then by McCone and Call. After his appointment had been agreed upon by those three, he began hiring his staff, primarily from among the prosecuting attorneys and investigators with whom he had worked in the past. A few days later Christopher called Sheridan and asked him if he knew Professor Harold Horowitz of the UCLA Law School, telling Sheridan that the commission was thinking of hiring Horowitz as Sheridan's assistant. Horowitz's background was in teaching law plus a few years in Washington with the Department of Health, Education and Welfare. He had also served on a number of state commissions and written on cases involving civil liberties.

Sheridan states that the choice of Horowitz was to balance the top staff: "Hal was coming from the academic community . . . and my legal career being on the prosecution side, dealing with investigators, etc., etc., . . . well, then I think the balance comes in this way—that if you'd try to characterize Sheridan, you'd probably end up characterizing him as pro law enforcement, which is a bad way to characterize anybody, I guess; and Hal, you'd characterize as the liberal academician. And then maybe the two will balance . . . Well, I don't know if we ever balanced or not . . ."

As it turned out the "balance" was precarious at best and in the long run the "pro law enforcement" man, the prosecutor, won out easily over the "liberal academician." And Horowitz's dilemma during the life of the commission was the classic one faced by every other "liberal academician" in such situations: they see their choice only as either quietly quitting the commission or remaining on the staff in the hope of being able to influence the results. Most eventually concede that their hopes have been vain and their influence upon the results minimal, except perhaps in an isolated case or two.

(Two people did quit the commission staff: Bryant Cushing and Carol Ratner, neither of whom were attorneys or investigators. Cushing was a management consultant with an interest in race relations who had done some work with employers in the South; Miss Ratner had some university background in social science. Both had worked on the study of the conflict between the Free Speech Movement and the administration of the University of California at Berkeley. Authorized by the Board of Regents, that study had resulted in a serious, in-depth analysis of the basic issues confronting the American universities today and had been hailed as a real contribution to the field. On the basis of that experience they had accepted an invitation to work on the McCone Commission, believing that a similar kind of report would be made at the conclusion of its investigation.)

To Sheridan the entire investigation was focused on gathering "hard facts," and in his view "hard facts" included the "underlying" causes of the riots. "Take a look at the governor's charge," he says. "Circumstances around the arrests; the riots; why did it spread; what did law enforcement do; what did private individuals do to control the riots; ordering up the National Guard; action taken by law enforcement and the National Guard to control the riots; circumstances surrounding the deaths which took place; personal injuries; damages done by fire; weapons used; how they got them; disturbances of a similar nature in other parts of the nation; arraignments; trials of persons apprehended during the riots. That's all just pure fact investigation.

"Then secondly, the physical and sociological conditions of the area, the way it's phrased, are really fact questions. At least the physical one—what's the physical area look like; what's involved; opportunities for Negroes in employment; public and private welfare programs available. Pertinent facts to be gotten on the persons involved in the riots, their background—which is again a straight fact thing; attitude of the rioters toward the community.

"Before we could get to the underlying causes, our whole feeling was 'underlying cause of what?' Underlying cause of the riots? Who was arrested? Let's first get those facts; when you've got the facts, present it to the sociologists, psychiatrists, and so on across the board . . ."

Sam Williams, the third member of the staff to be hired, epitomized a role as clearly as Sheridan and Horowitz. Williams was the prototype of the young Negro who from the white viewpoint is becoming integrated properly into the society. A good-looking, husky young man, Williams was a former football hero at the University of California who went on to an outstanding career at law school. After law school he went to work for the State Attorney General and then became the first Negro attorney to be hired by a large "downtown" law firm in Los Angeles. From the moment the governor had announced the appointment of the commission Williams had been very anxious to work with it; his interest had become known to Christopher, and he was hired after the usual interviewing process had been completed. But he was never able to play more than a secondary role, for he was not a narrow "facts" man; his emphasis was on looking at social conditions.

By this time the pace of activity had become feverish in the commission's offices. Dozens of people were volunteering for work, the phones were ringing continually, administrative procedures were unknown or uncertain, and no one even knew exactly how much money was available for the commission's work. The governor had allocated $100,000 from his own emergency funds, but it seemed certain that more money would be needed, and so contact was made with the Ford Foundation for additional help in financing the operation. The foundation sent its representatives to California a number of times, and fairly quickly allocated $150,000 to the commission.

The first task Sheridan and Horowitz faced was putting together a staff. Sheridan assumed the responsibility for hiring the attorneys and investigators, who were going to get "the facts," while Horowitz was assigned the task of employing consultants to whom "the facts" were to be presented. But as was obvious fairly early, far more importance was given to gathering the "facts" than to their interpretation.

Of the eleven attorneys hired by the commission, three were from the U.S. Attorney's office; one came from the State Attorney General and one from a background as a court clerk; the others came from specialized backgrounds. Only two had done any work in race relations, and only one had any prior experience with welfare problems. Four of the ten investigators were former FBI men, two were former agents of the Federal Narcotics Bureau, one had been a deputy sheriff, and the three others were private detectives. Indeed, the full-time staff did not include a single professional working in the field of social sciences.

One explanation for this lack of social scientists on the full-time staff was that it was difficult to get such people away from their assignments at the universities where most of them worked. As a substitute, therefore, the decision was made to hire them as consultants. But the social scientist consultants were always downgraded by McCone and Sheridan, who viewed them as dreamers and visionaries.

By instinct, training, and professional activity men like McCone and Sheridan distrust or feel uncomfortable with social science and theory. McCone prides himself on being a pragmatist, a man who gets things done. Sheridan was a prosecuting attorney, whose professional life had necessarily been concerned with getting convictions. And since McCone was chairman of the commission and Sheridan its chief counsel, it was inevitable that their views would dominate the commission and its staff. As a result serious tensions developed among the staff as they divided themselves into two rough groupings: the one whose primary emphasis was on gathering facts and making limited recommendations, and the one which sought to probe below the surface and explore a wider range of possible solutions.

That conflict came to a head quickly. At a staff meeting held shortly after the commission began operating, the subject of housing was being discussed. Cushing spoke up: "We are working with a pretty big problem here. I feel that housing is one of the central aspects of the whole problem. And it would be very helpful to us if we can gain from the commission some view as to what range of recommendations you're willing to consider. Not necessarily make, but are willing to consider."

A silence followed and then McCone asked, "Well, tell us what you mean by that."

"Here's the possible range," replied Cushing. "At one end of the spectrum your report can suggest that the way to solve this problem is to encourage little groups not to get into block-busting. At the other end, you can recommend that the President exercise his executive powers in tying non-discrimination in housing into every bank and savings and loan account guarantee in the United States. Now that's the range and there are a lot of things in between. Where does the commission want to fall?"

Once again, silence. Then the meeting adjourned. The next day McCone and Christopher appeared before the staff and gave them a short lecture, the gist of it being that the commission was only interested in "hard facts," not staff thinking on social problems. "We are not here to revolutionize society," they said. "We are not going to recommend any major social changes. We want to come up with some things that can be done right now."

The following day the same point was stressed again when Sheridan responded to a comment by Cushing that the commission had a great opportunity in carrying out its task.

"Mr. McCone and those in charge of the commission have declined that opportunity," answered Sheridan.

Another early source of disagreement in the staff was whether or not the commission should hold open hearings. McCone, supported by Christopher and Call plus a few other members of the commission, was completely opposed to such open hearings—a position shared vehemently by Sheridan. Horowitz, Williams, Cushing, and Ratner wanted open hearings, but their position was given little or no weight.

"We decided not to have any open hearings," states McCone, "for the simple reason that emotions were running high, and open hearings would have produced nothing but a forum for extremes on either side, or let's say all four sides, to come and use the commission as a platform. There had been open hearings held by various organizations, the City Council had had some hearings and I believe the Board of Supervisors, and we were cognizant of the extent to which they had been abused and used. We felt it would be unproductive."

Christopher is more uncertain today than McCone or Sheridan about the decision not to hold open hearings. "We thought that the situation might be aggravated. You have to put yourself back into that period of the fall, when there were still a couple of fires a day down in that area. The amount of press attention when our people went out of the hearings and some of the things that were said just outside the hearings in the press conferences rather led us to feel that open hearings might have incendiary effects on the area and also might not lead to maximum candor and assistance to the commission.

"But it's a very close question, and I don't feel completely comfortable about the lack of open hearings. I think we can argue that both ways."

Like McCone, Sheridan was opposed to the idea of open hearings, which, he believed, "couldn't accomplish as much" as closed ones. "As soon as you go to open hearings, how many people will try and use the commission for posturing, to take public positions, and then just use the commission to make a lot of noise?"

Sheridan's model in preparing for the closed sessions seemed to have been the Kefauver Hearings or those conducted by the McClellan Committee, in which a large staff of investigators gathered information to be used by the committee's counsel in questioning witnesses. But in the actual conduct of the sessions McCone played the dominant role, allowing Sheridan very little opportunity for questioning witnesses.

As a substitute for open hearings the commission members did have some meetings, in the two offices which had been set up in the Negro section, at which people in the community were invited to appear. But this operation was never more than half-hearted; when the commission members did appear, one at a time, most of the people to whom they talked had already been screened by the staff. And the general impression in the community was that going to the office was just a waste of time. The fact that on a few occasions Asa Call arrived at the Watts office in his limousine with a white chauffeur who parked outside the office didn't do much to mitigate the Negroes' feeling that talking to such white people was useless.

Implicit, too, in the character of the closed hearings was the commission's, or at least McCone and Sheridan's, view of whom it was important to listen to. The list of witnesses who appeared before the commission is very revealing: primarily the heads of government agencies who came to defend themselves and their roles either in the rioting or in the events that preceded it. And many of the Negroes who testified fitted the white society's notion of what constitutes Negro leadership; they were not the people who play the real leadership roles in the Negro quarters.

As one white staff member put it, "McCone sees as the Negro leaders the few people who are visible to the whites. He doesn't understand that maybe they're just the tip of a pyramid, and because he doesn't understand that, he doesn't even realize the pyramid exists."

A Negro staff member says, "McCone's whole concept of leadership disturbs me. I think he, like the majority community, think they help build Negro leaders. And to the extent that they do, their Negro leaders are going to have certain built-in defects; because in order for a Negro to be acceptable as a leader to people like McCone, you have to meet certain standards of the white community, you have to make sure you stay in your place and do all the other things which have always been characteristic of the 'Uncle Tom.' And once you build this kind of person, one who can communicate with the white power structure, he can't communicate with his own people because he's out of touch with their real problems. And so it's just a fantastic vicious circle; and then when you end up, as McCone did, blaming those people for what happened, it's like blaming a creation of your own for not being able to control the masses. It's ridiculous.

"I started out having a lot of respect for McCone, but I lost it very rapidly. He did one thing that really threw me: one day he came into the office and told us that he sees things just a little more clearly now. Why did he see things a little more clearly? Because, he said, he'd gone and received an interpretation of these problems from his maid! She'd told him something that had convinced him he was on the right track. And he didn't understand that this maid is dependent upon him for a livelihood; in all probability she likes him because he's probably a good employer, and how could he think she's going to stand up and tell him anything that would in any way disturb him?"

McCone seems to have been disturbed neither by anything his maid told him nor by what was presented in testimony at the sixty-four hearings the commission held in the auditorium of the State Office Building under strict security conditions. In general, the hearings were defensive of the existing agencies of government, and sought to balance any criticism of them with evidence supporting their activities.

While the hearings were going on, attended regularly by most of the commission members, tensions among the staff were growing worse. Administratively, the commission operated like an hourglass, a military operation with the commission members, the officers, on the top, and on the staff, the enlisted personnel, below them. Between the two groups, at the center of the hourglass, was Sheridan, the top sergeant.

"We worked out a chain of command right from the beginning," says Sheridan. "Because we had to deal with normal kinds of problems, not serious ones. I drew a little diagram at one of the early commission meetings, and I said, 'This is the commission up here, all the commissioners; this is all the staff, down here; this is me, in the middle. If the people on the commission have anything they want the staff to do, any communications, correspondence, or anything like that with the staff, it's got to go through me. And I'm instructing the staff that if they've got anything for the commission, it goes through me, not because I'm important or anything else, but because if we don't have this kind of a thing, then I'll never know what the hell is going on and neither will the commission.' The commission agreed with this kind of approach, so that after a while McCone and myself had any number of meetings, any number of sessions."

The pressure on the commission members was great, for they were attending the hearings plus the occasional commission meetings called by the chairman. And because they all had to cram their normal week's work into a day or two at the most so that they could spend time on commission activities, most of them were willing to allow McCone, Call, and Christopher, together with Sheridan, to continue making all the daily decisions. Indeed, McCone, a very energetic man, was spending almost all of his time on commission business, flying to Washington frequently to meet with government officials, conferring with people from the Warren Commission about their experiences, and talking to his friends in the Washington scene. Even when Mc-Cone was in California, he kept in constant touch with the White House, discussing the progress of the investigation with Joseph Califano, a top Presidential advisor. Liaison with state officials was maintained through Christopher, who was always regarded as the governor's voice on the commission.

But the abdication of responsibility by the other commission members resulted not only from their crowded schedules and McCone's willingness to put in hundreds of hours on commission work; other factors were involved, too.

John McCone is not only a strong personality but a powerful one as well, a member of that group in America who exert much influence on the nation's life. Because he combines prestige in business, one of the highest forms of status in the country, with influence in government, he is not a man to be lightly challenged. And few of the other commission members were in a position to do so, even if they had wanted to fight him. The only one who did, and then only at the end and not very seriously, was Reverend Jones.

The original division of staff work had been that Sheridan was to assume primary responsibility for the investigations and hearings, Horowitz for the work being done by the consultants, and Williams for the operations of the field offices. But Sheridan was the overall director of all the staff activities, and this created stress between him and Horowitz, for according to some of the staff, he believed Horowitz was breaking the chain of command by going directly to Mc-Cone and some of the commissioners, discussing with them the work of the consultants.

This stopped when Horowitz was relieved of his responsibility for dealing with the consultants and replaced by Cushing, who was in turn replaced by Sheridan himself. And while all this internal tension was growing, time was getting shorter, the offices more and more chaotic, and the staff more and more disorganized and depressed. Memos were written and ignored, plans outlined and forgotten, consultants called in and never seen again. Perhaps the only consistent daily action was the nightly emptying of all the wastepaper baskets and the destruction of their contents by a waste disposal company brought in by Sheridan.

In desperation, for the deadline was growing closer and closer, members of the staff were assigned areas of responsibility without any relationship to their experience or expertise in the field. The result was more chaos, of course, with an enormous amount of effort wasted in writing memos eventually discarded and conducting useless interviews.

" 'Give us a memo,' they'd say," reports one staff member, "so I'd prepare a memo. Then they'd tell me, 'No, that's not what we want. It's too long.' So I'd write another and they'd come back with, 'No, that's no good either; what we want is just an outline.' And once I wrote a very long memorandum, but when I got it back it was just a précis and a lousy one at that of what I'd said. That was when I began to understand that the report wasn't going to have a lot in it."

In addition, the prior attitudes and training of the staff necessarily skewed their views of the problems. The investigators were busy looking for signs of a plot behind the riots and writing reports of their "interrogations" of "subjects," while the attorneys tended to see the areas to which they'd been assigned primarily in legal terms. And the consultants, too, necessarily had to write their reports on the basis of their already established views, for there was neither the time nor the opportunity for them to do any further research in their special areas. The only exception was Dr. Kenneth Martyn, the consultant on education, who received funds to complete his research work.

One of the few consultants actively involved with the commission was Paul Bullock, an economist on the staff of the Institute of Industrial Relations at UCLA. Bullock had been one of the men chiefly responsible for making a detailed report on the Negro and Mexican-American community of Los Angeles commissioned by the Area Redevelopment Administration in 1963. That report had covered, in great detail, employment, housing, consumer practices, transportation, and a variety of other problems in the south and south central ghettos. Bullock's own special interest was employment, and he was considered to be the most knowledgeable person in all of Los Angeles on the situation in the Negro areas.

Bullock was contacted by Horowitz soon after the commission was created and asked to report on such questions as the impact on the area of various training programs, the kinds of jobs that had been developed, where the jobs had been located and what the transportation problems were in getting to them. Since so little time was available to do any new research, Bullock was forced to use whatever data he had already gathered in connection with his ARA report and his continuing interest in the situation.

Fortunately, he had quite a lot of data, and so he prepared a preliminary report and then added a supplemental report to it, following this up with an appearance before the commission members to summarize his reports. By this time it was November and the situation at the commission was one of terrible anxiety, since the deadline for the report was only a few weeks away.

The notion McCone and Sheridan had of the relationship between the staff and the commission members extended over their attitude toward the consultants. "Facts" not opinions were what was demanded of the staff, and "facts" not opinions were all that was wanted from the consultants, too.

As Sheridan says of the consultants, "A lot of material, a lot of information that was coming in at that stage wasn't in the practical world. And when we wanted hard facts, some of the consultants couldn't give you hard facts. So, what they wanted to give you was their opinions. And of course their opinions weren't important. They're important but they're not important. It's the commissioners' opinion that became important . . ."

In the meantime, too, Horowitz had been removed from liaison with consultants such as Bullock and had been replaced by Cushing. But then Cushing and Miss Ratner both quit, convinced that they and the others who shared their viewpoint had lost the battle. Believing that the commission's report was going to be useless, they wanted no connection with it. Unfortunately, however, they left without explaining their position, thus leaving themselves open to all sorts of rumors about their reasons for resigning.

Sheridan then took over the liaison role with the consultants at the time when the staff was beginning work on writing the report. Members of the commission were also designated to accept responsibility for making certain that specific sections of the report were written. In the case of the employment section, for example, one of the men formerly with the U.S. Attorney's staff, an ex-FBI agent, and commission member Asa Call had been designated as the staff members responsible.

As the deadline came closer and closer, the atmosphere of the commission's offices grew more frantic and tense. As Sheridan describes it, "At this stage we had no end product in mind. We didn't know what we were working toward; we didn't know when we were working toward it. We didn't know the exact date; are we going to turn out a book, are we going to turn out a forty-page report, or are we going to do the same thing as the Welfare Commission did—put out its report, its recommendations, and a separate volume with the consultants' reports attached to it? And all of these suggestions, of course, were discussed with the commissioners. . . . So we drew up several drafts, formats, this kind of thing, for the commissioners to decide what it wanted . . ."

"We had assembled a mass of data," recalls McCone. "We had a great number of witnesses; we had our offices; we had consultants' reports, and we had reports from investigators. And we had a study on education, a study on employment, and we had assembled a lot of information from studies that had gone before us . . .

"So, then we sat around and we took the various areas of importance—employment, education, housing, transportation, various sections of the report—and we concluded among ourselves just what our general recommendations would be. And those were written maybe on one piece of paper. And in fact I dictated most of them and then brought them down and tried them on for size, and we modified them or added to them to meet the will of the commission.

"We found we were in quite general agreement and then we set out to write the report. Now, I wanted a report that would be an interesting, readable document, so I asked a friend of mine to come out and assist in writing the report. And he did. Unfortunately, he was taken violently ill the day after he arrived, and as a consequence the writing of the report fell pretty much on the shoulders of Warren Christopher and myself. And then I insisted that we take the draft that was produced by whoever produced it and that we go over it line by line and word by word with the commission. Now, this was very tedious for them but having had some experience in getting out national estimates for the United States Intelligence Board, I know how to do that. And so we went over it line by line and while we were together, we changed it and agreed to it, and if some wording had to be changed to make a special point or emphasize or de-emphasize something the writer had emphasized, we did that. When all of that was done, then the thing was put to bed."

McCone's calm recital represents one view of the process by which the report was written. From the consultants' viewpoint, the process looked quite different.

Many of them who undertook their responsibilities very seriously believe that they were used by the commission primarily because their names would lend an aura of intellectual respectability to the report. In fact, with one notable exception, the report of the consultant on education, the commission's final report does not contain very much of either what some staff members produced for it or of the lengthy reports submitted to it by the consultants referred to in the final document. In the overwhelming majority of cases, the consultants' work was either ignored or contradicted in the commission's final document. . . .

I 2.

ROBERT M. FOGELSON

White on Black: A Critique of the McCone Commission Report

On August 11, 1965, a white California highway patrolman arrested a young black for drunken driving in the south central ghetto known as Watts. A scuffle involving the youth, his mother, and the patrolman followed, attracting a large crowd which was further incited by the arrival of the Los Angeles police. From about eight that evening to one the next morning, mobs stoned passing automobiles, assaulted white motorists, and threatened a police command post. On August 12, after a tumultuous meeting called by the Los Angeles County Human Relations Commission, the rioting, accompanied by looting, arson, and assault, spread through the ghetto. At great personal risk many moderate black leaders, some from Los Angeles and others of national renown, pleaded with the rioters to end the violence, but to little or no avail. The next day the disorder was so widespread that Los Angeles Police Chief William Parker asked California Lieutenant

SOURCE: From Robert M. Fogelson, *Violence as Protest* (New York: Doubleday & Company, 1971), pp. 192-216. Reprinted with the permission of author and publisher.

Governor Glenn Anderson (standing in for vacationing Governor Edmund Brown) to order in the National Guard. Rioters and guardsmen besieged Watts that evening, and after Anderson imposed a curfew, the authorities slowly suppressed the nation's worst racial riot in a generation. On August 15—with 34 dead, over 1,000 injured, and almost 4,000 arrested, 600 buildings damaged, and $20 million to $40 million in property destroyed order was restored.[1]

Four days later Governor Brown (by then returned to California) appointed a commission consisting of six whites and two blacks and headed by John A. McCone, a prominent industrialist and former director of the CIA, to make "an objective and dispassionate study of the Los Angeles riots." Brown instructed the commission to "prepare an accurate chronology and description of the riots . . . probe deeply the immediate and underlying causes of the riots . . . [and] develop recommendations for action designed to prevent a recurrence of these tragic disorders." The commission, which was allocated $250,000, hired twenty-nine staff members, sixteen clerks and secretaries, and twenty-six consultants, and then launched its investigation. It heard seventy-nine witnesses, including Governor Brown and his advisers, local politicians, police administrators, civil libertarians, teachers, black spokesmen, and Watts residents; its staff members interviewed several hundred persons, including ninety arrested during the riots, and its consultants questioned another 10,000 people. Working at an extremely, perhaps unduly, rapid pace, the commission completed its investigation in three months. And on December 2, 1965, it presented its interpretations and recommendations in an eighty-six page report entitled *Violence in the City—an End or a Beginning?*[2]

Put bluntly, *Violence in the City* claimed that the rioters were marginal people and the riots meaningless outbursts. The rioters were marginal people because they were a small and unrepresentative fraction of the black population, namely, the unemployed, ill-educated, juvenile, delinquent, and uprooted. What provoked them to riot were not the conditions endemic to black ghettos (i.e., police harassment and consumer exploitation), but rather problems peculiar to immigrant groups (i.e., insufficient skills and inferior education) and irresponsible agitation by black leaders. Also, the riots were a meaningless outburst, according to the McCone Commission, not simply because there was no connection between the blacks' grievances and their violence, but also because the rioting was unwarranted. Watts, for all its inadequacies, is not, like Harlem, a slum—its streets are wide and clean, and its houses are detached one- and two-story dwellings; nor are its residents, like Southern Negroes, subject to racial discrimination—to the contrary, they enjoy full legal and political equality.[3] Thus, to prevent a repetition of rioting in south central Los Angeles, *Violence in the City* concluded, requires that police-civilian relations be improved, unemployment reduced, education upgraded, and civil rights protest suppressed.

Less than two months later, the California Advisory Committee to the United States Civil Rights Commission challenged the McCone Commission's findings and recommendations. Shortly thereafter Bayard Rustin, the well-known civil rights spokesman, Robert Blauner, a Berkeley sociologist, and Harry Scoble, a U.C.L.A. political scientist, criticized the report, too.[4] Notwithstanding a few differences, these critics agreed on the following crucial points. First, that a much larger and more representative segment of the ghetto populace than the McCone Commission estimated joined the rioting and that many others who did not participate supported the rioters. Second, that the blacks rioted, because they could not passively accept conditions in the ghetto any longer and not because they were unprepared for urban life or because their leaders were contemptuous of law and order. Third, that the rioting, and especially the looting and burning, were articulate protests against genuine grievances and, as such, meaningful protests against the south central ghetto. Fourth, that the Watts vicinity is, by any physical or psychological criteria, a slum, in which Los Angeles' blacks are rigorously and involuntarily segregated. Hence, to maintain public order in Los Angeles, these critics countered, demands fundamental changes not only in the black ghetto but in the white metropolis as well.

The controversy between the McCone Commission and its critics was resolved late in 1966 when the U.C.L.A. Institute of Government and Public Affairs completed a survey of the Los Angeles riots for the U. S. Office of Economic Opportunity, and I finished a report on the riots of the 1960s for the President's Commission on Law Enforcement and Administration of Justice.[5] Together these studies left little doubt that the McCone Commission completely misunderstood the character and implications of the Los Angeles riots. Yet, as the McCone Commission archives were inaccessible for several months after the investigation, none of the critics (nor, for other reasons, either of the studies) made it clear why the commission failed. Accordingly, it was not until the summer of 1966, when the archives—which consist of the report, a chronology of the rioting, twelve volumes of staff interviews, and two volumes of consultants' papers—were deposited in the California State Library in Sacramento and the University of California Library in Los Angeles, that it was possible to reconstruct the Commission's investigation and to discern where and why it went wrong.

The archives indicate that the investigation failed for more profound reasons than the critics presumed. To begin with the most obvious explanation, the commission was unduly hasty in its work. The schedule, which allowed only slightly more than three months for the investigation,[6] was exceedingly tight and the pace excessively rapid. And the commission presented an extremely sketchy report, a document much less impressive than the exhaustive study of the Chicago riots of 1919 and even the modest account of the Harlem riots of 1935.[7] But during the three months available, a careful reading of the report, hearings, interviews, and consultants' papers reveals that the McCone Commission collected enough information for a satisfactory explanation of the rioting. And so completely did the commissioners ignore or misinterpret this information that there is no reason to believe that if given three years rather than three months they would have prepared a better report.[8]

To turn to another obvious explanation, the commission was not inclined to probe deeply into the riots anyway. Governor Brown, who was gravely concerned about his political future (with good cause, it turned out), knew that the riots were an explosive issue. Hence he appointed a conservative Commission. In addition to McCone, who, by virtue of his prestige, dominated the deliberations, it consisted of a prominent attorney, the chairman of the Pacific Mutual Life Insurance Company, the president of Loyola University, the dean of U.C.L.A. Medical School, and a former president of the California League of Women Voters (the six whites) as well as a Los Angeles judge and a Presbyterian pastor (the two blacks). Except for the blacks, who were anything but militant and exerted little influence anyway, the commissioners were representative of California's establishment. This was hardly auspicious because blue-ribbon commissions in the United States, unlike royal commissions in Great Britain, have as a rule sought political, as opposed to literal, truth.[9] And the McCone Commission was no exception.

There is, however, a more crucial explanation for the Commission's failure. The commissioners were not altogether unsympathetic to the plight of the south central ghetto, nor were they unintelligent or irresponsible. But they were mainly upper-middle-class whites who brought to their task assorted preconceptions about violence, law enforcement, ghettos, and slums—preconceptions which they shared with others of their class and race. These preconceptions filtered the testimony and other information received by the commission and enabled it to draw conclusions based on the flimsiest material while ignoring more substantial but less reassuring data. And therefore they prevented the Commission from perceptively analyzing the evidence and correctly interpreting the riots. Hence, a reconsideration of the investigation is worthwhile not only because *Violence in the City* is the official statement of the Los Angeles riots but also because the McCone Commission's fiasco sharply illuminates why most whites have not understood the 1960s riots.

I

At the outset of the investigation the Commission reached the conclusion that only 10,000, or approximately 2 percent, of Los Angeles County's 650,000 blacks joined the rioting. Moreover, the rioters were not representative of the black community; they were the unemployed, ill-educated, delinquent, juvenile, and uprooted—in short, the riffraff.[10] The overwhelming majority of blacks, the Commission implied, were law-abiding, that is, non-riotous; doubtless they disapproved of the disturbances. The riffraff theory, it should be noted, was not formulated for the first time by the McCone Commission. It had been adopted a year earlier by Paul Screvane, Acting Mayor of New York City, and Nelson Rockefeller, Governor of New York State, in order to explain the Harlem, Bedford-Stuyvesant, and Rochester riots.[11] Nevertheless, for the McCone Commission (as well as for the Brown administration and most white Californians), the conclusion that the riffraff was primarily responsible for the riots was highly reassuring.

For if the rioters were only a small group of unemployed, ill-educated, delinquent, juvenile, and uprooted blacks, the Los Angeles riots were less serious than would otherwise be the case. It follows that the rioting was not only peripheral to the issue of black-white relations, but also a manifestation of problems of poverty, which is alterable, rather than race, which is immutable. It also follows that the riots reflected not so much the social problems inherent in black ghettos as the personal disabilities of recent newcomers. It follows further that the violent acts, the looting, arson, and assault, were not expressions of legitimate grievances and that they were, in the Commission's words, "formless, quite senseless," and, by implication, meaningless.[12] Hence future riots could be prevented in south central Los

Angeles merely by elevating the riffraff without transforming the ghetto—without, in effect, radically changing greater Los Angeles or seriously inconveniencing its white majority.

Given the profound implications of the riffraff theory, its foundations should have been based on solid evidence. Yet little evidence, solid or otherwise, is contained in *Violence in the City*. For all its hearings, interviews, and consultants, the McCone Commission made no surveys of riot participation. Instead, it derived its estimate that only 2 percent of the blacks rioted from the impressions of Mayor Samuel Yorty, Police Chief Parker, and other officials who had good reason to minimize the extent of participation.[13] What is more, the Commission based its conclusion that the rioters were the riffraff on nothing more than a breakdown of the persons arrested during the rioting according to age, prior criminal record, and place of birth. It did not present the comparable statistics for the south central ghetto which would have shown that the number of juveniles, criminals, and newcomers involved was not disproportionately large.[14] Nor did it compile any data about the employment rates and educational levels. Finally, the Commission offered no proof that the great majority of blacks disapproved of the rioting, and even ignored the testimony of many middle-class blacks who did not riot but fully sympathized with the rioters.[15]

Why then, in the absence of corroborating evidence, did the McCone Commission adopt the riffraff theory? The answer, I believe, can be traced to its conviction that no matter how grave the grievances, there are no legitimate grounds for violent protest—a conviction, shared by most whites and, until recently, most blacks which reflects the nation's traditional confidence in orderly social change.[16] To have accepted, indeed, even to have raised, the possibility that a substantial and representative segment of the blacks participated in the riots would have compelled the commission to draw either of two conclusions. One, that the deterioration of the south central ghetto has destroyed the prospect for gradual progress and provided the justification for violent protest; the other, that even if the Commission does not believe that the situation is so desperate, a large number of ordinary blacks do. Neither conclusion could have been reconciled with the Commission's commitment to orderly (and extremely limited) social change. And to have accepted either would have obliged the commissioners to reexamine a fundamental feature of the ideology of their class, race, and country. Not surprisingly, they were disinclined to do so.

The riffraff theory is wrong, however. On the basis of statistical and other data now available, the Commission's estimate that only 10,000, or approximately 2 percent, of Los Angeles County's 650,000 blacks participated in the riots is wholly farfetched. For to claim that only 10,000 rioted when almost 4,000 were arrested is to presume that the police apprehended fully 40 percent of the rioters, a presumption which, as Harry Scoble has pointed out, is inconsistent with the first-hand descriptions of the rioting.[17] Indeed, recent surveys conducted by David O. Sears, a U.C.L.A. political scientist, and John F. Kraft, Inc., an opinion research organization, reveal that the figure is at least 20,000 and perhaps as high as 50,000.[18] Of the 650,000 blacks then living in Los Angeles County, moreover, no more than 450,000 resided in the curfew area; and of these, roughly 180,000—namely, children under ten and adults over sixty—did not participate in the rioting.[19] Thus, of the potential rioters (the male and female adolescents and young and middle-age adults)—and the McCone Commission notwithstanding, potential rioters, not total population, is the appropriate base on which to compute riot participation—a substantial minority joined in the riots.

Arrest data and survey research also refute the McCone Commission's conclusion that the rioters were the unemployed, ill-educated, delinquent, juvenile, and uprooted. The Commission's profile is not internally consistent—a study prepared for the Area Redevelopment Administration by the U.C.L.A. Institute of Industrial Relations reveals that the newcomers tend to be better educated and more regularly employed than the older residents.[20] Nor is it otherwise accurate. Young adults and not minors made up the large majority of the arrestees; that most of them had prior records reflects not so much their criminality as the high incidence of arrest in the ghetto. Evidence about educational achievement suggests that the rioters were, if anything, slightly better educated than their peers; so, survey research indicates, were their parents. And data on residence and employment, also based on arrest records, show that the great majority of the rioters had lived in Los Angeles for at least five years and were currently employed. For these reasons the U.C.L.A. Institute of Government and Public Affairs concluded that the rioters were very much in "the mainstream of modern Negro urban life."[21]

Recent public opinion surveys also contradict the McCone Commission's implication that an overwhelming proportion of the blacks disapproved of the riots. Not only did a substantial and representative minority participate in the rioting, but many others who did not riot sympathized with the rioters.[22] Nor did attitudes in the ghetto change later. Whereas a small majority of blacks interviewed after the rioting expressed confidence in non-violence, nearly as many believed that the riots had improved the blacks' position. Also, many who disapproved of the rioting gave as their reason that blacks, not whites, suffered most of the personal injuries. Asked what impact the riots had on them, a slight majority answered that they felt more pride, a large minority reported no change, and almost none said that they felt less pride.[23] Contrary to the McCone Commission's findings, then, the Los Angeles riots were made by a large minority of the potential rioters, typical of the young adult population, which received widespread support within the ghetto.

This conclusion has very different, but no less profound, implications than the riffraff theory. If the rioters were a substantial and representative minority, sympathetically regarded by the black community, the riots were clearly of the utmost importance. They were not only central to the issue of black-white relations but also manifestations of problems of race even more than class. Indeed, there is considerable evidence that working- and middle-class blacks resent the indignities of ghetto life more than lower-class blacks do. The rioting also reflected social problems endemic to black ghettos rather than personal disabilities peculiar to immigrant groups (or, as Bayard Rustin put it, the unpreparedness not of the newcomers but of the cities). And the violent acts were expressions of genuine grievances and, as such, meaningful protests. If these implications are valid, future riots can be prevented only by transforming the south central ghetto, not simply by elevating the riffraff—a recommendation which is highly irresponsible when exploited, as it was by the McCone Commission, to obscure the ghetto's legitimate grievances.

II

The riots made it quite clear that many blacks in the south central ghetto regard the conduct of the local police as one of these grievances. The incident which precipitated the rioting—a routine and, were it not for what followed, trivial arrest for drunken driving—is otherwise incomprehensible. Why else did hundreds of blacks gather at the site of the arrest, shout abuse at the patrolman, attempt to free the prisoners, and hurl bricks at the police cars? Why else did so many blacks believe the wild rumors that the patrolmen were mistreating other blacks which swiftly spread through the ghetto? Why else did the arrival of police reinforcements attract a thousand or so blacks to the scene and transform the crowd into a mob? And why else did the rioters later vent their hostility against local patrolmen and not, with some exceptions, against National Guardsmen?[24] So overwhelming is the evidence that even the McCone Commission realized that police action has an incendiary effect in the south central ghetto that it has nowhere else in Los Angeles. And for this reason the commission spent many of its sessions investigating the blacks' resentment of the police.

Several middle-class blacks conceded at these sessions that many blacks are resentful of the police because of their earlier experience in the South. But, they insisted, even in Los Angeles, blacks are victims of brutality and harassment so often that their resentment is justified. These witnesses also admitted that for the patrolmen who work there (as for the people who live there) the south central ghetto is a very dangerous place. Even so, they pointed out, blacks are convinced, and with good reason, that the police enforce the law less rigorously in their community than elsewhere in Los Angeles.[25] It is because, as Assemblyman Mervyn M. Dymally told the commission, blacks have "generally expected the worst from the police and generally received it"[26] that they resent them so. To ease this resentment, Dymally and the other black witnesses urged the Commission to recommend that brutality and harassment be eliminated, law enforcement tightened, and a civilian review board established.

The Los Angeles Police Department spokesmen, Chief Parker, John Ferraro, President of the Board of Police Commissioners, and Mayor Yorty replied that these charges were altogether unfounded. Indeed, to Parker they were manifestations of the dwindling respect for law and order in the United States and attempts to undermine the effectiveness of law enforcement in Los Angeles. Police brutality is extremely uncommon, they argued, police harassment is deplored and discouraged, and a single standard of law enforcement is maintained everywhere in Los Angeles. The blacks' resentment, they claimed, is due to their past mistreatment in the South and present maladjustment in the North, and not to the conduct of the police in the ghetto. Blacks vent their hostility toward patrolmen not as patrolmen, but as representatives of white society and white authority; the police are the recipients, not the source, of black resentment. Past practices aside, the police department's spokesmen assured the Commission, Los Angeles' blacks have no genuine grievances against the police; and no major departmental reforms are necessary.[27]

The McCone Commission endorsed the police department's position.[28] It dismissed the charges of brutality and harassment, ignored the allegations of inadequate law enforcement, and concluded that the problem of police-community relations was a problem not of misconduct but of misunderstanding. To alleviate this misunderstanding the Commission recommended that the police department's complaint procedure be revised. But it rejected demands for a civilian review board—on the grounds that such boards have not worked well in two other cities (both of which were unnamed) and that they tend to demoralize patrolmen (though black, not police, morale was the issue)—and proposed instead the creation of an "inspector general" under the jurisdiction of the chief of police. It also recommended the professionalization of the Board of Police Commissioners, the non-salaried agency which has ultimate responsibility for the police force, and the expansion of the police department's current community relations program.[29]

To reach these conclusions was no mean task. The McCone Commission had to do more than just reject the testimony of many middle-class blacks. It also had to disregard the affidavits and other evidence submitted by the southern California chapter of the American Civil Liberties Union substantiating the allegations of police misconduct and to ignore the statement of one Los Angeles policeman who reluctantly admitted that most white patrolmen cannot distinguish between law-abiding and lawless blacks.[30] And it had to accept without qualification the testimony of Chief Parker, a man whose antipathy to the civil rights movement was exceeded only by his devotion to the Los Angeles police, whose professional views were extremely conservative even for a conservative profession, and whose personal behavior at the Commission's hearings bordered on the paranoid.[31] That the McCone Commission or, more accurately, Chairman Mc-Cone—for the other commissioners deferred to him on the problem of police-community relations—overcame these obstacles without the benefit of any surveys or other data refuting the blacks' complaints or supporting the department's replies is indeed remarkable.

What is even more remarkable is that McCone had already resolved this problem by the start of the investigation. Questioning George Slaff of the American Civil Liberties Union, to whom he was inexcusably rude,[32] McCone remarked that as CIA director he had found that in all recent domestic riots and overseas insurrections the issue of police brutality was raised in order to destroy effective law enforcement. This tactic is reprehensible, he explained, because society is held together by respect for law, and respect for law is maintained by effective law enforcement, an assertion which reappeared almost verbatim in *Violence in the City*,[33] even though Slaff and others challenged its fundamental premise at the hearings. If brutality is admitted, McCone reasoned, authority will be undermined, law will be disregarded, society will be disrupted, and, in the words of the report, "chaos might easily result"—a prospect for which the Commission was unwilling to assume responsibility. That effective law enforcement is only one source of respect for law, that respect for law is only one basis for public order, and that society is simply a collection of predatory individuals and groups, McCone did not realize. Given his preconceptions and the other commissioners' deference, the Commission could not have reached any other conclusions.

These conclusions are untenable, however, not only because they are inconsistent with the testimony and evidence offered by black witnesses and Civil Liberties Union spokesmen, but also because they are contradicted by two independent surveys of police conduct in the south central ghetto subsequently prepared by the Kraft organization and U.C.L.A. psychologist Walter J. Raine. These surveys reveal that most blacks, middle-class as well as lower-class and law-abiding as well as lawless, have suffered brutality or harassment at one time or another.[34] These surveys also indicate that few blacks believe that they receive adequate police protection, a belief supported by the crime statistics Chief Parker submitted to the McCone Commission. Hence, without analyzing the blacks' complaints or the patrolmen's conduct at this point, it is possible to define brutality, harassment, and inadequate protection as the primary problems underlying resentment of the police which precipitated the Los Angeles riots.

These problems are problems of substance, not misunderstanding, which the Commission's recommendations do little to alleviate. Professionalization of the Board of Police Commissioners is irrelevant because it is not intrinsically related to the questions of brutality, harassment, and inadequate police protection in the ghetto. Establishment of an "inspector general," as opposed to a civilian review board, is valueless because the blacks will not place their trust in any police official, no matter how impressive his title. And expansion of the police department's community-relations program is at best beneficial and at worst, if exploited, as it was by the McCone Commission, to avoid the real issue, misguided. That issue is to provide south central Los Angeles with the same law enforcement as the rest of the metropolis, a policy which would reduce brutality and harassment and at the same time enhance police protection. This is not easy, politically or otherwise. But if the relationship between the police and blacks in Los Angeles is to be improved so that routine incidents do not trigger terrible confrontations in the future, it is imperative.

III

The McCone Commission did not do much better in its investigation of the other reasons underlying the riots. That there were other reasons no one, not the Commission and not its critics, seriously doubted. Although only a thousand blacks gathered at the scene of the triggering incident, thousands more, few of whom had witnessed the initial arrest, subsequently joined in the rioting. Night after night, for almost a week, they left their homes and, with a camaraderie and jubilation usually reserved for festive occasions, thronged the streets. There they not only attacked patrolmen (flinging bricks and Molotov cocktails and occasionally firing rifles from the rooftops), but also assaulted white passersby and looted and burned neighborhood stores.[35] These actions transformed a minor disturbance into a full-scale riot. This transformation was not inevitable, however: there are too many instances in which bands of Americans, often adolescent members of ethnic minorities, challenged police authority without provoking widespread disorder for this to be so.[36] But neither was it accidental. It was rather a violent manifestation of the fact that the blacks resent other conditions in the south central ghetto just as keenly as they resent police misconduct. To discern these conditions, and to recommend action to remedy them, was the McCone Commission's principal responsibility.

To this end the Commission received from its witnesses and consultants sixteen volumes of testimony and reports which, for all its inconsistencies, made certain points quite clear. First, that in addition to police misconduct the crucial problems of Los Angeles' blacks, and not only its lower-class blacks, are economic deprivation, consumer exploitation, inadequate accommodations, and racial discrimination. Second, that these problems are deeply rooted in the conditions of ghetto life, especially in the high rates of unemployment, extreme risks of business enterprise, rigid patterns of residential segregation, and the profound weakness of moderate leadership. Third, that the rioters were so selective in their violence that, with few exceptions, they looted and burned only white-owned stores which charged outrageous prices, sold inferior goods, and applied extortionate credit arrangements.[37]

But for the McCone Commission it was one thing to receive information and quite another to accept it. A few examples illustrate this difference. Jeffery Nugent and Michael DePrano, University of Southern California economists, suggested that the rioting was generated by the disparity between the black's educational achievements and his employment opportunities.[38] An imaginative hypothesis, but one incompatible with the riffraff theory, it was completely ignored by the Commission. Paul Schrade, a United Automobile Workers official, argued that unemployment in the ghetto is due primarily to job shortages in greater Los Angeles, an assertion which contradicts the assumption that individual disabilities, not social conditions, provoked the rioting.[39] McCone sharply dissented, claiming that the problem is a function of insufficient training, and the Commission adopted his position. Thomas Reddin, deputy chief of the Los Angeles Police Department, testified that the theft and arson were directed at unscrupulous white merchants.[40] His testimony ran counter to the presumption that the rioting was meaningless, and, though confirmed by half a dozen witnesses, it too was disregarded by the Commission.

Rejecting this and other evidence inconsistent with its preconceptions, the McCone Commission found three main reasons for the riots (other than police-community misunderstanding and irresponsible black leadership): excessive unemployment, inferior education, and inadequate transportation. Jobless blacks cannot attain a decent standard of living, the Commission argued, nor can they assume responsibility for their families. Hence, their self-esteem wanes, and their community ties erode; welfare, which feeds their children, intensifies their dependency. Training black workers to compete in the labor market is one solution. Also, the Commission insisted, black youngsters cannot understand what is taught in schools because they are culturally deprived. Nor can the schools help; they have insufficient equipment and a limited curriculum, too few experienced teachers, and too many double sessions. To educate the black students so that they can be trained for skilled employment is another solution. Finally, the Commission contended, the blacks are sorely inconvenienced as workers and as students, because the ghetto is isolated from Los Angeles. In a metropolis which lacks adequate mass transit facilities only 14 percent of the families in south central Los Angeles, as opposed to over 50 percent in Los Angeles County, own automobiles. Improving transportation to facilitate movement in and out of the ghetto is yet another solution.[41]

The McCone Commission's recommendations are also consistent with its preconceptions. To reduce unemployment it proposed that government, business, and labor create a job training and placement center in south central Los Angeles, that federal and state authorities insure due advantage is taken of available training programs and job opportunities, and that the California legislature require employers and unions to disclose the racial composition of their employees and members. To upgrade education it urged that a permanent pre-school program be established in the ghetto to assist three-year-olds to develop the skills required to learn to read and write, and that certain elementary and junior high schools there, designated "emergency schools," be authorized to set up literacy programs with classes limited to twenty-two students and special services provided by supplementary personnel. To improve transportation it recommended that all the transit companies in greater Los Angeles be consolidated with the Southern California Rapid Transit District, and that public authority subsidize the District to expand service in the ghetto[42]—a recommendation partially implemented when the U.S. Department of Housing and Urban Development granted $2.7 million for the District in May 1966.[43]

These recommendations are unsatisfactory, however. Unemployment in south central Los Angeles—which, by the U.S. Census Bureau's conservative estimate, is over 10 percent—is very high. But inadequate training is only one among many reasons for unemployment, and unemployment is only one among many economic problems in the ghetto.[44] About these reasons—job shortage, racial discrimination, and criminal records—and these problems—irregular employment and inadequate wages—the McCone Commission said virtually nothing. Education in the ghetto—where, according to commission consultant Kenneth A. Martyn, test scores in all subjects and at all grades are extremely low—is inferior, too. But approximately one black in four who graduates from high school cannot find employment anyway, and many others must settle for menial jobs.[45] To urge blacks to acquire an education under these conditions, as the McCone Commission did, is unfair and perhaps even unsafe. Lastly, mass transit is awful in south central Los Angeles as well as in greater Los Angeles. But according to a 1965 census, fully 65 percent of the families in the ghetto, and not, as reported by the McCone Commission, only 14 percent, own one or more cars.[46] The south central ghetto is isolated, but not for reasons as simple and reassuring as dreadful bus service.

The McCone Commission's findings are particularly incomplete with regard to consumer exploitation and racial discrimination. The

Commission admitted that many witnesses charged that white merchants systematically exploit black consumers in south central Los
Angeles. But it insisted that low-income consumers are at a disadvantage everywhere, not only in the ghetto, and denied that there was a
correlation between consumer exploitation and the looting and burning.[47] To relieve consumer exploitation it recommended establishment of educational programs and expansion of legal services. The
Commission's findings do not withstand careful scrutiny, however.
Consumer exploitation is a function of race as well as poverty, of
customers without credit, high-risk businesses, and merchants without
scruples. The correlation between rioting (and especially arson) and
consumer exploitation is imperfect, but, the archives reveal, convincing just the same.[48] And the Commission's recommendations are inadequate because, if implemented, they would not increase consumer
credit, reduce business risks, or curtail mercantile cupidity in south
central Los Angeles.

If the McCone Commission minimized consumer exploitation, it
ignored racial discrimination. For this the witnesses were not to
blame. One after another, and sometimes with great eloquence, they
spoke of discrimination. They testified that it started when the blacks
first migrated to southern California at the turn of the century and
still persists today, fully fifty years and a half a million people later.
They also testified that most whites, not only patrolmen, politicians,
realtors, and merchants, treat most blacks as unworthy, undesirable,
and even inferior.[49] Yet their testimony, which, while subjective, was
quite restrained, made no impact on the McCone Commission—and
for good reason. The Commission could not concede that resentment
of racial discrimination (as well as economic deprivation and consumer exploitation) was justified, or that assaults on white passersby
and looting and burning of neighborhood stores were manifestations
of these grievances, without abandoning its preconceptions about the
riots. Hence the McCone Commission failed to discover the conditions underlying the riots and to devise recommendations which might
prevent future rioting.

IV

The McCone Commission also failed to explain why the customary
restraints on rioting were inoperative in the south central ghetto. To
be sure, it did devote a large part of its limited time to investigate the
ineffectiveness of the external restraints, namely, police and military
power. It questioned Chief Parker, Lieutenant Governor Anderson,

and Lieutenant General Roderic Hill, commander of the California National Guard, about the coordination of local, state, and national forces. And it examined their activities during the riots to determine why the National Guard was not ordered in earlier, which it assumed would have ended the rioting sooner.[50] To an observer who considers the Los Angeles riots a problem of black ghettos and not of police strategy, the questioning seems wide of the mark. The Commission's finding, that Lieutenant Governor Anderson delayed unduly in responding to Chief Parker's request for the National Guard, appears beside the point. And so does its conclusion that local law enforcement agencies and National Guard units should prepare plans for a quicker commitment and better deployment of troops in the event of future emergencies.[51]

Far more serious, the McCone Commission spent little or no time analyzing the ineffectiveness of the internal restraints in the ghetto. It was so concerned about the damage done by the riots that it was oblivious to the risks run by the rioters. To riot with the support of the police, as the Irish did in New York in 1900, is one thing; to riot in the face of the opposition of the police and the military, as the blacks did in Los Angeles in 1965, is quite another.[52] To discount this difference on the grounds that the patrolmen were outnumbered at the initial disturbance, that at first they attempted merely to contain the rioting, and that afterwards they exercised commendable restraint is to beg the question. However safe the rioters were during the first few days, they were in grave peril during the last few days. By then all available police personnel and over 15,000 National Guardsmen were assigned to south central Los Angeles with orders to fire when fired upon and to take whatever action necessary, short of indiscriminate slaughter, to quell the rioting.[53] Thus for several days the ghetto was so dangerous a place that by the time the authorities pacified it 34 were dead, over 1,000 injured, and nearly 4,000 arrested, almost all of whom were black.

Given the grave dangers to life, limb, and liberty at the peak and near the end of the riots, it is not surprising that a majority of ghetto residents sought the safety of their homes. What is surprising is that a large minority, totaling tens of thousands of people, congregated in the streets and participated in the rioting anyway. The McCone Commission implied that their action reflected the growing desperation of the black riffraff. This implication is unacceptable, however, not only because it misconstrues the composition of the rioters and discounts the risks in the rioting but also because the history of native

Americans in Appalachia, Puerto Ricans in New York, Mexicans in southern California and other under-privileged groups in the United States reveals that poverty and illiteracy do not necessarily lead to rioting.[54] It is unacceptable, too, because it does not explain why Los Angeles' blacks, however intense their resentment, refused to abide by the time-honored strategy expressed in the aphorism "Cheese it, the cops!" why they, unlike other ethnic minorities, insisted instead on a direct confrontation with the authorities—why, in sum, they disregarded the customary restraints on rioting in the United States.

Among these restraints are the fear of arrest, and possible conviction and imprisonment, which is inconvenient at the time and burdensome later on; the concern for personal safety, the reluctance to risk life and limb, especially when the opposition is much stronger; and the commitment to orderly social change, the conviction that necessary changes can be secured through legitimate channels and that there is no point at which violence is the only recourse. To riot, as the blacks did in Los Angeles, means not only that the grievances provoking them were intolerable but also that the restraints inhibiting them were ineffective. To claim that these circumstances were complementary and equally crucial prerequisites for the riots is not to deny that the grievances generated the resentment which weakened the restraints. Indeed, this is just what happened in south central Los Angeles. It is rather to insist that there are certain other conditions overlooked by the McCone Commission which have further undermined these restraints in the ghetto. And the reason why these conditions were overlooked helps explain the Commission's failure.

Why the restraints on rioting were ineffective can be briefly outlined. The fear of arrest did not restrain the rioters because the overwhelming majority of them, or at any rate of the men, had already been arrested, if not convicted and imprisoned. The exact proportion has not been calculated, but 70 percent is a reasonable estimate; and whether it is a trifle too low or too high is not critical, because the other 30 percent presume that they too will be arrested sooner or later and if not for rioting then for something else.[55] The concern for personal safety did not restrain the rioters either because they had been hardened to the point of indifference by the relentless assaults on life and limb in the ghetto. The rioting, tumultuous though it was, did not mark a fundamental discontinuity in their experience, nor pose an extraordinary threat to their security.[56] And the commitment to orderly social change did not restrain the rioters because, whatever their objective circumstances, they were convinced that their trust was misplaced. And according to surveys conducted in the ghetto shortly after the riots, a substantial majority of the residents believed that violence was either necessary or, if not, probable just the same.[57]

The reasons for these conditions can be briefly summarized too. The extreme incidence of arrest is due in large part to preventive patrolling in the ghetto, a police practice which, in the name of rigorous law enforcement, often subjects the blacks to intensive surveillance, unwarranted suspicion, and outright harassment. The high level of violence is a consequence of the blacks' tendency to resort to illegitimate enterprises when legitimate channels to success are closed, and to express through aggression against blacks resentment which cannot be directed against whites. And the dwindling confidence in orderly change is a reflection of the disparity between the rapid rise in the blacks' expectations and the more gradual advance in their achievements, a disparity more pronounced in the 1960s than at any other time in the twentieth century.[58] From this summary one conclusion emerges: the conditions undermining the restraints and the reasons underlying the conditions are all manifestations of slum life in south central Los Angeles. For it is only in the slums, though not only in Los Angeles slums, that preventive patrolling is practiced so intensively, illegitimate enterprises operate so openly, and minority groups are frustrated so frequently in their quest for a better life.

To the McCone Commission, however, south central Los Angeles was not a slum—not an urban gem, it conceded, but not a slum either.[59] Hence there was no reason for the Commission to probe for the conditions which weakened the restraints on rioting there. Commissioner Warren M. Christopher's examination of Judge Loren Miller is illuminative here. Christopher remarked that he returned from a recent visit to other ghettos reassured. "I wouldn't say that this (Watts) is a garden spot of South Los Angeles," he said, "but I see street after street of small well-kept homes and I find the contrast between that and the large tenement structures in New York and Philadelphia . . . quite striking."[60] What about this contrast, he asked? Miller, who was less impressed, answered that Watts did not resemble Harlem, but neither did Los Angeles resemble New York: in any case the south central ghetto was a slum. Other witnesses agreed, insisting that a close look at the Watts vicinity revealed that one of every three houses was dilapidated or deteriorated. And so did others, who stressed that by any social, economic, or psychological, as opposed to physical criteria, south central Los Angeles was unquestionably a slum.[61]

On what, if not the testimony of the witnesses, did the McCone Commission base its conclusion that south central Los Angeles was not a slum? The Commission's observation that the streets were wide, clean, and lined with trees and that the houses were one- and two-family dwellings begs the question. For what the Commission observed depended on what it deemed worth observing, which, in turn, depended on how it conceived of a slum. And despite a rash of studies showing that physical condition is only one, and by no means the principal, measure of a slum, the Commission's conception was purely environmental.[62] By this conception, which the Commission shared with most Americans, a slum is defined by its deviation from a middle-class residential suburb. And on the surface Watts does not deviate very much, a fact which no doubt helps explain why many whites found the 1965 riots beyond belief. This conception of a slum is altogether oblivious to the wide range of social, economic, and psychological indicators of community pathology; and so, accordingly, was the McCone Commission. For this reason it overlooked the extreme incidence of arrest, high level of violence, and dwindling confidence in orderly social change which have undermined the restraints of rioting in south central Los Angeles.

V

The McCone Commission also misinterpreted the black leaders' role in the Los Angeles riots. The leaders, the Commission argued, incited the ghetto residents by various inflammatory activities. They denounced the disparities between the grandiose promises of the anti-poverty program and the patent inadequacy of its provisions and protracted bickering over its implementation. They also encouraged the blacks to feel affronted by the passage of Proposition 14, a state-wide referendum which repealed California's fair housing act and precluded future fair housing legislation. (The Commission's choice of words was perplexing: given the obvious implications of Proposition 14, the blacks needed no encouragement to feel affronted.) And inspired by reports of civil disobedience and outright violence elsewhere in the United States, they exhorted blacks to devise extreme and illegal remedies for wrongs in Los Angeles. On the basis of these findings, the McCone Commission recommended that the black leaders curb their extremism and—in the phrase of one commissioner, the black pastor, who disagreed with this recommendation—"put the lid on protest."[63]

These findings are not corroborated by the testimony offered at the hearings, however. The moderate blacks leaders, witnesses pointed out, had attempted to channel the ghetto's discontent into orderly outlets long before the riots.[64] They were middle-class in outlook, personally confident in orderly change and professionally committed to non-violent protest. They also realized that rioting would endanger the rioters and, by alienating friends and comforting enemies, undermine the civil rights movement. Once the riots erupted, moreover, the moderate leaders perceived that, their position notwithstanding, they were not leading. They understood that the rioters were challenging their leadership in the black community and subverting their position vis-à-vis the white society. They could, and did, denounce conditions responsible for the riots, but the intensity of the outbursts demanded something stronger. Hence, other than to join in the rioting and assume its direction, which they were unwilling to do, the moderate leaders had no alternative but to try to restrain the rioters. And from the very beginning of the riots, witnesses testified, these leaders roamed the streets of Los Angeles doing precisely that.[65]

Yet none of them was successful.[66] In stressing that local leadership (not to mention national leadership) was incapable of restraining the rioters, I am not implying that the rioters were easily restrained; the excitement was too great, the grievances too strong, and the customary restraints too weak. But I am suggesting that the outbreak of rioting in south central Los Angeles revealed that the moderate leaders had failed not only to alleviate ghetto conditions but also to confine black resentment to non-violent channels. I am suggesting, too, that the timing of the riots, which started late in the evening and stopped early in the morning, provided the moderate leaders with an opportunity to meet with the ghetto residents under relatively calm circumstances and that they failed to exploit this opportunity. Taken together these failures highlight the weakness of moderate leadership, in south central Los Angeles, a problem much more serious than the McCone Commission's unfounded allegations about the extremism and irresponsibility of black leaders.

There are several reasons why moderate leadership is so weak in the south central ghetto. There is the intransigence of white Los Angeles, which is responsible for the approval of Proposition 14 and other discriminatory actions which have impaired the moderate leaders' prestige. There is the lower- and working-class blacks' antagonism to the middle-class blacks who alone have the time, money, and energy to organize cohesive groups and fill positions of leadership. There is also the weakness of the ghetto's voluntary associations, which is largely due to the assumption of their traditional functions by public authority, private enterprises, and the mass media. There are the competition of militant black nationalists and the absence of a distinctive black culture in the United States too.[67] These reasons need not be described at any length here. But one other reason is, however, worth discussing in more detail because it has implications for an examination of the McCone Commission as well as for a consideration of black leadership. And that is, the indifference of middle-class blacks to the problems of the residents and institutions of south central Los Angeles.

Although middle-class blacks have not been unsympathetic to the plight of lower- and working-class blacks in Los Angeles, they have not displayed the same concern for the south central ghetto that middle-class Italians and Jews in Boston and New York showed for the North End and Lower East Side.[68] Middle-class blacks in Los Angeles have left the ghetto physically and spiritually. They have left it physically not only because of social conditions there which do not meet middle-class standards, but also because housing there is vastly inferior to housing elsewhere in Los Angeles. According to the U.S. Census of 1965, houses in south central Los Angeles are the most overcrowded, substandard, and overpriced in the metropolis.[69] Middle-class blacks have also left the Los Angeles ghetto spiritually to dissociate themselves not only from lower- and working-classes, a common practice of middle-class Americans whatever their color, but from the ghetto itself. It is for them, as the plantation was for their fathers, the embodiment of the blacks' ignominious position in American society, the symbol of their subordination and segregation.[70] Within or without the south central ghetto, the middle-class is not of it, and thus cannot lead it.

What underlies the physical and spiritual flight from the south central ghetto is the system of residential segregation. Just how widespread the system is has been too well documented elsewhere to require further proof here,[71] but its involuntary character is worth stressing. Unlike Mexicans and other newcomers, blacks did not choose to live as a group in Los Angeles; far from choosing at all, they were compelled to reside together.[72] And the consequences were as unfortunate as they were inevitable. So long as blacks were denied access to the metropolitan real estate market and so long as they were deprived of the chance to move freely if dissatisfied with the quality or cost of their housing, they were confined to overcrowded, substandard, and overpriced dwellings. Also, so long as they lived in south central Los Angeles only because there were no alternatives and so long as they regarded it as a place of confinement, they perceived the ghetto as the emblem of their subordination and segregation. Under these circumstances middle-class blacks have fled the ghetto whenever they could do so.

The McCone Commission did nothing more than admit that involuntary residential segregation is practiced in metropolitan Los Angeles.[73] It did not consider its consequences or recommend its elimination; nor did it point out the implications of Proposition 14. For this the witnesses were again free of fault. One after another they explained how involuntary residential segregation is implemented in Los Angeles and how the black community is victimized by this practice. The McCone Commission ignored them because their testimonies revealed the tremendous stakes that many whites have in perpetuating the black ghetto. Merchants who overcharge customers, manufacturers who underpay laborers, and landlords who exploit tenants are only the most obvious beneficiaries. Less evident but more numerous are the homeowners who spend their lives in all-white suburbs and the parents who send their children to all-white schools. But for the McCone Commission to have investigated involuntary residential segregation would have obliged it to abandon its preconceptions that the Los Angeles riots were manifestations of economic, not racial, problems and individual, not social, deficiencies.

Here as elsewhere the McCone Commission offered inadequate recommendations based on erroneous analyses derived from untenable assumptions. And in so doing it demeaned the rioters, belittled their grievances, misunderstood the ghetto, misconstrued the riots, and thereby discouraged efforts to devise imperative and more drastic reforms. As the official version of the Los Angeles riots, moreover, *Violence in the City* has not only shaped public policy—witness the federal subsidy to the Transit District—but also guided popular opinion. From it the residents of Los Angeles have either taken the conclusion that the rioting was meaningless or drawn the implication that the blacks somehow lack the qualifications for responsible citizenship. That the McCone Commission provided them no other alternative was not the least of its disservices. Worse still, the Commission reflected middle-class, white ideas and values so well that its findings and recommendations, or facsimiles thereof, have appeared in many official comments on other recent riots, and with more validity.[74] Not until white America abandons the preconceptions about rioting, law enforcement, slums, and ghettos which misled the McCone Commission, will it recognize the 1960s riots as articulate protests against genuine grievances in the black ghettos.

NOTES

1. Jerry Cohen and William S. Murphy, *Burn, Baby, Burn! The Los Angeles Race Riot August, 1965* (New York, 1966), pp. 78-222; Governor's Commission on the Los Angeles Riots, *Archives*, II, in the University of California Library, Los Angeles (hereafter referred to as *MCA*).

2. *Violence in the City—an End or a Beginning?* A *Report by the Governor's Commission on the Los Angeles Riots*, December 2, 1965 (hereafter referred to as *MCR*). For Governor Brown's charge, see ibid., pp. i-iii.

3. Ibid., pp. 2-9.

4. California Advisory Committee to the United States Commission on Civil Rights, "An Analysis of the McCone Commission Report" (January 1966); Bayard Rustin, "The Watts 'Manifesto' and the McCone Report," *Commentary* 41 (1966): 29-35; Robert Blauner, "Whitewash Over Watts," *Trans-action* 3 (1966): 3 ff.; Harry Scoble, "The McCone Commission and Social Science" (unpub. paper, U.S. Office of Economic Opportunity, August 1966).

5. Robert M. Fogelson, "The 1960s Riots: Interpretations and Recommendations" (report prepared for the President's Commission on Law Enforcement and Administration of Justice, 1966). The Institute's study was prepared under the supervision of Professor Nat Cohen who kindly allowed me to read the findings.

6. Blauner, "Whitewash Over Watts," p. 2.

7. Chicago Commission on Race Relations, *The Negro in Chicago* (Chicago, 1922); Mayor's Commission on Conditions in Harlem, "The Negro in Harlem: A Report on Social and Economic Conditions Responsible for the Outbreak of March 19, 1935" (New York, 1936).

8. Rustin, "The Watts 'Manifesto'," pp. 33-34; Blauner, "Whitewash Over Watts," pp. 2-3.

9. Charles J. Hanser, *Guide to Decision: The Royal Commission* (Totowa, N.J., 1965), chapter 10.

10. *MCA*, III, Testimony of Lieutenant Governor Glenn M. Anderson, p. 22; *MCR*, pp. 1, 3, 5, 24.

11. New York *Times*, July 22 and August 4, 1964; Newark *Evening News*, July 20, 1964; New York *Journal-American*, July 26, 1964.

12. *MCR*, pp. 4-5.

13. *MCA*, III, Testimony of Lieutenant Governor Glenn M. Anderson, pp. 22-23; XI, Testimony of Police Chief William H. Parker, pp. 87-89; XIV, Testimony of Mayor Samuel W. Yorty, pp. 58-61.

14. Bureau of Criminal Statistics, California Department of Justice, "Summary of a Preliminary Report of Persons Arrested in the Los Angeles Riots" (November 1965), *MCA*, II; *MCR*, p. 24; U.S. Bureau of the Census, *Current Population Reports*, "Characteristics of the South and East Los Angeles Areas: November 1965," series P-23, no. 18 (Washington, D.C., 1966), p. 38; idem, *United States Census of Population: 1960. Detailed Characteristics. California. Final Report* (Washington, D.C., 1962), pp. 478, 485; President's Commission on Law Enforcement and Administration of Justice, *The Challenge of Crime in a Free Society* (Washington, D.C., 1967), p. 75.

15. *MCA*, XV, Interview 29; XVI, Interview 90.

16. *MCR*, pp. 6-7. See also Louis Hartz, *The Liberal Tradition in America* (New York, 1955), chapter I; Gresham M. Sykes, *Crime and Society* (New York, 1966), p. 79.

17. Scoble, "The McCone Commission," p. 11.

18. John F. Kraft, Inc., "Attitudes of Negroes in Various Cities" (report prepared for the U.S. Senate Subcommittee on Executive Reorganization, 1966), pp. 5-6; David O. Sears, "Riot Activity and Evaluation: An Overview of the Negro Survey" (unpub. paper, U.S. Office of Economic Opportunity, 1966), pp. 1-2.

19. U.S. Bureau of the Census, "Characteristics of the South and East Los Angeles Areas," p. 38.

20. Institute of Industrial Relations, University of California, Los Angeles, "Hard-Core Unemployment and Poverty in Los Angeles" (Washington, D.C., 1965), pp. 143-45.

21. Sears, "Riot Activity and Evaluation," pp. 1-13; Los Angeles County Probation Department, "Riot Participation Study: Juvenile Offenders" (November 1965); Bureau of Criminal Statistics, California Department of Criminal Justice, "Watts Riots Arrests: Los Angeles August 1965" (June 30, 1966).

22. *MCA*, XVI, Interview 90.

23. John F. Kraft, Inc., "Attitudes of Negroes," pp. 4, 6, 7; Sears, "Riot Activity and Evaluation," 5-6.

24. *MCR*, pp. 10-12; *MCA*, XII, Testimony of Benjamin Peery, a

longtime Watts resident, pp. 5-6; Cohen and Murphy, *Burn, Baby, Burn*, pp. 50-59.

25. *MCA*, III, Testimony of Councilman Thomas Bradley, pp. 29-36; V, Testimony of John A. Buggs, Executive Director of the Los Angeles County Human Relations Commission, pp. 18-23; VI, Testimony of Assemblyman Mervyn M. Dymally, pp. 48-49; VIII, Testimony of Congressman Augustus F. Hawkins, pp. 82-85; X, Testimony of Councilman Billy G. Mills, pp. 9-10.

26. Mervyn M. Dymally, "Statement Prepared for the Governor's Commission on the Los Angeles Riots" (October 11, 1965), p. 2.

27. *MCA*, VI, Testimony of John Ferraro, President of the Los Angeles Board of Police Commissioners, pp. 5-8; XI, Testimony of Police Chief William H. Parker, pp. 3-36; XIV, Testimony of Mayor Samuel W. Yorty, pp. 58-61.

28. *MCR*, pp. 27-28.

29. Ibid., pp. 29-37.

30. *MCA*, XIII, Testimony of Richard Simon, Los Angeles Police Department, pp. 8-9; Testimony of George Slaff, American Civil Liberties Union, pp. 9-12.

31. For indications of Parker's paranoia, see *MCA*, XI, Testimony of Police Chief William H. Parker, pp. 16, 37-38, 119, and especially 121, where he claimed that black leaders "seem to think that if Parker can be destroyed officially, then they will have no more trouble in imposing their will upon the police of America, and that's about what it amounts to, because nobody else will dare stand up."

32. *MCA*, XIII, Testimony of George Slaff, American Civil Liberties Union, pp. 9-11.

33. See McCone's statement in *MCA*, pp. 26-27, and the Commission's position in *MCR*, pp. 28-29.

34. John F. Kraft, Inc., "Attitudes of Negroes," pp. 12-14, 23-25; Walter J. Raine, "The Perception of Police Brutality in South Central Los Angeles Following the Revolt of August 1965" (unpub. paper, U.S. Office of Economic Opportunity, 1966), pp. 2-12; California Advisory Committee to the United States Commission on Civil Rights, "Report on California: Police-Minority Group Relations" (August 1963), pp. 7-31.

35. *MCR*, pp. 12-20; *MCA*, II; XVI, Interview 29; Cohen and Murphy, *Burn, Baby, Burn*, pp. 85-175.

36. Harrison Salisbury, *The Shook-up Generation* (New York, 1958), chapters 2, 5, 6, 11.

37. Bayard Rustin, "The Watts 'Manifesto'," pp. 29-30; Alex Rosen, "The Riots in Watts, Los Angeles," p. 7 (paper presented at the 13th National Institute on Crime and Delinquency, Atlantic City, N.J., June 14, 1966); Fogelson, "The 1960s' Riots," chapter III.

38. Michael E. DePrano and Jeffery B. Nugent, "Economic Aspects of the L.A. Riots and Proposed Solutions," *MCA*, XVII.

39. Ibid., Testimony of Paul Schrade, United Automobile Workers, pp. 42-44.

40. Ibid., Testimony of Thomas Reddin, Los Angeles Police Department, p. 21.

41. *MCR*, pp. 38-47, 49-60, 65-67.

42. Ibid., pp. 47-48, 60-61, 67-68.

43. New York *Times*, May 28, 1966.

44. U.S. Department of Labor, "Sub-Employment in the Slums of Los Angeles" (Washington, D.C., 1966). For the Commission's remarks on criminal records and employment opportunities, see *MCR*, p. 47.

45. Kenneth A. Martyn, "Report on Education to the Governor's Commission on the Los Angeles Riots" (November, 1965), pp. 2-30, *MCA*, XVIII; U.S. Department of Labor, *The Negroes in the United States: Their Social and Economic Situation* (Washington, D.C., 1966), pp. 24-25.

46. U.S. Bureau of the Census, *Current Population Reports*, "Special Census Survey of the South and East Los Angeles Areas: November 1965," series P-23, no. 17 (Washington, D.C., 1966), p. 13.

47. *MCR*, pp. 62-65.

48. *MCA*, V, Testimony of Harvey Claybrook, an accountant formerly employed in Watts, pp. 8-13; XII, Testimony of Thomas Reddin, Los Angeles Police Department, pp. 21-22; XIII, Testimony of Helen Nelson, Consumer Counsel, State of California, pp. 1-14. See also Rustin, "The Watts 'Manifesto'," pp. 29-30; Cohen and Murphy, *Burn, Baby, Burn*, pp. 111, 132; David Caplovitz, *The Poor Pay More: Consumer Practices of Low-Income Families* (New York, 1963).

49. Loren Miller, "Relationship of Racial Residential Segregation to Los Angeles Riots," *MCA*, X; ibid., XIV, Testimony of Sue Welch, a junior high school teacher in Watts, pp. 17-22, 47-48.

50. Ibid., III, Testimony of Lieutenant Governor Glenn M. Anderson; VIII, Testimony of Lieutenant General Roderic L. Hill; XI, Testimony of Police Chief William H. Parker.

51. *MCR*, pp. 17, 19.

52. Citizens Protective League, *Story of the Riot* (1900); Gilbert Osofsky, *Harlem: The Making of a Ghetto* (New York, 1966), pp. 46-52.

53. *MCR*, pp. 17-20; *MCA*, II; Cohen and Murphy, *Burn, Baby, Burn*, chapters 15-21.

54. The McCone Commission lumped the Mexicans and blacks together just the same. See *MCR*, p. 5.

55. For nationwide estimates see President's Commission on Law Enforcement, *The Challenge of Crime*, p. 75, and Ronald Christensen, "Projected Percentages of U.S. Population with Criminal Arrest and Conviction Records" (report prepared for the Commission, August 18, 1966). See also Cohen and Murphy, *Burn, Baby, Burn*, p. 208.

56. President's Commission on Law Enforcement, *The Challenge of Crime*, p. 62; Marvin E. Wolfgang, *Crime and Race: Conceptions and Misconceptions* (New York, 1964), pp. 38-44.

57. *MCA*, II, p. 32; Cohen and Murphy, *Burn, Baby, Burn*, p. 207; John F. Kraft, Inc., "Attitudes of Negroes," p. 7.

58. Diane Fisher, "Police Investigatory Practices" (report prepared for the President's Commission on Law Enforcement and Administration of Justice, 1966); Richard A. Cloward and Lloyd E. Ohlin, *Delinquency and Opportunity* (Glencoe, Ill., 1960), chapters 1, 2, 4; Abraham Kardiner and Lionel Ovesey, *The Mark of Oppression* (Cleveland, 1962), chapter 5; William Brink and Louis Harris, *The Negro Revolution in America* (New York, 1964), chapters 1 and 2.

59. *MCR*, p. 3.

60. *MCA*, X, Testimony of Judge Loren Miller, pp. 17-18.

61. Ibid., III, Testimony of Herb Atkinson, Vice-President, South Los Angeles Transportation Company, p. 25; X, Testimony of John C. Monning, Superintendent, Los Angeles Department of Building and Safety, pp. 5-8; Testimony of Winston Slaughter, Compton Junior College student, pp. 5-29; XIV, Testimony of Edward Warren, Watts real estate broker, pp. 9-11.

62. *MCR*, pp. 3, 75-80; *MCA*, X, Testimony of Judge Loren Miller, pp. 17-18. See also Herbert J. Gans, *The Urban Villagers* (Glencoe, Ill., 1962), chapters 1 and 14.

63. *MCR*, pp. 2, 85-88.

64. *MCA*, IV, Testimony of the Reverend Hartford H. Brookins, pp. 24-32; Harry M. Scoble, "Negro Leadership Study: Tentative Findings" (unpub. paper, U.S. Office of Economic Opportunity, 1966), p. 9.

65. *MCA*, V, Testimony of Wendell Collins, first vice-chairman of

C.O.R.E., pp. 6-25; Dymally, "Statement"; Cohen and Murphy, *Burn, Baby, Burn*, pp. 119-20.

66. Ibid., pp. 130-31. Nor were moderate black leaders in other cities; see Federal Bureau of Investigation, "Report on the 1964 Riots" (September 18, 1964), p. 3.

67. *MCA*, III, Testimony of Herb Atkinson, p. 25; statement by Gloster B. Current in "Community Unrest: Causes, Effects, Prevention, Cure" (transcript of N.A.A.C.P. seminar, Columbus, Ohio, April 2, 1966), pp. 27-28.

68. Gans, *Urban Villagers*, p. 298; Arthur Aryeh Goren, "The New York Kehillah: 1908-1922" (Ph.D. diss., Columbia University, 1966); Moses Rischin, *The Promised City* (Cambridge, Mass., 1962), chapter 6.

69. U.S. Bureau of the Census, "Characteristics of the South and East Los Angeles Areas," pp. 34-37. See also Fred E. Case, "Housing in the Los Angeles Riot Area," *MCA*, XVII.

70. *MCA*, III, Testimony of Herb Atkinson, p. 25. See also E. Franklin Frazier, *Black Bourgeoisie* (Chicago, 1957), part II; Louis E. Lomax, *The Negro Revolt* (New York, 1962), p. 202.

71. Karl E. Taeuber and Alma F. Taeuber, *Negroes in Cities* (Chicago, 1965).

72. Robert M. Fogelson, *The Fragmented Metropolis: Los Angeles, 1850-1930* (Cambridge, Mass., 1967), chapter 9. See also Charles Abrams, *Forbidden Neighbors* (New York, 1955), chapters XII-XIV, XVI–XVIII; Commission on Race and Housing, *Where Shall We Live* (Berkeley and Los Angeles, 1958), p. 36.

73. *MCR*, pp. 75-80.

74. See P. W. Homer, City Manager, "Report to the Rochester City Council on the Riots of July 1964" (April 27, 1965); New York *Times*, July 22 and August 4, 1964.

13.

PAUL JACOBS

Postscript to the McCone Commission

The story of the McCone Commission does not end with the publication of its report. After the report was issued the staff was dissolved; only Sheridan and a few of the investigators remained on the payroll, answering correspondence and handling accounting problems. Sheridan is also acting as the commission's attorney in a lawsuit in which it has become involved: a number of insurance companies are suing the City of Los Angeles and have demanded the right to see the documents accumulated by the commission during the investigation but not made public afterwards. The commission has refused to allow access to these documents.

That refusal is not limited to the insurance companies but extends to everyone else. After the commission report was issued Sheridan was given the blanket authority to decide what other documents the commission would make public, what documents should be saved,

SOURCE: From Paul Jacobs, *Prelude to Riot: A View of Urban America from the Bottom* (New York: Random House, 1966), pp. 281-83. Reprinted with permission of the author and publisher.

and what should be destroyed. Acting on this authority, he went through the materials, chose those he felt should be copied, and deposited the copies in nine libraries throughout the state. Thus, it is possible to read the consultants' reports, for example, or study the transcripts of testimony either at one of the libraries or by getting a microfilm copy.

But, and a big but it is, future scholars would have no way of knowing, from looking at the eleven volumes of materials available in the libraries, that Sheridan had taken out such key exhibits as John Buggs's chronology of events. Sheridan states that he destroyed only "drafts" of reports and memoranda, but that edited versions of interviews and other materials were saved. Unfortunately, until access to the materials is given, no one will know what was destroyed and what was kept but for a variety of reasons not included in the documents the commission did deposit in the libraries.

The commission is still operating at the public relations level, too, defending itself against some of the attacks which have been made upon it. That defense has devolved upon McCone, the conservative Republican, and Christopher, the liberal Democrat, who have acted in the name of the commission, even though they do not consult with the other commission members. Thus, for example, in August 1966 a "Staff Report of Actions Taken to Implement the Recommendations in the Commission's Report" was issued in the name of the commission. It was signed by McCone and Christopher but seen for the first time by the other commissioners on the day it was released to the press.

Considering that the commission never functioned like a British Royal Commission, perhaps nothing more could be expected from it than what was produced. From its start, as an idea of the governor's staff, the commission was given a limited responsibility to perform, and it was hampered even in that by the needs of short-term political expediency and anticipated acceptance; it was assumed that the whole truth should not be told to the community, lest it be rejected. And so instead of acting like a responsible public body, the *Governor's* Commission became John A. McCone's Commission. As a reflection of McCone's views the commission report is accurate; as a reflection of truth and reality it is unreliable. And its recommendations are useful only in that the commission acknowledges the need to spend money on strengthening such institutions as schools or on building a hospital. But in every case where fundamental change, not just more money, is required, the commission was silent.

But the greatest tragedy of the commission is that it may become the model for all the other commissions that have been set up by governors and the President. Indeed, Warren Christopher went to Detroit along with Cyrus Vance; shortly afterwards the President announced the formation of his Commission. It's not hard to predict what its report will be.

VII

U.S.A.,
1968

INTRODUCTION

Following the numerous and devastating riots during the 1960s, President Johnson established The National Advisory Commission on Civil Disorders (popularly known as the "Kerner Commission," after its chairman, Otto Kerner) and instructed it to investigate the "basic causes and factors" leading to civil disorders, to develop "methods and techniques for averting or controlling such disorders," and to make recommendations for local, state, and federal action.

Unlike previous official inquiries into civil disorders, the Kerner Commission was the first federally funded, national and Presidential-level examination of race relations in the United States. The size and scope of the Commission's lengthy final report is comparable to Gunnar Myrdal's *An American Dilemma*, published twenty-four years earlier. The Kerner Report, which was to become identified by the news media as an indictment of "white racism," was completed in less than a year of hearings, field investigations, research and consultants' reports, and laborious data collection.

The Report has been generally well-received by both the public (who have made it a best-seller) and liberal critics. In terms of its scholarly seriousness and consistency, it is reminiscent of *The Negro in Chicago*, prepared by the Chicago Commission on Race Relations in 1919. Gary Marx, writing in *Trans-action*, called the Report "the most significant and far-reaching statement of a programmatic nature ever made by a governmental unit on American race relations. It is a major call for a new will and resources and a re-ordering of the nation's priorities."[1]

Critics of the Kerner Report have questioned its liberal ideology, theoretical assumptions, and political relevance. As Robert Fogelson has observed,[2] the Kerner Commission assumed an integrationist perspective on race relations, a progressive view of government, a commitment to welfare capitalism, and an abiding faith in the capacity and flexibility of established political and economic institutions. Given these assumptions, notes Fogelson, "the Kerner Commission did a good, but not splendid, job. . . . [I]n view of the public opinion polls, the Kerner Commission did a better job than the country deserves. It offered a comprehensive and plausible interpretation of the riots when it could have explained them away as the product of outside agitators and irresponsible riffraff. It also offered elaborate and reasonable recommendations for the ghettos when it could have written them off with vague phrases about private enterprise and local initiative. And had the commission abandoned its liberal perspective and submitted a more original interpretation and more radical recommendations, it would probably have been rejected outright by most Americans."

The ideology and internal politics of the Kerner Commission are discussed in the selection from Andrew Kopkind who suggests that the Report's liberalism was predictable from the beginning and that the Commission's analysis and recommendations are grounded in a fundamentally elitist and managerial view of American society. Kopkind's analysis of the organizational and structural conditions underlying riot commission politics has general applicability.

NOTES

1. Gary T. Marx, "A Document With a Difference," *Trans-action* (September 1968), pp. 56-58.

2. Robert M. Fogelson, "Review Symposium," *American Political Science Review* 63 (December 1969): 1269-75.

14.

NATIONAL ADVISORY COMMISSION ON CIVIL DISORDERS

The Kerner Report

SUMMARY

Introduction

The summer of 1967 again brought racial disorders to American cities, and with them shock, fear, and bewilderment to the Nation.

The worst came during a two-week period in July, first in Newark and then in Detroit. Each set off a chain reaction in neighboring communities.

On July 28, 1967, the President of the United States established this Commission and directed us to answer three basic questions:

What happened?

Why did it happen?

What can be done to prevent it from happening again?

To respond to these questions, we have undertaken a broad range of studies and investigations. We have visited the riot cities; we have heard many witnesses; we have sought the counsel of experts across the country.

SOURCE: From The National Advisory Commission on Civil Disorders, *Report* (Washington, D.C.: Government Printing Office, 1968), pp. 1-13.

This is our basic conclusion: Our Nation is moving toward two societies, one black, one white—separate and unequal.

Reaction to last summer's disorders has quickened the movement and deepened the division. Discrimination and segregation have long permeated much of American life; they now threaten the future of every American.

This deepening racial division is not inevitable. The movement apart can be reversed. Choice is still possible. Our principal task is to define that choice and to press for a national resolution.

To pursue our present course will involve the continuing polarization of the American community and, ultimately, the destruction of basic democratic values.

The alternative is not blind repression or capitulation to lawlessness. It is the realization of common opportunities for all within a single society.

This alternative will require a commitment to national action—compassionate, massive, and sustained, backed by the resources of the most powerful and the richest nation on this earth. From every American it will require new attitudes, new understanding, and, above all, new will.

The vital needs of the Nation must be met; hard choices must be made, and, if necessary, new taxes enacted.

Violence cannot build a better society. Disruption and disorder nourish repression, not justice. They strike at the freedom of every citizen. The community cannot—it will not—tolerate coercion and mob rule.

Violence and destruction must be ended—in the streets of the ghetto and in the lives of people.

Segregation and poverty have created in the racial ghetto a destructive environment totally unknown to most white Americans.

What white Americans have never fully understood—but what the Negro can never forget—is that white society is deeply implicated in the ghetto. White institutions created it, white institutions maintain it, and white society condones it.

It is time now to turn with all the purpose at our command to the major unfinished business of this Nation. It is time to adopt strategies for action that will produce quick and visible progress. It is time to make good the promises of American democracy to all citizens—urban and rural, white and black, Spanish-surname, American Indian, and every minority group.

Our recommendations embrace three basic principles:

To mount programs on a scale equal to the dimension of the problems;

To aim these programs for high impact in the immediate future in order to close the gap between promise and performance;

To undertake new initiatives and experiments that can change the system of failure and frustration that now dominates the ghetto and weakens our society.

These programs will require unprecedented levels of funding and performance, but they neither probe deeper nor demand more than the problems which called them forth. There can be no higher priority for national action and no higher claim on the Nation's conscience.

We issue this report now, 5 months before the date called for by the President. Much remains that can be learned. Continued study is essential.

As Commissioners we have worked together with a sense of the greatest urgency and have sought to compose whatever differences exist among us. Some differences remain. But the gravity of the problem and the pressing need for action are too clear to allow further delay in the issuance of this report.

I. What Happened?

CHAPTER 1.——PROFILES OF DISORDER

The report contains profiles of a selection of the disorders that took place during the summer of 1967. These profiles are designed to indicate how the disorders happened, who participated in them, and how local officials, police forces, and the National Guard responded. Illustrative excerpts follow:

NEWARK

It was decided to attempt to channel the energies of the people into a nonviolent protest. While Lofton promised the crowd that a full investigation would be made of the Smith incident, the other Negro leaders began urging those on the scene to form a line of march toward the city hall.

Some persons joined the line of march. Others milled about in the narrow street. From the dark grounds of the housing project came a barrage of rocks. Some of them fell among the crowd. Others hit persons in the line of march. Many smashed the windows of the police station. The rock throwing, it was believed, was the work of youngsters; approximately 2,500 children lived in the housing project.

Almost at the same time, an old car was set afire in a parking lot. The line of march began to disintegrate. The police, their heads protected by World War I-type helmets, sallied forth to disperse the crowd. A fire engine, arriving on the scene, was pelted with rocks. As police drove people away from the station, they scattered in all directions.

A few minutes later a nearby liquor store was broken into. Some persons, seeing a caravan of cabs appear at city hall to protest Smith's arrest, interpreted this as evidence that the disturbance had been organized, and generated rumors to that effect.

However, only a few stores were looted. Within a short period of time, the disorder appeared to have run its course.

On Saturday, July 15, [Director of Police Dominick] Spina received a report of snipers in a housing project. When he arrived he saw approximately 100 National Guardsmen and police officers crouching behind vehicles, hiding in corners, and lying on the ground around the edge of the courtyard.

Since everything appeared quiet and it was broad daylight, Spina walked directly down the middle of the street. Nothing happened. As he came to the last building of the complex, he heard a shot. All around him the troopers jumped, believing themselves to be under sniper fire. A moment later a young Guardsman ran from behind a building.

The director of police went over and asked him if he had fired the shot. The soldier said "Yes," he had fired to scare a man away from a window; that his orders were to keep everyone away from windows.

Spina said he told the soldier: "Do you know what you just did? You have now created a state of hysteria. Every Guardsman up and down this street and every state policeman and every city policeman that is present thinks that somebody just fired a shot and that it is probably a sniper."

A short time later more "gunshots" were heard. Investigating, Spina came upon a Puerto Rican sitting on a wall. In reply to a question as to whether he knew "where the firing is coming from?" the man said:

"That's no firing. That's fireworks. If you look up to the fourth floor, you will see the people who are throwing down these cherry bombs."

By this time four truckloads of National Guardsmen had arrived and troopers and policemen were again crouched everywhere looking for a sniper. The director of police remained at the scene for 3 hours, and the only shot fired was the one by the Guardsman.

Nevertheless, at 6 o'clock that evening two columns of National Guardsmen and State troopers were directing mass fire at the Hayes housing project in response to what they believed were snipers.

DETROIT

A spirit of carefree nihilism was taking hold. To riot and destroy appeared more and more to become ends in themselves. Late Sunday afternoon it appeared to one observer that the young people were "dancing amidst the flames."

A Negro plainclothes officer was standing at an intersection when a man threw a Molotov cocktail into a business establishment at the corner. In the heat of the afternoon, fanned by the 20 to 25 miles per hour winds of both Sunday and Monday, the fire reached the home next door within minutes. As residents uselessly sprayed the flames with garden hoses, the fire jumped from roof to roof of adjacent two- and three-story buildings. Within the hour the entire block was in flames. The ninth house in the burning row belonged to the arsonist who had thrown the Molotov cocktail.

Employed as a private guard, 55-year-old Julius L. Dorsey, a Negro, was standing in front of a market when accosted by two Negro men and a woman. They demanded he permit them to loot the market. He ignored their demands. They began to berate him. He asked a neighbor to call the police. As the argument grew more heated, Dorsey fired three shots from his pistol into the air.

The police radio reported: "Looters—they have rifles." A patrol car driven by a police officer and carrying three National Guardsmen arrived. As the looters fled, the law-enforcement personnel opened fire. When the firing ceased, one person lay dead.

He was Julius L. Dorsey.

As the riot alternately waxed and waned, one area of the ghetto remained insulated. On the northeast side the residents of some 150 square blocks inhabited by 21,000 persons had, in 1966, banded to-

gether in the Positive Neighborhood Action Committee (PNAC).
With professional help from the Institute of Urban Dynamics, they
had organized block clubs and made plans for the improvement of the
neighborhood.

When the riot broke out, the residents, through the block clubs,
were able to organize quickly. Youngsters, agreeing to stay in the
neighborhood, participated in detouring traffic. While many persons
reportedly sympathized with the idea of a rebellion against the "system" only two small fires were set—one in an empty building.

According to Lieutenant General Throckmorton and Colonel Bol-
ling, the city, at this time, was saturated with fear. The National
Guardsmen were afraid, the citizens were afraid, and the police were
afraid. Numerous persons, the majority of them Negroes, were being
injured by gunshots of undetermined origin. The general and his staff
felt that the major task of the troops was to reduce the fear and
restore an air of normalcy.

In order to accomplish this, every effort was made to establish
contact and rapport between the troops and the residents. The soldiers
—20 percent of whom were Negro—began helping to clean up the
streets, collect garbage, and trace persons who had disappeared in the
confusion. Residents in the neighborhoods responded with soup and
sandwiches for the troops. In areas where the National Guard tried to
establish rapport with the citizens, there was a similar response.

NEW BRUNSWICK

A short time later, elements of the crowd—an older and rougher
one than the night before—appeared in front of the police station.
The participants wanted to see the mayor.

Mayor [Patricia] Sheehan went out onto the steps of the station.
Using a bull horn, she talked to the people and asked that she be
given an opportunity to correct conditions. The crowd was boisterous.
Some persons challenged the mayor. But, finally, the opinion, "She's
new! Give her a chance!" prevailed.

A demand was issued by people in the crowd that all persons
arrested the previous night be released. Told that this already had
been done, the people were suspicious. They asked to be allowed to
inspect the jail cells.

It was agreed to permit representatives of the people to look in the
cells to satisfy themselves that everyone had been released.

The crowd dispersed. The New Brunswick riot had failed to materialize.

CHAPTER 2.——PATTERNS OF DISORDER

The "typical" riot did not take place. The disorders of 1967 were unusual, irregular, complex, and unpredictable social processes. Like most human events, they did not unfold in an orderly sequence. However, an analysis of our survey information leads to some conclusions about the riot process.

In general:

> The civil disorders of 1967 involved Negroes acting against local symbols of white American society, authority, and property in Negro neighborhoods—rather than against white persons.

> Of 164 disorders reported during the first nine months of 1967, eight (5 percent) were major in terms of violence and damage; 33 (20 percent) were serious but not major; 123 (75 percent) were minor and undoubtedly would not have received national attention as riots had the Nation not been sensitized by the more serious outbreaks.

> In the 75 disorders studied by a Senate subcommittee, 83 deaths were reported. Eighty-two percent of the deaths and more than half the injuries occurred in Newark and Detroit. About 10 percent of the dead and 36 percent of the injured were public employees, primarily law officers and firemen. The overwhelming majority of the persons killed or injured in all the disorders were Negro civilians.

> Initial damage estimates were greatly exaggerated. In Detroit, newspaper damage estimates at first ranged from $200 to $500 million; the highest recent estimate is $45 million. In Newark, early estimates ranged from $15 to $25 million. A month later damage was estimated at $10.2 million, 80 percent in inventory losses.

In the 24 disorders in 23 cities which we surveyed:

> The final incident before the outbreak of disorder, and the initial violence itself, generally took place in the evening or at night at a place in which it was normal for many people to be on the streets.

Violence usually occurred almost immediately following the occurrence of the final precipitating incident, and then escalated rapidly. With but few exceptions, violence subsided during the day, and flared rapidly again at night. The night-day cycles continued through the early period of the major disorders.

Disorder generally began with rock and bottle throwing and window breaking. Once store windows were broken, looting usually followed.

Disorder did not erupt as a result of a single "triggering" or "precipitating" incident. Instead, it was generated out of an increasingly disturbed social atmosphere, in which typically a series of tension-heightening incidents over a period of weeks or months became linked in the minds of many in the Negro community with a reservoir of underlying grievances. At some point in the mounting tension, a further incident—in itself often routine or trivial—became the breaking point and the tension spilled over into violence.

"Prior" incidents, which increased tensions and ultimately led to violence, were police actions in almost half the cases; police actions were "final" incidents before the outbreak of violence in 12 of the 24 surveyed disorders.

No particular control tactic was successful in every situation. The varied effectiveness of control techniques emphasizes the need for advance training, planning, adequate intelligence systems, and knowledge of the ghetto community.

Negotiations between Negroes—including young militants as well as older Negro leaders—and white officials concerning "terms of peace" occurred during virtually all the disorders surveyed. In many cases, these negotiations involved discussion of underlying grievances as well as the handling of the disorder by control authorities.

The typical rioter was a teenager or young adult, a life-long resident of the city in which he rioted, a high school dropout; he was, nevertheless, somewhat better educated than his nonrioting Negro neighbor, and was usually underemployed or employed in a menial job. He was proud of his race, extremely hostile to both whites and middle-class Negroes and, although informed about politics, highly distrustful of the political system.

A Detroit survey revealed that approximately 11 percent of the total residents of two riot areas admitted participation in the rioting, 20 to 25 percent identified themselves as "bystanders," over 16 percent identified themselves as "counterrioters" who urged rioters to "cool it," and the remaining 48 to 53 percent said they were at home or elsewhere and did not participate. In a survey of Negro males between the ages of 15 and 35 residing in the disturbance area in Newark, about 45 percent identified themselves as rioters, and about 55 percent as "noninvolved."

Most rioters were young Negro males. Nearly 53 percent of arrestees were between 15 and 24 years of age; nearly 81 percent between 15 and 35.

In Detroit and Newark about 74 percent of the rioters were brought up in the North. In contrast, of the noninvolved, 36 percent in Detroit and 52 percent in Newark were brought up in the North.

What the rioters appeared to be seeking was fuller participation in the social order and the material benefits enjoyed by the majority of American citizens. Rather than rejecting the American system, they were anxious to obtain a place for themselves in it.

Numerous Negro counterrioters walked the streets urging rioters to "cool it." The typical counterrioter was better educated and had higher income than either the rioter or the noninvolved.

The proportion of Negroes in local government was substantially smaller than the Negro proportion of population. Only three of the 20 cities studied had more than one Negro legislator; none had ever had a Negro mayor or city manager. In only four cities did Negroes hold other important policy-making positions or serve as heads of municipal departments.

Although almost all cities had some sort of formal grievance mechanism for handling citizen complaints, this typically was regarded by Negroes as ineffective and was generally ignored.

Although specific grievances varied from city to city, at least 12 deeply held grievances can be identified and ranked into three levels of relative intensity:

First level of intensity:

1. Police practices.
2. Unemployment and underemployment.
3. Inadequate housing.

Second level of intensity:

4. Inadequate education.
5. Poor recreation facilities and programs.
6. Ineffectiveness of the political structure and grievance mechanisms.

Third level of intensity:

7. Disrespectful white attitudes.
8. Discriminatory administration of justice.
9. Inadequacy of Federal programs.
10. Inadequacy of municipal services.
11. Discriminatory consumer and credit practices.
12. Inadequate welfare programs.

The results of a three-city survey of various Federal programs—manpower, education, housing, welfare and community action—indicate that, despite substantial expenditures, the number of persons assisted constituted only a fraction of those in need.

The background of disorder is often as complex and difficult to analyze as the disorder itself. But we find that certain general conclusions can be drawn:

> Social and economic conditions in the riot cities constituted a clear pattern of severe disadvantage for Negroes compared with whites, whether the Negroes lived in the area where the riot took place or outside it. Negroes had completed fewer years of education and fewer had attended high school. Negroes were twice as likely to be unemployed and three times as likely to be in unskilled and service jobs. Negroes averaged 70 percent of the income earned by whites and were more than twice as likely to be living in poverty. Although housing cost Negroes relatively more, they had worse housing—three times as likely to be overcrowded and substandard. When compared to white suburbs, the relative disadvantage was even more pronounced.

A study of the aftermath of disorder leads to disturbing conclusions. We find that, despite the institution of some postriot programs:

Little basic change in the conditions underlying the outbreak of disorder has taken place. Actions to ameliorate Negro grievances have been limited and sporadic; with but few exceptions, they have not significantly reduced tensions.

In several cities, the principal official response has been to train and equip the police with more sophisticated weapons.

In several cities, increasing polarization is evident, with continuing breakdown of interracial communication, and growth of white segregationist or black separatist groups.

CHAPTER 3.——ORGANIZED ACTIVITY

The President directed the Commission to investigate "to what extent, if any, there has been planning or organization in any of the riots."

To carry out this part of the President's charge, the Commission established a special investigative staff supplementing the field teams that made the general examination of the riots in 23 cities. The unit examined data collected by Federal agencies and congressional committees, including thousands of documents supplied by the Federal Bureau of Investigation, gathered and evaluated information from local and state law enforcement agencies and officials, and conducted its own field investigation in selected cities.

On the basis of all the information collected, the Commission concludes that:

The urban disorders of the summer of 1967 were not caused by, nor were they the consequence of, any organized plan or "conspiracy."

Specifically, the Commission has found no evidence that all or any of the disorders or the incidents that led to them were planned or directed by any organization or group, international, national, or local.

Militant organizations, local and national, and individual agitators, who repeatedly forecast and called for violence, were active in the spring and summer of 1967. We believe that they sought to encourage violence, and that they helped to create an atmosphere that contributed to the outbreak of disorder.

We recognize that the continuation of disorders and the polarization of the races would provide fertile ground for organized exploitation in the future.

Investigations of organized activity are continuing at all levels of government, including committees of Congress. These investigations relate not only to the disorders of 1967 but also to the actions of groups and individuals, particularly in schools and colleges, during this last fall and winter. The Commission has co-operated in these investigations. They should continue.

II. Why Did It Happen?

CHAPTER 4.—THE BASIC CAUSES

In addressing the question "Why did it happen?" we shift our focus from the local to the national scene, from the particular events of the summer of 1967 to the factors within the society at large that created a mood of violence among many urban Negroes.

These factors are complex and interacting; they vary significantly in their effect from city to city and from year to year; and the consequences of one disorder, generating new grievances and new demands, become the causes of the next. Thus was created the "thicket of tension, conflicting evidence, and extreme opinions" cited by the President.

Despite these complexities, certain fundamental matters are clear. Of these, the most fundamental is the racial attitude and behavior of white Americans toward black Americans.

Race prejudice has shaped our history decisively; it now threatens to affect our future.

White racism is essentially responsible for the explosive mixture which has been accumulating in our cities since the end of World War II. Among the ingredients of this mixture are:

> *Pervasive discrimination and segregation* in employment, education, and housing, which have resulted in the continuing exclusion of great numbers of Negroes from the benefits of economic progress.
>
> *Black in-migration and white exodus,* which have produced the massive and growing concentrations of impoverished Negroes in our major cities, creating a growing crisis of deteriorating facilities and services and unmet human needs.
>
> *The black ghettos,* where segregation and poverty converge on the young to destroy opportunity and enforce failure.

Crime, drug addiction, dependency on welfare, and bitterness and resentment against society in general and white society in particular are the result.

At the same time, most whites and some Negroes outside the ghetto have prospered to a degree unparalleled in the history of civilization. Through television and other media, this affluence has been flaunted before the eyes of the Negro poor and the jobless ghetto youth.

Yet these facts alone cannot be said to have caused the disorders. Recently, other powerful ingredients have begun to catalyze the mixture:

Frustrated hopes are the residue of the unfulfilled expectations aroused by the great judicial and legislative victories of the civil rights movement and the dramatic struggle for equal rights in the South.

A *climate that tends toward approval and encouragement of violence* as a form of protest has been created by white terrorism directed against nonviolent protest; by the open defiance of law and Federal authority by state and local officials resisting desegregation; and by some protest groups engaging in civil disobedience who turn their backs on nonviolence, go beyond the constitutionally protected rights of petition and free assembly, and resort to violence to attempt to compel alteration of laws and policies with which they disagree.

The frustrations of powerlessness have led some Negroes to the conviction that there is no effective alternative to violence as a means of achieving redress of grievances, and of "moving the system." These frustrations are reflected in alienation and hostility toward the institutions of law and government and the white society which controls them, and in the reach toward racial consciousness and solidarity reflected in the slogan "Black Power."

A *new mood* has sprung up among Negroes, particularly among the young, in which self-esteem and enhanced racial pride are replacing apathy and submission to "the system."

The police are not merely a "spark" factor. To some Negroes police have come to symbolize white power, white racism, and white repression. And the fact is that many police do reflect and express these white attitudes. The atmosphere of hostility and cynicism is reinforced by a wide-spread belief among Negroes in the existence of police brutality and in a "double standard" of justice and protection—one for Negroes and one for whites.

To this point, we have attempted only to identify the prime components of the "explosive mixture." In the chapters that follow we seek to analyze them in the perspective of history. Their meaning, however, is clear:

In the summer of 1967, we have seen in our cities a chain reaction of racial violence. If we are heedless, none of us shall escape the consequences.

CHAPTER 5.——REJECTION AND PROTEST:
AN HISTORICAL SKETCH

The causes of recent racial disorders are embedded in a tangle of issues and circumstances—social, economic, political, and psychological—which arise out of the historic pattern of Negro-white relations in America.

In this chapter we trace the pattern, identify the recurrent themes of Negro protest and, most importantly, provide a perspective on the protest activities of the present era.

We describe the Negro's experience in America and the development of slavery as an institution. We show his persistent striving for equality in the face of rigidly maintained social, economic, and educational barriers, and repeated mob violence. We portray the ebb and flow of the doctrinal tides—accommodation, separatism, and self-help —and their relationship to the current theme of Black Power. We conclude:

The Black Power advocates of today consciously feel that they are the most militant group in the Negro protest movement. Yet they have retreated from a direct confrontation with American society on the issue of integration and, by preaching separatism, unconsciously function as an accommodation to white racism. Much of their economic program, as well as their interest in Negro history, self-help, racial solidarity and separation, is reminiscent of Booker T. Washington. The rhetoric is different, but the ideas are remarkably similar.

CHAPTER 6.—THE FORMATION OF THE RACIAL GHETTOS[1]

Throughout the 20th century the Negro population of the United States has been moving steadily from rural areas to urban and from South to North and West. In 1910, 91 percent of the Nation's 9.8 million Negroes lived in the South and only 27 percent of American Negroes lived in cities of 2,500 persons or more. Between 1910 and 1966 the total Negro population more than doubled, reaching 21.5 million, and the number living in metropolitan areas rose more than fivefold (from 2.6 million to 14.8 million). The number outside the South rose elevenfold (from 885,000 to 9.7 million).

Negro migration from the South has resulted from the expectation of thousands of new and highly paid jobs for unskilled workers in the North and the shift to mechanized farming in the South. However, the Negro migration is small when compared to earlier waves of European immigrants. Even between 1960 and 1966, there were 1.8 million immigrants from abroad compared to the 613,000 Negroes who arrived in the North and West from the South.

As a result of the growing number of Negroes in urban areas, natural increase has replaced migration as the primary source of Negro population increase in the cities. Nevertheless, Negro migration from the South will continue unless economic conditions there change dramatically.

Basic data concerning Negro urbanization trends indicate that:

Almost all Negro population growth (98 percent from 1950 to 1966) is occurring within metropolitan areas, primarily within central cities.[2]

The vast majority of white population growth (78 percent from 1960 to 1966) is occurring in suburban portions of metropolitan areas. Since 1960, white central-city population has declined by 1.3 million.

As a result, central cities are becoming more heavily Negro while the suburban fringes around them remain almost entirely white.

The 12 largest central cities now contain over two-thirds of the Negro population outside the South, and almost one-third of the Negro total in the United States.

Within the cities, Negroes have been excluded from white residential areas through discriminatory practices. Just as significant is the withdrawal of white families from, or their refusal to enter, neighborhoods where Negroes are moving or already residing. About 20 percent of the urban population of the United States changes residence every year. The refusal of whites to move into "changing" areas when vacancies occur means that most vacancies eventually are occupied by Negroes.

The result, according to a recent study, is that in 1960 the average segregation index for 207 of the largest U.S. cities was 86.2. In other words, to create an unsegregated population distribution, an average of over 86 percent of all Negroes would have to change their place of residence within the city.

CHAPTER 7.—UNEMPLOYMENT, FAMILY STRUCTURE, AND
SOCIAL DISORGANIZATION

Although there have been gains in Negro income nationally, and a decline in the number of Negroes below the "poverty level," the condition of Negroes in the central city remains in a state of crisis. Between 2 and 2.5 million Negroes—16 to 20 percent of the total Negro population of all central cities—live in squalor and deprivation in ghetto neighborhoods.

Employment is a key problem. It not only controls the present for the Negro American but, in a most profound way, it is creating the future as well. Yet, despite continuing economic growth and declining national unemployment rates, the unemployment rate for Negroes in 1967 was more than double that for whites.

Equally important is the undesirable nature of many jobs open to Negroes and other minorities. Negro men are more than three times as likely as white men to be in low-paying, unskilled, or service jobs. This concentration of male Negro employment at the lowest end of the occupational scale is the single most important cause of poverty among Negroes.

In one study of low-income neighborhoods, the "sub-employment rate," including both unemployment and underemployment, was about 33 percent, or 8.8 times greater than the overall unemployment rate for all U.S. workers.

Employment problems, aggravated by the constant arrival of new unemployed migrants, many of them from depressed rural areas, create persistent poverty in the ghetto. In 1966, about 11.9 percent of the Nation's whites and 40.6 percent of its nonwhites were below the poverty level defined by the Social Security Administration (in 1966,

$3,335 per year for an urban family of four). Over 40 percent of the nonwhites below the poverty level live in the central cities.

Employment problems have drastic social impact in the ghetto. Men who are chronically unemployed or employed in the lowest status jobs are often unable or unwilling to remain with their families. The handicap imposed on children growing up without fathers in an atmosphere of deprivation is increased as mothers are forced to work to provide support.

The culture of poverty that results from unemployment and family breakup generates a system of ruthless, exploitative relationships within the ghetto. Prostitution, dope addiction, and crime create an environmental "jungle" characterized by personal insecurity and tension. Children growing up under such conditions are likely participants in civil disorder.

CHAPTER 8.—CONDITIONS OF LIFE IN THE RACIAL GHETTO

A striking difference in environment from that of white, middle-class Americans profoundly influences the lives of residents of the ghetto.

Crime rates, consistently higher than in other areas, create a pronounced sense of insecurity. For example, in one city one low-income Negro district had 35 times as many serious crimes against persons as a high-income white district. Unless drastic steps are taken, the crime problems in poverty areas are likely to continue to multiply as the growing youth and rapid urbanization of the population outstrip police resources.

Poor health and sanitation conditions in the ghetto result in higher mortality rates, a higher incidence of major diseases, and lower availability and utilization of medical services. The infant mortality rate for nonwhite babies under the age of 1 month is 58 percent higher than for whites; for 1 to 12 months it is almost three times as high. The level of sanitation in the ghetto is far below that in high-income areas. Garbage collection is often inadequate. Of an estimated 14,000 cases of rat bite in the United States in 1965, most were in ghetto neighborhoods.

Ghetto residents believe they are exploited by local merchants; and evidence substantiates some of these beliefs. A study conducted in one city by the Federal Trade Commission showed that higher prices were charged for goods sold in ghetto stores than in other areas.

Lack of knowledge regarding credit purchasing creates special pitfalls for the disadvantaged. In many states, garnishment practices compound these difficulties by allowing creditors to deprive individuals of their wages without hearing or trial.

CHAPTER 9.——COMPARING THE IMMIGRANT AND
NEGRO EXPERIENCE

In this chapter, we address ourselves to a fundamental question that many white Americans are asking: Why have so many Negroes, unlike the European immigrants, been unable to escape from the ghetto and from poverty?

We believe the following factors play a part:

The maturing economy.—When the European immigrants arrived, they gained an economic foothold by providing the unskilled labor needed by industry. Unlike the immigrant, the Negro migrant found little opportunity in the city. The economy, by then matured, had little use for the unskilled labor he had to offer.

The disability of race.—The structure of discrimination has stringently narrowed opportunities for the Negro and restricted his prospects. European immigrants suffered from discrimination, but never so pervasively.

Entry into the political system.—The immigrants usually settled in rapidly growing cities with powerful and expanding political machines, which traded economic advantages for political support. Ward-level grievance machinery, as well as personal representation, enabled the immigrant to make his voice heard and his power felt.

By the time the Negro arrived, these political machines were no longer so powerful or so well equipped to provide jobs or other favors, and in many cases were unwilling to share their remaining influence with Negroes.

Cultural factors.—Coming from societies with a low standard of living and at a time when job aspirations were low, the immigrants sensed little deprivation in being forced to take the less desirable and poorer paying jobs. Their large and cohesive families contributed to total income. Their vision of the future—one that led to a life outside of the ghetto—provided the incentive necessary to endure the present.

Although Negro men worked as hard as the immigrants, they were unable to support their families. The entrepreneurial opportunities had vanished. As a result of slavery and long periods of unemployment, the Negro family structure had become matriarchal; the males played a secondary and marginal family role—one which offered little compensation for their hard and unrewarding labor. Above all, segregation denied Negroes access to good jobs and the opportunity to leave the ghetto. For them, the future seemed to lead only to a dead end.

Today, whites tend to exaggerate how well and quickly they escaped from poverty. The fact is that immigrants who came from rural backgrounds, as many Negroes do, are only now, after three generations, finally beginning to move into the middle class.

By contrast, Negroes began concentrating in the city less than two generations ago, and under much less favorable conditions. Although some Negroes have escaped poverty, few have been able to escape the urban ghetto.

III. What Can Be Done?

CHAPTER 10.—THE COMMUNITY RESPONSE

Our investigation of the 1967 riot cities establishes that virtually every major episode of violence was foreshadowed by an accumulation of unresolved grievances and by widespread dissatisfaction among Negroes with the unwillingness or inability of local government to respond.

Overcoming these conditions is essential for community support of law enforcement and civil order. City governments need new and more vital channels of communication to the residents of the ghetto; they need to improve their capacity to respond effectively to community needs before they become community grievances; and they need to provide opportunity for meaningful involvement of ghetto residents in shaping policies and programs which affect the community.

The Commission recommends that local governments:

> Develop Neighborhood Action Task Forces as joint community-government efforts through which more effective communication can be achieved, and the delivery of city services to ghetto residents improved.
>
> Establish comprehensive grievance-response mechanisms in order to bring all public agencies under public scrutiny.

Bring the institutions of local government closer to the people they serve by establishing neighborhood outlets for local, state, and Federal administrative and public service agencies.

Expand opportunities for ghetto residents to participate in the formulation of public policy and the implementation of programs affecting them through improved political representation, creation of institutional channels for community action, expansion of legal services, and legislative hearings on ghetto problems.

In this effort, city governments will require State and Federal support.

The Commission recommends:

State and Federal financial assistance for mayors and city councils to support the research, consultants, staff, and other resources needed to respond effectively to Federal program initiatives.

State cooperation in providing municipalities with the jurisdictional tools needed to deal with their problems; a fuller measure of financial aid to urban areas; and the focusing of the interests of suburban communities on the physical, social, and cultural environment of the central city.

CHAPTER 11.—POLICE AND THE COMMUNITY

The abrasive relationship between the police and minority communities has been a major—and explosive—source of grievance, tension, and disorder. The blame must be shared by the total society.

The police are faced with demands for increased protection and service in the ghetto. Yet the aggressive patrol practices thought necessary to meet these demands themselves create tension and hostility. The resulting grievances have been further aggravated by the lack of effective mechanisms for handling complaints against the police. Special programs for bettering police-community relations have been instituted, but these alone are not enough. Police administrators, with the guidance of public officials, and the support of the entire community, must take vigorous action to improve law enforcement and to decrease the potential for disorder.

The Commission recommends that city government and police authorities:

Review police operations in the ghetto to ensure proper conduct by police officers, and eliminate abrasive practices.

Provide more adequate police protection to ghetto residents to eliminate their high sense of insecurity and the belief in the existence of a dual standard of law enforcement.

Establish fair and effective mechanisms for the redress of grievances against the police and other municipal employees.

Develop and adopt policy guidelines to assist officers in making critical decisions in areas where police conduct can create tension.

Develop and use innovative programs to insure widespread community support for law enforcement.

Recruit more Negroes into the regular police force, and review promotion policies to insure fair promotion for Negro officers.

Establish a "Community Service Officer" program to attract ghetto youths between the ages of 17 and 21 to police work. These junior officers would perform duties in ghetto neighborhoods, but would not have full police authority. The Federal Government should provide support equal to 90 percent of the costs of employing CSO's on the basis of one for every 10 regular officers.

CHAPTER 12.——CONTROL OF DISORDER

Preserving civil peace is the first responsibility of government. Unless the rule of law prevails, our society will lack not only order but also the environment essential to social and economic progress.

The maintenance of civil order cannot be left to the police alone. The police need guidance, as well as support, from mayors and other public officials. It is the responsibility of public officials to determine proper police policies, support adequate police standards for personnel and performance, and participate in planning for the control of disorders.

To maintain control of incidents which could lead to disorders, the Commission recommends that local officials:

Assign seasoned, well-trained policemen and supervisory officers to patrol ghetto areas, and to respond to disturbances.

Develop plans which will quickly muster maximum police

manpower and highly qualified senior commanders at the outbreak of disorders.

Provide special training in the prevention of disorders, and prepare police for riot control and for operation in units, with adequate command and control and field communication for proper discipline and effectiveness.

Develop guidelines governing the use of control equipment and provide alternatives to the use of lethal weapons. Federal support for research in this area is needed.

Establish an intelligence system to provide police and other public officials with reliable information that may help to prevent the outbreak of a disorder and to institute effective control measures in the event a riot erupts.

Develop continuing contacts with ghetto residents to make use of the forces for order which exist within the community.

Establish machinery for neutralizing rumors, and enabling Negro leaders and residents to obtain the facts. Create special rumor details to collect, evaluate, and dispel rumors that may lead to a civil disorder.

The Commission believes there is a grave danger that some communities may resort to the indiscriminate and excessive use of force. The harmful effects of over-reaction are incalculable. The Commission condemns moves to equip police departments with mass destruction weapons, such as automatic rifles, machine guns, and tanks. Weapons which are designed to destroy, not to control, have no place in densely populated urban communities.

The Commission recommends that the Federal Government share in the financing of programs for improvement of police forces, both in their normal law enforcement activities as well as in their response to civil disorders.

To assist government authorities in planning their response to civil disorder, this report contains a Supplement on Control of Disorder. It deals with specific problems encountered during riot control operations, and includes:

Assessment of the present capabilities of police, National Guard and Army forces to control major riots, and recommendations for improvement.

Recommended means by which the control operations of those forces may be coordinated with the response of other agencies, such as fire departments, and with the community at large.

Recommendations for review and revision of Federal, state and local laws needed to provide the framework for control efforts and for the callup and interrelated action of public safety forces.

CHAPTER 13.—THE ADMINISTRATION OF JUSTICE UNDER EMERGENCY CONDITIONS

In many of the cities which experienced disorders last summer, there were recurring breakdowns in the mechanisms for processing, prosecuting, and protecting arrested persons. These resulted mainly from long-standing structural deficiencies in criminal court systems, and from the failure of communities to anticipate and plan for the emergency demands of civil disorders.

In part, because of this, there were few successful prosecutions for serious crimes committed during the riots. In those cities where mass arrests occurred, many arrestees were deprived of basic legal rights.

The Commission recommends that the cities and states:

Undertake reform of the lower courts so as to improve the quality of justice rendered under normal conditions.

Plan comprehensive measures by which the criminal justice system may be supplemented during civil disorders so that its deliberative functions are protected, and the quality of justice is maintained.

Such emergency plans require broad community participation and dedicated leadership by the bench and bar. They should include:

Laws sufficient to deter and punish riot conduct.

Additional judges, bail and probation officers, and clerical staff.

Arrangements for volunteer lawyers to help prosecutors and to represent riot defendants at every stage of proceedings.

Policies to insure proper and individual bail, arraignment, pretrial, trial, and sentencing proceedings.

Adequate emergency processing and detention facilities.

CHAPTER 14.—DAMAGES: REPAIR AND COMPENSATION

The Commission recommends that the Federal Government:

> Amend the Federal Disaster Act—which now applies only to natural disasters—to permit Federal emergency food and medical assistance to cities during major civil disorders, and provide long-term economic assistance afterwards.
>
> With the cooperation of the states, create incentives for the private insurance industry to provide more adequate property insurance coverage in inner-city areas.

The Commission endorses the report of the National Advisory Panel on Insurance in Riot-Affected Areas: "Meeting the Insurance Crisis of our Cities."

CHAPTER 15.—THE NEWS MEDIA AND THE DISORDERS

In his charge to the Commission, the President asked: "What effect do the mass media have on the riots?"

The Commission determined that the answer to the President's question did not lie solely in the performance of the press and broadcasters in reporting the riots. Our analysis had to consider also the overall treatment by the media of the Negro ghettos, community relations, racial attitudes, and poverty—day by day and month by month, year in and year out.

A wide range of interviews with Government officials, law enforcement authorities, media personnel and other citizens, including ghetto residents, as well as a quantitative analysis of riot coverage and a special conference with industry representatives, leads us to conclude that:

> Despite instances of sensationalism, inaccuracy and distortion, newspapers, radio and television tried on the whole to give a balanced, factual account of the 1967 disorders.
>
> Elements of the news media failed to portray accurately the scale and character of the violence that occurred last summer. The overall effect was, we believe, an exaggeration of both mood and event.
>
> Important segments of the media failed to report adequately on the causes and consequences of civil disorders and on the underlying problems of race relations. They have not communicated to the majority of their audience—which is

white—a sense of the degradation, misery, and hopelessness of life in the ghetto.

These failings must be corrected, and the improvement must come from within the industry. Freedom of the press is not the issue. Any effort to impose governmental restrictions would be inconsistent with fundamental constitutional precepts.

We have seen evidence that the news media are becoming aware of and concerned about their performance in this field. As that concern grows, coverage will improve. But much more must be done, and it must be done soon.

The Commission recommends that the media:

Expand coverage of the Negro community and of race problems through permanent assignment of reporters familiar with urban and racial affairs, and through establishment of more and better links with the Negro community.

Integrate Negroes and Negro activities into all aspects of coverage and content, including newspaper articles and television programing. The news media must publish newspapers and produce programs that recognize the existence and activities of Negroes as a group within the community and as a part of the larger community.

Recruit more Negroes into journalism and broadcasting and promote those who are qualified to positions of significant responsibility. Recruitment should begin in high schools and continue through college; where necessary, aid for training should be provided.

Improve coordination with police in reporting riot news through advance planning, and cooperate with the police in the designation of police information officers, establishment of information centers, and development of mutually acceptable guidelines for riot reporting and the conduct of media personnel.

Accelerate efforts to insure accurate and responsible reporting of riot and racial news, through adoption by all newsgathering organizations of stringent internal staff guidelines.

Cooperate in the establishment of a privately organized and funded Institute of Urban Communications to train and educate journalists in urban affairs, recruit and train more

Negro journalists, develop methods for improving police-press relations, review coverage of riots and racial issues, and support continuing research in the urban field.

CHAPTER 16.—THE FUTURE OF THE CITIES

By 1985, the Negro population in central cities is expected to increase by 68 percent to approximately 20.3 million. Coupled with the continued exodus of white families to the suburbs, this growth will produce majority Negro populations in many of the Nation's largest cities.

The future of these cities, and of their burgeoning Negro populations, is grim. Most new employment opportunities are being created in suburbs and out-lying areas. This trend will continue unless important changes in public policy are made.

In prospect, therefore, is further deterioration of already inadequate municipal tax bases in the face of increasing demands for public services, and continuing unemployment and poverty among the urban Negro population:

Three choices are open to the Nation:

We can maintain present policies, continuing both the proportion of the Nation's resources now allocated to programs for the unemployed and the disadvantaged, and the inadequate and failing effort to achieve an integrated society.

We can adopt a policy of "enrichment" aimed at improving dramatically the quality of ghetto life while abandoning integration as a goal.

We can pursue integration by combining ghetto "enrichment" with policies which will encourage Negro movement out of central city areas.

The first choice, continuance of present policies, has ominous consequences for our society. The share of the Nation's resources now allocated to programs for the disadvantaged is insufficient to arrest the deterioration of life in central-city ghettos. Under such conditions, a rising proportion of Negroes may come to see in the deprivation and segregation they experience, a justification for violent protest, or for extending support to now isolated extremists who advocate civil disruption. Large-scale and continuing violence could result, followed by white retaliation, and, ultimately, the separation of the two communities in a garrison state.

Even if violence does not occur, the consequences are unacceptable. Development of a racially integrated society, extraordinarily difficult today, will be virtually impossible when the present black central-city population of 12.1 million has grown to almost 21 million.

To continue present policies is to make permanent the division of our country into two societies: one, largely Negro and poor, located in the central cities; the other, predominantly white and affluent, located in the suburbs and in outlying areas.

The second choice, ghetto enrichment coupled with abandonment of integration, is also unacceptable. It is another way of choosing a permanently divided country. Moreover, equality cannot be achieved under conditions of nearly complete separation. In a country where the economy, and particularly the resources of employment, are predominantly white, a policy of separation can only relegate Negroes to a permanently inferior economic status.

We believe that the only possible choice for America is the third—a policy which combines ghetto enrichment with programs designed to encourage integration of substantial numbers of Negroes into the society outside the ghetto.

Enrichment must be an important adjunct to integration, for no matter how ambitious or energetic the program, few Negroes now living in central cities can be quickly integrated. In the meantime, large-scale improvement in the quality of ghetto life is essential.

But this can be no more than an interim strategy. Programs must be developed which will permit substantial Negro movement out of the ghettos. The primary goal must be a single society, in which every citizen will be free to live and work according to his capabilities and desires, not his color.

CHAPTER 17.——RECOMMENDATIONS FOR NATIONAL ACTION
Introduction

No American—white or black—can escape the consequences of the continuing social and economic decay of our major cities.

Only a commitment to national action on an unprecedented scale can shape a future compatible with the historic ideals of American society.

The great productivity of our economy, and a Federal revenue system which is highly responsive to economic growth, can provide the resources.

The major need is to generate new will—the will to tax ourselves to the extent necessary to meet the vital needs of the Nation.

We have set forth goals and proposed strategies to reach those goals. We discuss and recommend programs not to commit each of us to specific parts of such programs, but to illustrate the type and dimension of action needed.

The major goal is the creation of a true union—a single society and a single American identity. Toward that goal, we propose the following objectives for national action:

Opening up opportunities to those who are restricted by racial segregation and discrimination, and eliminating all barriers to their choice of jobs, education, and housing.

Removing the frustration of powerlessness among the disadvantaged by providing the means for them to deal with the problems that affect their own lives and by increasing the capacity of our public and private institutions to respond to these problems.

Increasing communication across racial lines to destroy stereotypes, halt polarization, end distrust and hostility, and create common ground for efforts toward public order and social justice.

We propose these aims to fulfill our pledge of equality and to meet the fundamental needs of a democratic and civilized society—domestic peace and social justice.

Employment

Pervasive unemployment and underemployment are the most persistent and serious grievances in minority areas. They are inextricably linked to the problem of civil disorder.

Despite growing Federal expenditures for manpower development and training programs, and sustained general economic prosperity and increasing demands for skilled workers, about 2 million—white and non-white—are permanently unemployed. About 10 million are underemployed, of whom 6.5 million work full time for wages below the poverty line.

The 500,000 "hard-core" unemployed in the central cities who lack a basic education and are unable to hold a steady job are made up in large part of Negro males between the ages of 18 and 25. In the riot cities which we surveyed, Negroes were three times as likely as whites to hold unskilled jobs, which are often part time, seasonal, low paying and "dead end."

Negro males between the ages of 15 and 25 predominated among the rioters. More than 20 percent of the rioters were unemployed, and many who were employed held intermittent, low status, unskilled jobs which they regarded as below their education and ability.

The Commission recommends that the Federal Government:

Undertake joint efforts with cities and states to consolidate existing manpower programs to avoid fragmentation and duplication.

Take immediate action to create 2 million new jobs over the next 3 years—1 million in the public sector and 1 million in the private sector—to absorb the hard-core unemployed and materially reduce the level of underemployment for all workers, black and white. We propose 250,000 public sector and 300,000 private sector jobs in the first year.

Provide on-the-job training by both public and private employers with reimbursement to private employers for the extra costs of training the hard-core unemployed, by contract or by tax credits.

Provide tax and other incentives to investment in rural as well as urban poverty areas in order to offer to the rural poor an alternative to migration to urban centers.

Take new and vigorous action to remove artificial barriers to employment and promotion, including not only racial discrimination but, in certain cases, arrest records or lack of a high school diploma. Strengthen those agencies such as the Equal Employment Opportunity Commission, charged with eliminating discriminatory practices, and provide full support for Title VI of the 1964 Civil Rights Act allowing Federal grant-in-aid funds to be withheld from activities which discriminate on grounds of color or race.

The Commission commends the recent public commitment of the National Council of the Building and Construction Trades Unions, AFL–CIO, to encourage and recruit Negro membership in apprenticeship programs. This commitment should be intensified and implemented.

Education

Education in a democratic society must equip children to develop their potential and to participate fully in American life. For the community at large, the schools have discharged this responsibility well. But for many minorities, and particularly for the children of the ghetto, the schools have failed to provide the educational experience which could overcome the effects of discrimination and deprivation.

This failure is one of the persistent sources of grievance and resentment within the Negro community. The hostility of Negro parents and students toward the school system is generating increasing conflict and causing disruption within many city school districts. But the most dramatic evidence of the relationship between educational practices and civil disorders lies in the high incidence of riot participation by ghetto youth who have not completed high school.

The bleak record of public education for ghetto children is growing worse. In the critical skills—verbal and reading ability—Negro students are falling further behind whites with each year of school completed. The high unemployment and underemployment rate for Negro youth is evidence, in part, of the growing educational crisis.

We support integration as the priority education strategy; it is essential to the future of American society. In this last summer's disorders we have seen the consequences of racial isolation at all levels, and of attitudes toward race, on both sides, produced by three centuries of myth, ignorance, and bias. It is indispensable that opportunities for interaction between the races be expanded.

We recognize that the growing dominance of pupils from disadvantaged minorities in city school populations will not soon be reversed. No matter how great the effort toward desegregation, many children of the ghetto will not, within their school careers, attend integrated schools.

If existing disadvantages are not to be perpetuated, we must drastically improve the quality of ghetto education. Equality of results with all-white schools must be the goal.

To implement these strategies, the Commission recommends:

Sharply increased efforts to eliminate de facto segregation in our schools through substantial federal aid to school systems seeking to desegregate either within the system or in cooperation with neighboring school systems.

Elimination of racial discrimination in Northern as well as

Southern schools by vigorous application of Title VI of the Civil Rights Act of 1964.

Extension of quality early childhood education to every disadvantaged child in the country.

Efforts to improve dramatically schools serving disadvantaged children through substantial federal funding of year-round quality compensatory education programs, improved teaching, and expanded experimentation and research.

Elimination of illiteracy through greater Federal support for adult basic education.

Enlarged opportunities for parent and community participation in the public schools.

Reoriented vocational education emphasizing work-experience training and the involvement of business and industry.

Expanded opportunities for higher education through increased federal assistance to disadvantaged students.

Revision of state aid formulas to assure more per student aid to districts having a high proportion of disadvantaged school age children.

The Welfare System

Our present system of public welfare is designed to save money instead of people, and tragically ends up doing neither. This system has two critical deficiencies:

First, it excludes large numbers of persons who are in great need, and who, if provided a decent level of support, might be able to become more productive and self-sufficient. No Federal funds are available for millions of unemployed and underemployed men and women who are needy but neither aged, handicapped nor the parents of minor children.

Second, for those included, the system provides assistance well below the minimum necessary for a decent level of existence, and imposes restrictions that encourage continued dependency on welfare and undermine self-respect.

A welter of statutory requirements and administrative practices and regulations operate to remind recipients that they are considered untrustworthy, promiscuous, and lazy. Residence requirements prevent assistance to people in need who are newly arrived in the state. Searches of recipients' homes violate privacy. Inadequate social services compound the problems.

The Commission recommends that the Federal Government, acting with state and local governments where necessary, reform the existing welfare system to:

> Establish, for recipients in existing welfare categories, uniform national standards of assistance at least as high as the annual "poverty level" of income, now set by the Social Security Administration at $3,335 per year for an urban family of four.
>
> Require that all states receiving Federal welfare contributions participate in the Aid to Families with Dependent Children-Unemployed Parents Program (AFDC-UP) that permits assistance to families with both father and mother in the home, thus aiding the family while it is still intact.
>
> Bear a substantially greater portion of all welfare costs—at least 90 percent of total payments.
>
> Increase incentives for seeking employment and job training, but remove restrictions recently enacted by the Congress that would compel mothers of young children to work.
>
> Provide more adequate social services through neighborhood centers and family-planning program.
>
> Remove the freeze placed by the 1967 welfare amendments on the percentage of children in a State that can be covered by Federal assistance.
>
> Eliminate residence requirements.

As a long-range goal, the Commission recommends that the Federal Government seek to develop a national system of income supplementation based strictly on need with two broad and basic purposes:

> To provide, for those who can work or who do work, any necessary supplements in such a way as to develop incentives for fuller employment.
>
> To provide, for those who cannot work and for mothers who decide to remain with their children, a minimum standard of decent living, and to aid in saving children from the prison of poverty that has held their parents.

A broad system of supplementation would involve substantially greater Federal expenditures than anything now contemplated. The cost will range widely depending on the standard of need accepted as the "basic allowance" to individuals and families, and on the rate at which additional income above this level is taxed. Yet if the deepening cycle of poverty and dependence on welfare can be broken, if the children of the poor can be given the opportunity to scale the wall that now separates them from the rest of society, the return on this investment will be great indeed.

Housing

After more than three decades of fragmented and grossly underfunded Federal housing programs, nearly 6 million substandard housing units remain occupied in the United States.

The housing problem is particularly acute in the minority ghettos. Nearly two-thirds of all nonwhite families living in the central cities today live in neighborhoods marked by substandard housing and general urban blight. Two major factors are responsible:

First: Many ghetto residents simply cannot pay the rent necessary to support decent housing. In Detroit, for example, over 40 percent of the nonwhite-occupied units in 1960 required rent of over 35 percent of the tenants' income.

Second: Discrimination prevents access to many nonslum areas, particularly the suburbs, where good housing exists. In addition, by creating a "back pressure" in the racial ghettos, it makes it possible for landlords to break up apartments for denser occupancy, and keeps prices and rents of deteriorated ghetto housing higher than they would be in a truly free market.

To date, Federal programs have been able to do comparatively little to provide housing for the disadvantaged. In the 31-year history of subsidized Federal housing, only about 800,000 units have been constructed, with recent production averaging about 50,000 units a year. By comparison, over a period only 3 years longer, FHA insurance guarantees have made possible the construction of over 10 million middle and upper income units.

Two points are fundamental to the Commission's recommendations:

First: Federal housing programs must be given a new thrust aimed at overcoming the prevailing patterns of racial segregation. If this is not done, those programs will continue to concentrate the most impoverished and dependent segments of the population into the central-city ghettos where there is already a critical gap between the needs of the population and the public resources to deal with them.

Second: The private sector must be brought into the production and financing of low and moderate-rental housing to supply the capabilities and capital necessary to meet the housing needs of the Nation.

The Commission recommends that the Federal Government:

Enact a comprehensive and enforceable Federal open-housing law to cover the sale or rental of all housing, including single-family homes.

Reorient Federal housing programs to place more low- and moderate-income housing outside of ghetto areas.

Bring within the reach of low- and moderate-income families within the next 5 years 6 million new and existing units of decent housing, beginning with 600,000 units in the next year.

To reach this goal we recommend:

Expansion and modification of the rent supplement program to permit use of supplements for existing housing, thus greatly increasing the reach of the program.

Expansion and modification of the below-market interest rate program to enlarge the interest subsidy to all sponsors, provide interest-free loans to nonprofit sponsors to cover pre-construction costs, and permit sale of projects to nonprofit corporations, co-operatives, or condominiums.

Creation of an ownership supplement program similar to present rent supplements, to make home ownership possible for low-income families.

Federal writedown of interest rates on loans to private builders constructing moderate-rent housing.

Expansion of the public housing program, with emphasis on small units on scattered sites, and leasing and "turnkey" programs.

Expansion of the Model Cities program.

Expansion and reorientation of the urban renewal program to give priority to projects directly assisting low-income households to obtain adequate housing.

Conclusion

One of the first witnesses to be invited to appear before this Commission was Dr. Kenneth B. Clark, a distinguished and perceptive scholar. Referring to the reports of earlier riot commissions, he said:

I read that report * * * of the 1919 riot in Chicago, and it is as if I were reading the report of the investigating committee on the Harlem riot of '35, the report of the investigating committee on the Harlem riot of '43, the report of the Mc-Cone Commission on the Watts riot.

I must again in candor say to you members of this Commission—it is a kind of Alice in Wonderland—with the same moving picture reshown over and over again, the same analysis, the same recommendations, and the same inaction.

These words come to our minds as we conclude this report.

We have provided an honest beginning. We have learned much. But we have uncovered no startling truths, no unique insights, no simple solutions. The destruction and the bitterness of racial disorder, the harsh polemics of black revolt and white repression have been seen and heard before in this country.

It is time now to end the destruction and the violence, not only in the streets of the ghetto but in the lives of people.

NOTES

1. The term "ghetto" as used in this Report refers to an area within a city characterized by poverty and acute social disorganization and inhabited by members of a racial or ethnic group under conditions of involuntary segregation.

2. A "central city" is the largest city of a standard metropolitan statistical area, that is, a metropolitan area containing at least one city of 50,000 or more inhabitants.

15.

ANDREW KOPKIND

White on Black: The Riot Commission and the Rhetoric of Reform

"As America gets worse and worse," Murray Kempton once wrote, "its reports get better and better." No report of a commission investigating America's recent crises has found so warm a public welcome as the Kerner Commission's study of the season of civil disorders in the summer of 1967. In its official and private editions the "Riot Commission" Report has sold almost two million copies. Countless critiques and analyses have greeted it in the press, and it has turned to grist for thesis mills in the nation's graduate schools and colleges. The careers of several commissioners, staff officials, and consultants have been considerably enhanced by their association with the Report (and only a few reputations have suffered). All in all, the Report has become a basic document in the platform of American liberals for social reform, a catalogue of problems and a program of solutions.

SOURCE: From Andrew Kopkind, "White on Black: The Riot Commission and the Rhetoric of Reform," Hard Times 44 (September 15-22, 1969): 1-4. Copyright 1969, The New Weekly Project, Inc. Reprinted with the permission of the author and publisher.

But by and large, those who were cheered by the Report's solemn platitudes or impressed by its torrent of statistics missed its essential political functions and its crucial social consequences. It presented— and legitimized—a specific view of the riots and a particular under- standing of America that now constitutes the standard approach to the treatment of social ills. The Commission was able to do that job because of the way it was set up, staffed, manipulated, and termi- nated; because of the promises and rewards it offered those who worked for it; because of its punishments for criticism and dissention; and because of its calculated presentation to the public through press and mass media.

Reportage and analysis of the Commission's work have largely failed, and for the same reasons: Reporters and analysts became deeply implicated in the "success" of the Report. Although there was an unusual amount of reportable conflicts during the Commission's seven months of operation, reporters never got past the vague rumors of friction between liberal and conservative forces, or the whispered hints of White House interference. The firing of 120 staff members in late 1967 was never explained; the substantial hostility of black staffers towards the Commission's own "institutional" racism was never mentioned; the "underground" Commission document, "The Harvest of American Racism," was never examined; the White House veto on employment of staff and consultants active in anti-war work was never disclosed; the tacit agreement to "forget" the war in Viet- nam throughout the Commission's investigations and its Report was overlooked; and the secret plan of Commissioner Charles ("Tex") Thornton to torpedo the Report just before launching is still an untold story.

In similar ways, the political analysts who pored over the long document never got past its liberal rhetoric and its profuse program- matics to see its political role. No one has yet detailed the Report's lasting effect on the set of signals it delivered to corporations, founda- tions, and government planners to manage urban affairs on the model of foreign aid and counter-insurgency programs of the early 1960s.

The Report does not exist outside of its political context. It can logically escape neither the conflicts which informed its operations, nor the uses to which it will be put. Strictures on thinking "unthinka- ble" thoughts about Vietnam (among other unthinkables) made im- possible a realistic assessment of the nature of riotous America. Total concern for the way resources of the society are allocated—rather than control of the allocation process—eliminated discussion of the possibilities of serious social change. Acceptance of pluralistic myths about the operation of American institutions limited the Report to the exposition of a narrow ideology. Failure to analyze in any way the "white racism" asserted by the commissioners in the Report's summary transformed that critical category into a cheap slogan. And overall, the Report's mindless attention to documenting conventional perceptions and drowning them in conventional wisdom made meaningless the commissioners' demands for social reconstruction.

The very acceptance—and acceptability—of the Report is a clue to its emptiness. It threatens no real, commanding interests. It demands, by implication or explication, no real shifts in the way power and wealth are apportioned among classes; it assumes that the political and social elites now in control will (and should) remain in their positions. By avoiding an approach to the riots as events of political insurrection, or as part of a worldwide response to an overbearing United States empire, the Report makes sure that social therapy will be applied only to surface effects, not systemic faults.

President Johnson chose eleven members for his National Advisory Commission on Civil Disorders, a collection remarkable chiefly for its predictable moderation. There could, and would, be no surprises. The list was comprised of men (and one woman) representing various aspects of economic and political elites in the United States: expansive corporatism (Charles B. Thornton, the President, Director and Chairman of Litton Industries); bureaucratic labor (I.W. Abel, President of the United Steel Workers); the pre-1965 civil rights establishment (Roy Wilkins, Executive Director of the NAACP); Republicans (Rep. William M. McCulloch of Ohio and Sen. Edward W. Brooke of Massachusetts); Democrats (Rep. James Corman of California and Sen. Fred Harris of Oklahoma); old-style machine politics (Chairman Otto Kerner, Governor of Illinois); new-style urban politics (Vice-Chairman John Lindsay, Mayor of New York City); the police (Chief Herbert Jenkins of Atlanta); and women-in-politics (Katherine Graham Peden, then Commerce Commissioner of the State of Kentucky).

Like all presidential commissions, the Kerner Commission was designed not to study questions but to state them, not to conduct investigations but to accept them, not to formulate policy but to confirm it. Although the Commission conducted hundreds of hours of official "hearings" and traveled in groups of two and three commissioners to riot cities, the basic work was done by the staff—and by the scores of outside consultants, specialists, and experts who were directed into the really critical policy-making roles. Together, the outsiders made up the elite of professional "urbanists" which has become the command group for the management of social crises.

·Staff Director David Ginsburg was chief political cadre for the administration. His assignment was to manipulate the internal and external operations of the Commission so as to produce a forward-looking report and avoid the worst pitfalls of controversy, bickering, and career damage. President Johnson himself appointed Ginsburg as the Director, shortly after he announced the names of the commissioners. It was an unusual move, and a source of some suspicion afterwards; commissions like to hire their own hands. But the job of political organizer was too important to be left to any bureaucrat. The White House had to keep control of the Commission, even indirectly —*preferably* indirectly. David Ginsburg filled the required role to perfection. A quiet, commanding West Virginia lawyer, he had first met Johnson in New Deal days and became one of his pool of Jewish lawyers (cf. Abe Fortas, Edwin Weisl) who are always available for odd jobs, big deals, and general counsel (myths of ethnic attributes grow tall in Texas).

As Ginsburg was the political manager and manipulator of the Commission, his deputy, Victor Palmieri, was the administrator and theoretician. Palmieri was a young Southern California lawyer, very much in the hard-living, aggressive Kennedy style. By the time he was 35, he had become president of the Janss Corporation, one of the West's biggest landholding and development corporations.

If Ginsburg had a broad rhetorical view of the Commission's purposes, Palmieri had a much more specific notion of what it was supposed to do: "We thought we had a damn good chance of moving to a major racial conflagration. . . . The most important thing was what the response would be in the white police forces. The objective was to affect the posture of local authorities in the next summer."

President Johnson had called for two separate products from the Commission: an "interim" document in March 1968 and a final Report by August 1. But Palmieri and Ginsburg came to believe that the schedule of separate reports would have to be discarded if the Commission was to influence events in the summer of 1968.

It fell to Palmieri to assemble a crew of social scientists to document and analyze the "causes" of the riots, on which everyone had agreed before the Commission's work ever started. President Johnson's television speech on July 27—written in part and edited by Justice Abe Fortas—asserted that the riots then engulfing scores of cities were "caused" by "ignorance, discrimination, slums, poverty, disease, not enough jobs."

It should not have been difficult to find social scientists who accepted the Commission's premises. Until very recently, there has been no tradition of radical analysis in the social sciences. Many of the most important figures in academic and political social science in the United States came of age in the late 1940s and 1950s, when the "end of ideology" was proclaimed. But while many social science stars agreed to "consult" with the Commission, none would undertake a full-time commitment. The staff finally had to settle for a National Institute of Mental Health psychologist, Robert Shellow, who was a commissioned officer in the Public Health Service.

There was also some question about the acceptability to the administration of those academics who agreed to work in any capacity on the Report. Herbert Gans, for instance, was "vetoed" by the White House as a regular consultant because he had indulged in anti-war activities. Palmieri (who was personally very much against the war, too) succeeded in hiring Gans on a "contract" basis. The White House veto operation was run by Presidential Assistant Marvin Watson, the notorious hatchet man of the late Johnson years, who kept names of anti-war activists in a computer file in the basement of the executive offices. Gans's name turned up as a member of a group of artists, writers and academics who declared that they would refuse tax payments as a protest against the war in Vietnam.

Within the Commission staff, Palmieri tried a management device designed to provide alternate circuits and prevent overloading of the "social science input." He laid out his system of "fail-safes" in an attempt to treat conclusively the data received from field researchers. According to Palmieri's plan, the investigative and research material would be worked over in three ways: sociologically, by Robert Shellow; journalistically, by Robert Conot, co-author of a book on the Watts riots of 1965; and practical-politically, by staff lawyers, such as Ginsburg, Palmieri, and Stephen Kurzman.

What happened in the end, as Palmieri once said, was that the system had an "abort" in its critical center—the social scientific, "intellectual" effort. The fail-safe failed. To Palmieri's way of thinking, that failure gutted the whole Report. The journalistic accounts, the statistical tables, and the political suggestions were never bound in a coherent analytical structure.

It was more than a month after the commissioners were appointed that the "critical" social scientific staff began its work. Having failed to enlist the undivided attentions of the top men at the universities and research centers around the country, Director Robert Shellow called for their recommendations for bright young assistants to round out his department. In time, he was provided with six full- and part-time men, three undergraduate "interns" from Antioch College, and scores of consultants who would fly to Washington at $100 or $150 per diem.

Like many government agencies, bureaus, and departments plowing the new fields of "social technology"—education, urban development, anti-poverty, welfare, health, and civil rights—the Commission drew to it every academic entrepreneur with a scheme to sell. Some were more successful than others: Washington is full of small research firms where returned VISTAs, Peace Corpsmen or Appalachian Volunteers can earn $12,000 or $15,000 a year trading on their brief associations with the poor, black, and oppressed. Such operations are often run by the returnees' old bosses at the various government agencies which funded the volunteer projects in the first place.

The Commission signed a contract, quite early in the game, with the Trans-Century Corporation, a Washington-based research, training, and job placement company run by Warren Wiggins, a former deputy director of the Peace Corps, and staffed in large measure by returned volunteers and their friends. Several Trans-Centurians joined the Commission staff. The company itself won its $18,000 contract to recruit staff.

Hundreds of thousands of dollars went into research contracts. The Bureau of Applied Social Science Research at Columbia (where several Commission contractors and consultants, including Herbert Gans now work) got $45,540 for a study of arrest records of rioters. A University of Michigan spin-off research department got $45,488 for a study of the life habits of rioters. The International Association of Chiefs of Police won a $38,000 contract for a study of police preparedness.

One of the most important Commission research contracts was given to Systemetrics, a subsidiary of the Real Estate Research Corporation, of Chicago. Systemetrics is run by Anthony G. Downs, an old friend of Palmieri's. Downs is on the "new breed" side of a family connected with Mayor Daley's Chicago. He is a major ideologist of "downtownism" and "urban land reform."

Systemetrics was assigned two jobs: to design research and management programs for the Commission, and to combine and summarize the field research reports on twenty-four riots in twenty-three cities. The way the Systemetrics researchers perceived the riots in the twenty-four summaries could profoundly affect the commissioners' understanding of the processes of conflict. If the summaries portrayed ghetto blacks as pitiable victims, surrounded by rats and roaches, and put upon by evil and prejudiced predators, that would be how the commissioners ultimately would perceive the situation.

Systemetrics did use that approach, of course, and it was the theme of the final Report. That theme grows out of the "middle position" between reactionary and revolutionary ideologies. It expresses the notion that since the conflicts of black and white America are non-ideological, no real shifts of power are needed to correct them. The problems which were seen in the American cities in the summer of 1967 did not represent contradictions within the whole political economy, but malfunctions of one or another institution—the failure to get food or money or jobs to the black people and whites in the same income group, to establish lines of communication between "control authorities" and the people they "serve." Racial prejudice, practiced by individuals alone or in groups, compounds the problems. But there is no real answer to prejudice; the "solution" to racial and urban problems must always be put in technical terms. And although it may be extremely difficult, solutions can be produced by the existing political elites.

Much of the foundation for that "middle position" was laid in an early paper written for the Commission by Howard Margolis, of the Institute for Defense Analysis, the secret war research corporation. The memorandum—never made public—reportedly laid out three possible perspectives for the Commissioners to ponder: 1) the "right-wing" theory that a conspiracy lay behind the riots, and that program recommendations should emphasize the restoration of "law and order"; 2) the "left-wing" theory, that the riots represented a para-political rebellion of the black poor in America, and that only radical social change could integrate that rebellion into a new American "system"; and 3) the "middle position," focusing on the presumably "neutral" problems of migration, urban overpopulation, and historical black underprivilege. Programs designed to deal with those problems implied no threat to the current organization of corporate capitalism in America.

The central contradiction of the entire Commission operation was embedded in the "middle position." As Margolis—and other staff assistants who read it in the first months of the Commission's autumn

—understood, the position did not fit the realities of the black rebellions of the summer. The problem was not that it was "wrong," but
that it did not represent the forces at work in the country. Its presentation was meant to serve a single political purpose.

For that reason, its unquestioned reception created a constellation
of problems for the Commission staff, for the commissioners themselves, and for the final Report. The contradiction between theory and
reality hampered the work of the field investigators, who felt themselves pulled apart between the blacks they were interviewing and the
Commission they were serving. It created fatal tensions within the
social science section, which was charged with integrating research
materials and historical perspectives in a framework which was ab-
stracted from real conditions. It made the official "hearings" before
the full Commission quite irrelevant, for it gave values to the parameters of testimony before anyone ever was heard. And finally, it denied
meaning to the Report, for it based programs on unrealistic theories.

The field investigation teams were the first to feel the tensions.
Teams of six investigators were sent to each of twenty-three cities. In
each city, "sub-teams" of two people would speak with officials, private citizens in positions of power, and ghetto residents and activists.
The teams were organized on racial lines. According to a memorandum from David Ginsburg to the Commission staff, it was to be
assumed that "only Negroes would be able to obtain information from
residents in the ghetto areas." Whites, Ginsburg added, would be sent
to interview officials and private citizens.

It was not long, however, before the black investigators began to
sense that they were being used for purposes of which they were at
least partly suspicious; specifically, they were worried that the reports
of their interviews would be misrepresented when shown to the higher
levels of the Commission staff or that information on militants might
ultimately be passed on to law enforcement agencies, despite official
assurances that it would go only as far as the National Archives.

Many black staffers remained convinced that "the whole thing was
a racist operation," as one of the field investigators put it. All the top
policy-making jobs were held by whites, except for the post of general
counsel, which had been given to a black man, Merle McCurdy.
There were only a few "token" black consultants in the long list
appended to the Report. Overall, the Report was always thought of as
a white document written by white writers and aimed at a white
audience—*about* black people. It was primarily a response to the

white response to the riots. It was supposed to prescribe policy for black people, not for whites. Although it named "white racism," it did not describe white racist society.

The central contradiction of the Commission—between what was politic and what was real—was felt most strongly by the social science section, under Research Director Robert Shellow. It was expressed primarily in the drafting of the document, "The Harvest of American Racism," and "Harvest's" eventual rejection by Palmieri; and by the firing of Shellow and his entire staff in late December 1967. Although perceptions of the reasons for the findings differ widely, the context of contradictions is hardly arguable: the Report was intended to serve particular political ends, and "Harvest" and the social scientists interfered.

Shellow had four assistants working on "Harvest": David Boesel, Louis Goldberg, Gary T. Marx, and David Sears. All of them were young social scientists with liberal or radical tendencies. To them, the riots were not incoherent freakouts, but rather specific (though unplanned) responses to oppression. They could not be understood without a conception of black struggle against white domination; and the "causes" could not be found in the obviously bad living conditions, but in the distribution of power in the total system. In other words, the riots were rebellions.

By early November, the Shellow section began to feel the critical press of time. No underlings had yet been told that there would be only one Report—instead of the March interim document and the August final version—so the summary analysis of the whole summer of riots would have to be finished by the end of November to meet the interim deadline. "We were working around the clock," Boesel said. "We slept in our offices—they brought in cots—and we never left. It was crazy. We'd be found in our underwear darting across the hall in the mornings, just before people came to work. But we were really excited. We thought our case studies would be the guts of the Report. We thought our original doubts about how the Commission would operate were proving unfounded, and that we'd be able to say what we wanted."

What they wanted to say was contained in a 176-page document of forceful impressions, if somewhat limited analysis. "The Harvest of American Racism" was hardly the kind of work that a government agency would be happy to endorse. It did not couch its ideology in the conventions of "neutrality," but stated its positions boldly. It also was confused and inconsistent even in its own terms, and mixed traditional liberal assumptions which even the Commission would find perfectly acceptable with radical notions about the nature of oppression and the development of rebellion. The most extraordinary part was the last chapter, "America on the Brink: White Racism and Black Rebellion." Written in rather heated language, it went further than most top staff officials thought prudent in charging that racism infused all American institutions, and characterized the riots as a first step in a developing black revolution, in which Negroes will "feel it is legitimate and necessary to use violence against the social order. A truly revolutionary spirit has begun to take hold . . . an unwillingness to compromise or wait any longer, to risk death rather than have their people continue in a subordinate status."

Both Palmieri and Ginsburg admit that they were appalled when they read "Harvest." Ginsburg, who was thought to be the soul of genteel manners and quiet control, spoke of the document in four-letter words. Palmieri said he fairly threw it across the room when Shellow gave it to him. The real problem was not that it was poorly done (it was no worse a job than much of the finished Report) but that it defied the categories that the top officials had established for the "social science input."

Palmieri "fired" Shellow on the spot, although the actual process of separation was much more ambiguous and drawn out. But from that point on, Shellow was excluded from all important Commission activities. "Harvest" was popped down a memory hold.

At length, Palmieri gave up entirely on "social science input," a notion in which he once placed so much confidence, and gave the analysis section of the Report to Stephen Kurzman, a lawyer who was a deputy director of the Commission, to complete. Kurzman turned out a quick, lawyer-like job, incorporating those notions in the "Harvest" thesis which were acceptable from the start, but removing the more threatening ideas.

Many of the 120 investigators and social scientists "released" from the Commission staff in December 1967 will always believe that the firings were ordered by the Johnson administration. But there is every reason to believe that the action was undertaken by Palmieri (with Ginsburg concurring) because of the failure of Shellow's group to produce an "acceptable" analytical section.

The commissioners themselves knew little of the firings, or of the controversy surrounding them, until the few speculative reports in the press were seen. On December 8, Ginsburg gave the Commission the news: "It was simply flabbergasting," a staff member reported. "Ginsburg said that the publication of the Report in March wouldn't really mean the end of the Commission, that there would be supplemental reports and such. And the Commissioners allowed themselves to be deluded. 'Oh, well,' Kerner said, 'if it's not really going to be the end of the Commission, then I guess it's all right.' He fell right in line, then Harris behind him, then Brooke. The rest of them sort of looked at one another. The decision was made in just fourteen minutes."

From the beginning, it was clear that John Lindsay was the chief spokesman for the liberal position, and Tex Thornton was the heavy for the conservatives. Lindsay's closest allies were Senator Harris, Chief Jenkins, and Roy Wilkins. Thornton had only Mrs. Peden as a full-time cohort. The others roamed around the middle, or, like Brooke, who had the worst attendance record, roamed elsewhere.

What the "liberal" side meant first of all was a full acceptance of the "middle position" as laid out long before in the Margolis memo. Beyond that, it entailed a rhetorical emphasis on the horrors of life for ghetto blacks, and a sense—as Hubert Humphrey once expressed it—that things were bad enough to explain (but not excuse) rioting. There was no agreement, however, that the riots were a positive or beneficial political act (as "Harvest" had proposed), nor, of course, was there any idea that the failure of black Americans to achieve equality with whites was a structural failure of the American political and economic system.

The "conservative" side grudgingly accepted that same "middle position" thesis but emphasized the bad character of the criminal element in the ghettoes rather than the conditions of life there. Secret minutes of a Commission meeting of November 10, 1967, taken by a staff member, illustrate Thornton's attitudes; in this instance, he was responding to a discussion on "what causes riots":

> In re "bitterness and despair": we're playing right into the hands of the militants who will use it as justification for violence. Maybe bitterness and an element of despair; but only 2 or 3 percent actually start the riots. It's also the rewards, the benefit from free burglary. Put in . . . "an increasing lack of respect for the law": that's what it is, and the Report has to bring this out loud and clear. There's little restraint to participation in disorders. . . . Improve the police departments: the military should train soldiers about to come out of the service in law enforcement work. Help solve big

recruitment problem. There are up to 60,000 coming out per year. . . . No question that show of restraining force, quickly applied, actually has restraining effect. Show of military force (even with no bullets or bayonets fixed) quickly stopped militants. We should provide maybe that federal troops be made available on standby basis as a precautionary measure.

Let's not mention about the slave background and the poor Negro. Sins of forefathers idea will fall on deaf ears. Only 10 to 15 percent of whites had slave-owning forefathers.

No law and no courts will change the attitude of the whites. Labor unions have this very bad attitude, as does the so-called establishment. . . . Open housing helps force Negroes onto whites and releases hostile attitudes. . . . If we voice poverty, etc. as a cause of riots, thirty million poor people will use it as an excuse to riot.

On the other hand, Lindsay thought that the Report, even in its finished form, was "wishy-washy." He was particularly angry that no mention was made of the war in Vietnam as a contributing factor to the riot process. But in a meeting of the Commission to debate the point of "mentioning" the war, Lindsay was voted down. Although there is no reason to think that President Johnson directed Ginsburg to avoid mention of the war, it is clear that Ginsburg was doing Johnson's bidding. That, indeed, was his function, and the reason he was picked to head the Commission staff—by the President himself. Early fears that Lindsay entertained about Ginsburg's "daily" contact with Johnson were irrelevant. Ginsburg did not *have* to see Johnson.

There was, however, one exception. Late in 1967, Thornton grew anxious about the final Report's "liberalism." He was particularly worried that it would suggest legislation for enormous federal expenditures; and, more than that, that it would generate "expectations" in the black community which could never be fulfilled, and which would lead to more rioting. Thornton went to George Mahon, the Texas Democrat who heads the House Appropriations Committee, and asked him to intercede with the White House on behalf of the "conservative" side of the Commission. Mahon, Thornton, and the President were, of course, all Texans. Mahon and Thornton were also allied through Litton Industries' intense interest in government appropriations.

On the night before the final meeting, Lindsay and his personal staff put together what he describes as an "end game." The plan was that Lindsay would "assume" at the next day's meeting that a summary would precede the full Report. He would then read just such a summary—written in an all-night session by his aides. In promoting the summary, Lindsay would tell how deeply he felt about the issues it raised. The implication was that he would not sign the Report if the summary were not included. The move had three objectives. First, Lindsay's "support" of the Report (with summary) would put the burden of "dissent" on the conservative side. Secondly, Lindsay got his own summary into the hopper before any others. Finally, the gambit would lay the emotional and intellectual basis for Lindsay's personal dissent, should his summary be defeated, or if the conservatives won their points.

But the game worked smoothly. At first, Thornton and Corman argued against Lindsay's summary, but Thornton's attempt to put together a majority against it (and, by implication, against the Report as it stood) came to nothing.

Could the Report have gone either way? Palmieri, for instance, thought there was a real danger that it could turn into an obviously illiberal document. But the structure of the Commission and the context in which it operated suggest that its tone could have hardly been other than "liberal." The finished product almost exactly reproduced the ideological sense given it by President Johnson more than half a year earlier. The choice of commissioners, staff, consultants, and contractors led in the same direction. The political constituency foremost in the directors' minds—the audience to which the Report was played —had been conditioned to expect and accept a catalogue of ills and a list of reforms.

According to the directors, the real fights in the Commission came over the introduction to the "Recommendations for National Action." That seventy-page chapter was supposed to outline the scope of a national program of social reforms, in employment, education, welfare, and housing, with no "price tag" attached.

The chapter was based on a thorough memorandum of program recommendations drawn up for the Commission by Anthony Downs of Systemetrics.

The importance of the Downs strategy is not in the specifics of its programs, which in many cases are considered desirable by most right-thinking people, but in the nature of its political demands. Continuing, reinforcing—and to some degree setting the ideology of the Commission—it assumes the dominance of the same elites now in power, minus the old fogeys and plus the new technocrats. While its theory of programming may be dynamic, its theory of power is static.

VIII

U.S.A.,
1969

INTRODUCTION

"After the assassination of Robert Kennedy," wrote Richard Drinnon in *The Nation*, "Mr. Johnson followed what had become standard operating procedure: he quickly announced the appointment of 'a commission of most distinguished Americans to immediately examine this tragic phenomenon'. . . . and a new team took over."[1]

In terms of both its mandate and composition, the "new team" was decidedly more conservative than the Kerner Commission. President Johnson instructed the Violence Commission to "investigate and make recommendations with respect to:

(a) The causes and prevention of lawless acts of violence in our society, including assassination, murder and assault;

(b) The causes and prevention of disrespect for law and order, of disrespect for public officials, and of violent disruptions of public order by individuals and groups; and

(c) Such other matters as the President may place before the Commission."

The political tenor of the commissioners supported the rumor that President Johnson wanted to repudiate the Kerner Report because he felt, according to a Presidential aide, that it "over-dramatized the white racism theme" and was "counter-productive in terms of programs for society as a whole."[2] The Commission was chaired by Dr. Milton Eisenhower, a university administrator and brother of the late President, and included: A. Leon Higginbotham, a black federal judge; Hale Boggs, a southern Congressman and former member of the Warren Commission; Terence Cardinal Cooke, Archbishop of New York; Philip A. Hart, a senator and liberal Democrat from Michigan; Eric Hoffer, a conservative philosopher and longshoreman; Roman Lee Hruska, a conservative Republican senator from Nebraska; Patricia Robert Harris, a black lawyer, formerly Dean of Howard University's Law School and Ambassador to Luxembourg; Leon Jaworski, a Texan lawyer and personal adviser to the President, formerly a member of the National Crime Commission; Albert E. Jenner, Jr., a prominent midwestern lawyer and former Senior Counsel to the Warren Commission; William McCulloch, a conservative

Congressman from Ohio, formerly a member of the Kerner Commission; Ernest William McFarland, a Justice of the Arizona Supreme Court, formerly Governor of Arizona and Senate Majority Leader; and Dr. W. Walter Menninger, a psychiatrist and staff member of the Menninger Foundation.

The Commission's work was completed under President Nixon, who granted the Commission an additional six months, and released in December, 1969. According to Milton Eisenhower, the Violence Commission even surpassed the Kerner Commission in terms of research, documentation, and resources: "Our Report is based on penetrating research by two hundred leading scholars and on eighteen months of hearings, conferences, and some sixty days of arduous working sessions by members of the Commission. . . . The detailed data and findings of the scholars who helped us are set forth in more than fifteen volumes of printed reports." Of the latter reports, the news media gave the most attention to *Rights in Conflict* (Daniel Walker's investigation of the riot in Chicago during the Democratic National Convention) and *The Politics of Protest* (Jerome Skolnick's task force report on collective dissent in American society).

The final report of the Violence Commission justified the worst fears of political commentators and shocked many scholars who had expected the Report to at least imitate the serious and scholarly tone of the Kerner Report. The Report is primarily an ideological tract, badly written and composed, often inconsistent and whimsical, and completely lacking in serious scholarship. The selections from the Violence Commission clearly indicate that the Report adopts a counterinsurgency perspective on dissent and identifies ghetto blacks as the major source of violence in the United States. In this respect, the Violence Commission follows a tradition established by previous riot commissions in which the violence of blacks is defined as the major subject of condemnation and explanation, whereas the violence of whites and governments is either ignored or defended.

Elliott Currie is well qualified to write a critique of the Violence Commission's final report. As Assistant Director for Jerome Skolnick's task force, which produced *The Politics of Protest*, Currie was responsible for writing many important sections of the Skolnick Report and gave considerable thought to ideological and theoretical issues in the "riot" literature. The Report receives the kind of critique that it deserves—disrespectful, abrasive, and devastating.

NOTES

1. Richard Drinnon, "The Rhetoric of Evasion," *The Nation* (October 13, 1969), pp. 370-74.

2. Joseph A. Califano, Jr., quoted in the *Washington Post* (October 17, 1968), p. 17.

16.

NATIONAL COMMISSION ON THE CAUSES
AND PREVENTION OF VIOLENCE

To Establish Justice, to Insure
Domestic Tranquility

INTRODUCTION

Violence in the United States has risen to alarmingly high levels. Whether one considers assassination, group violence, or individual acts of violence, the decade of the 1960s was considerably more violent than the several decades preceding it and ranks among the most violent in our history. The United States is the clear leader among modern, stable democratic nations in its rates of homicide, assault, rape, and robbery, and it is at least among the highest in incidence of group violence and assassination.

This high level of violence is dangerous to our society. It is disfiguring our society—making fortresses of portions of our cities and dividing our people into armed camps. It is jeopardizing some of our most precious institutions, among them our schools and universities—

SOURCE: From the National Commission on the Causes and Prevention of Violence, *To Establish Justice, To Insure Domestic Tranquility* (Washington, D.C.: U.S. Government Printing Office, 1969), pp. xv-xxxii, 17-30, 34-43, 57-85.

poisoning the spirit of trust and cooperation that is essential to their proper functioning. It is corroding the central political processes of our democratic society—substituting force and fear for argument and accommodation.

We have endured and survived other cycles of violence in our history. Today, however, we are more vulnerable to violence than ever before. Two-thirds of our people live in urban areas, where violence especially thrives. Individual and group specializations have intensified our dependence on one another. Men are no longer capable of solitary living and individual self-defense; men must live together and depend upon one another to observe the laws and keep the peace.

The American people know the threat. They demand that violence be brought to a halt. Violence must be brought under control—to safeguard life and property, and to make possible the creation of the understanding and cooperation needed to remedy underlying causes. No society can remain free, much less deal effectively with its fundamental problems, if its people live in fear of their fellow citizens; it is ancient wisdom that a house divided against itself cannot stand.

In this Report we suggest a number of specific measures for the better control of violence. We urge, for example, that the nation should double its investment in the prevention of crime and the administration of justice, as rapidly as that investment can be wisely planned and utilized. We recommend that central offices of criminal justice be created at the metropolitan level to make all parts of the criminal justice process—police, courts, corrections—function more effectively, and that private citizens' organizations be formed to work as counterparts of these offices in every major city in the nation. We urge that public officials, including law enforcement officers, intensify their efforts to develop more effective tactics in handling both peaceful demonstrations and violent disturbances. As we show by comparing successful and unsuccessful strategies of control of major mass demonstrations of the past few years, official behavior may determine whether protest remains peaceful or erupts into serious violence.

Further, we recommend the adoption of a national firearms policy that will limit the general availability of handguns. . . .

Necessary as measures of control are, they are only a part of the answer. They do not cure the basic causes of violence. Violence is like a fever in the body politic: it is but the symptom of some more basic pathology which must be cured before the fever will disappear.

Indeed, if measures of control were this society's only response to violence, they would in the long run exacerbate the problem. The pyramiding of control measures could turn us into a repressive society, where the peace is kept primarily through official coercion rather than through willing obedience to law. That kind of society, where law is more feared than respected, where individual expression and movement are curtailed, is violent too—and it nurtures within itself the seeds of its own violent destruction.

In this Report, we analyze basic causes which underlie the chief varieties of contemporary violence. We make a number of recommendations directed to removing these causes. They cannot be eliminated entirely; even in a perfectly just society in which all have a fair and nondiscriminatory stake, there will always be some violent individuals, in rural as well as in urban areas, and measures of control will always be required to restrain them. But we can improve the conditions and opportunities of life for all citizens and thus reduce sharply the number who will commit violent acts.

Thus, we urge that young people must be given a greater role in determining their own destiny and in shaping the future course of our society. Responsible participation in decision-making may, for many, be a substitute for the violence that is born in frustration. We propose lowering the voting age, reforming the draft, and providing a massive expansion in opportunities for youth to engage in public service activities whose goals young people wholeheartedly embrace.

While we categorically condemn all illegal violence, including group violence,[1] as incompatible with the survival of a just, democratic, and humane society, we state emphatically that aggrieved groups must be permitted to exercise their constitutional rights of protest and public presentation of grievances. Accordingly, we believe the President should seek legislation that would confer jurisdiction upon the United States District Courts to grant injunctions, upon the request of the Attorney General or private persons, against the threatened or actual interference by any person, whether or not under color of state or federal law, with the rights of individuals or groups to freedom of speech, freedom of the press, peaceful assembly, and petition for redress of grievances.

We must have the perception to recognize injustices when they are called to our attention, and we must have the institutional flexibility to correct those injustices promptly. To enable the less affluent to obtain effective and peaceful redress of grievances, we recommend that additional steps should be taken to meet their needs for lawyers, and that state and local jurisdictions should be encouraged to experiment with the establishment of grievance agencies to serve all citizens.

The way in which we can make the greatest progress toward reducing violence in America is by taking the actions necessary to improve the conditions of family and community life for all who live in our cities, and especially for the poor who are concentrated in the ghetto slums. It is the ghetto slum that is disproportionately responsible for violent crime, by far the most acute aspect of the problem of violence in the United States today.

To be a young, poor male; to be undereducated and without means of escape from an oppressive urban environment; to want what the society claims is available (but mostly to others); to see around oneself illegitimate and often violent methods being used to achieve material gain; and to observe others using these means with impunity —all this is to be burdened with an enormous set of influences that pull many toward crime and delinquency. To be also a Negro, Puerto Rican or Mexican-American and subject to discrimination and segregation adds considerably to the pull of these other criminogenic forces.

Safety in our cities requires nothing less than progress in reconstructing urban life. We must meet the 1968 Housing Act's goal of a decent home for every American within a decade. We must take more effective steps to realize the goal, first set in the Employment Act of 1946, of a useful job at a reasonable wage for all who are able to work. We must provide better educational opportunities for all our children. We must act on current recommendations that those American families who cannot care for themselves receive a basic annual income. We must restructure our local governments, restore their fiscal vitality and accomplish a host of other major tasks of the kind discussed in this Report. . . .

As these brief introductory comments indicate, we believe that the twin objectives of the social order must be to make violence both unnecessary and unrewarding. To make violence unnecessary, our institutions must be capable of providing justice for all who live under them—of giving all a satisfactory stake in the normal life of the community and the nation. To make violence unrewarding, our institutions must be able to control violence when it occurs, and to do so firmly, fairly, and within the law.

The Preamble of our Constitution does not speak merely of justice or merely of order; it embraces both. Two of the six purposes set forth in the Preamble are to "establish justice" and to "insure domestic tranquility." If we are to succeed in preventing and controlling violence, we must achieve both of these goals.

We are well aware that our recommendations for attaining these objectives—and the recommendations of other national commissions before us—will require far-reaching improvements in our institutions and unprecedented levels of public funding. We adopt as our own the verdict which the Kerner Commission pronounced upon the scope and costs of its recommendations:

> [T]hey neither probe deeper nor demand more than the problems which called them forth. There can be no higher priority for national action and no higher claim on the nation's conscience.

For the past three decades, the primary concerns of the federal government have been the national defense, the conduct of wars and foreign affairs, the growth of the economy, and, more recently, the conquest of space. These problems have consumed the major part of the public attention. They currently devour more than two-thirds of federal expenditures and approximately 50 percent of federal, state, and local expenditures combined.

Traditionally we have left the problems of social justice, provision of essential community services, and law enforcement primarily to the states and cities. In recent years, the federal government has made some major efforts in diverse fields such as rural development, civil rights, medical care, housing, employment, and education, but these efforts have been subordinated to the claims of the "national security."

Yet the federal government still collects the lion's share (about 65 percent) of all tax receipts. Tax revenue available to the states and cities falls woefully below what is needed to discharge their responsibilities. Each one percent rise in the Gross National Product increases the income of the federal government by one and one-half percent, while the normal income of state and city governments increases by less than half that percentage. Concentration on "national" and international problems at the expense of "local" and domestic concerns has left us with an enormous deficit of unmet social needs and deeply-felt social injustices.

Ironically, this gap has appeared despite rapidly accelerating technological, economic and social gains. For the first time in man's history, this nation is nearing the capability of releasing all citizens from the poverty and social privation that hitherto have been accepted as the inevitable lot of mankind. We have also achieved an enormous capacity to communicate: the poor, the black, and other deprived groups among us can see daily on their television sets what they are missing, and how near their release from bondage can be. But our institutions have not yet made it possible for an expectant populace to achieve what our economy and technology are becoming capable of providing.

In our judgment, the time is upon us for a reordering of national priorities and for a greater investment of resources in the fulfillment of two basic purposes of our Constitution—to "establish justice" and to "insure domestic tranquility." . . .

We solemnly declare our conviction that this nation is entering a period in which our people need to be as concerned by the internal dangers to our free society as by any probable combination of external threats. We recognize that substantial amounts of funds cannot be transferred from sterile war purposes to more productive ones until our participation in the Vietnam war is ended. We also recognize that to make our society essentially free of poverty and discrimination, and to make our sprawling urban areas fit to inhabit, will cost a great deal of money and will take a great length of time. We believe, however, that we can and should make a major decision now to reassess our national priorities by placing these objectives in the first rank of the nation's goals.

The decision that has the greatest effect on the level of our expenditures for these objectives is what we decide to spend on the national defense. For three decades, the national defense has ranked first by far in our scale of priorities, much of the time necessarily so. With occasional exceptions, whatever the Administration has requested for the Armed Forces has been readily granted. Since 1939 there have been a number of occasions when the Administration's budget requests for the Armed Forces have been exceeded by Congressional appropriations; for most other federal programs the opposite is true. For example, actual appropriations for the general welfare (health, labor, education, housing, pollution, and law enforcement) are currently running more than five billion dollars annually below the amounts previously authorized by the Congress.

Our Commission is not competent to recommend a specific level of national defense expenditures. We recognize that without the deterrent capability essential for security against external attack, internal freedom and security would not be possible. It is to be expected that our military leaders will, like other government officials, stress the extreme urgency of the programs under their charge. But we believe the time has come to question whether expenditures for the general welfare should continue to be subordinated to those for national defense.

Defense expenditures, stated in 1968 prices, fell from about 78 billion dollars in 1953 (at the end of the Korean War) to about 60 billion dollars in 1954 and remained at that level for the decade 1955 to 1964. But by 1968 they had risen again to the present 81 billion dollar annual level as the result of our major commitment of troops to Vietnam.[2]

Federal expenditures for the general welfare, while they have increased substantially over the past several years, are now approximately 60 billion dollars, of which $25 billion represents social security payments.

As a first step, we should try to reverse this relationship. When our participation in the Vietnam War is concluded, we recommend increasing annual general welfare expenditures by about 20 billion dollars (stated in 1968 dollars), partly by reducing military expenditures and partly by use of increased tax revenues resulting from the growth of the Gross National Product. We suggest this only as an initial goal: as the Gross National Product and tax revenues continue to rise, we should strive to keep military expenditures level (in constant dollars), while general welfare expenditures should continue to increase until essential social goals are achieved.[3]

Based on estimates of the Council of Economic Advisers,[4] the funds needed to achieve this goal without inflationary consequences could be obtained from two sources:

(1) The end of the Vietnam war should reduce defense expenditures by 19 billion dollars annually. The Council anticipates that this reduction will be offset in part by war-end program adjustments and deferred weapons programs. Hence, defense expenditures should go down to about 65 billion dollars (at 1968 prices).[5]

(2) The Gross National Product is expected to increase over the next decade (in constant dollars) at the rate of about four percent a year. The same should be true of fed-

eral tax revenues, which should grow in real terms at an annual increment of approximately 15 billion dollars.[6] Of this amount, approximately half will be required to meet expected annual increases for "baseline" federal non-defense expenditures other than general welfare programs. Hence, about seven or eight billion dollars more each year than the preceding year should be available for new and expanded programs in the general welfare field.

Whether somewhat more or less than the amounts we have indicated should be provided to overcome social ills is not the important point.[7] What is important is that the people of this nation recognize both the possibilities and the need for choice. For an entire generation, we have necessarily been more aware of and responsive to the external dangers to our society than to the internal dangers. In this Commission's opinion, the internal dangers now demand a greater awareness and a more substantial response—one that can only be made if we face the need to reorder our priorities. It is time to balance the risks and precautions we take abroad against those we take here at home.

The Department of Health, Education, and Welfare has made a suggestion which merits careful consideration as a potentially valuable supplemental step toward reordering national priorities, namely, the preparation of an "Annual Social Report."[8] The Annual Social Report, comparable to the present Annual Economic Report, would provide us with a set of measurements—of "social indicators"—on how well we have done in providing housing, education, health care, public safety, and opportunities for the upward advancement of all sectors of our population. It would tell us whether the disadvantaged groups among us have been advancing at a rate sufficient to foster hope and to quiet the desperation that drives men to violence. It would significantly aid the nation and its leaders in establishing national priorities.

The Social Report would be prepared by social scientists recruited for stated periods of public service from among the nation's best scholars, just as the members and staff of the Council of Economic Advisers are today. They could be organized as a Council of Social Advisers, as are the Economic Advisers, or in some other visible and independent form. A major function of the social science staff would be to develop tools for measuring the comparative effectiveness of social programs. While we have learned a good deal about social stresses and the gross causative factors that require correction, we still know very little about whether particular remedial programs work at all, which ones work better than others, and why. We lack practicable means for measuring cost-benefit ratios, for establishing and observing parallel programs with significant variables, and for putting an end to programs which have failed to justify their continuance.[9] A central staff charged with this responsibility could do much to improve the accuracy of our social planning and the efficacy of on-going programs.

Two decades ago, the Council of Economic Advisers was created by the Full Employment Act of 1946, amid much skepticism about the "science" of economics and particularly about the wisdom and effect of governmental efforts to stimulate or restrain economic activity. Today we recognize the importance of the government's economic role and of national economic measurements, imprecise and imperfect as the economist's tools still are. The other social sciences may now have as much potential for informing wise government policy as economics had twenty years ago. . . .

In a democratic society, the citizens possess the basic social power, and national priorities reflect the value judgments of the majority. Skeptics may thus take a pessimistic view of this Commission's recommendation that our national priorities be reordered. They will point, for example, to the reluctance of the public, despite the penetrating reports and the excellent recommendations of previous presidential commissions, to take the comprehensive actions needed to curb crime, eliminate racial discrimination, and alleviate the problems of the ghetto poor. They will point especially to middle-class America —to the "forgotten American"—and his concern over some consequences of racial integration, his rebellion against rising taxes, his distrust of dissent on the campus and protest movements in the capital. How realistic is it, they will ask, to think that the majority of Americans will support a reallocation of our national resources to deal with social problems?

Skepticism is understandable. But the majority of Americans have always responded constructively to national crises when they have been fully informed and responsibly led. The "silent majority," like most other Americans, do not wish to surrender any of the most important freedoms of our open society—freedom of movement, freedom from harm, freedom from fear. They stand to benefit from the programs necessary to retain these freedoms just as much as any disadvantaged minority. All Americans—the majority and our various minorities—must come to grips with the basic causes of violence in our society and do what must be done to achieve liberty and justice for all.

Some, with little faith in our nation, predict that majority indifference will result in a violent revolution of some kind. Indeed, nihilists and anarchists openly espouse this course. We see signs, however, that a peaceful revolution is already under way: a spirit of needed reform is rising steadily among the people and in the ranks of local and national leaders. We see a growing readiness to formulate new values, to set new priorities, and to make firm commitments now, to be honored as soon as resources are available.

Some ordinary citizens feel they can do nothing to influence the direction and the destiny of their nation. But more and more Americans are proving this to be a myth. A growing number of our citizens have found they need not stand idle while our cities rot, people live in fear, householders build individual fortresses, and human and financial resources flow to less urgent endeavors. A new generation of Americans is emerging, with the energy and the talent and the determination to fulfill the promise of the nation. As it ever was, the young—idealistic but earnest, inexperienced but dedicated—are the spearheads of the drive toward change, and increasing numbers of adult Americans are joining their ranks.

When in man's long history other great civilizations fell, it was less often from external assault than from internal decay. Our own civilization has shown a remarkable capacity for responding to crises and for emerging to higher pinnacles of power and achievement. But our most serious challenges to date have been external—the kind this strong and resourceful country could unite against. While serious external dangers remain, the graver threats today are internal: haphazard urbanization, racial discrimination, disfiguring of the environment, unprecedented interdependence, the dislocation of human identity and motivation created by an affluent society—all resulting in a rising tide of individual and group violence.

The greatness and durability of most civilizations has been finally determined by how they have responded to these challenges from within. Ours will be no exception. . . .

VIOLENT CRIME: HOMICIDE, ASSAULT, RAPE, ROBBERY

When citizens express concern about high levels of violence in the United States, they have in mind a number of different types of events: homicides and assaults, rioting and looting, clashes between demonstrators and police, student seizures of university buildings, violence in the entertainment media, assassinations of national leaders. Foremost in their minds, no doubt, is what appears to be a rising tide of individual acts of violent crime, especially "crime in the streets."

Only a fraction of all crime is violent, of course. Major crimes of violence—homicide, rape, robbery, and assault—represent only 13 percent (or 588,000) of the Federal Bureau of Investigation's Index of reported serious crimes (about 4.5 million in 1968).[10] Moreover, deaths and personal injuries from violent crime cause only a small part of the pain and suffering which we experience: one is five times more likely to die in an auto accident than to be criminally slain, and one hundred times more likely to be injured in a home accident than in a serious assault.

But to suffer deliberate violence is different from experiencing an accident, illness or other misfortune. In violent crime man becomes a wolf to man, threatening or destroying the personal safety of his victim in a terrifying act. Violent crime (particularly street crime) engenders fear—the deep-seated fear of the hunted in the presence of the hunter. Today this fear is gnawing at the vitals of urban America.

In a recent national survey, half of the women and one-fifth of the men said they were afraid to walk outdoors at night, even near their homes. One-third of American householders keep guns in the hope that they will provide protection against intruders. In some urban neighborhoods, nearly one-third of the residents wish to move because of high rates of crime, and very large numbers have moved for that reason. In fear of crime, bus drivers in many cities do not carry change, cab drivers in some areas are in scarce supply, and some merchants are closing their businesses. Vigilante-like groups have sprung up in some areas.

Fear of crime is destroying some of the basic human freedoms which any society is supposed to safeguard—freedom of movement, freedom from harm, freedom from fear itself. Is there a basis for this fear? Is there an unprecedented increase in violent crime in this country? Who and where are most of the violent criminals and what makes them violent? What can we do to eliminate the causes of that violence?

I. Profile of Violent Crime

Between 1960 and 1968, the national rate of criminal homicide per 100,000 population increased 36 percent, the rate of forcible rape 65 percent, of aggravated assault 67 percent, and of robbery 119 percent. These figures are from the *Uniform Crime Reports* published by the Federal Bureau of Investigation. These Reports are the only national indicators we have of crime in America. But, as the FBI recognizes, they must be used with caution.

There is a large gap between the reported rates and the true rates. In 1967 the President's Commission on Law Enforcement and Administration of Justice stated that the true rate of total major violent crime was roughly twice as high as the reported rate.[11] This ratio has probably been a changing one. Decreasing public tolerance of crime is seemingly causing more crimes to be reported. Changes in police practices, such as better recording procedures and more intensive patrolling, are causing police statistics to dip deeper into the large well of unreported crime. Hence, some part of the increase in reported rates of violent crime is no doubt due to a fuller disclosure of the violent crimes actually committed.

Moreover, while current rates compare unfavorably, even alarmingly, with those of the 1950s, fragmentary information available indicates that at the beginning of this century there was an upsurge in violent crime which probably equaled today's levels. In 1916, the city of Memphis reported a homicide rate more than seven times its present rate. Studies in Boston, Chicago and New York during the years of the First World War and the 1920s showed violent crime rates considerably higher than those evident in the first published national crime statistics in 1933.

Despite all these factors, it is still clear that *significant and disturbing increases in the true rates of homicide and, especially, of assault and robbery have occurred over the last decade.*

While the reported incidence of forcible rape has also increased, reporting difficulties associated with this crime are too great to permit any firm conclusion on the true rate of increase.

Violent crimes are not evenly distributed throughout the nation. Using new data from a Victim-Offender Survey conducted by our staff Task Force on Individual Acts of Violence, standard data from the FBI, and facts from other recent studies, we can sketch a more accurate profile of violent crime in the United States than has hitherto been possible. We note, however, that our information about crime is still unsatisfactory and that many critical details in the profile of violent crime remain obscure. Moreover, we strongly urge all who study this profile to keep two facts constantly in mind. First, violent crime is to be found in all regions of the country, and among all groups of the population—not just in the areas and groups of greatest concentration to which we draw attention. Second, despite heavy concentrations of crime in certain groups, the overwhelming majority of individuals in these groups are law-abiding citizens.

(1) *Violent crime in the United States in primarily a phenomenon of large cities. This is a fact of central importance.*

The twenty-six cities with 500,000 or more residents and containing about 17 percent of our total population contribute about 45 percent of the total reported major violent crimes. Six cities with one million or more residents and having ten percent of our total population contribute 30 percent of the total reported major violent crimes.

Large cities uniformly have the highest reported violent crime levels per unit of population.[12] Smaller cities, suburbs and rural areas have lower levels. The average rate of major violent offenses in cities of over 50,000 inhabitants is eleven times greater than in rural areas, eight times greater than in suburban areas, and five and one-half times greater than in cities with 50,000 to 100,000 inhabitants.

For cities of all sizes, as well as for suburbs and rural areas, there has been a recent upward trend in violent crime; the increase in the city rate has been much more dramatic than that for the other areas and subdivisions.

The result in our larger cities is a growing risk of victimization: in Baltimore, the nation's leader in violent crime, the risk of being the victim of a reported violent crime is one in forty-nine per year. Thus, in the context of major violent crimes, the popular phrase "urban crisis" is pregnant with meaning.

(2) *Violent crime in the city is overwhelmingly committed by males.*

Judgments about overall trends and levels of violent crime, and about variations in violent crime according to city size, can be based upon reported offense data. But conclusions about the sex, age, race and socioeconomic status of violent offenders can be based only on arrest data. Besides the gap previously mentioned between true offense rates and reported offense rates, we must now deal also with the even larger gap between *offenses reported* and *arrests made.* Accordingly, conclusions in these areas must be drawn with extreme care, especially since arrests, as distinguished from convictions, are made by policemen whose decisions in apprehending suspects thus determine the nature of arrest statistics.[13]

In spite of the possibly wide margins of error, however, one fact is clearly indisputable: violent crimes in urban areas are disproportionately caused by male offenders. To the extent that females are involved, they are more likely to commit the more "intimate" violent crimes like homicide than the "street crimes" like robbery. Thus, the 1968 reported male homicide rate was five times higher than the female rate; the robbery rate twenty times higher.

(3) *Violent crime in the city is concentrated especially among youths between the ages of fifteen and twenty-four.*

Urban arrest rates for homicide are much higher among the 18-24 age group than among any other; for rape, robbery and aggravated assault, arrests in the 15-24 age group far outstrip those of any other group. Moreover, it is in these age groups that the greatest increases in all arrest rates have occurred. Surprisingly, however, there have also been dramatic and disturbing increases in arrest rates of the 10-14 age group for two categories—a 300 percent increase in assault between 1958 and 1967, and 200 percent in robbery in the same period.

(4) *Violent crime in the city is committed primarily by individuals at the lower end of the occupational scale.*

Although there are no regularly collected national data on the socioeconomic status of violent offenders, local studies indicate that poor and uneducated individuals with few employment skills are much more likely to commit serious violence than persons higher on the socioeconomic ladder. A forthcoming University of Pennsylvania study of youthful male offenders in Philadelphia, for example, will show that boys from lower income areas in the city have delinquency rates for assaultive crimes nearly five times the rates of boys from higher income areas; delinquency rates for robbery are six times higher.[14] Other studies have found higher involvement in violence by persons at the lower end of the occupational scale. A succession of studies at the University of Pennsylvania, using Philadelphia police data, show that persons ranging from skilled laborers to the unemployed constitute about 90-95 percent of the criminal homicide offenders, 90 percent of the rape offenders and 92-97 percent of the robbery offenders. A St. Louis study of aggravated assault found that blue collar workers predominate as offenders. The District of Columbia Crime Commission found more than 40 percent of the major violent crime offenders to be unemployed.

(5) *Violent crime in the cities stems disproportionately from the ghetto slum where most Negroes live.*

Reported national urban arrest rates are much higher for Negroes than for whites in all four major violent crime categories, ranging from ten or eleven times higher for assault and rape to sixteen or seventeen times higher for robbery and homicide.[15] As we shall show, these differences in urban violent crime rates are not, in fact, racial; they are primarily a result of conditions of life in the ghetto slum. The gap between Negro and white crime rates can be expected to close as the opportunity gap between Negro and white also closes—a development which has not yet occurred.

The large national urban differentials between Negroes and whites are also found in the more intensive Philadelphia study previously cited. Of 10,000 boys born in 1945, some 50 percent of the three thousand non-whites had had at least one police contact by age 18, compared with 20 percent of the 7,000 whites. (A police contact means that the subject was taken into custody for an offense other than a traffic violation and a report recording his alleged offense was prepared and retained in police files.) The differences were most pronounced for the major violent offenses: of fourteen juveniles who had police contacts for homicide, all were non-whites; of 44 who had police contacts for rape, 86 percent were non-whites and 14 percent whites; of 193 who had police contacts for robbery, 90 percent were non-whites and 10 percent whites; and of 220 who had police contacts for aggravated assault, 82 percent were non-whites and 18 percent whites. When the three sets of figures for rape, robbery and assault are related to the number of non-whites and whites, respectively, in the total group studied (3,000 vs. 7,000), the differences between the resulting ratios closely reflect the differentials in the national urban arrest rates of non-whites and whites in the 10–17 age group.

> (6) *The victims of assaultive violence in the cities generally have the same characteristics as the offenders: victimization rates are generally highest for males, youths, poor persons, and blacks. Robbery victims, however, are very often older whites.*

There is a widespread public misconception that most violent crime is committed by black offenders against white victims. This is not true. Our Task Force Victim-Offender Survey covering seventeen cities has confirmed other evidence that serious assaultive violence in the city—homicide, aggravated assault and rape—is predominantly between white offenders and white victims and black offenders and black victims. The majority of these crimes involves blacks attacking blacks, while most of the remainder involve whites victimizing whites. Indeed, our Survey found that 90 percent of urban homicide, aggravated assaults and rapes involve victims and offenders of the same race.

In two-thirds of homicides and aggravated assaults in the city, and in three-fifths of the rapes, the victim is a Negro. Rape victims tend strongly to be younger women; the victims of homicide and aggravated assault are usually young males but include a higher proportion of older persons. Nearly four-fifths of homicide victims and two-thirds of the assault victims are male. Generalizing from these data, we may say that the typical victim of a violent assaultive crime is a young Negro male, or in the case of rape, a young Negro woman.

Robbery, on the other hand, is the one major violent crime in the city with a high inter-racial component: although about 38 percent of robberies in the Survey involve Negro offenders and victims, 45 percent involve Negroes robbing whites—very often young black males robbing somewhat older white males. In three-fifths of all robberies the victim is white and nearly two-thirds of the time he or she is age 26 or over. Four-fifths of the time the victim is a man.

Data collected by the Crime Commission indicate that victimization rates for violent crimes are much higher in the lower-income groups. This is clearly true for robbery and rape, where persons with incomes under $6,000 were found to be victimized three to five times more often than persons with incomes over $6,000. The same relation held, but less strongly, for aggravated assault, while homicide victimization rates by income could not be computed under the investigative techniques used.

(7) *Unlike robbery, the other violent crimes of homicide, assault and rape tend to be acts of passion among intimates and acquaintances.*

The Victim-Offender Survey shows that homicide and assault usually occur between relatives, friends or acquaintances (about two-thirds to three-fourths of the cases in which the relationship is known). They occur in the home or other indoor locations about 50-60 percent of the time. Rape is more likely to be perpetrated by a stranger (slightly over half of the cases), usually in the home or other indoor location (about two-thirds of the time). By contrast, robbery is usually committed outside (two-thirds of the cases) by a stranger (more than 80 percent of the cases).

The victim, the offender, or both are likely to have been drinking prior to homicide, assault, and rape, and the victim often provokes or otherwise helps precipitate the crime. The ostensible motives in homicide and assault are often relatively trivial, usually involving spontaneous altercations, family quarrels, jealous rages, and the like. The two crimes are similar; there is often no reason to believe that the person guilty of homicide sets out with any more intention to harm than the one who commits an aggravated assault. Except for the seriousness of the final outcomes, the major distinction is that homicides most often involve handguns while knives are most common in assault.[16]

(8) *By far the greatest proportion of all serious violence is committed by repeaters.*

While the number of hard-core repeaters is small compared to the number of one-time offenders, the former group has a much higher rate of violence and inflicts considerably more serious injury. In the Philadelphia study, 627 of the 10,000 boys were chronic offenders, having five or more police contacts. Though they represented only six percent of the boys in the study, they accounted for 53 percent of the police contacts for personal attacks—homicide, rape and assault—and 71 percent of the contacts for robberies.

Offenders arrested for major criminal violence generally have long criminal histories, but these careers are mainly filled with offenses other than the final serious acts. Generally, though there are many exceptions, the more serious the crime committed, the less chance it will be repeated.

(9) *Americans generally are no strangers to violent crime.*

Although it is impossible to determine accurately how many Americans commit violent crimes each year,[17] the data that are available suggest that the number is substantial, ranging from perhaps 600,000 to 1,000,000—or somewhere between one in every 300 and one in every 150 persons. Undoubtedly, a far greater number commit a serious violent crime at some time in their lives. The Philadelphia study found that of about 10,000 boys 35 percent (3,475) were taken into police custody for delinquency, and of the delinquents 10 percent (363) were apprehended once or more for a major crime of violence before age eighteen.

A comparison of reported violent crime rates in this country with those in other modern, stable nations shows the United States to be the clear leader. Our homicide rate is more than twice that of our closest competitior, Finland, and from four to twelve times higher than the rates in a dozen other advanced countries including Japan, Canada, England and Norway. Similar patterns are found in the rates of other violent crimes: averages computed for the years 1963–1967 show the United States rape rate to be twelve times that of England and Wales and three times that of Canada; our robbery rate is nine times that of England and Wales and double that of Canada; our aggravated assault rate is double that of England and Wales and eighteen times that of Canada.

II. Causes of Violent Crime

Violent crime occurs in many places and among all races, but we have just shown that it is heavily concentrated in large cities and especially among poor black young men in the ghettos. We must therefore focus on the conditions of life for the youth of the inner-city to find the root causes of a high percentage of violent crime.

Much has been written about inner-city slums where crime and delinquency are bred.[18] Social scientists have analyzed slum conditions and their causal link to crime and violence, writers and artists have dramatized the sordidness and the frustrations of life in the inner cities, and a number of Commissions prior to this one have produced comprehensive reports on this subject. In its 1967 Report the Crime Commission described the linkage between violent crime and slum conditions in large cities as "one of the most fully documented facts about crime." Referring to numerous studies conducted over a period of years, the Commission found that violent crime, its offenders and its victims are found most often in urban areas characterized by:

low income
physical deterioration
dependency
racial and ethnic concentrations
broken homes
working mothers
low levels of education and vocational skills
high unemployment
high proportions of single males
overcrowded and substandard housing
low rates of home ownership or single family dwellings
mixed land use
high population density.[19]

A series of studies by Clifford Shaw and Henry McKay remains the classic investigation of these ecological patterns.[20] Extensive data on the distribution of delinquency among neighborhoods were collected in a number of large American cities, and the results for Chicago have recently been updated to cover the period from 1900 through 1965. Finding uniformly high correlations between delinquency and areas having the characteristics listed above, Shaw and McKay focused on the process of change in the communities studied.

Neighborhoods disrupted by population movements and social change contained high proportions of delinquents. Although the same central core areas tended to experience social change and high delinquent rates over time, high or low delinquent rates were not permanently associated with any particular ethnic or racial group. The newest immigrant or migrant groups tended to settle initially in the core areas and be responsible for the highest delinquency rates in each city; yet the rates for these groups went down as the groups either moved outward to better areas or achieved a more stable community structure. In Chicago, first the Germans and Irish, then the Poles and Italians, and finally southern Negroes and Spanish-speaking peoples replaced one another as the newest groups settling in the inner-city and producing the highest delinquency rates. Consistent with these findings has been a regular decline in delinquency rates from the innermost to the outermost areas around the centers of each city examined.[21] Crime and delinquency are thus seen as associated with the disorganization and deprivation experienced by new immigrant or migrant groups as they strive to gain a foothold in the economic and social life of the city.

Negroes, however, have not been able, even when they have improved their economic condition, to move freely from the central cities. Therefore, movement of Negroes with higher income has tended merely to extend the ghetto periphery. The southern Negro migrants who have now been concentrated in the cities for two generations—as well as Negroes who have been living under conditions of urban segregation even longer—have experienced the same disorganizing forces as the earlier European settlers, but there are a number of reasons why the impact of these forces has been more destructive in the case of the Negro. Discrimination by race in housing, employment and education has been harder to overcome than discrimination based on language or ethnic background. With changes in the economy, there has been less demand for the Negro's unskilled labor than for that of the earlier immigrants. The urban political machines which furthered the political and economic interests of earlier immigrants had declined in power by the time the Negroes arrived in large numbers. The cultural experience which Negroes brought with them from the segregation and discrimination of the rural South was of less utility in the process of adaptation to urban life than was the cultural experience of many of the European immigrants. The net effect of these differences is that urban slums have tended to become *ghetto* slums from which escape has been increasingly difficult. . . .

When poverty, dilapidated housing, high unemployment, poor education, over-population, and broken homes are combined, an interrelated complex of powerful criminogenic forces is produced by the ghetto environment. These social forces for crime are intensified by the inferiority-inducing attitudes of the larger American society—attitudes that today view ghetto blacks as being suspended between slavery and the full rights and dignity of free men.

The competitive road to success is accorded great emphasis in American life. Achievement often tends to be measured largely in material terms. Our consumer-oriented culture pressures us to desire goods and services and to feel successful if one obtains them, unsuccessful if one does not. The network of mass communications spreads a culture of consumer desires over a vast audience. Happiness, we are endlessly reminded, is obtaining and having things. Most Americans operate on the premise that in the race to material success all men have an equal chance at the starting line, and that anyone who falls behind has only himself to blame. Yet not all can be at the front of the pack, especially not those who started far behind in the first place. And the race has different rules for different participants.

There are many ways of coping with the frustration of failure. Some take solace in the fact that others are even further behind. Some withdraw entirely from the race: alcohol, drugs, mental illness and even suicide are avenues of escape. Others, especially college youth whose parents have succeeded in the race, experiment with "alternative life-styles" such as those associated with the hippie phenomenon. In the inner city, where the chances of success are less, many adopt illegal means in the effort to achieve their goals of securing more money and higher status among their peers.

To be a young, poor male; to be undereducated and without means of escape from an oppressive urban environment; to want what the society claims is available (but mostly to others); to see around oneself illegitimate and often violent methods being used to achieve material success; and to observe others using these means with impunity—all this is to be burdened with an enormous set of influences that pull many toward crime and delinquency. To be also a Negro, Mexican or Puerto Rican American and subject to discrimination and segregation adds considerably to the pull of these other criminogenic forces.

Believing they have no stake in the system, the ghetto young men see little to gain by playing according to society's rules and little to lose by not. They believe the odds against their success by legitimate means are greater than the odds against success by crime. The step to violence is not great, for in an effort to obtain material goods and services beyond those available by legitimate means, lower-class persons without work skills and education resort to crimes for which force or threat of force has a functional utility, especially robbery, the principal street crime.

But the slum ghetto does more than generate frustration that expresses itself in violent acquisitive crime. It also produces a "subculture" within the dominant American middle-class culture in which aggressive violence tends to be accepted as normal in everyday life, not necessarily illicit. In the contemporary American city we find the necessary conditions not only for the birth but also for the accelerated development of violent subcultures, and it is in these settings that most violent aggressive crimes in fact occur.[22]

From the perspective of dominant middle-class standards, the motives in most criminal homicides and other assaults—altercations, family quarrels, jealousy—are cheap issues for which people give their lives or suffer serious injury. Similarly, the transient gratifications to be obtained from the rape or the robbery do not seem to warrant the risk of punishment or the burden of guilt that is presumably involved. Yet these events are much more reasonable to those in the ghetto slum subculture of violence, where a wide range of situations is perceived as justifying violent responses. An altercation with overtones threatening a young man's masculinity, a misunderstanding between husband and wife, competition for a sexual partner, the need to get hold of a few dollars—these "trivial" events can readily elicit a violent response in an environment that accepts violence as a norm, allows easy access to weapons, is physically and culturally isolated from the rest of the wider American community, and has limited social controls—including inadequate law enforcement.[23]

Violence is actually often used to enable a young man to become a successful member of ghetto society. In the subculture of violence, proving masculinity may require frequent rehearsal of the toughness, the exploitation of women, and the quick aggressive responses that are characteristic of the lower-class adult male. Those who engage in subcultural violence are often not burdened by conscious guilt, because their victims are likely to belong to the same subculture or to a group they believe has exploited them. Thus, when victims see their assaulters as agents of the same kind of aggression they themselves represent, violent retaliation is readily legitimized.

Moreover, if the poor, young, black male is conditioned in the ways of violence by his immediate subculture, he is also under the influence of many forces from the general, dominant culture. As we have said in another statement, violence is a pervasive theme in the mass media.

The frequency of violent themes in myriad forms in the media tends to foster permissive attitudes toward violence. Much the same can be said about guns in American society. The highest gun-to-population ratio in the world, the glorification of guns in our culture, and the television and movie displays of guns by heroes surely contribute to the scope and extent of urban violence.

Taking all the foregoing facts and circumstances into account, perhaps we should marvel that there is not more violent crime in the cities of our nation.

III. The Rise in Violent Crime

If, as we believe, the conditions of life for inner-city populations are responsible for the sharp difference in violent crime rates between these populations and other groups in our society, there remains a puzzling paradox to be considered: Why, we must ask, have urban violent crime rates increased substantially during the past decade when the conditions that are supposed to cause violent crime have not worsened—have, indeed, generally improved? . . .

In seeking an acceptable answer, we must keep in mind two qualifications which to a degree mitigate the seriousness of the discrepancy: first, while, as we have said, serious increases have occurred in major crimes involving violence, these increases are not so dramatic as FBI data suggest. Undoubtedly our crime reporting system is gradually dipping deeper into the well of previously unreported crime. Second, substantial portions of such increases as have occurred are to some extent attributable to demographic shifts in the population, particularly increases in the young population and increasing urbanization of the population.[24]

Even with these two factors taken into account, however, an important part of the original question remains. Why, if a high percentage of the crime in our cities is caused by factors such as poverty and racial discrimination, has it increased in a period of unprecedented prosperity for most Americans and in a time of painfully slow and uneven but genuine progress toward racial equality? These questions are not susceptible to precise scientific answers, but it is possible to offer informed judgments about them. In our considered opinion, the following factors have been significantly operative in the increasing levels of violent crime in the inner cities:

(1) The United States has been changing with bewildering rapidity —scientifically, technologically, socially, and politically. Americans literally are changing how we work, how we live, how we think, how

we manage our vast enterprise. Other rapidly changing nations— Israel, Japan, Western European countries—also have experienced rapid rise in crime rates, though at a much lower level than ours. Sociologists and anthropologists have long observed that rapid social change leads to a breakdown of traditional social roles and institutional controls over the behavior of young and old alike—but particularly the young, who, because of the social change, are less likely to be socialized into traditional ways of doing things (and not doing them) and, hence, ineffectively constrained by these traditional ways. This process includes the breakdown in traditional notions of civility, respect for elders and the institutions and patterns of conduct they represent, property rights, ways of settling disputes, relations between the sexes and many other matters.

With economic and technical progress in the United States has come increased affluence for most—but not all—of the members of our society. This combination of rapid social change and unevenly distributed affluence is devastating. At a time when established ways of doing things, traditions of morality, and attitudes about personal and property rights are changing, rising levels of affluence, interacting with public promises of a better life and television displays of still more affluence, have created expectations that have outstripped reality, particularly among the poor and especially the poor black. Rising income statistics look reassuring until one focuses on the continuing gap between black and white incomes.

We have in this country what has been referred to as a "revolution of rising expectations" born of unprecedented prosperity, changes in the law, wars on poverty, space spectaculars, and a host of other features of contemporary life. But, as one of the research contributions in this Commission's Task Force on Historical and Comparative Perspectives points out,[25] a rapid increase in human expectations followed by obvious failure to meet those expectations has been and continues to be a prescription for violence. Disappointment has manifested itself not only in riots and violent demonstrations—but may also be reflected in the increasing levels of violent crime.

(2) Our agencies of law enforcement have not been strengthened sufficiently to contain the violence that normally accompanies rapid social change and the failure to fulfill human expectations. The criminal justice process, suffering from an insufficiency of resources and a lack of management, has become less effective as a deterrent to crime and as an instrument for rehabilitating those who are apprehended and convicted.

As we analyze in other parts of our reports, we are allowing law enforcement to falter, the handgun census to approach 25 million, and an increasing number of crimes to go unpunished. Every successful crime is an inducement to further crime: it advertises society's inability to enforce generally accepted rules of conduct. Weaknesses of our criminal justice system have had a multiplier effect upon the rise of violent crime.

(3) Public order in a free society does not and cannot rest solely on applications or threats of force by the authorities. It must also rest on the people's acceptance of the legitimacy of the rule-making institutions of the political and social order and of the rules these institutions make. Persons obey the rules of society when the groups with which they identify approve those who abide by the rules and disapprove those who violate them. Such expressions of approval and disapproval are forthcoming only if the group believes that the rule-making institutions are in fact entitled to rule—that is, are "legitimate." What weakens the legitimacy of social and political institutions contributes to law-breaking, including violent crime.

In recent years a number of forces have converged to weaken the legitimacy of our institutions. We repeat what was said elsewhere: the spectacle of governors defying court orders, police unlawfully beating demonstrators, looters and rioters going unapprehended and unpunished, and college youth attacking society's rules and values, makes it easier, even more "logical," for disadvantaged young people, whose attachment to law-abiding behavior already is tenuous, to slip into law-breaking behavior when the opportunity presents itself. Too, the pervasive suspicion that personal greed and corruption are prevalent among even the highest public officials has fed the idea among the poor that nearly everyone is "on the take," and that the real crime is getting caught.

The beliefs that some claim to be widely held among poor young ghetto males—that the "system" in the United States is collectively guilty of "white racism" and of prosecuting an "immoral" war in Vietnam—have also tended to impair the moral impact upon them of our nation's institutions and laws and weakened the sense of guilt that otherwise would have restrained the commission of violent crimes against society.

These three factors—disappointments of minorities in the revolution of rising expectations, the weakening of law enforcement, and the loss of institutional legitimacy in the view of many—have had their effects on crime rates throughout our society. It is not surprising, however, that their greatest impact has been in the inner cities, among the young, the poor, the male, the black. It is there that reality most frustrates expectations, that law enforcement provides the least protection, and that the social and political institutions of society serve the needs of the individual least effectively. It is in the inner city that a subculture of violence, already flourishing, is further strengthened by the blockage of aspirations whose fulfillment would lead out of the subcultural, by the failure of a criminal justice system that would deter adherence to undesirable subculture values, and by the weakness of institutions which would inculcate a competing set of values and attitudes. . . .

GROUP VIOLENCE

I. Causes: Historical and Comparative Aspects

We tend to think of group violence[26] as a major aberration in a democratic society, as a sickness that comes only in extraordinary times. A deeper reading of the past belies this notion. In man's political history, group violence has accompanied periods of serious social stress from Homer to this morning's newspaper. Group violence runs through the American experience, as it always has, in varying degrees and manifestations, for every society. Violence has been used by groups seeking power, by groups holding onto power, and by groups in the process of losing power. Violence has been pursued in the defense of order by the satisfied, in the name of justice by the oppressed, and in fear of displacement by the threatened.

At the outset, it must be made clear that group violence has no necessary relationship to group protest, although there continue to be those who decry the one as though it were the other. The right to protest is an indispensable element of a free society; the exercise of that right is essential to the health of the body politic and its ability to adapt itself to a changing environment. In this country, we have endowed the right of protest with constitutional status. The very first Amendment to the Constitution protects freedom of speech and press and "the right of the people peaceably to assemble and to petition the government for a redress of grievances." The Amendment protects much more than the individual right of dissent; it guarantees the right of groups to assemble and petition, or, in the modern phrase, to demonstrate.

Group violence, on the other hand, is dangerous to a free society. All too frequently, it is an effort not to persuade, but to compel. It has no protected legal status; indeed, one purpose of law is to prevent and control it. Nor is group violence a necessary consequence of group protest. The violence of the Ku Klux Klan—the lynching of Negroes at the rate of almost 100 per year from 1890 to 1910—had little to do with protest; if anything, it was more a cause of protest than a response. The same may be said of the harsh treatment of Orientals on the Pacific frontier and the common use of violence to settle property and political disputes among competing groups in the early days of the American West.

It is true, of course, that group protest sometimes results in group violence. Violence may be committed by groups opposed to the aims of the protesters (as in the Southern murders of civil rights workers by groups of white militants); excessive force may be used by the public authorities, as in Selma in 1965; violence may be committed by some within the protesting group itself (as in the case of the Weatherman faction of the SDS). But the widely held belief that protesting groups usually behave violently is not supported by fact. Of the multitude of occasions when protesting groups exercise their rights of assembly and petition, only a small number result in violence.

Thus, our Task Force Report on Historical and Comparative Perspectives reports that over the five year period from mid-1963 to mid-1968, protests or counter-protests and ghetto riots involved more than two million persons. Civil rights demonstrations mobilized 1.1 million, anti-war demonstrations 680,000, and ghetto riots an estimated 200,000. Nine thousand casualties resulted, including some 200 deaths.[27] Ghetto riots were responsible for most of these casualties, including 191 deaths. Almost all other deaths, an estimated 23, resulted from white terrorism against blacks and civil rights workers. These casualty figures are for a five-year period, and apart from the ghetto riots, they are comparatively infinitesimal. While they are not to be condoned, in a country with 250,000 aggravated assaults and 12,000 homicides per year, group protest cannot be considered as accounting for a major part of the deliberate violence we experience.[28]

Do we have a greater amount of group violence today than in earlier periods of our history? While a precise quantitative answer cannot be provided, we may conclude with confidence that, while group violence in the 1960's was at a higher level than in the decades immediately preceding, several earlier decades of American history were marked by higher levels of group violence—in terms of casualties per 100,000 population—than has been true of the decade now ending.

Ever since the Boston Tea Party, occasional group violence has been a recurring—though not a continuous—feature of American political and social history.

From 1740 to 1790, Appalachian farmers, protesting against debt and tax collectors from the seaboard centers of political and economic power, engaged in a series of violent disorders, of which the Whiskey Rebellion in Pennsylvania is best known.

Southern landowners and northern Abolitionists engaged in a variety of skirmishes, from "bleeding Kansas" to John Brown's raid on Harper's Ferry, that were the violent prelude to the Civil War.

During Reconstruction, The Ku Klux Klan and other elements of the defeated white majority in the South conducted a campaign of terrorism against the freed blacks, government officials and Southerners who cooperated with them.

So-called "Native Americans" of the original colonial stocks resorted to group violence when they perceived their status as threatened by European Catholic and Jewish immigrants in the East and Orientals in the West; the immigrant groups occasionally engaged in violence such as the New York Draft Riots in 1863.

As the freed Negro migrants from the South began settling in border and Northern cities after the Civil War, white residents (including the most recent of the European immigrants) launched occasional attacks on black sections of the city.

The growth of organized labor in the half century from 1880 to 1930 was marked by unusually severe episodes of violence in which employers, workers and public authorities were all occasional aggressors. In the three year period 1902-1904, about 200 persons were killed and 2,000 injured in the violence accompanying various strikes and lockouts.

During each of these episodes, most of the community continued to live in peace. The violent episodes themselves were sporadic. At any given time they probably involved minor percentages of the total population—certainly not more than a small fraction of the number who were then engaging in various sorts of group protest.

While it is probably true that protest by one or more groups seeking to advance or defend its status in society has been a continuous feature of American life, group violence has not. Indeed, it is group protest, not group violence, that is as American as cherry pie.

Do we have more group violence than other modern nations? Comparisons with other countries are difficult. Our Task Force Report shows a group violence casualty rate in seventeen other industrially advanced nations for the first half of this decade that is only one-fourth the United States rate.[29] (The average for all nations, however, was forty times the United States rate.) Yet few advanced democratic nations are free from group violence, as the riots in France, Germany, Italy, Canada and Japan during the past two years and the continuing strife in Northern Ireland remind us. Unlike many other countries, (including some advanced ones) strife in the United States is usually aimed at particular policies, conditions or groups rather than at overthrow of the government; indeed, the United States has been free of anything resembling insurrection for more than a century. Except for Great Britain, this country has the longest record of government continuity in the world.

Why does group violence occur in an advanced democratic society? We may accept that men naturally possess aggressive tendencies without concluding that group violence is inevitable. Nature provides us with the capacity for violence; material, social and political circumstances are the determinants of whether and how we exercise that capacity. Men's frustration over some of these circumstances is a necessary precondition of group protest. Whether that frustration will erupt into violence depends largely on the degree and consistency of social control and the extent to which social and political institutions afford peaceful alternatives for the redress of group grievances.

All societies generate some discontent because organized life by its very nature inhibits most human beings. Group violence occurs when expectations about rights and status are continually frustrated and when peaceful efforts to press these claims yield inadequate results. It also occurs when the claims of groups who feel disadvantaged are viewed as threats by other groups occupying a higher status in society. Greater expectations and frustrations for disadvantaged groups, and greater fears of threatened groups, are more likely to occur in times of rapid social change than in times of social stability.

America has always been a nation of rapid social change. We have proclaimed ourselves a modern promised land, and have brought millions of restless immigrants to our shores to partake in its fulfillment. Persistent demands by these groups—by the western farmers of the revolutionary period, later by the Irish, the Italians and the Slavs, and more recently by Puerto Rican, Mexican, and Negro Americans—and resistance to these demands by other groups, have accounted for most of the offensive and defensive group violence that marks our history.

This analysis, however, does not adequately explain why some upper class and middle class students engage in group violence. Some affluent students doubtless perceive themselves as disadvantaged—by the draft and forced service in the Vietnam war, by their small voice in college governance, by their lack of identity and purpose in what they perceive as a complex, computerized and highly materialistic urban society. But for many students, the causes that attract them most are not their own grievances but those of the other groups and problems of the society as a whole. To a high degree, they are motivated by a sense of guilt for being privileged and by the desire of many young people to share with others in the experience of serving a noble cause. For most of those so motivated, participation in peaceful protest fulfills this need. Those few who are particularly impatient or cynical about the "system" or are committed to revolution resort to violence.

As we have noted, discontent is only one prerequisite of group violence. Whether violence actually occurs also depends on popular attitudes and how effectively political institutions respond to the threat of violence and to demands for the redress of group grievances. Although we have an open political and social system, more dedicated than most to the dream of individual and group advancement, the majority are sometimes unwilling either to hear or to redress the just grievances of particular minorities until violent advocacy or repression calls them to the forefront of our attention.

And for all our rhetoric to the contrary, we have never been a fully law-abiding nation. For example, some measure of public sympathy has often been with the night-riders who punished the transgressor of community mores and with the disadvantaged who sought to remedy obvious injustices by violent means. Lack of full respect for law and at least tacit support for violence in one's own interest have helped to make the United States, in the past as at present, somewhat more tumultuous than we would like it to be.

II. The Rationale of Group Violence

Those who engage in group violence as a political tactic advance several reasons to support it. Some of the current justifications, have been summarized by our Task Force on Violent Aspects of Protest and Confrontation.[30] They are stated as the militants themselves might make them.

1. Militants argue that the creation of turmoil and disorder can stimulate otherwise quiescent groups to take more forceful action in their own ways. Liberals may come to support radical demands while opposing their tactics; extreme tactics may shock moderates into self re-examination.

2. Militants point out that direct action is not intended to win particular reforms or to influence decision makers, but rather to bring out a repressive response from authorities—a response rarely seen by most white Americans. When confrontation brings violent official response, uncommitted elements of the public can see for themselves the true nature of the "system." Confrontation, therefore, is a means of political education.

3. Militants believe that if the movement really seriously threatens the power of political authorities, efforts to repress the movement through police-state measures are inevitable. The development of resistant attitudes and action toward the police at the present time is a necessary preparation for more serious resistance in the future.

4. Militants state that educated, middle-class, non-violent styles of protest are poorly understood by working-class youth, black youth, and other "drop-outs." Contact with these other sectors of the youth population is essential and depends upon the adoption of a tough and aggressive stance to win respect from such youth.

5. Militants recognize that most middle-class students are shocked by aggressive or violent behavior. In the militant view, this cultural fear of violence is psychologically damaging and may be politically inhibiting. To be a serious revolutionary, they say, one must reject middle-class values, particularly deference toward authority. Militant confrontation gives resisters the experience of physically opposing institutional power, and it may force students to choose between

"respectable" intellectual radicalism and serious commitment to revolution, violent or otherwise.

6. Militants respond to those who point to the possibility of repression as a reaction to confrontation tactics by accusing them of wishing to compromise demands and principles and dilute radicalism. Militants believe that repression will come in any case, and to diminish one's efforts in anticipation is to give up the game before it starts.

Somewhat different arguments are advanced by those among threatened groups to justify defensive private violence and the use of excessive force by public authorities. They believe that the disadvantaged group will cease to exert pressure only if protesters are firmly and decisively repressed and that strong evidence of superior force and willingness to use it will succeed in defending the status quo.

These arguments for group violence—offensive or defensive[31]—are not sustained by history, contemporary reality, logic or law. They are inconsistent with the basic principles of democratic government.

We put to one side the efficacy of violence in overturning a government or maintaining it in power, for this has not been the main thrust of American group violence. The thornier question—one that is more pertinent to American practitioners of group violence who usually aim not at seizing or defending the government but at altering or continuing its policies—is whether group violence is an effective, albeit illegal, tactic for winning or preventing a significant change of status.

History provides no ready answer to this question. There have been a great many protest movements marked by violence which eventually achieved some of their aims. But whether offensive violence by the protesting group helped or hindered the subsequent achievement remains a matter of conjecture, as does the question of whether defensive violence by the threatened group hindered or helped the eventual change. In the history of the American labor movement, for example, violence persistently accompanied the struggle of workingmen to gain decent working conditions and recognition for their unions; both ends were eventually achieved, but there are differences of opinion whether pro-labor violence helped the cause or whether anti-labor violence hindered it.[32] Labor leaders themselves doubted the effectiveness of violence, and no major labor organization in American history advocated violence as a policy. Typically, pro-labor violence was a response to the use of excessive force by militia or private police or strikebreakers. While violence proved to be a better short-run weapon for employers than for workers, the escalation of counter-violence it produced was a factor in the passage of the laws that eventually established the rights of labor.

It is no doubt true that in the 1960s policy changes advantageous to dissident groups have sometimes followed in the wake of urban riots and campus disturbances. These gains, however, may have been attributable more to the validity of the protest goals than to the violent outbreaks when they came. Moreover, to the extent violence may have contributed to these gains, the use of excessive force against peaceful demonstrators—as in Birmingham—may have been more decisive than any violence by the demonstrators themselves. No one will ever know whether as much or more might have been won without resort to violence by either side. The advocacy and practice of deliberate violence by some radical black militants and some student and anti-war activists have certainly created antagonism and resulted in the loss of sympathy for these causes among large sectors of the public. Leaders of many protesting groups recognize the counterproductivity of violence; before the November Peace Mobilization in Washington, many of the protest leaders sought diligently to discourage violence by such groups as the Weatherman faction and the Youth International Party. When these factions did resort to violence, leaders of the Mobilization expressly disavowed and condemned them.

If the lessons of history are ambiguous on the short-term effectiveness of violence as a political tactic, they are clear on its long-term dangers. . . . Violence tends to feed on itself, with one power group imposing its will on another until repressive elements succeed in reestablishing order. The violent cycles of the French and Russian Revolutions and the decade resulting in the Third Reich are dark abysses of history to ponder. Violence tends to become a style, with many eager followers. German students setting fire to cars in West Berlin chanted in English: "Burn, baby, burn." When students last year violently took control of the telephone system at Brandeis University, within ten days British, French, German and Italian students attempted to do the same thing. Violently disruptive tactics that began inappropriately in universities have been copied even more inappropriately in high schools and churches.

As our Task Force on Law and Law Enforcement has found, the danger of this contagion is that extreme, unlawful tactics will replace normal legal processes as the usual way of pressing demands. Given present trends, it is not impossible to imagine an America in which the accepted method for getting a traffic light installed will be to disrupt traffic by blocking the intersection, where complaints against businessmen will call for massive sit-ins, where unsatisfactory refuse collection will cause protesting citizens to dump garbage in the street. We do not believe that a healthy society can result from the widespread use of such techniques.

As our Task Force concluded, group violence as a tactic to advance or restrain protest by discontented groups does not contribute to the emergence of a more liberal and humane society but produces an opposite tendency. The fears and resentments created by these tactics have strengthened the political power of some of the most destructive elements in American society.

As one of this nation's most thoughtful leaders has observed:

> No society can live in constant and destructive tumult. . . . The anarchist plays into the hands of the authoritarian. Those of us who find authoritarianism repugnant have a duty to speak out against all who destroy civil order. The time has come when the full weight of community opinion should be felt by those who break the peace or coerce through mob action.[33]

III. Elements of Prevention and Control

What steps should a representative constitutional society take to prevent and control group violence? Our political institutions should be so framed and managed as to make violence as a political tactic both unnecessary and unrewarding. To make violence an unnecessary tactic, our institutions must be capable of providing political and social justice for all who live under them and of correcting injustice against any group by peaceful and lawful means. To make violence an unrewarding tactic, our political and social institutions must be able to cope with violence when it occurs and do so firmly, fairly, and within the law.

Our Constitution was written after the violent overthrow of a colonial government which followed one of these imperatives, but ignored the other. Its Preamble does not speak merely of justice, or merely of order; it embraces both. Two of the six purposes set forth in the Preamble are to "establish justice" and to "insure domestic tranquility." The First Amendment sets forth a third and closely related goal—to protect the rights of free speech and peaceable assembly and the right to petition the government for redress of grievances. If we are to succeed in controlling group violence, we must navigate by all three of these stars.

History is full of violent disasters that occurred because channels for peaceful presentation of grievances were blocked and because governments did not or could not act to correct the underlying injustices or to control disorder; history also contains examples of disasters that were averted by governments, which kept the channels of protest open and applied a judicious combination of reform and control.

The French and Russian Revolutions reached extraordinary peaks of violence because absolutist governments concentrated on efforts to restore order and refused to redress grievances or transfer a sufficient share of power to the emerging lower classes. The British, on the other hand, averted a similar disaster by judicious measures of control and by more flexible development of their political institutions to accommodate the rights and needs of all their people.[34] In Germany, after World War I, the Weimar Republic was too weak either to control street fighting between right wing and left wing students and workers or to remedy their grievances; the emergence of Hitler to "restore order" proved to be a disaster for the entire world.

In our own country, we have on some occasions failed to take the necessary measures of reform and control; on other occasions we have succeeded. We proved unable to abolish the injustice of Negro slavery without a bloody war—a conflict which released currents of violence that continue to flow a century later. The Reconstruction governments in the southern states were too weak to enforce the newly won rights of black people against a hostile community or to prevent the Ku Klux Klan from reestablishing white supremacy by violence. The struggle of the labor unions was marked by extensive restrictions on peaceful protest and by repressive violence in the absence of laws to provide minimum standards of justice for working people and legal machinery for the resolution of disputes; the violence largely subsided after such laws were enacted. And in the wake of the Depression, after relatively few violent incidents such as the Bonus March and the farmers' defense of their lands against foreclosure, we averted further violence by fashioning major alterations in the rights of individuals to government assistance and in the responsibilities of government for directing the course of our private enterprise economy.

When group violence occurs, it must be put down by lawful means, including the use of whatever force may be required. But when it occurs—better still, before it occurs—we must permit aggrieved groups to exercise their rights of protest and public presentation of grievances; we must have the perception to recognize injustices when they are called to our attention, and we must have the institutional flexibility to correct those injustices promptly.

We do not mean, of course, that the mere making of a demand entitles it to be granted, or that the particular remedy proposed by those aggrieved should be adopted. Some "non-negotiable" demands by students, by radical black militants, by anti-war demonstrators and others are unrealistic and unfair to the rights of others; some proposed remedies are self-defeating or administratively unworkable. What is essential is that when the basic justice of the underlying grievance is clear, an effort to take suitable measures of accommodation and correction must be made. The effort must be made even though other groups feel threatened by the proposed correction, and even though they may resort to violence to prevent it. We cannot "insure domestic tranquility" unless we "establish justice"—in a democratic society one is impossible without the other.

We therefore put forth our suggestions as to how these three goals—controlling disorder, keeping open the channels of protest, and correcting social injustices—can be more successfully pursued.

IV. Strategies of Control

Many feel that rioters should be dealt with harshly. At least two-thirds of white Americans, according to one poll, believe that looters and fire-bombers should simply be shot down in the streets.[35] Many believe that even peaceful demonstrators are "agitators" or "anarchists." In a poll conducted for this Commission, 56 percent agreed that "any man who insults a policeman has no complaint if he gets roughed up in return."

As recent history illustrates, the prompt, prudent deployment of well-trained law enforcement personnel can extinguish a civil disorder in its incipiency. But history also demonstrates that excessive use of force is an unwise tactic for handling disorder. To the generalization made earlier, that violence is an always dangerous and sometimes ineffective tactic for dissident groups pressing their demands or for threatened groups resisting those demands, may be added this corollary: the use of excessive and illegal force is an always dangerous and usually ineffective tactic for authorities seeking to quell unrest. Both in the short and in the long run, the use of excessive force to repress group violence often has the effect of magnifying turmoil, not diminishing it.

It is useful to contrast the official response to the anti-war protest in Chicago during the Democratic National Convention of 1968 and the "counter-inaugural" in Washington on January 20, 1969. These two events were organized by many of the same protesting groups and attended by many of the same individuals, in roughly equal numbers. Yet the results of these events were markedly different. In Chicago, the authorities were restrictive in granting demonstration permits; some of the police, deliberately goaded by verbal and physical attacks of small militant groups, responded with excessive force not only against the provocateurs but also against peaceful demonstrators and passive bystanders. Their conduct, while it won the support of the majority, polarized substantial and previously neutral segments of the population against the authorities and in favor of the demonstrators.[36]

In Washington, demonstration permits were liberally issued. Although there was also provocative violence by some of the demonstrators, the police used only that force clearly necessary to maintain order. As a result, there was little criticism of police behavior. Our analysis leads to the conclusion that the amount of violence that occurred during these demonstrations and the resulting effects on public opinion were directly related to the kind of official response that greeted them.[37]

In both instances a small number—no more than a few hundred in either case—intended to provoke a "confrontation" with authorities by provocative acts, aimed especially at policemen. A majority of the participants intended to demonstrate peacefully and, in fact, did so.

In response to reports that violence and disruptive conduct would occur, Chicago authorities adopted tight, well-publicized security measures designed to dissuade protesters from coming to the city. To discourage the protesters further, they prolonged the negotiations for demonstration permits and exercised their discretionary powers restrictively. The limited, begrudging dialogue with protesting groups reduced the opportunity of the authorities to assess and separate the component groups in the demonstration (many of which intended to demonstrate peacefully) and to learn the details of their plans. This resistant posture served to discourage more mature and responsible protesters from coming while firing the determination of young militants to attend and confront. To some of the police and some Chicago citizens, the official posture of resistance signified that the protest activities as such were dangerous or illegitimate; they tended to view protesters as troublemakers and law-breakers, thus failing to discriminate between the small number of radicals seeking trouble and the great majority of peaceful citizens exercising their constitutional rights.

In preparation for the Inaugural in Washington five months later, intelligence reports were carefully evaluated. Genuine threats were sorted from theatric exaggerations. Troublemakers were identified and watched closely, but no attempt was made to interfere with the activities of the majority of peaceful demonstrators. Authorities negotiated conscientiously with protest leaders and arrived at agreements on the scope of permits for parades and meetings that were acceptable to all parties. The protest leaders, impressed with the reasonableness of the government spokesmen, made substantial efforts to cooperate with officials and ensure peace.

As the Chicago and Washington events differed in preparation, they differed in outcome. After minor skirmishes, trouble in Chicago escalated when throngs of demonstrators, having been denied permits to remain overnight, refused to leave Lincoln Park, their main gathering place. Dozens of police attempted to clear the park on three successive nights. In response to serious and deliberate provocations, but without coherent planning, some policemen clubbed and teargassed guilty and innocent alike, chasing demonstrators through streets some distance from the park. Particularly on the side streets, some bystanders who had taken no part in the demonstrations were attacked by police officers. Several media representatives were clubbed and had their cameras smashed. Predictably, tensions and anger rose. Extremists who would otherwise have been ignored began to attract audiences. They urged demonstrators to fight back. The police were exposed to more and more jeers and obscenities and had to withstand heavier barrages of rocks and other missiles. During one of the first nights, fifteen policemen were injured; two nights later, 149 were injured.

In Washington, the cycle of escalating violence never got started. Both verbal and physical provocations by demonstrators were frequently intense, but they were met with restraint. Provocation by policemen was rare; when it occurred it was terminated by police and city officials who intervened quickly to restore discipline. In general, police withstood physical and verbal abuse with great calm. In the end, the behavior of Washington officials and the police won praise in newspaper editorials and from leaders of the demonstrations.

There were some radical leaders, however, who were more grateful for the official response in Chicago, for it appeared to validate their characterizations of government as being "reactionary" and "repressive" and to increase support from other protesting groups. The chaos at Chicago also gave solidarity to the ranks of those who regard all demonstrators, however peaceful, as irresponsible "punks." The overall effect was to increase polarization and unrest, not diminish them.

This comparison between Chicago in August of 1968 and Washington last January can be closed on two encouraging notes. Permits for peace marches in Chicago were sought and granted in October 1969. The marches were organized by the "Weatherman," an extremely militant faction of the Students for a Democratic Society. In the course of the demonstrations, Chicago police had to face four days of intense provocation and wanton violence. This time, however, the police acted with calm and restraint. No injuries to residents, bystanders or newsmen were reported; on the contrary, the police took steps to safeguard bystanders from the violence. As a result of the professional conduct of Chicago police, violence was effectively contained, and blame for the damage and injuries that did occur fell squarely upon the violent group among the demonstrators, many of whom were arrested.

The Peace Moratorium Parade and assembly in Washington on November 15 was another example of intelligent and restrained official response. Although the government had reason to expect that some elements among the protesting groups were bent on violence, reasonable permits were ultimately negotiated with the responsible demonstration leaders, and ample police and military force were provided to preserve order if necessary. In the largest single protest demonstration in American history, the overwhelming majority of the participants behaved peacefully. Their activities were facilitated rather than restrained by the police. When the few extremists did attempt violent attacks on two occasions, the police responded quickly and firmly but, on the whole, without excessive force.[38] As a result, order was maintained, the right to protest was upheld, and it was possible to judge both the peaceful and the violent aspects of the protest in their true proportion.

Civil governments must, of course, act promptly and decisively against threats to public order. As the National Advisory Commission on Civil Disorders stated: "Individuals cannot be permitted to endanger the public peace and safety, and public officials have a duty to make it clear that all just and necessary means to protect both will be used."[39]

A parallel duty exists for colleges and universities: they must have firm, well-publicized plans for dealing swiftly and decisively with campus disorders. The practice of keeping rules fuzzy so that dissident groups are "kept off balance" has failed demonstrably. . . . We recommend that students, faculty and administrators develop acceptable standards of conduct and responses appropriate to deviations from those standards, including the circumstances under which they will resort to (i) campus disciplinary procedures, (ii) campus police, (iii) court injunctions, (iv) other court sanctions, and (v) the city police. We believe genuine progress is presently being made in this direction.

Police manuals recognize that when the police are needed—as in urban riots, demonstrations that threaten violence, and campus disorders in which court injunctions must be enforced—their behavior must be calm and impartial, however intense the provocation. Panic, overt expressions of anger, and inflammatory use of force are serious breaches of police discipline. The FBI riot control manual states that:

> The basic rule, when applying force, is to use only the minimum force necessary to effectively control the situation. Unwarranted application of force will incite the mob to further violence, as well as kindle seeds of resentment for police that, in turn, could cause a riot to recur.[40]

The National Advisory Commission on Civil Disorders has provided excellent, detailed prescriptions for improving police practices, especially in handling urban riots.[41] Despite notable progress since the Commission issued its report in March 1968, many police departments in American cities are still ill-prepared to handle riots and other civil disorders.

In a survey of sixteen major cities, this Commission's Task Force on Law and Law Enforcement found that few city governments had established formal, dependable communication links with dissident groups. Few had adequate plans for dealing with disorders, and effective planning staffs were rare. Though all have added riot control to the curriculum of police training, the number of hours devoted to training per man has not increased significantly.

We therefore urge police departments throughout the nation to improve their preparations for anticipating, preventing and controlling group disorders, and to that end to study the approaches that have been employed successfully on the three most recent occasions in Washington and Chicago.[42]

V. Keeping Open the Channels of Peaceful Protest

We have pointed out the fundamental distinction between protest and violence, the fact that there is no necessary connection between them, and the need to vindicate the former while opposing the latter. As we have quoted, the First Amendment to the Constitution protects freedom of speech, freedom of the press, and the "right of the people peaceably to assemble and to petition the government for a redress of grievances." In the Supreme Court's words, the First Amendment entails a "profound national commitment to the principle that debate on public issues should be uninhibited, robust and wide open."[43]

Obstructions to peaceful speech and assembly—whether by public officials, policemen, or unruly mobs—abridge the fundamental right to free expression. On the other hand, speech, assembly and other forms of conduct that become coercive or intimidating invade the fundamental First Amendment rights of other citizens. When a mob forces a university to suspend classes, the rights of teachers to teach and students to learn are abridged; when a speaker is shouted down or forced from a platform, he is deprived of freedom to speak, and the great majority of the audience is deprived of freedom to listen.

Society's failure to afford full protection to the exercise of these rights is probably a major reason why protest sometimes results in violence. Although these rights are expressly safeguarded by the federal Constitution, the existing remedies available to aggrieved persons are not adequate. The only approximation to an effective remedy at the federal level is a court injunction authorized under 42 U.S.C. sec. 1983, a Reconstruction era civil rights statute that creates a private cause of action for the "deprivation of any rights, privileges, or immunities secured by the Constitution" by any person acting "under color of" state law. The relative ineffectiveness of this private remedy is indicated by the rarity with which injunctions have been sought in the thirty years since the statute was first interpreted to apply to interference with First Amendment rights. Moreover, state officials acting under color of state law are not alone in posing threats to First Amendment rights; on college campuses, for example, the protesters themselves have obstructed free speech and peaceful assembly. No present federal law affords a remedy for private abridgement of First Amendment rights.[44]

> *Accordingly, we recommend that the President seek legislation that would confer jurisdiction upon the United States District Courts to grant injunctions, upon the request of the Attorney General or private persons, against the threatened or actual interference by any person, whether or not under color of state or federal law, with the rights of individuals or groups to freedom of speech, freedom of the press, peaceful assembly and petition for redress of grievances.*

Under present law private citizens can seek federal injunctions in instances where the complainant alleges unreasonable denial of permits for parades or meetings by state or federal officials or their issuance only on excessively restrictive conditions. Private persons can also obtain federal injunctive relief on proof of suppression by government agencies or their employees of publications or communications (including the seizure or destruction of newsmen's cameras or film) or the use by law enforcement officials of excessive or unauthorized force to arrest or disperse individuals who seek to make lawful expressions of their views. Our proposal would authorize the Attorney General, as well as private persons, to initiate such proceedings in appropriate cases involving state or federal action. It would also authorize suits for injunctions, both by the Attorney General and by private persons, against private obstruction of the exercise of free expression by pushing speakers off platforms, by the making of deliberately excessive noise, or by seizure of or denial of access to buildings or other facilities, streets and public areas—a type of interference with First Amendment rights not now covered by any federal statute.

The statute should also authorize suits for either damages or an injunction by the persons aggrieved and allow the Attorney General to intervene in such suits on request of the parties or the court or on his own motion. State and federal courts should be given concurrent jurisdiction to enforce the statute.

Our proposal suggests a greater federal role in preserving freedom of expression. We do so because federal district courts, which often deal with somewhat comparable provisions in other areas of federal law, are experienced in handling requests for injunctions expeditiously and fashioning careful and effective decrees. The use of federal court injunctions would also provide for greater uniformity in the judicial treatment of those infringing the constitutional rights of others. It would increase the likelihood that the experience of one community or institution would be readily available and useful in handling subsequent problems elsewhere.

State remedies against private misconduct involving infringement of First Amendment rights are usually based not on the First Amendment but on trespass statutes or disorderly conduct ordinances. Such laws were not written to deal with acts of physical obstruction, particularly those committed for demonstrative purposes, and are not always effective in handling such conduct. Moreover, where acts of violence or obstruction are committed in the name of righting fundamental grievances, those engaging in such conduct may find it harder to justify disobedience of court orders issued to uphold the First Amendment than would be true of orders based upon the laws against trespass and disorderly conduct.

In recent legislation, Congress has given the Attorney General an increasingly active role in protecting certain vital individual rights. This approach seems particularly appropriate for the protection of First Amendment rights, since the mechanism of peaceful dispute, debate, compromise, and change is so essential to the preservation of a just and orderly society and since private persons are often unable to protect their First Amendment rights without some assistance.

For speech, petition and assembly to be effective, they must be heard and seen. In 1789 this was a regular consequence of exercising one's First Amendment rights. In today's crowded and complex society, however, being seen and heard depends almost entirely upon the printed and electronic news media, which are necessarily selective in picking out the relatively few items in a day's or a week's events that can be fitted into the space or time available for reporting "news." The *New York Times* daily receives 1.25 to 1.5 million words of news material from its correspondents and news services; of that amount, only about one-tenth is printed.

Moreover, the number of separate, independent news "voices" has not kept up with the growing size and diversity of the nation. Economic factors have forced down the number of regularly published daily newspapers and weekly magazines despite substantial population increases. The number of radio and television stations in any area is greater but still relatively small; more importantly, there is little difference among them in their reporting of the "news." Protesting groups can and do print their own newspapers and handbills, but their circulation is rarely extensive. All in all, the number of efforts to gain attention through the exercise of free speech and assembly far exceeds the number that impact upon the public consciousness as news. For example the *New York Times* received over 37,000 letters to the editor last year; only six percent were published, though at least 85 percent were, in the words of the *Times* motto, considered "fit to print." Had they all been printed, they would have completely filled 135 daily issues of the newspaper.

The difficulties presented by today's society for those who want their protests and demonstrations to be seen and heard leave most people unaware of how deeply felt many grievances have become. A decade ago it would have been fair to say—as many thoughtful journalists have since admitted—that the press did too little reporting of the existence of social injustice and of the grievances of protesting groups. It was generally thought that open conflict—especially violent conflict—was the most important kind of news. Too few news reports went beyond a description of "who-what-when-where" into the "why" of social and political analysis. The national press, for example, has acknowledged its past shortcomings in covering the life and the problems of our black, Indian and Latin American minorities and their efforts to redress their grievances.

Today, in-depth analysis of underlying social conditions is now a regular and welcome part of the best of our print and broadcast media. Many responsible journalists now recognize more fully the challenge of their crucial role in creating the public understanding of complex modern problems that is a necessary precondition for informed democratic decisions on the timing and content of peaceful social and institutional change. Indeed, some critics—wrongly in our opinion—complain that the media now go too far in reporting protests and in commentary on their causes.

Like the Kerner Commission before us, this Commission has struggled with the question of what public or private measures a governmental body might recommend to improve the efforts of the press to report on the problems facing individuals and groups in American society and alternative means proposed for solving them, as well as on protest and its underlying causes. We have concluded the indispensable element of a free press is pluralism and diversity: we need more effective and different voices, not fewer and fewer standardized or homogenized ones.

Accordingly, we recommend that private and govern-
mental institutions encourage the development of competing
news media and discourage increased concentration of con-
trol over existing media.

Apart from such strictly limited measures of government intervention as the "fairness doctrine" for broadcasters who operate under
public license—which deals not with the substance of broadcast
speech but only with the broadcaster's duty to present all sides—we
oppose official attempts to control how the media present and inter-
pret the news. Governmental interference with the free press is no
way to cure its defects. The need is rather for constant self-appraisal
and for responsible, effective criticism of the media by private entities
such as university schools of journalism and by any group or individual, public or private, aggrieved by any aspect of media performance.

We urge that the members of the journalism profession
continue to improve and re-evaluate their standards and
practices, and to strengthen their capacity for creative self-
criticism, along the lines suggested in the staff report of our
Media Task Force.[45]

An observer of the current journalistic scene has recently observed:

It ought to be plain, but seemingly it is not, that the
quality of journalism depends primarily on journalists—not
on government and not on the legal owners of media. . . .
Journalism will always need artistry to reach the public's
mind and heart. Indeed, what is now required is a higher
level of art, a boldness that will get journalism unstuck from
forms of communication developed in and for a social context very different from the present. Nobody except journalists can develop such forms.[46]

VI. *Establishing Justice*

The third element in any program for reducing group violence is to
see to it that our political and social institutions "establish justice"
and that valid grievances of disadvantaged groups of citizens are
redressed in a timely manner.

Man's progress has reached a stage in which several forces combine to create critical stresses in our social and political structure. First, technological advances and population growth have wrought profound and complex changes in our physical environment and our ability to control it so as to meet basic human needs. Second, an extended period of considerable progress in raising standards of living and education for all and in providing greater social justice for disadvantaged groups—however unevenly—has created rising expectations of still further progress and demands that it be brought about. Third, our political and social institutions and the programs they manage are not changing rapidly enough to keep up with the speed of change in the environment they are intended to control. Although we now have the technological and economic capability of releasing all our citizens from poverty and social deprivation, we have not been willing or able to fashion the changes in our political institutions and public programs that will bring to the disadvantaged the liberation that is almost within their grasp. This combination of forces creates demands for change that are not being met, and leads to protests that sometimes result in group violence.

To appreciate the magnitude of these forces and the stresses that result, we need look back no further than the beginning of this century. In 1900, within the memory of men still alive, we were a nation of 75 million people, of whom less than forty percent lived in metropolitan areas. We rode in carriages or trains. We communicated by mail and the printed word.

Today, within the same land space, we have almost tripled our number. Two-thirds of us live in urban concentrations. We motor at high speeds over a nation paved with freeways. We fly across and between the continents. We communicate by telephone, radio and television. Our resources and the demands we place upon them have increased enormously; so has our individual specialization of function and our dependence on one another for shelter and food, for personal safety, and even for the purity of the air we breathe.

But our political and social institutions and programs have not kept pace. We have achieved the phenomenal forward leap to the moon, but we have not managed the flow of traffic in New York. Most of us now live in metropolitan areas, but . . . we have made few, if any, advances in the art of governing the urban environment. We desire peace, but we are now engaged in the fourth war of this century. Science has shown us how to provide so much food that surpluses embarrass us economically, yet millions are hungry. We boast of our dedication to the concept that all men are created equal, yet inequality of opportunity remains our most persistent problem.

Despite our special penchant for economic and technological innovation, we tend like other peoples to resist political and social change. Thomas Jefferson noted this phenomenon and its relationship to violence. After a lifetime of public service, he observed:

> I am certainly not an advocate for frequent and untried changes in laws and constitutions. . . . But I know also, that laws and institutions must go hand in hand with progress of the human mind. As that becomes more developed, more enlightened, as new discoveries are made, new truths disclosed, and manners and opinions change with the change of circumstances, institutions must advance also and keep pace with the times. We might as well require a man to wear still the coat which fitted him when a boy, as civilized society to remain ever under the regimen of their barbarous ancestors. It is this preposterous idea which has lately deluged Europe in blood. Their monarchs, instead of wisely yielding to the gradual change of circumstances, of favoring progressive accommodation to progressive improvement, have clung to old abuses, entrenched themselves behind steady habits, and obliged their subjects to seek through blood and violence rash and ruinous innovations, which, had they been referred to the peaceful deliberations and collected wisdom of the nation, would have been put into acceptable and salutary forms.[47]

We strongly urge all Americans to reflect upon Jefferson's observations, and their special relevance to the causes and prevention of group violence. Today, the pace of change has become far more rapid than when Jefferson wrote, and the need for adapting our institutions to the changing environment has become greater still. Today, more than ever before, we need to strengthen and utilize our institutions for peaceful redress of grievances and peaceful accommodation to the quickening pace of social change.[48]

NOTES

1. We define group violence as the unlawful threat or use of force by any group that results or is intended to result in the injury or

forcible restraint or intimidation of persons, or the destruction or forcible seizure of property.

2. For fiscal 1970, the budgeted figure is $77 billion.

3. Some experts believe that since military expenditures were successfully held to an annual level of 60 billion dollars (in 1968 prices) for the decade from 1955 to 1964, a comparable plateau can and should be maintained for the decade of the seventies. Indeed, it has been urged that, assuming the success of strategic arms limitation talks and a revaluation of our foreign commitments, it would be feasible to hold the military budget for the early 1970s to 50 billion dollars (at 1969 prices). See Kaysen, "Military Strategy, Military Forces and Arms Control," in *Agenda for the Nation* (Washington, D.C.: Brookings Institution, 1969), p. 549.

4. Annual Report of the Council of Economic Advisers, January, 1969, pp. 199-200.

5. At estimated 1972 prices, for example, actual outlays would be 73 billion. At this point, defense expenditures would be at seven percent of forecast GNP, as compared to perhaps eight percent at present. In other industrially advanced democratic countries, according to the Institute for Strategic Studies, defense expenditures (in 1966) were 6.4 percent of GNP for the United Kingdom, 4.4 percent in France, 3.6 percent in West Germany, 3.3 percent in Italy, 2.2 percent in Canada and 1.1 percent in Japan. For Soviet Russia, the estimated figure is 8.9 percent, but this represents a total 1966 defense outlay of less than 30 billion dollars as compared to about 68 billion dollars for the United States.

6. This estimate assumes that the present 10 percent surcharge will have been repealed, but that other tax reform measures will be neutral in their effect on aggregate revenues. Any substantial reduction in federal tax revenues incidental to tax reform will make it more difficult to reorder our priorities as we have proposed.

7. We further note that the same point can be strongly made for other non-military categories of expenditure that have been built into the federal budget, including agricultural and maritime subsidies, the postal service as presently structured, and space exploration. See Schultze, "Budget Alternatives After Vietnam" in *Agenda for the Nation* (Brookings, 1969), p. 44.

8. *Toward a Social Report*, Government Printing Office, 1969.

9. Daniel P. Moynihan, *Maximum Feasible Misunderstanding* (New York: Macmillan, 1968), pp. 190-203.

10. The FBI Index of Reported Crime classifies seven offenses as

"serious crimes"—homicide, forcible rape, robbery, aggravated assault, burglary, larceny of more than $50 and auto theft. It classifies the first four—homicide, rape, robbery and assault—as "violent crimes" because they involve the doing or threatening of bodily injury.

11. Reasons for the gap include failure of citizens to report crimes because they believe police cannot be effective in solving them; others do not want to take the time to report, some do not know how to report, and others fear reprisals.

12. The direct correlation between city size and violent crime rates may not be as uniform in the South as in other regions. Available data indicate higher suburban violent crime rates relative to city rates in the South, suggesting the possibility that smaller city rates may also be higher relative to larger city rates in the South (although direct evidence on this point is not presently available).

Also, it should be kept in mind that the relationships noted in the text are for cities within certain population ranges (e.g., more than 250,000, 100,000–250,000, etc.), not for individual cities. Thus the five cities with the highest metropolitan violent crime rates in 1968—Baltimore, Newark, Washington, San Francisco and Detroit—had smaller populations than some very large cities with somewhat lower rates of violent crime.

13. According to the FBI *Uniform Crime Reports,* about half of all arrests for serious crimes result in pleas of guilty or convictions; in only 88 percent of all arrests does the prosecutor decide he has sufficient evidence to try the case, and of those cases that are prosecuted, only 62 percent result in a plea of guilty or conviction, often for a lesser offense than the one originally charged. A wide margin of error thus exists between the making of an arrest and proof that the person arrested has committed an offense.

14. This is a study of 9945 males born in 1945 and who lived in Philadelphia at least from age 10 to 18. Of this group, 3475, or 35 percent, were taken into custody by the police for delinquent offenses other than traffic violations. Race, socio-economic status and many other variables are analyzed in this study, supported by NIMH, to be published shortly by Thorsten Sellin and Marvin E. Wolfgang under the title, *Delinquency in a Birth Cohort.*

15. Because some police commonly associate crime with Negroes more than with whites, Negroes may be disproportionately arrested on suspicion, thus producing a higher reported Negro involvement in crime than is the true situation.

16. . . . Gun attacks are fatal in one out of five cases, on the average; knife attacks are fatal in one out of twenty.

17. The FBI has reported that in 1968 588,000 violent crimes occurred. This is about 300 crimes of major violence per each 100,000 Americans. It is generally estimated that only about half of all violent crimes are reported; if this is true, the total number of violent crimes per year is in the range of 1,200,000 or 600 per 100,000 people. These are *offenses*, not *offenders*. Since violent crimes often involve several offenders committing a single crime—particularly among the large number of juvenile offenders—a fair guess might be that twice as many offenders (2,400,000) were involved. But some offenders account for more than one crime per year. If we assume the commission of two crimes per year per offender, the total number of offenders drops back to 1,200,000; if we assume the commission of four crimes per year per offender, the total number of offenders is 600,000. Thus the number of Americans who commit violent crimes each year appears to be somewhere between these figures—between one in every 150 and one in every 300 Americans. Since children under twelve and adults over 45 commit relatively few crimes, the rate for persons between 12 and 45 is even higher.

18. President's Commission on Law Enforcement and Administration of Justice, *The Challenge of Crime in a Free Society* (Washington, D.C.: Government Printing Office, 1967); *Report of the National Advisory Commission on Civil Disorders* (Washington, D.C.: Government Printing Office, 1968); National Commission on Urban Problems, *Building the American City* (Washington, D.C.: Government Printing Office, 1968).

19. *The Challenge of Crime in a Free Society, op. cit.*, p. 35.

20. Shaw and McKay, *Juvenile Delinquency and Urban Areas* (Chicago, 1969).

21. One expert testifying before this Commission reported his finding in Chicago: a person living in the inner-city faced a risk each year of 1 in 77 of being assaulted; a risk of only 1 in 2,000 in the better areas of the city, and 1 in 10,000 in the rich suburbs.

22. The subculture of violence is not the product of our cities alone: the Thugs of India, the *vendetta barbaricina* in Sardinia, the *mafiosi* in Sicily and the Ku Klux Klan, for example, have existed for many years. Nor is violence absent from the established middle-class culture of the majority in our society. It is simply the greater frequency and approval of illegitimate violence that distinguishes the subculture of violence from the dominant cultural pattern.

23. We are here drawing upon Marvin E. Wolfgang and Franco Ferracuti, *The Subculture of Violence* (New York: Barnes and Noble; London: Tavistock Publications, 1967).

24. Computations set forth in *Crimes of Violence*, the Report of our staff Task Force on Individual Acts of Violence, suggest that 18% of the increase in the volume of violent crime between 1950 and 1965 is attributable solely to urbanization, and 12% to age redistribution alone.

25. See James C. Davies, "The J—Curve of Rising and Declining Satisfactions as a Cause of Some Great Revolutions and a Contained Rebellion," in *Violence in America*, the Report of the Task Force on Historical and Comparative Perspectives (Washington, D.C.: Government Printing Office, 1969).

26. For present purposes we define group violence as the unlawful threat or use of force by any group that results or is intended to result in the injury or forcible restraint or intimidation of persons, or the destruction or forcible seizure of property.

27. Report of the Task Force on Historical and Comparative Perspectives, *Violence in America*, Vol. 2 (U.S. Government Printing Office: Washington, D.C., 1969), pp. 445-6. The Department of Justice recorded 22 deaths in civil disturbances in the last 6 months of 1968 and the first 3 months of 1969; 11 of these deaths occurred in a single disturbance—the Cleveland "shoot-out" in July of 1968. Similarly, while most of the nation's 2,300 college campuses probably experienced some kind of demonstrative protest during the academic year 1968-1969, the American Council on Education has found that only about six percent of the colleges experienced any violence. *Campus Disruption During 1968-1969*, ACE Research Reports, Vol. 4, No. 3 (1969), p. 8.

28. Comparative figures for property damage as the result of group protests are not available. But when measured against property damage resulting from more than 1,000,000 annual robberies and burglaries reported in crime statistics, it also seems likely that group protest accounts for a very small part of the deliberate property damage we experience.

29. *Violence in America*, p. 448. This comparison is based on available data that may not be fully comparable on a cross-national basis.

30. *The Politics of Protest* (U.S. Government Printing Office: Washington, D.C., 1969), pp. 81-82.

31. We use the term "offensive" violence as violence used to advance the cause of a protesting group, and the term "defensive" vio-

lence as violence used to defend the position of the group threatened by protest. Occasionally, a peacefully protesting group meeting defensive violence as so defined may engage in counter-violence as a means of self defense, as is true of the Negro Deacons for Defense in Mississippi and Alabama.

32. In *Violence in America*, p. 290, Philip Taft and Philip Ross conclude: "The effect of labor violence was almost always harmful to the union. There is little evidence that violence succeeded in gaining advantages for strikers."

33. John W. Gardner, *No Easy Victories* (New York: Harper and Row, 1968), p. 5.

34. See B. C. Roberts, "On the Origins and Resolution of English Working-Class Protest," in *Violence in America*, pp. 197-220.

35. Report of the Task Force on Law and Law Enforcement, *Law and Order Reconsidered* (U.S. Government Printing Office: Washington, D.C., 1969), p. 335.

36. The Democratic Convention and the possible desire of some demonstrators to influence its outcome by violence may have intensified the disorder in Chicago—a circumstance absent during the Washington Inaugural.

37. The Washington authorities had also dealt successfully with the large-scale antiwar march on the Pentagon in October 1967.

38. The bulk of the actual work of maintaining the peacefulness of the proceedings was performed by the demonstrators themselves. An estimated five thousand "marshals," recruited from among the demonstrators, flanked the crowds throughout. Their effectiveness was shown when they succeeded in stopping an attempt by the fringe radicals to leave the line of march in an effort to reach the White House during the Saturday parade.

Fringe groups among the demonstrators, numbering approximately 100, provoked two confrontations by throwing rocks at police on Friday night, November 14, as they unlawfully attempted to march on the Embassy of South Vietnam, and again on Saturday evening when rocks and paint bombs were used during an otherwise lawful assembly at the Justice Department. On both occasions, police used tear gas to disperse the crowds among which the extremists were mingled.

39. *Report of the National Advisory Commission on Civil Disorders* (U.S. Government Printing Office: Washington, D.C., 1968), p. 171.

40. *Law and Order Reconsidered*, p. 352.

41. *Report*, Chapter 12.

42. See generally, *Law and Order Reconsidered*, Chapters 15 and 16.

43. *New York Times* v. *Sullivan*, 376 U.S. 254.

44. The Supreme Court has suggested that federal statutory remedies against such private acts of interference are constitutional but that no statute yet enacted provides them. *United States* v. *Guest*, 383 U.S. 745.

45. These suggestions include more attention to in-depth, interpretive news reporting; hiring and training newsmen from minority groups and providing equivalent regular coverage of minority group activities including births and deaths, business promotions and social functions, as well as larger issues; and creation of vehicles for responsible criticism of news media performance, including internal grievance machinery within news organizations, community press councils, professional journalism reviews, and a national center for media study. See *Mass Media and Violence*, to be published.

46. Max Ways, "What's Wrong with News? It Isn't New Enough," *Fortune Magazine*, October 1969.

47. Letter to Samuel Kerchival, July 12, 1816. *Writings of Thomas Jefferson* (Lippincott, 1871), Vol. VII, p. 15.

48. We present our recommendations for achieving this goal throughout this report.

17.

ELLIOTT CURRIE

Violence and Ideology: A Critique of the Final Report of the Violence Commission

I

We live in an age of commissions. Up to now, this has not been completely unfortunate. The governmental commission can provide information unobtainable elsewhere; moreover, it can establish (in the sense of official validation) certain minimum levels of public and governmental concern about important social problems. Thus, the Kerner Report, despite its flaws, is a useful compendium of information on racial violence and on the socio-economic condition of black Americans, and it did much to establish permanent concern over "white racism" (though the Report itself was never very clear about the exact *meaning* of "white racism"). Therefore, it is especially depressing to find inflicted upon the public a document so dismissable as the final report of the Naional Commission on the Causes and Preven-

SOURCE: This paper, specially prepared for this book, was written at and supported by the Center for the Study of Law and Society, University of California, Berkeley.

tion of Violence, misleadingly entitled *To Establish Justice, to Insure Domestic Tranquility.*[1]

The title is supposed to indicate the Commission's message in a nutshell, namely that the government has as much responsibility for repressing "disorder" as it does for creating a just society. The Commission acknowledges the pressing need for social change, but insists, in the meantime, on the inalienable right of civil government to crack heads.

One hesitates to accept the Commission's reading of the meaning of that phrase about "Insuring Domestic Tranquility." In the Preamble to the Constitution, where it belongs, the phrase does *not* imply that "Justice" and "Order" were to be seen as separable items on a bureaucratic agenda. On the contrary, the Preamble suggests that a liberally- and well-designed Constitution will lead to both justice and tranquility as well as a number of other things. In the Preamble, both "Justice" and "Tranquility" are seen as *flowing from good government.* They are *not* considered as alternative policies that an established government may weigh, one against the other, in some sort of administrative balancing act.[2]

This suggests the fundamental problem with this Report. It is in no sense a serious analytical work, nor yet a clearly thought-out political manifesto. It is a hastily and carelessly constructed hodge-podge, composed of a limited amount of empirical evidence, a minimum of coherent theoretical analysis, and a great deal of rhetorical posturing in defense of authority. Its great mistake is in the *assumption* of the most important and problematic questions: the wisdom and goodwill of those now governing in the United States, and the basic soundness of contemporary American social and political institutions. Its main purpose seems to be to try to convince the rest of us of the validity of those assumptions. In this effort, the Report goes to great and sometimes disturbing lengths, systematically (if unsuccessfully) bending its analysis toward the ideological defense of the powerful, even to the extent of distorting the English language.

To some extent, this result was predictable. The mandate of the Violence Commission, as formulated by President Johnson, was to investigate and make recommendations regarding "the causes and prevention of lawless acts of violence in our society, including assassination, murder, and assault; [and] the causes and prevention of disrespect for law and order, of disrespect for public officials, and of violent disruptions of public order by individuals and groups."[3] From the beginning, therefore, the Commission was defined as a "law and order" commission, one that would conceive the problem of violence in America from the point of view of public officials threatened by challenges from below; one that would slap the wrists of militants and criminals of all colors and persuasions, while affirming the essential integrity of established authority. When the Commission was created in 1968, following the assassination of Robert Kennedy, there was some feeling that the administration conceived of the Violence Commission as a kind of rhetorical antidote to the Kerner Report, whose emphasis on the racism of American institutions had been unfavorably received by the Johnson administration.

The composition of the Violence Commission seemed to affirm this, since on the whole the commissioners were generally viewed as more conservative than the Kerner commissioners. But this is not always a useful indicator of the outcome of such commissions. Many people were pleasantly surprised by the outcome of the Kerner Report, despite the moderate political persuasions of the commissioners. Moreover, the wide range of issues selected for investigation and the diversity of the staff and researchers indicated that the Violence Commission would be at least presented with a variety of viewpoints.

The Commission created a number of task forces to deal with various aspects of the problem of violence in America. (The subject matter of those task forces corresponded roughly to that of the chapters of the Final Report—Historical and Comparative Perspectives, Violent Crime, Group Violence, Assassination, Law Enforcement, Firearms and Violence, Mass Media and Violence.) It also created several special investigative teams to deal with the Chicago convention riots, the Miami convention disorders, the inaugural demonstrations in Washington, the strike at San Francisco State College, and the "shoot-out" in Cleveland between police and militant blacks. The reports of these groups varied in quality, in character, and in impact. Several of them, however, provided materials suggesting that the matter of American violence was not nearly so cut-and-dried as the President's mandate seemed to suggest. In particular, several pointed to the significance of *official* violence, both in American history and in the contemporary behavior of the police and the military.

Consistent with what was apparently the original political aim, the Final Report of the Commission managed to ignore much of what was most significant in the earlier reports. We are left with a volume that concentrates on attacking "nihilists" and "anarchists" and "contemporary Cassandras who bemoan in self-flagellation how wretched we all are"[4] without once mentioning the violence of our overseas wars or the violence of authorities at home.

II

Perhaps the most remarkable feature of the Report is its curious use of the term "violence." What is especially noteworthy is the wide range of actions that the Commission includes under the rubric of "Group Violence," coupled with the absence of reference to the violence of constituted authorities.

In its chapter on the subject, the Commission defines "Group Violence" as "the unlawful threat or use of force by any group that results in or is intended to result in the injury or forcible restraint or intimidation of persons, or the destruction or forcible seizure of property."[5] That is, to say the least, a very inclusive definition. It includes not only those actions that we normally think of as "violence" but also a number of actions, threatened or actual, that may or may not even have a *forceful* outcome. The purpose of such a definition is clearly not analytical but ideological; it is to discredit those forms of *nonviolent* action that that Commission finds particularly disturbing. Such a definition covers, for example, sit-ins, the occupation of public buildings, locking up military recruiters, and the like. It conveniently blurs the common sense distinction between incivility and violence, presumably in order to justify severe responses by authorities to nonviolent but uncivil forms of protest.

By contrast, the Report never uses the term "violence" when discussing the behavior of police and other officials. Presumably, this is one function of the term "unlawful" in the Commission's definition of violence: it means that if violence is done by agents of the "law," it is not really violence. In several places the Report is regretful of the use of "excessive force" by police, but it does not mention police "violence." The Commission goes to great lengths to avoid using the word in this context; the chapter on "Campus Disorder," for example, speaks of the danger of student "nihilists" who for tactical reasons may try to "provoke counter-force to an excessive degree."[6]

The absence of serious recognition of official violence is especially remarkable given the emphasis placed on this subject in two of the earlier reports submitted to the Commission. The Walker Report on the 1968 Chicago convention disorders[7] did not hesitate to describe police violence in common sense terms. It spoke of a "police riot" and implicitly challenged the conventional idea that rioting and violence are characteristic of "mobs," while the police "preserve order." The Skolnick Report, prepared by the task force originally commissioned to study group violence,[8] also challenged the simplistic identification of "violence" with the actions of people who challenged authority rather than those who represented it. The Skolnick Report explicitly criticized careless use of the word "violence":

> Violence is an ambiguous term. . . . [T]he kinds of acts that become classified as "violent," and, equally important, those which do not become so classified, vary according to who provides the definition and who has superior resources for disseminating and enforcing his definitions. . . . The term "violence" is frequently employed to discredit forms of behavior considered improper, reprehensible, or threatening by specific groups which, in turn, may mask their own violent response with the rhetoric of order or progress.[9]

Moreover, the Skolnick Report also produced evidence suggesting that empirical examination of recent incidents of violence showed that violence was initiated *at least* as often by officials as by demonstrators.[10] Aware of these definitional pitfalls, the Skolnick Report adopted a precise and consistent definition of "violence"—"the intentional use of force to injure, to kill, or to destroy property"[11]—and proceeded to apply this definition uniformly and without exceptions.

The Commission, however, either did not read the Skolnick Report, or else deliberately chose to ignore it. Since the Skolnick Report was, after all, a document ordered by and submitted to the Commission, one would have thought that the Commission might have at least publicly acknowledged the differing point of view it expressed. Instead, the Commission chose to indulge in doublethink.

This doublethink is not merely an academic issue: it has consequences. It means that the Commission can ignore the question of controlling or otherwise dealing with the police, and for that matter can ignore the thorny problem of the war and its relation to domestic violence. Were the Commission to use the English language correctly, it would be forced to acknowledge the existence of official violence and indeed might be forced to take a position on it. As it is, the peculiar definition provides a way out. The Report, after all, is *about* violence; it is not *about* "excessive force." This also enables the

Commission to indulge in some remarkably disingenuous rhetoric, as in this passage:

> All history teaches us that as a conscious method of social reform, violence is a very dangerous weapon to employ. *That is why our nation has sought to avoid violent methods of effecting social change....*[12]

At one point, the Commission does note that violence may be used to maintain the power of an existing government, but goes on immediately to rule that "this has not been the main thrust of American group violence."[13] By any less evasive definition, of course, this *has* been the "main thrust" of American group violence, whether the government being maintained is our own or that of a friendly foreign regime.

A similar slanting of definitions permits the Commission to adopt uncritically the conventional wisdom that attributes violence and criminality primarily to the lower classes. The Report devotes its most serious attention to the question of violent crime in the cities. Violent crime is held to be "by far the most acute aspect of the problem of violence in the United States today." Moreover, "it is the ghetto slum that is disproportionately responsible for violent crime."[14] The first statement is true only if we accept the Commission's definition of violence, thereby excluding overseas war and domestic repression. The second statement is probably true if we accept conventional definitions of crime, thereby excluding genocidal warfare and corporate violence.

The Report's chapter on violent crime focusses on the high levels of violent crime among ghetto youth and purports to explain this primarily through a cliché-ridden examination of the culture of the lower class. (Loosely organized inner-city families make children subject to "premature autonomy," so that "resentment of authority figures, such as policemen and teachers, is not surprising."[15]) I am not suggesting that lower-class children are not violent, since it is patent that some of them sometimes are. And it may well be that they are more so, in the conventional ways, than other children. What is astonishing about this chapter is its implication that the routine use of violence to deal with problems is confined to the urban lower class and particularly lower-class youth. This is a matter of conventional political definitions being transformed into misleading sociological generalizations. The government uses violence on a massive scale to deal with its Asian difficulties; the police use it routinely at home; but only when ghetto kids (or, now, middle-class college students) use it does violence become a "social problem" requiring the establishment of presidential commissions. (This is the third such commission in recent years to be concerned *primarily*, when all is said and done, with the violent behavior of ghetto youth.) And only when lower-class youth use violence are we treated to analyses of the "undesirable subculture values"[16] impelling them to do so.

The refusal to give serious attention to the issue of official violence also undermines the Report's otherwise useful chapter on firearms.[17] This makes the intelligent point that it is ridiculous to expect a decrease in violence when everyone is allowed to run around armed. And it suggests, also intelligently, that our incredible distribution of guns ought to be somehow controlled. This is all very well, except that it says nothing whatever about controlling the use of guns by the *police*. Lacking even the most tentative suggestion that we ought to think about police violence, the firearms section loses impact and credibility. It is difficult to be enthusiastic about taking away *some* people's guns and not others, especially given the recent (and historical) record of the American police in regard to their use. But to consider this issue would have required the Commission to recognize forthrightly the problem of official violence, acknowledging that to be shot by a policeman makes one no less dead than to be shot by anyone else.

The Commission, however, chose to ignore this and to promote the position that violence is something poor people, student protestors, and black militants do. Even the language becomes emptied of precision as it is systematically bent to the purposes of social control.

III

These emphases, of course, are not accidental. They reflect the fact that this Report was commissioned as an exercise in the management of violence. From the managerial point of view, "violence" is whatever threatens the operation of current social arrangements. Seen from this perspective, violence becomes a social "problem" located in specific groups, and it becomes eligible for "treatment" in the way we generally treat social problems. Violence is seen as a property of certain kinds of people, in this case ghetto people and militant dissidents. "Underlying factors" are sought, generally in impersonal social processes, to explain its extraordinary incidence. Measures of "social

control" are also sought, where social control is defined as the extension of surveillance and organized restraint over populations considered to be dangerous or threatening.

In the Commission's treatment, these themes are presented in a way
that is less punitive, less moralistic, and more attuned to the grievances of discontented groups and to the need for some sort of social
change, than some more traditional approaches. Indeed, the central
point of the Report is the assertion of the government's supposed *dual*
responsibility, its commitment to the maintenance of order *and* the
establishment of justice. The Commission is careful to point out that
repression alone will not suffice, for violence is but "the lava flowing
from the top of a volcano fed by deeper fires of social dislocation and
injustice; it has not been stopped solely by capping the top."[18] What
is required is a "judicious combination of reform and control."[19]

The reader is struck immediately by a certain anomaly: if we are
serious about "establishing justice," if a genuine commitment to massive and basic institutional change is to be made, why should it *also*
be necessary to "double our investment" in the apparatus of repression? Isn't it reasonable to assume that "order" is intrinsically related
to "justice" and disorder to injustice? (The Commission, after all,
suggests this in several places.) And if so, doesn't the emphasis on
"order" betray a certain vacillation in the Commission's commitment
to "justice"?

The answer to this apparent anomaly is clear on a close reading of
the Report. This reveals that the issue of social control is dealt with
far more specifically, and far less equivocally, than the matter of
establishing justice. Taken together, the Report's ameliorative proposals—the eighteen-year-old vote, injunctions against interference with
First Amendment rights, expansion of the OEO legal services program, "seed money" for a few experimental citizen's grievance agencies, more programs (of the standard kind) for inner-city youth,
implementation of President Nixon's draft reforms—are simply not
very impressive.[20] They certainly do not amount to a "reconstruction
of urban life" of the kind that the Report rhetorically endorses, nor
does Daniel Patrick Moynihan's ten-point urban policy, which the
Commission presents as meriting "careful consideration."[21] But the
section on crime does contain a number of very specific proposals for
strengthening the agencies of social control in the ghetto. And while
the section on "Campus Disorder" contains not a single proposal that
can be seriously construed as aimed toward significant change in the
structure or operation of universities, it is quite specific on the need

for universities to develop "contingency plans" for handling campus disorders.[22]

In short, "Tranquility" is important because "Justice" is something we are not really ready to establish, and we are not sure when we *will* be ready, if at all. This is clear from the way the issues are phrased in the first place. The problem of violence is posed in the terms of domestic counterinsurgency. (Indeed, what is the idea of a "judicious combination of reform and control" but standard counterinsurgency procedure brought home?) "Justice" is presented not as an abiding social value, but as a practical "factor" to be weighed against others. The key passage in the Report, in this sense, is this one:

> We solemnly declare our conclusion that this nation is enter-
> ing a period in which our people need to be as concerned by
> the internal dangers of our free society as by any probable
> combination of external threats. We recognize that substan-
> tial amounts of funds cannot be transferred from sterile war
> purposes to more productive ones until our participation in
> the Vietnam war is ended.[23]

The passage is striking for two reasons: first, its imagery of "internal dangers" and the implication that we think of meaningful social change only inasmuch as we are afraid of what will happen otherwise; and second, its pragmatic and amoral covering of all bases. By invoking the war as an inevitable, essentially uncontrollable con-tingency, the Commission is able to say a great deal about the need for social change while justifying indefinite inaction. The passage is central, for it shows that the Commission has no intention of making *unequivocal* commitments except in the area of domestic social con-trol. Nothing of much importance will be done on the "Justice" side of the bureaucratic ledger until (unless) the war is ended. Needless to add, the Commission does not go on to suggest that the war *be* ended, though they grant that Vietnam is "hardly an open-and-shut case."[24]

This permits the Commission to declare itself for what must be the most painless "reordering of priorities" ever suggested: after the war is ended (presumably through divine intervention), we should "in-crease our general welfare expenditures by about 20 billion dollars," $19 billion of which will come from reduction of defense expenditures on ending the war and the rest from annual increments in the GNP.[25] Thus the Commission has promised nothing whatever while sounding quite progressive. We will have an extra $20 billion when the war is over. But the war is *not* over, so we do not have it. And we are certainly not going to take it from anywhere else in our budget or suggest an end to the war. The Commission's proposal is easy, politically safe, and cheap in all senses of the word.

The tendency to see certain aspects of the social world as relatively immutable and impersonal permeates the Report and structures its view of social problems and their possible resolution. Thus, "man's progress has reached a stage in which several forces combine to create critical stresses in our social and political structure."[26] The Report goes on to list population growth and technological advances and the fact that "our political and social institutions and the programs they manage are not changing rapidly enough to keep up with the speed of change in the environment they are intended to control" and that "we have not been willing or able" to refashion our institutions accordingly. "We tend like other peoples to resist political and social change."[27] (We?) The Commission here adopts the popular imagery of a bewildered society, full of innate goodwill but hampered by old-fashioned prejudices, slow to adjust to overpowering social forces, and therefore full of tension. Such imagery is very misleading, for it mystifies while maintaining a superficial plausibility. Its assumption of the goodwill of the "society" tends in practice to amount to an assertion of the congruence of the interests of those in authority with those who are likely to be classified as social problems. Its assumption of the relatively uncontrollable character of those large social forces amounts in practice to a rejection of basic institutional change, despite considerable rhetorical support.

In keeping with this emphasis, the Commission holds violent crime to be the result of "rapid social change," although it is then immediately admitted that other countries undergoing rapid social change have less violent crime than we do. This empirical difficulty is noted and then duly ignored, so that the idea that "rapid social change" causes crime can be invoked as part of a circular argument as to the second cause of violent crime: "our agencies of law enforcement have not been strengthened sufficiently to contain the violence that normally accompanies rapid social change."[28]

Lacking a strong commitment to serious institutional change, the Commission's specific recommendations on the control of violent crime focus on the ghetto and the strengthening of law enforcement therein. (After all, how can you control "rapid social change"?) The recommendations range from the banal to the terrifying. Increased foot patrols of the ghetto by interracial police teams, improved street lighting, community centers that would "provide activity so that city streets are not deserted in early evening hours" are among the banal. So is increased police-community relations activity in order to "secure greater understanding of ghetto residents by police, and of police by ghetto residents" (An equally plausible idea is that they understand each other all too well). Among the more terrifying proposals is the one suggesting

> Identification of specific violence-prone individuals for analysis and treatment in order to reduce the likelihood of repetition; provision of special schools for education of young people with violence-prone histories; special psychiatric services and employment programs for parolees and released offenders with a history of violent criminal acts.[29]

Note, here, the uncritical use of inordinately vague terms like "violence-prone." One can tell a great deal about a document such as this by noticing which terms are put in quotation marks—indicating, presumably, imprecision or inaccuracy—and which are presented unencumbered. This Report consistently puts quotes around "system," "white racism," and "immoral" (as applied to the Vietnam war),[30] but not around "violence-prone" or "stable positive male image."[31]

The Commission's tendency to see some social phenomena as controllable and others not does not reflect the old-fashioned conception of an invisible hand governing social and economic life, whose workings must not be tampered with. It suggests, instead, that social and political phenomena are *selectively* modifiable, and leaves the determination of *what* aspects of social life are modifiable, to what extent, and at what pace, to experts who, we are told, should be more heavily funded by the rest of us. In commission reports like this one, this amounts to self-boosting. The Commission tells us that more money ought to be poured into "extensive and sustained research into urban problems" and that "social science research is increasingly able to supply policy-makers and the public with empirical indicators of the nature of social problems and the success or failure of efforts to solve those problems."[32] This is not true, of course. Social science generally provides information about social problems once their "nature" has already been culturally and politically defined. And the tendency to see the larger issues as either predetermined or only limitedly modifiable (vide the Commission's approach to the war) means that "social problems" will generally be seen as confined to certain areas and kinds of people, as suggested earlier—"the cities" and the "ghetto," the "lower classes," "troublesome youth." This in turn means that greater investment in "research" will probably imply more of the same—studies of what is wrong with the poor, of what leads the lower-class boy to violence, or of the backgrounds of "protest-prone" students.

All of this implies the need for more research organizations, more money, and more high-level agencies of control and intervention. In its chapter on "Law Enforcement," the Commission recommends the establishment of a National Citizens Justice Center, to be staffed by people from the National Council on Crime and Delinquency, the American Bar Association, and—you guessed it—"the members, staffs, and consultants of the four Federal commissions which have recently studied the problems of crime, violence, and social disorder," including, not least, "this Commission."[33]

This illustrates an important point about the relationship between social science and government in an essentially conservative society like the United States. The needs of authority merge, all too often, with the needs of a rather barren, amoral social science on the make. Government has an interest in maintaining itself and therefore in keeping social analysis within "reasonable" bounds. Amoral social science is interested in maintaining (and enlarging) itself and therefore in making the simple sufficiently complex to justify "further research," continuing grants, and steady governmental support. Both stand to lose by concise critical analysis that points to basic levers of social and political change. Both stand to gain from the invocation of further commissions and the establishment of "justice centers" staffed by the politically harmless. Both, again, stand to lose if this kind of response to social problems is rejected in favor of genuinely far-reaching social action. This is not to suggest that there is no place for social science in a serious program of social change; only that we have for too long been subjected to the *substitution* of "further research" for obviously needed social action. This is getting to be a pretty big business and it is a business that flourishes in the absence of major social change.

IV

The *best* parts of this Report are *ideological*, in Karl Mannheim's sense: the social thought produced by a ruling group that is "so intensively interest-bound to a situation that they are simply no longer able to see certain facts which would undermine their sense of domination."[34] One of the best parts, for example, is the point at which the Commission begins to adopt an institutional perspective on the problem of violent crime.[35] Here the Commission begins to make the interesting and plausible point that when people no longer believe that "rule-making institutions are entitled to rule," they are more likely to break the law. The Commission then dissipates the point by listing a number of things that supposedly weaken the legitimacy of "our institutions"—including governors defying court orders, police beating demonstrators, looters going unpunished, college youth "attacking society's rules and values"—without offering a similar list of those aspects of our institutions *themselves*, rather than instances of disrespect for them, that might have something to do with the loss of legitimacy. The Commission's steadfast refusal to come to grips with that possibility is not just annoying, it is tragic. Violent crime is a serious matter, and the Commission's task force is to be commended for pointing out its devastating impact on the mentality of urban America and on the respect of the middle classes for civil liberties. In many respects, violent crime is the dirty secret of American society and one of the most compelling indicators of the inadequacy of its institutional life. To raise these issues and then smother them is a serious failure.

The worst parts of the Report, on the other hand, often read like self-caricature. Some of the Report is nothing more than a transparently biased attempt to convince us of the folly of challenging things as they are, and these sections are often unintentionally funny. Throughout the Report, much use is made of the appeal to status. There are constant references to the opinions of "one of this nation's most thoughtful leaders" or "a number of noted educators" or "the head of one of the nation's largest universities," or "the dean of one of the nation's largest law schools," as if these incantatory appeals would inspire us with such awe that we would ignore the Report's logical and empirical deficiencies.

Much of this appears in the chapter on "Civil Disobedience." That this chapter is included at all is curious; surely civil disobedience is not "violence," even by stretching definitions. The only reason for including a chapter denouncing civil disobedience in a report on violence would be if it could be shown that civil disobedience *leads* to violence or *results* in violence. The Commission knows that it has no evidence from which to argue this point, but tries to argue it anyway; and this lends the chapter its curiously inarticulate and tortuous character.

The first section speaks of the "cancerous growth of disobedi-
ences"[36] (what is *a* disobedience?), urging us to forego all collective
disobedience and obey the law—any law. This section is rejected by
Commissioners Milton Eisenhower, Philip Hart, Patricia Harris, Leon
Higginbotham, and Walter Menninger, to their credit. The second
section, however, is hardly better. It worries that civil disobedience
will not improve the "general level of morality in the country" (will
obedience improve it?) and that civil disobedience, moreover, will
destroy the normal legal process. This gloomy forecast, however, is
apparently based *wholly* on a consultant paper dealing with the alleged effects of civil disobedience in *India*.[37]

Aware that this line of argument, almost entirely lacking in sup-
portive evidence, is getting them nowhere, the Commission falls back
on sheer assertion:

> We agree with the overwhelming majority of the people in
> this country that our problems, serious as they are, are not
> the kind that make revolution even thinkable, let alone justi-
> fiable. We believe that political and social mechanisms do
> exist and have produced significant change in recent years.
> The remedy for the discontented, we believe, is to seek
> changes through lawful mechanisms. . . . [38]

To back *this* up, the Commission resorts to the useful old specter of
the crazy right wing. Civil disobedience has stirred up the nasties:

> The fears and resentments created by symbolic law violation
> have strengthened the political power of some of the most
> destructive elements in American society. Only naive and
> willful blindness can obscure the strength of these dark
> forces, which, but for the loosening of the bonds of law,
> might otherwise lie quiescent beneath the surface of our na-
> tional life.[39]

Strong language. This argument raises another interesting anomaly; if
our political and social institutions are in such sound shape as the
Commission keeps telling us they are, why is it that there are so many
"dark forces" waiting just under the surface to overwhelm us? Aside
from the absence, again, of any supporting evidence for the hint that
civil disobedience will lead to fascism, the Commission's adoption of
this imagery serves as a forceful reminder of what a conservative

country the United States has become, how afraid of its people and their presumably destructive appetites. The Report invokes the picture of fragile institutions under constant siege from all sorts of "elements." By the time they are finished, nearly *everybody* has been included under the rubric of dangerous elements; students, blacks, war protestors, even the great silent conservative mass, with its "dark" and "destructive" impulses. Nearly everybody is wrong, threatening, or dangerous. Only those manning the heights of our beleagured institutions—people like "the head of one of the nation's largest universities"—are free from taint.

Again, such an argument has sufficient plausibility to make it superficially attractive. Obviously there are some very destructive people in America. Obviously they can pose severe challenges to democratic institutions. The question is whether it makes sense to see these problems as rooted in the character of those "dangerous elements" rather than in the institutions themselves or in the absence of adequate institutional arrangements in the first place. The Skolnick Report, for example, also dealt with stirrings from the dangerous right, but tried to analyze these stirrings in the context of the social and economic sources of white political marginality[40] rather than in the "fears and resentments created by symbolic law violation." Rather than analyzing this problem, the Commission chose to use it as another device to discredit social protest.

The Commission's conservative imagery suggests the recurrent problem faced in this Report and in other attempts to offer a conservative justification for contemporary American social arrangements. It is difficult to square the conservative defense of overdeveloped contemporary power structures with the rhetorical resort to the American heritage, for the two do not mix well. Defense of the first requires real conservative language explicitly justifying elitism and the concentration of decision-making at the top. Defense of the second, however, requires affirmation of the values of popular participation in government and an assertion of faith in popular rationality and the restraint of authority. About the closest the Commission comes to the latter affirmation is the idea that students ought to have a "meaningful role in the governance of all noneducational, non-research functions" of the universities.[41]

The Commission therefore finds itself in the dilemma of trying to prove that traditional American libertarian principles do not apply (exactly) to contemporary dissent. Discussing "formative historical experiences" that are at the bottom of our contemporary problems, the Commission admits that after all our own history begins with revolution, and our Declaration of Independence asserts the rights of individuals against arbitrary authority. But,

> The revolutionary doctrine that our Declaration of Independence proudly proclaims is mistakenly cited as a model for legitimate violence by contemporary groups such as militant Negroes and radical students who confront a system of both private and public government that they regard as contemptuous of their consent. Entranced by the resurgence of revolution in the underdeveloped world and of international student unrest, radical students and blacks seize upon our early doctrine of the inherent right of revolution and self-determination to justify their rebellion. That their analogies are fatefully problematical in no way dilutes the majesty of our own proud Declaration.[42]

Caught in the unpleasant position of having to say either that there is or is not an inherent right of self-determination, and not daring to knock our proud Declaration, the Commission retreats into gibberish.

In this, as in many other things, the Report is altogether lacking in style. It is clumsy, badly put together, and occasionally completely inarticulate. In short, it is basically an *unserious* work. Moreover, it often betrays an unpleasant contempt for the intelligence of its readers. It is surely this contempt that is responsible for the inclusion in the Report of a section inspiringly entitled "The Strengths of America," written especially for this occasion by an English journalist. (America will prevail, writes this worthy; after all, it has absorbed millions of immigrants and "given them freedom to develop in their own manner—to chase an honest buck, build, aim at the moon, build a bomb, and dream their dreams."[43]) Such nonsense indicates an apparent assumption by the Commission of the incompetence of their readers, of the public's inability to distinguish between analysis and horseshit, or to care much one way or the other.

Indeed, the disaster of this Report suggests the wisdom of the remark by Judge Higginbotham, one of the two black commissioners, that we should have a "national moratorium on any additional temporary study commissions to probe the causes of racism, or poverty, or crime, or the urban crisis."[44] Federal commissions can be useful, but only insofar as they reflect a reasonably serious governmental effort to come to grips with pressing social problems. If this Report is any indication, there are some bleak years ahead.

NOTES

1. The National Commission on the Causes and Prevention of Violence, *To Establish Justice, To Insure Domestic Tranquility* (Washington, D.C.: U.S. Government Printing Office, 1969). Hereafter cited as "Violence Commission."

2. The entire passage is reprinted in ibid., p. i.

3. Ibid., p. v.

4. Ibid., p. 12.

5. Ibid., p. 57.

6. Ibid., p. 213.

7. The National Commission on the Causes and Prevention of Violence, Chicago Study Team, *Rights in Conflict* (New York: Bantam, 1968).

8. Jerome H. Skolnick, ed., *The Politics of Protest* (New York: Simon & Schuster, 1969); a task force report submitted to the National Commission on the Causes and Prevention of Violence.

9. Ibid., p. 4.

10. Ibid., pp. 3-4.

11. Ibid., p. 6.

12. Violence Commission, p. 213. (Emphasis added.)

13. Ibid., p. 65.

14. Ibid., p. xxi.

15. Ibid., p. 31.

16. Ibid., p. 43.

17. Ibid., pp. 169-85.

18. Ibid., p. 16.

19. Ibid., p. 69.

20. A list of all of those recommendations may be found in ibid., pp. 271-82.

21. This is presented, with modifications, in the Violence Commission's chapter on Violent Crime, pp. 48-54.

22. Ibid., p. 280.

23. Ibid., p. xxv.

24. Ibid., p. 96.

25. Ibid., pp. xxv-xxix.

26. Ibid., p. 83.

27. Ibid., pp. 83-84.

28. Ibid., p. 41.

29. Ibid., p. 47.

30. Ibid., p. 42.

31. Ibid., p. 31.

32. Ibid., p. 53.

33. Ibid., p. 165.

34. Karl Mannheim, *Ideology and Utopia* (London: Routledge & Kegan Paul, 1936), p. 40.

35. Violence Commission, pp. 41-42.

36. Ibid., p. 91.

37. Ibid., pp. 98-102.

38. Ibid., p. 103.

39. Ibid., p. 104.

40. Skolnick, *The Politics of Protest*, pp. 218-40.

41. Violence Commission, p. 218.

42. Ibid., p. 9.

43. Ibid., p. 261.

44. Ibid., p. 117.

IX

U.S.A., 1970

INTRODUCTION

During the first weekend in May 1970 there were widespread protests throughout the country in response to President Nixon's decision to extend the Indochina war into Cambodia. Protests in universities and colleges around the country were conducted on an unprecedented scale.[1] During predominantly peaceful protests at Kent State University on May 4, four students were killed by National Guard troops. Nine days later, two black students were similarly killed and several others injured by members of the Mississippi Highway Patrol at Jackson State College.

Although the Violence Commission's final Report, issued only five months earlier, included an extensive analysis of student protest and despite Commissioner Higginbotham's plea for a moratorium on commissions, the Cambodia crisis evoked demands for a presidential commission from diverse political sources, including HEW Secretary Robert Finch, Senator Edward Kennedy, Senate Majority Leader Mike Mansfield, Senate Minority Leader Hugh Scott, as well as the President of Kent State University and various educational spokesmen.[2] In response to these demands, on June 13 President Nixon appointed former Pennsylvania Governor William W. Scranton to head a nine-member Commission on Campus Unrest.

In addition to Scranton, the Commission included Bayless Manning, Dean of the Stanford Law School; James Ahern, Chief of Police in New Haven, Connecticut; Benjamin O. Davis, Cleveland's Public Safety Director and a former Air Force Lieutenant General; Erwin D. Canham, Editor-in-Chief of the *Christian Science Monitor*; Dr. James E. Cheek, President of Howard University; Martha A. Derthick, Associate Professor of Political Science at Boston College; Revius O. Ortique Jr., a New Orleans attorney; and Joseph Rhodes Jr., a junior fellow at Harvard University. It was a predominantly liberal commission—four blacks, four members affiliated with universities, four members under the age of 40 (and one under 25), and a liberal police chief from a university town.

The Commission was instructed by President Nixon to "study dissent, disorder, and violence on the campuses of higher learning." The duties of the Commission included:

> Identifying the principal causes of campus violence and the breakdown in the process of orderly expression of dissent on the campus.
>
> Suggesting specific methods and procedures through which grievances can be resolved by means other than the exertion of force.
>
> Suggesting ways to protect academic freedom, the right to obtain an education free from improper interference, and the right of peaceful dissent and protest.
>
> Proposing practical steps which can be taken by government at all levels, by the administrations of institutions of higher learning, and by students, through student governments or otherwise, to minimize dangers attendant upon expressions of dissent.

Like most "riot" commissions, the Scranton Commission worked under extraordinary time pressures; it was requested to complete its final report before the beginning of the fall quarter. Public hearings were held around the country in Washington, D.C., Los Angeles, Jackson, Mississippi, and Kent, Ohio. It held its first executive meeting on June 25 and consequently met another fourteen times in executive session. Two task force research teams were established in Kent and Jackson. The Commission released its final report on September 27—a comparatively short report of analysis and recommendations— followed a week later by two task force reports, mostly factual and descriptive, on the violence at Jackson State College and Kent State University.

The following selections from the Scranton Report include a summary of its findings and recommendations together with the full text of the task force report on "The Killings at Jackson State." A brief analysis of the Scranton Report and its political implications follows in the "Epilogue."

NOTES

1. *New York Times*, 3 October 1970, p. 35.
2. *Los Angeles Times*, 13 May 1970, p. 15.

18.

THE PRESIDENT'S COMMISSION ON CAMPUS UNREST

The Scranton Report

The crisis on American campuses has no parallel in the history of the nation. This crisis has roots in divisions of American society as deep as any since the Civil War. The divisions are reflected in violent acts and harsh rhetoric and in the enmity of those Americans who see themselves as occupying opposing camps. Campus unrest reflects and increases a more profound crisis in the nation as a whole.

This crisis has two components: a crisis of violence and a crisis of understanding. We fear new violence and growing enmity.

CRISIS OF VIOLENCE

On the nation's campuses, and in their neighboring communities, the level of violence has been steadily rising. Students have been killed

SOURCE: From The President's Commission on Campus Unrest, *The Scranton Report* (Washington, D.C.: U.S. Government Printing Office, 1970), *passim*.

and injured; civil authorities have been killed and injured; bystanders have been killed and injured. Valuable public and private property and scholarly products have been burned.

Too many Americans have begun to justify violence as a means of effecting change or safeguarding traditions. Too many have forgotten the values and sense of shared humanity that unite us. Campus violence reflects this national condition.

Much of the nation is so polarized that on many campuses a major domestic conflict or an unpopular initiative in foreign policy could trigger further violent protest and, in its wake, counterviolence and repression.

The Constitution protects the freedom of all citizens to dissent and to engage in nonviolent protest. Dissent is a healthy sign of freedom and a protection against stagnation. But the right to dissent is not the right to resort to violence.

Repression Is Unwise

Equally, to respond to peaceful protest with repression and brutal tactics is dangerously unwise. It makes extremists of moderates, deepens the divisions in the nation, and increases the chances that future protest will be violent.

We believe it urgent that Americans of all convictions draw back from the brink. We must recognize even our bitter opponents as fellow Americans with rights upon which we cannot morally or legally encroach and as fellow human beings whom we must not club, stone, shoot, or bomb.

We utterly condemn violence. Students who bomb and burn are criminals. Police and National Guardsmen who needlessly shoot and assault students are criminals. All who applaud these criminal acts share in the evil. We must declare a national ceasefire.

There can be no more "trashing," no more rock throwing, no more arson, no more bombing by protesters. No grievance, philosophy, or political idea can justify the destruction and killing we have witnessed. There can be no sanctuary or immunity from prosecution on the campus. If our society is to survive, criminal acts by students must be treated as such wherever they occur and whatever their purpose.

Crimes committed by one do not justify crimes committed by another. We condemn brutality and excessive force by officers and troops called to maintain order. The use of force by police is sometimes necessary and legal, but every unnecessary resort to violence is wrong, criminal, and feeds the hostility of the disaffected.

Our universities as centers of free inquiry are particularly vulnerable to violence. We condemn those groups which are openly seeking to destroy them.

We especially condemn bombing and political terrorism. The full resources of society must be employed to bring to justice those who commit terrorist acts. Anyone who aids or protects terrorists, on or off campus, must share the moral and legal responsibilities for the crimes they commit.

We find ominous and shocking reports that students are laying in supplies of weapons, and that others are preparing to take the law into their hands against protesters and minorities they dislike. There can be no place in our society for vigilantes, night-riders, or militants who would bring destruction and death upon their opponents. No one serves the law by breaking it.

Violence must stop, because it is wrong. It destroys human life and the products of human effort. It undermines the foundations of a just social order. No progress is possible in a society where lawlessness prevails.

Violence must stop because the sounds of violence drown out all words of reason. When students and officials resort to force and violence, no one can hear, and the nation is denied a vital call to conscience. It must stop, because no nation will long tolerate violence without repression. History offers grim proof that repression once started is almost impossible to contain.

CRISIS OF UNDERSTANDING

Campus protest has been focused on three major questions: racial injustice, war, and the university itself.

The first issue is the unfulfilled promise of full justice and dignity for blacks and other minorities. Blacks, like many others of different races and ethnic origins, are demanding today that the pledges of the Declaration of Independence and the Emancipation Proclamation be fulfilled now. Full social justice and dignity—an end to racism, in all its human, social, and cultural forms—is a central demand of today's students, black, brown, and white.

A great majority of students and a majority of their elders oppose the Indochina war. Many believe it entirely immoral. And if the war is wrong, students insist, then so are all policies and practices that support it, from the draft to military research, from ROTC to recruiting for defense industry. This opposition has led to an ever-widening wave of student protests.

A third target of student protest is the shortcomings of the American university. The goals, values, administration, and curriculum have been sharply criticized by many students. Students complain that their studies are irrelevant to the social problems that concern them. They want to shape their own personal and common lives, but find the university restrictive. They seek a community of companions and scholars, but find an impersonal multiversity. And they denounce the university's relationship to the war and to discriminatory racial practices.

Behind the student protest on these issues and the crisis of violence to which they have contributed lies the more basic crisis of understanding.

Americans have never shared a single culture, a single philosophy, or a single religion. But in most periods in our history, we have shared many common values, common sympathies, and a common dedication to a system of government which protects our diversity.

We are now in grave danger of losing what is common among us through growing intolerance of opposing views on issues and of diversity itself.

A "new" culture is emerging primarily among students. Membership is often manifested by differences in dress and life-style. Most of its members have high ideals and great fears. They stress the need for humanity, equality, and the sacredness of life. They fear that nuclear war will make them the last generation in history. They see their elders entrapped by materialism and competition, and prisoners of outdated social forms. They believe their own country has lost its sense of human purpose. They see the Indochina war as an onslaught by a technological giant upon the peasant people of a small, harmless, and backward nation. The war is seen as draining resources from the urgent needs of social and racial justice. They argue that we are the first nation with sufficient resources to create not only decent lives for some, but a decent society for all and that we are failing to do so. They feel they must remake America in its own image.

But among the members of this new student culture, there is a growing lack of tolerance, a growing insistence that their own views must govern, an impatience with the slow procedures of liberal democracy, a growing denial of the humanity and goodwill of those who urge patience and restraint, and particularly of those whose duty it is to enforce the law. A small number of students have turned to violence; an increasing number, not terrorists themselves, would not turn even arsonists and bombers over to law enforcement officials.

At the same time, many Americans have reacted to this emerging culture with an intolerance of their own. They reject not only that which is impatient, unrestrained, and intolerant in the new culture of the young, but even that which is good. Worse, they reject the individual members of the student culture themselves. Distinctive dress alone is enough to draw insult and abuse. Increasing numbers of citizens believe that students who dissent or protest, even those who protest peacefully, deserve to be treated harshly. Some even say that when dissenters are killed they have brought death upon themselves. Less and less do students and the larger community seek to understand or respect the viewpoints and motivations of the other.

If this trend continues, if this crisis of understanding endures, the very survival of the nation will be threatened. A nation driven to use the weapons of war upon its youth is a nation on the edge of chaos. A nation that has lost the allegiance of part of its youth is a nation that has lost part of its future. A nation whose young have become intolerant of diversity, intolerant of the rest of its citizenry, and intolerant of all traditional values simply because they are traditional has no generation worthy or capable of assuming leadership in the years to come. . . .

We urgently call for reconciliation. Tolerance and understanding on all sides must re-emerge from the fundamental decency of Americans, from our shared aspirations as Americans, from our traditional tolerance of diversity, and from our common humanity. We must regain our compassion for one another and our mutual respect.

There is a deep continuity between all Americans, young and old, a continuity that is being obscured in our growing polarization. Most dissenting youth are striving toward the ultimate values and dreams of their elders and forefathers. In all Americans there has always been latent respect for the idealism of the young. The whole object of a free government is to allow the nation to redefine its purposes in the light of new needs without sacrificing the accumulated wisdom of its living traditions. We cannot do this without each other.

Violence Must End

Despite the differences among us, powerful values and sympathies unite us. The very motto of our nation calls for both unity and diversity: from many, one.

Out of our divisions, we must now recreate understanding and respect for those different from ourselves.

Violence must end.

Understanding must be renewed.

All Americans must come to see each other not as symbols or stereotypes but as human beings.

Reconciliation must begin.

We share the impatience of those who call for change. We believe there is still time and opportunity to achieve change. We believe we can still fulfill our shared national commitment to peace, justice, decency, equality, and the celebration of human life.

We must start. All of us.

Our recommendations are directed toward this end.

MAJOR RECOMMENDATIONS

Far more important than the particular recommendations of this Commission are the underlying themes that are common to all:

Most student protesters are neither violent nor extremist. But a small minority of politically extreme students and faculty members and a small group of dedicated agitators are bent on destruction of the university through violence in order to gain their own political ends. Perpetrators of violence must be identified, removed from the university as swiftly as possible, and prosecuted vigorously by the appropriate agencies of law enforcement.

Dissent and peaceful protest are a valued part of this nation's way of governing itself. Violence and disorder are the antithesis of democratic processes and cannot be tolerated either on the nation's campuses or anywhere else.

The roots of student activism lie in unresolved conflicts in our national life, but the many defects of the universities have also fueled campus unrest.

Universities have not adequately prepared themselves to respond to disruption. They have been without suitable plans, rules, or sanctions. Some administrators and faculty members have responded irresolutely. Frequently, announced sanctions have not been applied. Even more frequently, the lack of appropriate organization within the university has rendered its response ineffective. The university's own house must be placed in order.

Issues of War and Race

Too many students have acted irresponsibly and even dangerously in pursuing their stated goals and expressing their dissent. Too many law enforcement officers have responded with unwarranted harshness and force in seeking to control disorder.

Actions—and inactions—of government at all levels have contributed to campus unrest. The words of some political leaders have helped to inflame it. Law enforcement officers have too often reacted ineptly or overreacted. At times, their response has degenerated into uncontrolled violence.

The nation has been slow to resolve the issues of war and race, which exacerbate divisions within American society and which have contributed to the escalation of student protest and disorder.

All of us must act to prevent violence, to create understanding, and to reduce the bitterness and hostility that divide both the campus and the country. We must establish respect for the processes of law and tolerance for the exercise of dissent on our campuses and in the nation.

We advance our recommendations not as cure-alls, but as rational and responsive steps that should be taken. We summarize here our major recommendations, addressed to those who have the power to carry them out.

For the President

We urge that the President exercise his reconciling moral leadership as the first step to prevent violence and create understanding. It is imperative that the President bring us together before more lives are lost and more property destroyed and more universities disrupted.

We recommend that the President seek to convince public officials and protesters alike that divisive and insulting rhetoric is dangerous. In the current political campaign and throughout the years ahead, the President should insist that no one play irresponsible politics with the issue of "campus unrest."

We recommend that the President take the lead in explaining to the American people the underlying causes of campus unrest and the urgency of our present situation. We recommend that he articulate and emphasize those values all Americans hold in common. At the same time we urge him to point out the importance of diversity and co-existence to the nation's health.

To this end, nothing is more important than an end to the war in

Indochina. Disaffected students see the war as a symbol of moral crisis in the nation which, in their eyes, deprives even law of its legitimacy. Their dramatic reaction to the Cambodian invasion was a measure of the intensity of their moral recoil.

Personal Support of the President

We urge the President to renew the national commitment to full social justice and to be aware of increasing charges of repression. We recommend that he take steps to see to it that the words and deeds of government do not encourage belief in those charges.

We recommend that the President lend his personal support and assistance to American universities to accomplish the changes and reforms suggested in this Report.

We recommend that the President take steps to assure that he be continuously informed of the views of students and blacks, important constituencies in this nation.

We recommend that the President call a series of national meetings designed to foster understanding among those who are now divided. He should meet with the governors of the states, with university leaders, with law enforcement officers, and with black and student leaders. Each participant in these meetings should be urged to bring with him practical suggestions for restoring trust and responsibility among those whom he represents, and commit himself to continue this process of national reconciliation in frequent meetings throughout the school year.

FOR GOVERNMENT

We strongly urge public officials at all levels of government to recognize that their public statements can either heal or divide. Harsh and bitter rhetoric can set citizen against citizen, exacerbate tension and encourage violence.

Just as the President must offer reconciling leadership to reunite the nation, so all government officials—at all levels—must work to bring our hostile factions together.

Like the President, the governors of the states should hold meetings and develop contacts throughout the school year to further the cause of reconciliation. Like the President, other federal, state, and local officials must be sensitive to the charge of repression and fashion their words and deeds in a manner designed to refute it.

Review of Federal Policies

We urge state and local officials to make plans for handling campus disorders in full cooperation with one another and with the universities. We urge the states to establish guidelines setting forth more precisely the circumstances that justify ordering the National Guard to intervene in a campus disorder.

We recommend that the federal government review all its current policies affecting students and universities to assure that neither the policies nor administration of them threatens the independence or quality of American higher education. At the same time government should increase its financial support of higher education.

We urge public officials to reject demands that entire universities be punished because of the ideas or excesses of some members and to honor their responsibility to help preserve academic freedom.

We recommend that the Department of Defense establish alternatives to ROTC so that officer education is available to students whose universities choose to terminate on-campus ROTC programs.

We recommend greatly increased financial aid for black colleges and universities. All agencies of government that support such institutions should massively increase their grants to enable these colleges to overcome past shortcomings.

We support the continuing efforts of formerly all-white universities to recruit black, Mexican-American, Puerto Rican, and other minority students, and we urge that adequate government-sponsored student aid be made available to them. We recommend that in the process of becoming more representative of the society at large, universities make the adjustments necessary to permit those from minority backgrounds to take maximum advantage of their university experience.

Strict Controls of Explosives Needed

Bombing and arson pose an increasing threat to lives and property on campus. We urge prompt enactment of strict controls over the sale, transfer, and possession of explosive materials. Such statutes are needed at both the federal and state levels.

FOR LAW ENFORCEMENT

We have deep sympathy for peace officers—local and state police, National Guardsmen, and campus security officers—who must deal with all types of campus disorder. Much depends on their judgment, courage, and professionalism.

We commend those thousands of law enforcement officers who have endured taunts and assaults without reacting violently and whose careful conduct has prevented violence and saved lives.

At the same time, we recognize that there have been dangerous and sometimes fatal instances of unnecessary harshness and illegal violence by law enforcement officers.

We therefore urge that peace officers be trained and equipped to deal with campus disorders, firmly, justly, and humanely. They must avoid both uncontrolled and excessive response.

Too frequently, local police forces have been undermanned, improperly equipped, poorly trained, and unprepared for campus disturbances. We therefore urge police forces, especially those in smaller communities, to improve their capacity to respond to civil disorders.

Shoulder Weapons Rarely Needed

We recommend the development of joint contingency plans among law enforcement agencies. They should specify which law enforcement official is to be in command when several forces are operating together.

Sending civil authorities on to a college campus armed as if for war—armed only to kill—has brought tragedy in the past. If this practice is not changed, tragedy will come again. Shoulder weapons (except for tear gas launchers) are very rarely needed on the college campus; they should not be used except as emergency equipment in the face of sniper fire or armed resistance justifying them.

We recommend that National Guardsmen receive much more training in controlling civil disturbances. During the last three years, the Guard has played almost no role in Southeast Asia, but has been called to intervene in civil disorders at home more than 200 times.

We urge that the National Guard be issued special protection equipment appropriate for use in controlling civil disorders. We urge that it have sufficient tactical capability and non-lethal weaponry, so that it will use deadly force only as the absolute last resort.

FOR THE UNIVERSITY

Every university must improve its capability for responding effectively to disorder. Students, faculty, and trustees must support these efforts. Universities must pull themselves together.

The university should be an open forum where speakers of every point of view can be heard. The area of permitted speech and conduct should be at least as broad as that protected by the First Amendment.

The university should promulgate a code making clear the limits of permissible conduct and announce in advance what measures it is willing to employ in response to impermissible conduct. It should strengthen its disciplinary process. It should assess the capabilities of its security force and determine what role, if any, that force should play in responding to disorder.

When criminal violence occurs on the campus, university officials should promptly call for the assistance of law enforcement agencies.

When faced with disruptive but nonviolent conduct, the university should be prepared to respond initially with internal measures. It must clearly understand the options available to it and be prepared to move from one to another if it is reasonably obvious that an earlier tactic has failed.

Students' Concerns Changed

Faculty members who engage in or lead disruptive conduct have no place in the university community.

The university, and particularly the faculty, must recognize that the expansion of higher education and the emergence of the new youth culture have changed the makeup and concerns of today's student population. The university should adapt itself to these new conditions. We urge that the university make its teaching programs, degree structure, and transfer and leave policies more flexible and more varied in order to enhance the quality and voluntariness of university study.

We call upon all members of the university to reaffirm that the proper functions of the university are teaching and learning, research and scholarship. An academic community best serves itself, the country, and every principle to which it is devoted by concentrating on these tasks.

Academic institutions must be free—free from outside interference, and free from internal intimidation. Far too many people who should know better—both within university communities and outside them— have forgotten this first principle of academic freedom. The pursuit of knowledge cannot continue without the free exchange of ideas.

Obviously, all members of the academic community, as individuals, should be free to participate actively in whatever campaigns or causes they choose. But universities as institutions must remain politically neutral, except in those rare cases in which their own integrity, educational purpose, or preservation are at stake.

One of the most valid criticisms of many universities is that their faculties have become so involved in outside research that their commitment to teaching seems compromised. We urge universities and faculty members to reduce their outside service commitments. We recognize that alternative sources of university funding will have to be developed to take the place of the money attached to these outside commitments. Realistically, this will mean more unrestricted government aid to higher education.

Large universities should take steps to decentralize or reorganize to make possible a more human scale.

University governance systems should be reformed to increase participation of students and faculty in the formulation of university policies that affect them. But universities cannot be run on a one man, one vote basis with participation of all members on all issues.

Universities must become true communities whose members share a sense of respect, tolerance, and responsibility for one another.

FOR STUDENTS

Students must accept the responsibility of presenting their ideas in a reasonable and persuasive manner. They must recognize that they are citizens of a nation which was founded on tolerance and diversity, and they must become more understanding of those with whom they differ.

Students must protect the right of all speakers to be heard even when they disagree with the point of view expressed. Heckling speakers is not only bad manners but is inimical to all the values that a university stands for.

Students must face the fact that giving moral support to those who are planning violent action is morally despicable.

Students should be reminded that language that offends will seldom persuade. Their words have sometimes been as offensive to many Americans as the words of some public officials have been to them.

Commitment to Majority Rule

Students should not expect their own views, even if held with great moral intensity, automatically and immediately to determine national policy. The rhetorical commitment to democracy by students must be matched by an awareness of the central role of majority rule in a democratic society and by an equal commitment to techniques of persuasion within the political process.

The Commission has been impressed and moved by the idealism and commitment of American youth. But this extraordinary commitment brings with it extraordinary obligations: to learn from our nation's past experience, to recognize the humanity of those with whom they disagree, and to maintain their respect for the rule of law. The fight for change and justice is the good fight; to drop out or strike out at the first sign of failure is to insure that change will never come.

This Commission is only too aware of America's shortcomings. Yet we are also a nation of enduring strength. Millions of Americans—generations past and present—have given their vision, their energy, and their patient labor to make us a more just nation and a more humane people. We who seek to change America today build on their accomplishments and enjoy the freedoms they won for us. It is a considerable inheritance; we must not squander or destroy it.

19.

THE PRESIDENT'S COMMISSION
ON CAMPUS UNREST

The Killings at Jackson State

Events of May 13, 1970
Disturbances began shortly after dusk on Wednesday, May 13. The triggering incident is undetermined, but by 9:00 P.M., rocks were being thrown at white motorists from a crowd of about 100 persons gathered on both sides of Lynch Street in front of Alexander Hall. Shortly thereafter, a Jackson City patrol car traveling west on Lynch Street was struck by a missile. By 9:45 P.M., there were approximately 150 persons, both men and women, in the Alexander Hall area. Most of them were students, and more than three-fourths of those present were passive onlookers.

At approximately 10:00 P.M., Jackson city police units established roadblocks on Lynch Street and on Pearl Street to seal off the campus. The rock-throwing stopped. But the number of persons in

SOURCE: From The President's Commission on Campus Unrest, *The Killings at Jackson State* (Washington, D.C.: U.S. Government Printing Office, 1970), pp. 7-69.

front of Alexander Hall continued to grow. A half block west on Lynch Street another larger group formed near Stewart Hall.

By 11:00 P.M. the number of persons in the street between Alexander and Stewart Halls would reach an estimated 700.

Members of Jackson State's eleven-man security force were harassed by small groups of students. Their attempts to quiet and disperse the growing crowds near Alexander and Stewart Halls proved futile. Jackson City Police made no attempt to enter the campus during the early stages of the disturbance.

At approximately 10:15 P.M., Edward Curtis, Dean of Men, accompanied by Sergeant M. P. Stringer of the security force, informed the crowd in front of Alexander Hall that President Peoples had imposed a 10:30 P.M. curfew. Some students went toward their dormitories, but many remained on the street. Little was done to enforce the curfew.

Jackson's Mayor Russell Davis spoke with the Governor at about this time and requested that the National Guard be mobilized and the Mississippi Highway Patrol placed on standby.

At about 10:30 P.M., security officer George Jones was driving onto the campus in his pickup truck when a rock struck and shattered his left vent window, as he passed in front of Stewart Hall, where about 200 persons were massed. Some in the crowd moved toward the truck. Jones fired three shots into the air with his revolver and then drove quickly to security police headquarters.

A little later, a group of perhaps a dozen corner boys and students broke out the rear window of a campus patrol car parked near Stewart Hall. They were attempting to turn it over when four security officers approached. The youths backed away when a security officer fired a shot into the air.

A trash trailer was pulled from behind one of the dormitories and into Lynch Street in front of the campus union. It was turned over and set afire. A second trash trailer was moved to the street in front of the east wing of Alexander Hall and set afire.

As the evening wore on, security officers increasingly heard reports that the students intended to march on the college ROTC building located some 150 yards south of Stewart Hall. At about 10:45 P.M., approximately 100 students and neighborhood youths broke from the crowd in the vicinity of Stewart Hall and moved toward the ROTC building. Dean Curtis and security officer Stringer went to the area, where they were joined by the commanding officer of the ROTC unit.

With assistance from student leaders, they managed to quiet and disperse most of the crowd.

Stringer moved to another area of the campus, but returned between 11:15 P.M. and 11:30 P.M. to find a small fire on the roof of a porch of the ROTC building and three black youths running from the area. After a bottle hit the gravel behind him, Stringer fired his revolver once into the air. He then smothered the fire with his shirt. He found two crude Molotov cocktails, one on the roof and one on the ground.

Around 11:00 P.M. TV newsman Bert Case was allowed to drive past the police barricades. His car was bombarded with rocks as he continued along Lynch Street through the campus.

Jackson city police units manning the blockades on Lynch and Pearl Streets were not released when their shift ended at 11:00 P.M. Shortly after the next shift of officers arrived at headquarters at 10:50 P.M., Dr. Peoples told Detective Chief M. B. Pierce of the march on the ROTC building. Pierce immediately ordered a squad under the command of Lieutenant Warren Magee to a police barricade northwest of the campus. Their instructions were to rendezvous with a unit of the Mississippi Highway Safety Patrol and then to move onto campus to secure the area around the ROTC building.

Magee's squad moved toward the campus area, some of them in "Thompson's tank"—an armored vehicle designed for riot control and equipped to dispense tear gas. The custom-made vehicle had been ordered by Jackson's former Mayor Thompson. The police have used the vehicle frequently on Lynch Street in the vicinity of the campus, but nowhere else in the city.

The city police and highway patrol units linked up before 11:30 P.M. They moved on foot to the ROTC building. As they passed Stewart Hall, the combined units were jeered by a crowd estimated at 250 to 300 persons. Rocks and other objects were thrown at them, but there were no injuries. Obscenities were shouted. There were statements that wives, mothers, and daughters of the officers were engaging in a variety of sexual relations with black men in dormitory rooms or at home.

Between 12:15 and 12:45 A.M., Magee's squad moved from the ROTC building east to the intersection of Rose and Lynch Streets to bar any attempt by the crowd to spread into Jackson's downtown area. The highway patrol unit remained at the ROTC building to secure the area. Magee avoided the shortest route, up Lynch Street through the heart of the campus, and chose instead to skirt the college. Sergeant Charles Lee, second in command of the police detachment, later testified that one reason for avoiding the campus was "not to harass or try to agitate in any way. I figured if we rode right back, all of these students out hollering and cutting up, that was just going to make the situation worse. . . ."

Police commanders were considering moving from the Rose/Lynch Street intersection back onto the campus to clear Lynch Street. Some police assembled in formation. However, Thompson's tank had broken down and Magee held his men back. Mayor Davis arrived at the police barricade.

Martel Cook, a black reporter and part-time student at Jackson State, came from the campus area to the barricade. He informed the Mayor that the situation was quieting down. Cook advised that there might be bloodshed if the police went in. Two other students also urged the Mayor not to send the police back into the campus.

Mayor Davis conferred with Chief Pierce, who was at police headquarters, and with Magee, about the advisability of ordering city policemen into the Lynch Street area of the campus. To some observers, it appeared that police commanders wanted to move in. However, Davis and Pierce agreed to keep the police out.

Sometime after midnight, the crowd gradually began to disperse. By the early hours of the morning the disturbance was over and the campus was quiet.

Around 1:00 A.M. Dr. Peoples met for more than an hour at his on-campus residence with about twenty-five students. They mentioned concern with the draft and the war in Southeast Asia, but agreed that the rock-throwing had started without a specific reason. No serious grievances against the college were mentioned.

At about 3:00 A.M. the Adjutant General of Mississippi, Major General Walter Johnson, visited Dr. Peoples at his home and informed him that the Mississippi National Guard had been placed on alert. He told Dr. Peoples that tear gas probably would be used if disorders developed on the 14th. Dr. Peoples was advised that gas masks would be brought to his home for him and members of his family.

During the disorder, security guards and some students reported hearing shots. Highway patrolmen heard shots fired while they remained at the ROTC building. At least four of the shots that were heard during the evening came in one burst when a black youth fired in the direction of a traffic light in front of Alexander Hall sometime between 10:00 and 11:00 P.M. Single shots were fired in the air by

Stringer at the ROTC building and by another security guard while students were attempting to overturn a campus patrol car. Three shots were fired in the air by security officer Jones after his truck was attacked in front of Stewart Hall.

No law enforcement officer or security guard reported being fired on during the disturbance, and there is no indication that any city policeman or highway patrolman fired a weapon on the 13th.

Events of May 14, 1970

There was some apprehension at Jackson State College on Thursday, May 14, but the campus was quiet and class attendance was normal.

At a 2:30 P.M. meeting with student leaders, Dr. Peoples stressed the seriousness of what happened the night before and told them the National Guard had been activated and was being mobilized. They reported to him that the general feeling among students was that there would be no disturbance on Thursday night. The students were unable to explain what caused the previous night's disturbance and told Peoples they had no new grievances.

Dr. Peoples issued a statement that afternoon designed to shame the students who had participated the night before in what he called "the annual riot." He said Wednesday night's "riot was perpetrated by a faceless, mindless mob of students and non-students bent on doing violence and destruction to the college. . . ."

Despite Dr. Peoples' request to Chief Pierce that Lynch Street be closed at dusk as a precautionary measure, police barricades were removed, and the street was open to traffic.

City police had earlier received reports from "confidential sources" that trouble was expected at Alexander Hall. Dr. Peoples knew nothing of such rumors, nor did any of the students subsequently interviewed by members of the Commission's staff. The police did not check these reports with college officials, but passed them on to highway patrol commanders. Detective Chief Pierce explained that the reports reflected a fear that male nonstudents escorting girls to the dormitory might be a source of trouble. He viewed the reports as being based on rumor. At the time he assigned no special significance to them. However, some policemen later claimed that events had borne out the truth of this rumor.

At 8:30 P.M., a National Guard log recorded that 647 Guardsmen were on duty and stationed at an armory in Jackson. The armory was more than a twenty-minute drive from the campus.

Around 9:30, a small group in the vicinity of Stewart Hall began throwing rocks at passing white motorists. Lynch Street soon was sealed off as it had been the night before. The crowd swelled to 100 to 200 persons, most of them onlookers who cheered the rock-throwers.

Around 10:00, an unidentified black man in a Volkswagen drove up to the crowd and announced—falsely—that Charles Evers, Mayor of Fayette, Mississippi and a civil rights leader, and his wife had been killed. Meanwhile, anonymous telephone calls to the same effect were made to several Lynch Street bars. Although many refused to believe this report, it spread quickly throughout the campus, and the level of tension rose.

Reports were coming in to the Jackson Police Department that the situation on campus was worsening. Around 10:15, a policeman gave a radio order: "Call that security guard out there at Jackson State and see if they can't scatter them niggers."

At the National Guard armory, an officer was monitoring the police radio reports. At some point between 10:30 and 11:00, he suggested to Adjutant General Johnson that National Guardsmen be put on trucks, ready to roll onto the campus. After General Johnson listened to the police radio for a few minutes, he ordered the Guardsmen to move to positions on Lynch Street near both ends of the campus. If called in, he wanted to be ready to move onto the campus at once. It was around 11:00 P.M.

Police radio reports were also telling of the movement of individuals from the Stewart Hall area to a dump truck at a nearby construction site. The truck was started; the vehicle jumped and sputtered and got as far as Stewart Hall, where the engine died. Then someone set the front seat afire. A nonstudent in the group pulled out a small pistol, knelt beside the truck, and began shooting at the gas tank.

At the other end of the campus, near the corner of Dalton and Lynch, two white newsmen were robbed and threatened by a gang of young blacks. Martel Cook and two other students rescued the two reporters and recovered $90 for them. One member of the gang fled with a tape recorder and another took $20.

At city police headquarters, the 11:00 P.M. shift had begun to arrive. A few minutes after 11:00, Chief Pierce ordered Lt. Magee to take Thompson's tank and a unit of twenty-six men to "clear the streets" on campus. On the way, they joined up with forty highway patrolmen under the command of Inspector Lloyd Jones. The two police groups moved onto the campus, and officers formed a line in front of Stewart Hall between the burning truck and the crowd.

A fire station on Lynch Street, 1.3 miles west of Stewart Hall, had been called by its dispatcher and directed to send a fire truck to the campus. As police waited for the fire truck to arrive, they radioed that they were being fired on. The fire truck proceeded slowly, without sounding the siren or flashing its red light. It moved in behind the officers, and firemen began dousing the fire. There was no interference by the demonstrators, and the firemen were able to extinguish the fire, but not before the dump truck was severely damaged.

The crowd at Stewart Hall grew in size. Students from the dormitory joined the demonstrators in jeering and yelling insults and obscenities. They repeated the references to wives, mothers, and daughters of the officers made the night before. Rocks and pieces of brick were thrown, but there were no serious injuries to firemen or police officers.

Lt. Magee repeatedly told the crowd to disperse, but with little success. College officials and student leaders, using a megaphone, also urged students to disperse and return to their dormitories.

Meanwhile, General Johnson had left the armory while the convoy of trucks was still being loaded with troops and equipment. He arrived at Stewart Hall ahead of the fire truck. A few minutes later, he rode through the campus on Lynch Street to the corner of Dalton, where a group had started a bonfire. He saw very few people on the street, but as he passed the front of Alexander Hall on his way back to the Stewart Hall area, his car was struck by a thrown object.

At 11:30, Chief Pierce called Mayor Davis to notify him that the situation on campus was worsening. The Mayor asked that the National Guard be sent in before the highway patrol or the city police, but was informed by Pierce that the patrol and police already were on campus. The Mayor said he wanted the Guardsmen to be sent in anyway. He drove to a barricade several blocks from the campus, where the convoy of National Guardsmen had taken positions. He was surprised to see them there rather than in the campus area.

Back at Stewart Hall, there was a barrage of bricks, rocks, bottles, and other objects, some of which came from dormitory windows. There were conflicting reports of small caliber gunfire from the area of Stewart Hall. Some highway patrolmen chased a group of persons into an alleyway adjoining Stewart Hall. Objects were thrown at them, and a patrolman fired a shotgun blast into a fourth-story window. No one was struck by the shot.

The gunfire from the highway patrol disturbed General Johnson, and he decided the National Guard should move onto campus and relieve the highway patrol and city police. He conferred with Magee and Jones and told them that the National Guard was coming in.

Two blocks away, Mayor Davis had also decided the National Guard should move onto the campus. He informed General Johnson's assistant, and the National Guardsmen began walking east on Lynch Street toward Stewart Hall, accompanied by the Mayor.

Meanwhile, as the firemen moved away from the Stewart Hall area after extinguishing the dump truck fire, they received a call to go to the bonfire in the middle of the intersection of Dalton and Lynch, at the opposite end of the campus. They drove around the campus to avoid arousing the students, and as they rounded a corner one block from the blaze, they and others heard the sound of small arms. They quickly extinguished the fire while a small crowd watched quietly. As the fire truck turned around to leave, it was hit by a barrage of thrown missiles, one of which made a loud sound when it struck and dented the top of the cab. The truck proceeded rapidly from the scene; none of the firemen was injured.

Magee stated that before the fire at the corner of Dalton had been put out, he had been informed of a request for police protection for the firemen. Magee testified that as he looked eastward down Lynch Street toward the bonfire, he saw a crowd he estimated at 200 milling around in front of Alexander Hall, some 300 yards away. Led by Thompson's tank, the city police and state patrolmen began moving eastward. Several newsmen trailed behind them.

At that time, Johnson, Magee, and Jones each had a different notion as to why police and highway patrol units were moving up Lynch Street. General Johnson thought the units were leaving the campus to permit Guardsmen who were securing the perimeter on the east side to enter the campus. Johnson's opinion was based on his understanding of discussions held that afternoon with representatives of the police and highway patrol, which he felt had resulted in the decision that, once the Guard had moved onto the campus, law enforcement groups would move off and secure the perimeter areas. The police and patrol did not understand this to be their mission.

Lieutenant Magee, under instructions from Chief Pierce to "clear the street and restore order," ordered the tank and his men to move "up to Alexander Hall" to disperse the crowd that he had seen gathered in that area. He intended to disperse the crowd prior to relieving the Guard at the perimeter. Magee later testified that he also intended to provide protection for the fire truck at the Dalton intersection.

Inspector Jones at no time was under the impression that the patrol was to withdraw from the campus when the Guard moved on. When he ordered his unit to move from Stewart Hall eastward on Lynch Street, his intention was to proceed directly to the Dalton intersection to protect the firemen. He did not hear Magee's directive to the tank—broadcast on a frequency different from that of the patrol—to stop at Alexander Hall, and therefore had no intention or expectation of doing so.

In addition to the confusion about objectives, there were crucial differences in procedure and training among the three law enforcement agencies concerning the use of firearms.

A basic policy of the National Guard is that no man can load or fire a weapon without an order from the senior commander. General Johnson believed that his men were well-trained and well-disciplined and would not load or shoot without an order. In the over six years he had served as their commanding officer—and in seven previous civil disorders—his men had not fired a shot. City policemen carried shotguns with shells in the magazine, but policy called for firing only upon order of the senior man on the scene, with the first shot over the heads of an advancing crowd and the second shot low and in front of the crowd. A separate order was required before each shot. The highway patrolmen carried loaded weapons and were authorized to decide on an individual basis if it was necessary to shoot to protect their own lives or those of other officers.

The National Guard was armed with special riot shotguns that hold seven rounds. The first four rounds are No. 9 birdshot, the smallest pellet used in shotguns, backed up by three rounds of double-O buckshot, the heaviest used in shotguns. City police carried shotguns loaded with heavy No. 1 buckshot. Most highway patrolmen were armed with shotguns loaded with double-O buckshot. Others carried personally owned rifles or carbines and two were armed with loaded submachineguns.

The National Guard and city police each had men specially assigned for antisniper duty, senior sharpshooters armed with rifles. Although the highway patrol manual indicates formal procedures for controlling sniper fire, Jones and a majority of his men considered each individual officer authorized to shoot any time he saw a sniper, if he believed lives were threatened.

After reaching Alexander Hall, the tank stopped in front of or slightly east of the west wing. With few exceptions, the city police were in a line south and east of the tank, and the highway patrolmen were in a line north and west of the tank, nearer the crowd. There were highway patrolmen within twenty feet of the nearest member of the crowd, most of whom had moved behind a three and one-half foot high chain-link fence along a sidewalk.

Estimates of the size of the crowd range all the way from 40 to 400. Along the fence in front of Alexander Hall, a campus security officer was urging students to disperse. There were jeers, obscene epithets, and a chant of "Pigs! Pigs!" Many girls inside the dormitory watched from their rooms and from stairwell landings in the west wing. Behind the police—on the south side of the street—a smaller group of demonstrators and onlookers stood near Roberts Dining Hall behind a chain-link fence which runs on top of a concrete retaining wall.

Soon after the peace officers and their tank stopped, the insults grew louder. Two TV newsmen, Bert Case and Jack Hobbs, moved into the area of the skirmish line. Magee then stepped forward with a megaphone to tell the students to go to their dormitories. He ordered them to disperse several times, but many students claimed that his words had been drowned out by the noise. Two officers staggered when struck on their helmets by thrown objects; one of them stated he was knocked to the ground. Inside the tank, an officer was loading a short-range tear gas shell, anticipating an order to fire gas.

Lieutenant Magee and other officers state that the students backed away, but Inspector Jones testified that the students were advancing toward the officers.

Someone threw a bottle from the lawn behind the fence in front of Alexander Hall. Almost simultaneously another bottle was lobbed from behind the retaining wall across the street, to the rear of the police line. One line of city police had turned to face that direction after some objects were thrown. A bottle shattered near the tank, and glass hit the ankle of TV cameraman Jack Hobbs. Frank James, a student standing on the south side of Lynch Street across from the campus Union, saw a rock almost hit the cameraman and strike the wall behind him. For his part, Hobbs stated that he heard a shot, then heard and felt an object whiz by his left ear that he strongly believed to be a bullet. He heard it ricochet on the wall behind him. An examination of this wall later failed to find evidence of a bullet mark there. Immediately thereafter, Hobbs heard shots fired by officers on his left.

Almost instantaneously, a general barrage of shotgun, carbine, rifle, and submachinegun fire began. Case, standing beside Hobbs, recalled that "the bottle crashed and the next thing I remember, they were firing."

Case looked toward the officers, saw their guns pointed upward, and his first impression was that the officers were firing into the air over Alexander Hall or possibly shooting tear gas.

When Case heard the shattering of glass in Alexander Hall, he realized that the officers were actually firing into the building. To him, it appeared they "systematically" shot into the windows from the top floor down to the bottom.

A college official who was standing a block away later said, "The whole sky lighted up."

The students at first thought that blanks or tear gas were being fired. Those outside began running for the hallway entrance, then began diving for cover.

In the doorway in front of the officers, one student, then others, fell. The entrance was blocked, as students struggled to find shelter.

Philip Gibbs, a married twenty-year-old junior and father of an eighteen-month-old son, was struck by a shotgun blast about fifty feet east of the west wing doorway of Alexander Hall. One buckshot pellet entered his left underarm area and two more entered his head, one just beneath the left eye, fatally penetrating the brain.

James Earl Green was standing in front of Roberts Hall, across Lynch Street from Alexander Hall. A student saw him run to the side of Roberts Hall, stop suddenly and fall. He was killed by a buckshot slug which entered his side and traveled through his liver, left lung, and heart. Green was a high school student.

Willie Woodward was wounded about 150 feet from the east wing of Alexander Hall as he fled toward the dormitory lobby door. Number one buckshot, probably fired by a Jackson city policeman, entered his chest from the back and collapsed a lung that filled with blood. Woodward, 31, was not a student; he explained his presence on the campus by saying he had driven a friend to the area to get a book.

Students Leroy Kenter and Vernon Steve Weakley were both struck in front of Alexander Hall. The large bone in Kenter's upper leg was shattered and pellet fragments remain in his leg and pelvis. Weakley was knocked from his feet by a slug striking him in the lower right leg. He was attempting to run from the firing when struck.

Fonzie Coleman, a freshman, ran inside the doorway for cover. He tripped over a fallen figure and then a bullet cut through his left thigh.

He passed out. According to hospital officials, he almost lost his life from shock and loss of blood.

Sophomore Lonzie Thompson ran into the dormitory after the shooting ended and only then realized he had been struck in the right thigh. Andrea Reese, a junior, dived into the bushes for cover no more than forty feet from the firing officers. A buckshot pellet passed through her armpit, leaving both entrance and exit wounds. Redd Wilson, Jr., another student, was hit in the left thigh as he ran toward the west wing entrance and tripped over one of those who had fallen.

Inside the dormitory at the foot of the stairs, nineteen-year-old Gloria Mayhorn was struck by a pellet in the right shoulder and struck in the scalp and back by hot fragments from ricocheting bullets. Patricia Ann Sanders ran from the first floor entranceway to calm a near-hysterical friend and then realized from a wetness on her shoulder that a bullet fragment had struck her. This fragment still is lodged in her shoulder.

Stella Spinks and Tuwaine Davis were wounded while in the dormitory stairwell. Miss Spinks was struck and burned on her back and arm by ricocheting fragments, as she lay huddled on the landing between the third and fourth floors. Miss Davis was cut and burned by ricocheting bullets as she ran down the stairs from the fourth floor landing.

Climmie Johnson was in the TV lounge on the second floor of the center section of the dormitory when the shooting began. She did not realize the officers were on Lynch Street until buckshot grazed her forehead.

Bert Case made a tape recording of the gunfire. The fusillade lasted twenty-eight seconds.

Many of the officers emptied shotguns containing four rounds of buckshot. One patrolman, who fired four rounds, reloaded and fired four more, and reloaded and fired again. He told a Commission staff investigator he did not know "how many times" he reloaded and emptied his gun.

In all, more than 150 rounds were fired. Most were fired into the air, but FBI investigation showed that nearly 400 bullets or pieces of buckshot struck Alexander Hall.

The area of the south end of the west wing alone contained 301 separate bullet marks. The upper floor level was hardest hit, with 105 marks or bullet holes in the windows, panels, and wall. There were 83 separate buckshot or bullet marks counted in the fourth floor area. There were 64 marks counted on the third floor, 36 on the second floor, and 13 separate bullet or buckshot marks in the windows, doors, and frames at ground level.

The glass in one of the doors to the ground entrance of the stairwell was splattered with blood. Blood stained the floor just inside the double glass doors of the entrance.

In addition to the firing at the west wing of Alexander Hall, shotgun blasts were fired into nearly every window in the first floor lobby of the center section of Alexander Hall. Windows in many student rooms in the center and east wings of the dorm were also hit.

According to a highway patrol investigator, a "majority" of the patrolmen fired into the west wing of Alexander Hall. They used buckshot, rifle slugs, a submachine gun, carbines with military ammunition, and two 30.06 rifles loaded with armor-piercing bullets. Several city police officers also fired, although each denied doing so during a police department investigation that night and in subsequent interviews with FBI agents.

After General Johnson rushed down from Stewart Hall, he approached Inspector Jones and asked who had issued the order to fire. Jones said, "No one."

There had been no order to fire and no warning given to students that shooting was being contemplated. Shortly after the shooting began, Lieutenant Magee began shouting, "Cease fire! Cease fire!" Several other officers who did not shoot repeated the order.

Immediately after the shooting, highway patrolmen began picking up empty shell casings. They explained that this was their training on the firing range and that they turned in empty casings for reloading. The patrolmen also picked up empty shell casings of the city police.

At highway patrol headquarters, a patrolman made the following entry in the log at 12:11 A.M.:

> Advise demonstrators threw rocks at them from a building. In return they tried to get them back into the building and they threw more rocks. Units had to hurt a few.

At the scene of the shooting, two newsmen recalled, the atmosphere among the officers was one of "some levity," and many officers engaged in casual small talk. Inspector Jones reported that two students were "10-7," radio code for "Out of Service." The radio tape continued:

Got one more female shot here—think it's serious.

A total of 6 injured there?

No, we got 2 more males, they say. . . .

I think there are about 3 more nigger males over there, one of 'em shot in the arm, one of 'em shot in the leg, and one of 'em somewhere else. They ain't hurt all that bad. Them gals, it was two nigger gals, two more nigger gals from over there shot in the arm I believe. One of 'em is over there in the east end. I told . . . there two nigger females and three males we just discovered, that's a total of 10. . . .

Here's another one, let me see what is this.

All persons killed or injured by gunshot were black.

FINDINGS

There are only a few disputed facts as to what happened on the night of May 14 at Jackson State College. Here we address ourselves to the six most significant of these: . . .

Was the Crowd Advancing?

Some highway patrolmen, including Inspector Jones, contend that, just prior to the shooting, the students were advancing on the law enforcement officers. Jones stated that the crowd was surging toward the officers and that the students were about to overwhelm the officers and cause them death or serious bodily harm.

This view is contradicted by the testimony of Lieutenant Magee and of all Jackson police officers interviewed by the staff, by the testimony of newsmen on the scene, by the statements of some highway patrolmen, and by the testimony and statements of students.

The crowd, with perhaps a few exceptions, was behind a chain-link fence which separates the grounds in front of Alexander Hall from the sidewalk and Lynch Street, where the officers were located.

No officer testified that he fired because the crowd was advancing. Each officer who did fire stated that he did so in response to sniper fire from Alexander Hall.

The Commission concludes that the crowd in front of Alexander Hall was not moving toward the police officers just prior to the shooting.

How Big Was the Crowd?

The Commission concludes that the best estimate of the size of the crowd in front of Alexander Hall is between 75 and 200. This finding is based on the radioed estimate by Lieutenant Magee, on the published estimates made that night by newsmen on the scene, and on an evaluation of the estimates of numerous other persons present.

How Soon Did the Shooting Begin?

The Commission concludes that approximately five minutes elapsed from the time peace officers arrived at Alexander Hall to the time they began firing. The first police log entry concerning the firing was made at eleven minutes after midnight, immediately after the shooting. Bert Case testified that he arrived in front of Alexander Hall at approximately seven minutes after midnight.

Case recorded his departure from the intersection of Valley and Lynch two blocks west of the campus, at 11:56 P.M. Subsequently, he retraced his steps and determined that it took eleven minutes to walk at the pace he walked May 14 to get to Alexander Hall. The police officers had been at Alexander Hall for approximately two minutes before Case arrived. Interviews conducted by Commission investigators confirmed that two other newsmen, who retraced their activities the night of May 14, were in front of Alexander Hall at least three minutes prior to the shooting.

Most students and officers gave statements indicating their belief that less time passed from the arrival of the officers to the shooting. Inspector Jones, for example, testified the elapsed time "could not" have been more than "ten to fifteen seconds."

Farries Adams, a student, stated:

> It was spontaneous, you know. . . . It [the tank] stopped in front of the west wing almost and these people positioned themselves and what have you . . . the front line . . . knelt to the ground and there they kneeled and started to fire into the dormitory to the west wing first.

Some officers gave longer time estimates, as did some students. However, it appears to the Commission that these varying estimates are a natural consequence of the confusion that inevitably attends a dramatic, emotional experience.

Were Officers Verbally Abused?

While some students deny hearing any abuse directed at the officers in front of Alexander Hall, the Commission concludes that the police officers were subject to vile verbal abuse. Not only did students chant, "Pig! Pigs! Pigs!" as Miss Andrea Reese testified, but some crowd members screamed obscenities and racial and sexual epithets at the officers. Few individual words are discernible on Bert Case's tape recording, but the fact that vile and obscene screaming did occur is clear from that tape, and one particularly offensive obscenity can be heard above the din.

Was Anything Thrown at the Officers in Front of Alexander Hall?

Earlier in the evening, a considerable number of rocks and other missiles were thrown at officers in front of Stewart Hall. There is conflict, however, over what, if anything, was thrown at officers in front of Alexander Hall.

Some students insisted in interviews with Commission staff members that there were no rocks, bottles, or other debris thrown at the police officers at Alexander Hall.

Some officers insisted there was a storm of debris. For example, Lieutenant Magee stated that when he was in front of Alexander Hall the debris "was coming directly in front of me, because I was having to dodge to keep from getting my brains knocked out." Inspector Jones testified that "bricks, bottles, rocks, and pieces of concrete . . . were thrown continuously from both sides of the street."

A tape recording that Bert Case made at the time of the incident has a sound that is unmistakably that of glass breaking near the tape recorder. Jack Hobbs felt shattered glass strike his ankle. Several students told Commission investigators that they saw a bottle thrown from the north side of the street, and it appears one was thrown also from the south side of the street. Frank James, a student from Vicksburg, saw a rock thrown near Jack Hobbs. Highway patrol officials recovered a brick that, laboratory examination proved, struck the helmet of patrolman William Turcotte. Jackson policeman Claude Gholson testified that a rock or brick thrown from the south side of Lynch Street struck his helmet and staggered him. Each of the four newsmen on the scene denies having seen or heard more than one or two objects thrown in front of Alexander Hall. The testimony of Bert Case is representative:

Q. Besides the bottle that you heard break in the street in front of you, did you see any bricks or other bottles flying through the air or striking the pavement?

A. The only thing I recall is the bottle breaking.

The city sent no special cleanup crew to the scene, and college officials responsible for keeping Lynch Street clean recall no unusual amount of debris the morning of May 15.

The Commission finds that some members of the crowd did throw a small number of bottles, rocks, and bricks at peace officers in front of Alexander Hall. However, the Commission also finds that the missile throwing was far short of the "constant barrage of flying missiles," highway patrol investigators reported to Governor John Bell Williams.

Was There Shooting Just Prior to the Police Fusillade?

The most difficult factual dispute to resolve is whether there was any shooting immediately preceding the firing by the officers. Clearly there was shooting on the campus while the dump truck was being burned. Frank James so testified, and other students have given similar statements. James also testified that there were shots fired while peace officers were in front of Stewart Hall. Police radio logs indicate two such incidents.

The evidence of shooting after the officers left Stewart Hall is much less clear. With one exception, only law enforcement officers state that they definitely heard any shooting from the campus after the officers arrived at Alexander Hall.

A number of officials, including Mayor Russell Davis, Lieutenant Warren Magee, and General Walter Johnson, heard no weapon fire after the officers arrived at Alexander Hall, prior to the fusillade.

On the other hand, most officers state that they did hear at least one shot from the campus before the officers' volley, and three of the four newsmen on the scene stated that they heard sounds that might have been shots. But two of them said the sounds they heard may have been firecrackers.

City policeman Charles Little told the Commission he observed from his position in Thompson's tank shots being fired from the east side of a third floor window of the stairwell:

> There was a colored male, ran to the window and . . .
> pushed the students in front of him away and apparently
> broke the window or a portion of the window with the back
> of his hand, or the butt of a weapon, I later found out, and it
> was a hand gun and I could tell when he stuck it out the
> window. . . . [H]e pointed directly at the men on the ground
> and fired it twice.

Little's testimony was corroborated by one highway patrolman who
saw a gun at the third floor window and by others who saw flashes or
heard sounds they believed came from the third floor. Another patrolman told Commission investigators he saw a gun fired from a stairwell
window but stated that it was on the west side of the fourth floor
window.

Stella Spinks, a junior at Jackson State, told the Commission that
she was standing on the landing identified by Little as the source of
the gunfire. She testified that she saw no one with a gun and heard no
talk of a gun. She did not hear any glass break before the officers
shot, and she heard no gun fired from that landing.

FBI agents who examined the third floor stairwell window reported
that all observable bullet holes in the window were made by shots
from outside the building. A portion of the window is broken, a fact
which offers possible corroboration of Little's testimony; but the
broken area is very small. And examination of the glass indicates that
the break was caused by incoming bullets or shotgun pellets.

TV cameraman Jack Hobbs gave the most persuasive testimony of
small arms fire from the area of Alexander Hall:

> At this point, a bottle shattered in the street just next to
> my foot, and I felt some pieces of it hit my ankle. At that
> point I heard a report, a bullet went past my ear and rico-
> cheted behind me.

Not only did Hobbs testify that he heard shooting, but Bert Case's
tape recording also reveals that Hobbs asked Case: "Did you hear
that bullet?"

While at the scene, Bert Case did not believe he had heard any
shots before the police fired. The tape recording, however, contains
two sounds immediately before the breaking of the bottle that Case
believes could be rounds of small arms fire. There are additional, less

distinct sounds on the tape between the breaking glass sound and the first shotgun blast. FBI laboratory analysts were unable to determine whether any of these sounds were made by shots.

There is no physical evidence of small arms fire in the area around Alexander Hall. On the basis of Jack Hobbs' report that a bullet had gone past his ear and struck a white-painted concrete wall behind him, highway patrolmen searched unsuccessfully with flashlights for a bullet or a bullet mark. FBI agents also examined that wall and found no evidence of any bullet having struck it.

Three .32 calibre cartridges and a .25 calibre cartridge were found on the south side of the chain-link fence. Because of the distance, it is unlikely that they were ejected from a weapon fired from Alexander Hall.

One unspent round of .22 calibre long rifle ammunition was found in the fifth floor hallway of Alexander Hall approximately two feet from the door leading out to the stairway. The bullet was discovered the next day beneath a pile of clothing, books, and other material discarded by students who left the dormitory when the school was closed.

One patrol officer reported being hit by a lead fragment. In reference to this Governor Williams stated on June 4, 1970, that "one spent, mashed bullet" was picked up after the shooting and that it had not been fired from an officer's weapon. However, laboratory examination established that the lead fragment—the mashed "bullet"—was actually mashed buckshot. Apparently it was fired by a police officer and had ricocheted into the street.

No other officer was struck by gunfire. Thompson's tank was not struck by gunfire.

Sergeant Charles Lee, the Jackson police officer second in command and responsible for locating and controlling sniper fire testified that while the officers were in front of Alexander Hall there may have been gunfire from another point on campus. He said he heard a shot that "sounded to me like it was more around the corner, which would be on the west side of the building. . . . I was more looking for flashes than anything else. . . . I never saw any."

It is significant to note that special agents of the FBI examined each of the rooms and stairs and stairwell landings behind the twenty-four windows and eighteen metal panels into which shots were fired and found no evidence of shooting *from* any of these locations. The Bureau's agents reported that every bullet mark which they could identify in every broken window and in every defaced panel was made by a bullet or pellet fired from outside the building.

The Commission is unable to determine positively whether there was, or was not, gunfire from Alexander Hall prior to the fusillade. The most favorable reading of the evidence tending to support a finding that there was such gunfire indicates that at most two shots were fired from one window.

CAUSES OF STUDENT CONDUCT

Jackson State College is a black school situated in a white-dominated state. This is the starting point for analyzing the causes of the student disorders of May 13 and 14, 1970.

The stark fact underlying all other causes of student unrest at Jackson State is the historic pattern of racism that substantially affects daily life in Mississippi.

The National Advisory Commission on Civil Disorders emphasized that racism is a fact in American society. No state or community is totally exempt. What happened in Jackson could have happened on any number of campuses where black students are protesting—on white campuses as well as black ones.

Dr. Margaret Walker Alexander, a native black Mississippian who is a poet and novelist and professor of English at Jackson State College, told the Commission at its hearings in Jackson:

> What is at issue is the issue of racism versus humanity. We have been educated for 350 years to think first in terms of race and property and almost never in terms of human lives. What is the value of human personality in this country? What would you give for a man's life? These two young men shot down, they could have been my sons. Of what value are they to the American society? Hundreds have been shot down. What does it mean? Is it tragic to other people, to anyone but the mother or the sister or the wife? What is the value of human life in America today?

It is important to emphasize that, in any normal sense of the term, "student unrest" does not exist on the Jackson State campus. There is virtually no student movement as such and no deep or serious grievance expressed by students with respect to the administration of the school. This is not because the students are insensitive to the issues that concern students on other campuses in this country. On the contrary, roughly 500 students attended the student-organized rally on May 7 protesting the move into Cambodia by American troops and expressing their sympathy for the four students who were slain at Kent State.

The rally and a proposed strike were called by a group of eight students, seven of them newly elected student body officers. Their statement to the student body calling for a strike was phrased in language of restraint. It said,

> To those of you who are sympathetic to this cause, we ask for your support. However, any students who feel otherwise and who would like to continue classes, no hostile efforts will be made to prevent you from doing so.

Interviews with black students reveal that in general they take for granted that the United States should withdraw from Indochina and that the social conditions which breed poverty and crime in this country should be eliminated. But Jackson State students do not agitate or protest or propagandize for these policies in any organized fashion. . . .

Several Jackson State students and black community leaders stated that although their faith in America continues, it is on the wane and can be sustained for only so long. They also were emphatic in pointing out that the basis of that faith has never been confidence in either state or local government, and that even the federal government is viewed more suspiciously today than in the 1950s and 1960s. Dr. Aaron Shirley, an advisor to the college's Committee of Concerned Students, expressed the view that the federal government indirectly contributed to the tragedies at Kent and Jackson by creating in the minds of both students and law enforcement officials a belief that dissent was no longer regarded with favor and that stringent measures to harness dissent were acceptable.

With hope waning and frustration growing, even those students who normally affect a pose of apathy sympathized with those few whose tempers reached a boiling point. Many students said that onlookers, including some girls who were leaning out of their windows in Alexander Hall, cheered on those who were throwing rocks.

While the decline in hope and the rise in frustration help to explain why some students condoned or participated in the violent actions that occurred on the Jackson State College campus, they do not provide sufficient explanation.

We do not know the specific cause of the first rock-throwing incident either evening.

However, one force behind the student actions of the 13th and 14th was closely akin to spring fever. In the weeks before May 13, freshman girls had been jokingly asking their boyfriends when the "spring riot" would be. President Peoples testified that students "look forward" to the spring disturbances. But spring fever exists every spring.

It does appear that some people wanted to exacerbate the trouble once it had started. On May 14, a black man about forty-five-years-old drove through campus spreading the false rumor that Charles Evers had been assassinated, as his brother Medgar Evers had been several years ago. The same false rumor was telephoned to several bars frequented by corner boys. Both nonstudents and some students responded to the rumor.

A small group of students believed that it would help focus attention on student concerns to engage in violent action that would bring the National Guard onto the campus. One student said:

> Some of the students wanted demonstrations on campus, not involving personal injury to anyone or extensive damage to property, but of sufficient magnitude to bring the National Guard on campus. It was felt that if the Guard came on campus, it would dramatize the students' position and create enough publicity to bring the matter to the attention of the President of the United States.

Spreading false rumors, urging rock-throwing, burning, and other violence, and taking violent action to focus attention on student concerns are deplorable and completely unjustified. Both false rumors and efforts to have the Guard called on campus contributed to the creation of a dangerous situation.

Before leaving the subject of the causes of student conduct on the nights of May 13 and 14, we re-emphasize the central role of anger and frustration, and the closely connected fact of racial antagonism.

One student, asked at the Commission hearings why the rock-throwing started, gave this response:

I mean like some people say the Vietnam issue and you know, it is a big thing on the campus, but I don't think that is true. I mean a lot of guys were upset, and, you know, something to the effect they wanted to step up the draft and there was a lot of—just a lot of tension.

When you go to class every day and in overcrowded class-rooms and it is hot and sweaty in there, you just get fed up with it and, you know, you should have had more classrooms and your classrooms should have been cool and you are sitting in a hundred-degree classroom and that night it is the same thing, and you ain't got nothing to do. You just got to do something, and it is just one thing led to another, so that is the way it was.

Another student said:

They throw rocks because they are angry. And they throw rocks at cars passing on Lynch Street, those cars carrying whites. Because I guess, always in the back of your head you are thinking that somebody hasn't been doing something right all along and if you can't get to the source, get to the next best thing. . . . If you are angry about anything that has political or social overtones, and if you can't get to the politicians and the government officials that are white here, and get them to do a little better, then you go to the next best thing; you get something that looks a little like them, I guess.

CAUSES OF POLICE CONDUCT

We have said it is impossible to understand the actions of the students who participated in the events of May 13 and 14 without recognizing the central role of racial antagonisms. That is equally true of the reaction of those peace officers who fired their weapons at Alexander Hall.

Many white Mississippi law enforcement officers—and all officers who fired were white—are afraid of what black men may do to them in hostile surroundings. Whether that fear is justified is of little con-sequence; the fear exists. That fear is intensified enormously in a violent confrontation—one in which foul language is made more threatening by thrown bricks and bottles and by the knowledge that there are blacks with guns in the immediate area.

Moreover, many white police officers are influenced by their disdain or hatred of blacks. One officer characterized the rock-throwing on Wednesday night as follows: "It's just a bunch of damn niggers." And Bert Case testified:

> I think that is probably the first time Mississippi patrolmen and Jackson policemen had been confronted at that close range with black people yelling obscenities at them. This is enough to put them in an infuriated mood, I am sure.

No white officer stated that he feels hostility toward blacks, but the chief highway patrol officer on the scene, Inspector Lloyd Jones, acknowledged that he has used the term "nigger" while on the job. He testified further that there is no highway patrol regulation prohibiting the use of such language.

We have previously quoted the catalog of injuries radioed by a highway patrolman shortly after the shooting. The attitude reflected in a statement of that type—"I think there are about three more nigger males over there, one of 'em shot in the arm, one of 'em shot in the leg, and one of 'em somewhere else"—is an attitude that blacks are not fully human.

Racial antagonism is aggravated by the all-white makeup of the Mississippi Highway Patrol and the nearly all-white makeup of the Jackson City Police Department. The highway patrol's director of personnel testified there has never been a black highway patrolman. The Jackson City Police Department has 19 uniformed black policemen, on a force of 279 members. No black policeman holds an officer rank. Of the 65 law enforcement officers in front of Alexander Hall, two were black; *they did not shoot.*

The Commission concludes that racial animosity on the part of white police officers was a substantial contributing factor in the deaths of two black youths and the gunshot injuries of twelve more.

One of the most tragic aspects of the Jackson State College deaths, however, is that—despite the obvious existence of racial antagonisms—the confrontation itself could have been avoided.

The Commission concludes that the twenty-eight-second fusillade from police officers was an unreasonable, unjustified overreaction.

Even if we were to assume that two shots were fired from a window in the west wing of Alexander Hall, the twenty-eight-second fusillade in response was clearly unwarranted. Peace officers should respond to sniper fire by taking cover and holding their fire. The Jackson City sniper team on the scene should have been used to deal with reported sniper fire. A broad barrage of gunfire in response to reported and unconfirmed sniper fire is never warranted.

Moreover, the Jackson City Police and Mississippi Highway Patrol lacked adequate planning, communications, training, and discipline—but not weapons—as they entered the Jackson State campus on May 14. . . .

The FBI manual, *Prevention and Control of Mobs and Riots*, emphasizes that,

> No aspect of the program [for mob and riot control] is more important than planning. Unless the plan is organized . . . the operation will be doomed to failure.

Similarly, the Mississippi Highway Patrol manual for crowd control states, "Never move into action without a plan." Following this elementary principle of effective law enforcement, action might have prevented gunfire and deaths at Jackson State College.

The National Advisory Commission on Civil Disorders also noted that:

> . . . No matter how well trained and skilled a police officer may be, he will be relatively ineffectual in dealing with civil disturbance so long as he functions as an individual.

The policy of the Mississippi Highway Safety Patrol—that each officer may decide for himself when he should fire his weapon because of danger to his or another's life—is contrary to this principle. More than twenty highway patrolmen fired, even though they had not received an order to do so. Later, each highway patrolman who fired told his superiors that he was firing in response to gunfire from one of two windows. The Jackson City Police Department has a standing rule that shotguns should be fired only upon the order of a commanding officer. Those city policemen who did fire were acting in clear violation of this rule. Sergeant Lee testified that immediately after the shooting ceased, he asked everyone, "Who gave the order to fire? Who gave the order to fire?" He said, "Nobody said anything." The only two city police officers who were assigned to respond to sniper fire, both of them armed with special rifles, did not shoot.

The FBI manual also states:

> Under no circumstances should firearms be used until all other measures for controlling the violence have been exhausted. Above all, officers should never fire indiscriminately into a crowd or mob.

Even if it is assumed that there were shooting from Alexander Hall, it is difficult to understand why officers fired "indiscriminately" into Alexander Hall. One officer, who did fire, told Commission investigators that if he saw a person in a crowd point a gun at him, he would fire his shotgun into the crowd, in the direction of the gun. Each load of double-O buckshot contains an equivalent of nine .33 calibre bullets, each of which travels along a different trajectory and can be lethal for a distance in excess of forty yards.

Lloyd Jones stated that he would have shot into the third floor window, if he had not been occupied reaching for a tear gas cannister and looking at a patrolman struck by a rock:

Q. And in those landings were several people, students or otherwise, and you could visibly see them, you said?
A. That is right.
Q. And you saw two flashes from the third floor; right?
A. Yes, sir. . . .
. . . I told you I would have fired into the third story window. There was people in it. I couldn't tell who was doing the firing.
Q. But would you fire into a crowd of people?
A. I would have fired into that third floor window; yes.
Q. Not knowing who was behind the window?
A. That is right.
Q. With a shotgun?
A. Right.
Q. With buckshot in it?
A. Yes.

But the peace officers who fired that night did not shoot only into the crowds in the windows of Alexander Hall. Some fired at the crowds on the campus behind the fences on both sides of Lynch Street.

Law enforcement officers stated that they did not fire to disperse the crowd in front of Alexander Hall, but rather were responding to what they believed was a sniper located in the west wing. Every officer who admits firing stated that he fired either into the west wing or into the air. The physical evidence and the positions of the victims, however, indicate that the officers were firing indiscriminately into the crowd at ground level on both sides of Lynch Street.

Even though the officers did fire into the crowd, it appears that no one would have been killed if birdshot had been used rather than buckshot. That the highway patrol used buckshot was the result of a change in its policy concerning ammunition. Inspector Jones said:

> Q. . . . in 1966 or '67, I believe you told me that the Highway Patrol used number 9 birdshot and that you yourself fired number 9 birdshot in the area of the Jackson State campus in 1967. Is that correct?
>
> A. Yes, sir.
>
> Q. And you also used number 9 birdshot at Alcorn College; is that correct?
>
> A. Yes.
>
> Q. What is the reason that the Highway Patrol now uses .oo buckshot, rather than number 9 birdshot?
>
> A. I haven't been given a reason. We use what is issued to us. We were issued buckshot this last time.

This change in policy lends some support to the view, widespread among Jackson State students, that police, particularly highway patrolmen, have become more hostile in recent years to blacks and more inclined to deal harshly with black protesters. Some students say that national, state, and local officials have created a favorable climate for such police attitudes.

Finally, the Commission concludes that a significant cause of the deaths and injuries at Jackson State College is the confidence of white officers that if they fire weapons during a black campus disturbance they will face neither stern departmental discipline nor criminal prosecution or conviction. . . .

After the highway patrol had completed its interviews, it made an oral report to Governor John Bell Williams. Governor Williams told Commission investigators that he relied exclusively on the highway patrol's oral report in making his television report on the Jackson State incident to the people of Mississippi on June 4, 1970. In that address, he characterized the highway patrol's inquest as a "complete and impartial investigation." The Governor explained the twenty-eight seconds and 150 rounds of gunfire by saying that "the officers felt compelled in the interest of self-preservation to return the fire." The Governor's chief conclusion was that "the officers . . . did not insti-gate the problem; they did not encourage it—the responsibility must rest with the protesters."

The report of the Hinds County grand jury was even more explicit in upholding the officers:

> We find that under the riot situation existing, the officers of both the Jackson Police and the Highway Patrol had a right and were justified in discharging their weapons. . . . [T]he officers used only that force that was necessary to protect themselves and to restore law and order on the cam-pus of Jackson State College.

The conclusions of the grand jury are based on a number of inac-curate findings. For example, the report states that "3 spent .32 calibre shell casings were found in the bushes in front of Alexander Hall by a member of the Mississippi Highway Patrol." In fact, Pa-trolman McComb informed a Commission investigator he found the shell casings on the sidewalk on the street side of the fence in front of Alexander Hall. The significance of the difference is that one could infer that spent cartridges in the bushes below the west wing stairwell were ejected from a weapon fired from that stairwell. No such infer-ence can be made when one knows that the cartridges were found more than twenty feet from the entry to the stairwell, on the other side of the fence.

The grand jury report further states that peace officer shooting was "at the area of the sniper." Photographs and diagrams, presented as exhibits to the grand jurors, indicate that there was shooting on both sides of Lynch Street and that shots on the north side of the street extended over an area more than 200 feet wide. Clearly the grand jury's conclusion that the officers "returned the fire" is a patently inadequate description of the extent of shooting that actually took place.

In the hours after the shooting and for months thereafter, the statements of some city police officers established a pattern of deceit. The night of the shooting, Mayor Davis and Chief Pierce decided to determine if any police officer had fired his weapon. Each officer who had been on the scene was interrogated and asked to turn in the ammunition he had been issued. Each officer replied that he had not fired a shot and returned the same amount of ammunition he had received. The following exchange occurred with Sergeant Lee during his testimony before the Commission:

> Q. Just to clarify this point, afterward you checked each man, checked the amount of ammunition he turned in to you and asked each man whether he had fired; and you got the same [amount] of ammunition back from each man, and each man told you he had not fired; is that correct?
> A. That is correct, sir.

(It later developed that officers had obtained shells from Thompson's tank to replace the bullets they had fired.)

The deception continued when sometime later, agents of the FBI interviewed each city policeman who was on the scene. Each was again asked if he had fired his weapon, and each repeated the denial he had made to Sergeant Lee.

Still later, policemen testified before a biracial lawyers' committee appointed by the mayor that they saw no city policemen fire. Newsmen testified to the same effect. While it is now clear that the newsmen were not in a position to see the policemen fire, and that their apparent corroboration was, in fact, meaningless, the committee concluded that the officers had told the truth.

The highway patrol, which collected empty number one buckshot shells on the street in front of Alexander Hall, did not release these shells—or publicly announce their existence—until required to turn them over to a federal grand jury. FBI laboratory tests proved that these shells had been fired from city police department shotguns. When confronted with this fact, at least three city policemen admitted shooting. Even now, those policemen who do admit firing claim to have shot only up into the air. Ballistics tests show that at least two of the victims, Green and Woodward, were shot with number one buckshot. The city police used this type of ammunition in their shotguns. The highway patrol was issued double-O shells, though some of the patrol may have used other types of shot.

Relying on the word of his police officers and the conclusions of the biracial committee, Mayor Russell Davis—a white Mississippi politician who urges whites and blacks to work together to improve Jackson—issued a public statement to the effect that there was no evidence that any city policeman had fired his weapon.

The reaction of the County Grand Jury to this chain of events was as follows:

> It was most unfortunate that the Mayor of the City of Jackson saw fit to appear on television and make statements to the press to the effect that the Jackson Police Department officers did not fire their weapons at Jackson State College. This statement was absolutely false and the Mayor, in making it, has brought extreme and unwarranted criticism upon the Mississippi Highway Patrol and its officers. This action of the Mayor in the opinion of this Grand Jury is reprehensible and should not be excused or cannot be justified.

Not only did the County Grand Jury condemn the Mayor for repeating what his officers had told him, but it did not suggest in any way that it had been improper for the police officers to lie. Instead, the Grand Jury report continues:

> . . . We feel strongly that insofar as investigations or other actions concerning statements that any of these twenty-two officers might have previously given be brought to an end with this Grand Jury report. We wish to make it clear that any future action of any kind against any of the twenty-two police officers involved by the Mayor of the City of Jackson or the Police Department of the City of Jackson would be unwarranted, unjustified, and political in nature.

This Commission understands why both white officers and black people in Mississippi gain the impression that policemen need not fear official punishment—or even censure—for repressive action against blacks.

One final observation as to the Grand Jury report. Its underlying philosophy is summarized in the following passage from the report, "When people . . . engage in civil disorders and riots, they must expect to be injured or killed when law enforcement officers are required to re-establish order."

That position, which the Grand Jury drew almost verbatim from Grand Jury charges by Federal District Judge Harold Cox and State Circuit Judge Russell Moore, may reflect the views of many Americans today. It is a view which this Commission urges Americans to reject.

The Commission categorically rejects rhetorical statements that students must "expect" injury or death during civil disorders. Such statements make no distinction between legitimate dissent and violent protest. It is the duty of public officials to protect human life and to safeguard peaceful, orderly, and lawful protest. When disorderly protest exists, it is their duty to deal with it firmly, justly, and with the minimum force necessary; lethal force should be used only to protect the lives of officers or citizens and only when the danger to innocent persons is not increased by the use of such force.

CONCLUSION

There must not be a repetition of the tragic incident at Jackson State.

We are heartened by the stated determination of Jackson city police and elected officials to take necessary steps to avoid the recurrence of tragedy at Jackson State College. It is imperative that this determination be reflected in action.

Mayor Davis described the first—and most difficult—task:

> I know truthfully in Jackson we do have a problem that the whole United States has of race relations, and somehow the solution to that problem simply lies in the determination of the black people and the white people to get along with each other. This is what it has got to come down to if it is going to be solved.

City officials also state they will take specific steps to improve the capability of their police officers to respond appropriately to any further incidents of disorder at Jackson State. The City Council has approved an extensive police training program for handling problems of campus disorder. The police department has taken steps to reduce the necessity of using lethal force; it has obtained protective vests for its officers and a new, improved tear gas dispenser.

Chief Pierce has made it clear that the department policies with respect to the use of buckshot rather than birdshot will be re-examined. He also stated that the policy of using Thompson's tank on the campus will be reevaluated in light of its inflammatory effects on crowds. He was receptive to the suggestion made by a number of students that, in the event of a disturbance, campus security forces be supported by student marshals to minimize the need for city or state policemen. Finally, the Chief testified that the police officers who lied to Sergeant Lee and to the FBI would be disciplined.

On the other hand, the reaction of the Mississippi Highway Safety Patrol to the deaths and injuries at Jackson State continues to be disturbing. Inspector Jones expressed the position of his patrol:

> Q. Do you have any recommendations to make to the Commission, particularly as it relates to command or control features for joint operation of law enforcement agencies, for this kind of thing if it should happen in the future?
>
> A. No, sir; I don't.
>
> Q. Does your department plan to take any corrective steps in view of what happened?
>
> A. Not that I know of. . . . There was no doubt in my mind that some of us would have been killed down there if the volley of shots hadn't gone off and I see no reason for disciplining a man for saving his own life.
>
> Q. . . . [D]oes your department . . . plan to take any corrective steps in the future to prevent this?
>
> A. Not that I know of.
>
> Q. How do you feel about it personally? Do you think they are needed?
>
> A. Not against any of our men, no, sir.

We urge a re-examination of this position. Every group or agency that participated in the Jackson State confrontation must learn from its errors of planning and judgment.

We are also concerned with the escalation of rhetoric on the part of certain Jackson State students. While we understand the profound emotional impact of the deaths and injuries of fellow students, we condemn statements to the effect that the next time something happens "all the pigs" will not walk away from campus, or statements suggesting that students arm themselves because of anticipated future confrontations with police. We condemn any action on the basis of such statements even more strongly.

Andrea Reese, a student who sustained gunshot wounds on May 14, warned:

> Unless somebody shows a little interest or a little common sense at looking at the whole problem of relationships be-

tween the white officers and the black people, if they can't establish some ground to meet on and to get a few things settled, it is going to happen again at Jackson State.

The Commission recommends that police and students commit themselves to end the hostility that presently divides them before it does, indeed, "happen again at Jackson State."

20.

Epilogue

The Scranton Commission on Campus Unrest illuminates many of the issues and problems discussed throughout this book. Many of its themes—condemnation of violence, social-psychological model of analysis, and criticism of police lawlessness—are identical to those raised by the 1917 congressional inquiry of the East St. Louis riots. The Scranton Commission differs from earlier riot commissions in subject matter, namely students, and in some of its procedures, but its essential characteristics remain unchanged. The recent publication of a satire on commission reports[1] indicates that "riot commissions" have already begun to achieve the status of an established government institution.

Like all riot commissions, the Scranton Commission was appointed immediately following a major political crisis. In this case, the crisis was generated by the government's decision to invade Cambodia at a time when most political and public opinion favored United States withdrawal from Vietnam. The decision was met with predominantly peaceful and far-reaching protests throughout the country. During such protests at Kent State University and Jackson State College, six students were killed and many others injured by police and troops. The government responded to these massive protests by justifying the invasion of Cambodia on grounds of military self-defense and by condemning student violence. In response to the murder of students at Kent, President Nixon curtly observed that "when dissent turns to violence it invites tragedy." Vice President Agnew similarly criticized students for the "grave dangers which accompany the new politics of violence."[2]

The government's analysis of "student violence" was widely criticized by the mass media and by various political and community leaders. A *New York Times* editorial was typical in its criticism of President Nixon for "placing the blame on the victims instead of the killers."[3] Various political spokesmen demanded the appointment of a "blue-ribbon" commission.[4] According to the *New York Times*, President Nixon turned to the American Bar Association for advice and, after meeting with A.B.A. leaders, agreed to appoint a commission.[5]

The Scranton Commission was decidedly more liberal than some of its predecessors. It included more black members (4 or 44%) than any previous national riot commission, one woman, fewer lawyers than usual, four persons associated with universities, and a police chief from a university town. Also, the average age of commissioners, 45 years, was far younger than the average of 54 years for previous commissions. Moreover, Joseph Rhodes (22 years), a black junior fellow at Harvard University, was the first person under 30 years ever to be appointed to a national or local riot commission. While it was a liberal commission, it was far from radical. It did not include any representatives from either the "new left" wing of the student movement or more militant black organizations. Commissioners such as William Scranton (lawyer, wealthy businessman, and Republican politician), Bayless Manning (Dean of Stanford Law School and a former member of the American Bar Association's conservative committee on campus disorders), and Benjamin Davis (a black career Air Force officer and strict advocate of "law and order" as Cleveland's Public Safety Director) guaranteed that the Commission's final report would be cautious and "balanced."

The appointment of a liberal commission by the Nixon administration appeared to indicate that the government intended to pursue contradictory policies on "student unrest," different policies for different audiences and constituencies. During the life of the Commission, representatives of the Nixon administration persistently attacked student dissent as irresponsible and prone to violence. At the same time, it was clearly expected that the Scranton Commission's final report would be at least partially sympathetic to the ideals and aspirations of students. This contradiction was evident from the earliest days of the Commission when Vice President Agnew demanded the resignation of Joseph Rhodes following a *New York Times* interview with Rhodes. Rhodes said that he intended to investigate charges that the government provoked campus violence. Agnew commented that Rhodes demonstrated a "transparent bias that will make him counterproductive to the work of the commission."[6] The White House refused to intervene and Rhodes refused to resign, but the incident undermined Rhodes' public credibility as an impartial investigator and identified him as the "house dissident."

The organizational format of the Scranton Commission was similar to previous commissions. A prominent lawyer and ex-federal prosecutor, Matthew Byrne, Jr., was hired as executive director to coordinate and administer the Commission's research program.[7] Research memoranda were commissioned from prominent social scientists and fact-finding task forces were established in Kent and Jackson. Unlike previous commissions, the Scranton Commission devoted considerable time to open public hearings in several parts of the country. The *New York Times* reported that:

> The prospect of open hearings is regarded with some surprise here (Washington, D.C.). Observers familiar with past commissions have doubted that the new panel could afford the time required for such hearings, usually slower and more ponderous than closed sessions.
>
> These observers speculated that the commission evidently believes that public hearings would lend credibility and authenticity to its work.[8]

The argument that hearings were used to establish political credibility is plausible, given Agnew's attack on Rhodes and criticism from other congressional quarters. The pattern of hearings was established in each city: spokesmen sympathetic to student dissent (students, liberal politicians, political activists, etc.) criticized administration policies at home and especially in Vietnam; equal time was given to more conservative spokesmen (university administrators, conservative social scientists, "law and order" politicians) who criticized students for provoking violence and bypassing "normal channels." The Commission appeared to be establishing a "record" for a moderate, middle-of-the-road report, comparable to the Kerner Commission's analysis of urban riots.

The format of the Scranton Commission's final report is somewhat different from those of the Kerner and Violence commissions. It is much shorter, more analytical than factual, and lacks the vast documentation of earlier commission reports. But its ideological premises are unchanged: it focuses on the violence of students and law enforcement agencies while ignoring the violence of American foreign policies in Indochina; it explains campus violence in social-psychological and collective behavior terms while dismissing its political and institutional context; it explains student protest against the war as a symptom of underlying social-psychological and identity problems, or as a problem of misunderstanding between generations, or as a result of the failure of universities to restrain students; and it recommends reconciliation and understanding without indicating how this is to be achieved. As in most commission reports, the Scranton Report is filled with optimistic rhetoric, inconsistent analysis, and a general belief in the fundamental worth of established political and economic institutions. It repeats the "two-pronged" fallacy of the Violence Commission, calling for more reform and more repression. Finally, as an act of unconscious irony, it calls upon the President to reconcile the country after he has demonstrated a unique ability for polarization and repression.

The non-analytical sections of the report are competent and valuable. The detailed report on "The Killings at Jackson State" is a thoroughly researched, well-documented and apparently impartial assessment of events surrounding the events of May 13 and 14. The report repudiates the findings of the Hinds County grand jury which justified police action and blamed students and "outsiders" for the violence.[9]

Considering the limited amount of time and a variety of political pressures, it is remarkable that the Commission was able to produce a unanimous report by the end of September. The press was continually reporting rumors of internal dissent and presidential censorship.[10] The Scranton Commission had the additional problem of competing with a national election campaign in which "law and order" was a prominent theme and "student violence" constituted the main platform of most Republican and many Democratic candidates. A number of politicians, in order to impress voters with their commitment to "law and order," criticized the Scranton Report before its contents were known or released. On August 26, Governor Reagan said that

Commission testimony was weighted "on the left";[11] on September 4, Senator Gordon Allott, Chairman of the Senate Republican Policy Committee, warned that the Scranton Report would be "a flaccid whitewash of the violent new-left political movement that is openly seeking to capture or destroy our great universities";[12] President Nixon's celebrated "Kansas speech" associated student violence with terrorism and airplane hijacking, and he called for an "uncompromising stand" against the "disease of violence and terror."[13] Following this important policy statement, the President sent a special letter to 900 university administrators, urging them to restore "order and discipline" on campuses. He also enclosed copies of a newspaper article by Sidney Hook, a critic of the student left, which argued *inter alia* that "the most important elements in the complex of causes of student violence are not objective social and political conditions but the mistaken ideas and ideological myths of militant extremists and their faculty allies." The President reaffirmed his position the following week by asking Congress to authorize the addition of 1,000 FBI agents to deal primarily with campus disorders.[14] The Nixon policy was the main theme of the 1970 electoral campaign; anti-student speeches by Vice President Agnew and Attorney General Mitchell set the tone for political rhetoric around the country.[15] Wealthy backers of the Nixon administration bought prime television time in nine cities to broadcast parts of the President's "Kansas speech."[16]

In an effort to halt premature criticism, Chairman William Scranton criticized Senator Goldwater and other conservatives for "setting up straw men and knocking them down, doing nothing but exacerbating the situation."[17] Scranton's modest criticism had no impact for the obvious reason that the anti-student theme originated from the highest levels of government, not just from the right-wing "lunatic fringe." As the election campaign proceeded, it became evident that the Scranton Report would receive little support from its sponsors if it was sympathetic to student dissent. By the time the Report was released, most political critics *assumed* that it was too liberal and its defenders were attacked for condoning student violence. In other words, the Scranton Report was symbolized as a "liberal" document, irrespective of its actual content.

The Administration in effect disowned the Scranton Report. On the day of its release, President Nixon left for a political tour of several European cities. Vice-President Agnew described the report as "imprecise, contradictory and equivocal," calling it "more pablum for the permissivists [*sic*]."[18] A predominantly Republican group of 66 members of the House of Representatives charged that the report was "erroneous and unfounded"; they demanded more discipline on campuses and the removal of "spineless college administrators."[19] Despite some support from such liberals as Senator Charles Goodell (later defeated in his bid for reelection), Edward Kennedy, and John Lindsay, the Scranton Report was generally dismissed without analysis. With the President's European tour, the sudden death of Egypt's Nasser, and the impending election, the report was no longer newsworthy and it quickly disappeared from public view.

The Scranton Commission is a fitting climax to the history of riot commissions. Like its predecessors, it is a failure as an intellectual resource because its analysis is too often inconsistent, uncritical and undermined by ideological imperatives. It is a failure as a political institution because its impact on the political process has been negligible. It has symbolized the hope and impression of major social and political change while affirming the strength of established institutions. It typifies the paradox and essential bankruptcy of modern liberalism.

NOTES

My thanks to Drew Humphries and John Pallas for their research assistance.

1. The Report to the Task Force on Pornography and Obscenity, *The Obscenity Report* (New York: Stein and Day, 1970).

2. *New York Times*, 5 May 1970, p. 17.

3. *New York Times*, 6 May 1970. See also, Tom Wicker's attack on Nixon's "obtuse and heartless" statement and on Agnew's "sustained and inflammatory" rhetoric in *New York Times*, 7 May 1970. An editorial in the *Washington Post*, 9 May 1970, adopts a similar position.

4. *Los Angeles Times*, 13 May 1970, p. 15.

5. *New York Times*, 7 July 1970, p. 25.

6. *New York Times*, 15 June 1970, p. 1; *New York Times*, 17 June 1970, p. 1; *Time*, 29 June 1970, p. 58.

7. *New York Times*, 7 July 1970, p. 24.

8. *New York Times*, 7 July 1970, p. 1.

9. *New York Times*, 30 July 1970,, pp. 1, 16.

10. See, for example, *New York Times*, 31 July 1970, pp. 1, 10; *San Francisco Chronicle*, 27 August 1970, p. 6; and *New York Times*, 27 September 1970, "Education" section.

11. *San Francisco Chronicle*, 27 August 1970, p. 6.

12. Ibid., 5 September 1970, p. 2.

13. Ibid., 17 September 1970, p. 1.

14. *New York Times*, 27 September 1970, "Education" section.

15. *San Francisco Chronicle*, 19 September 1970, p. 1 and 22 September 1970, p. 1.

16. Ibid., 25 September 1970, p. 5.

17. Ibid., 25 September 1970, p. 1.

18. *New York Times*, 30 September 1970, p. 1.

19. *New York Times*, 30 September 1970, p. 15.

Index

Index